PIONEERS OF THE PEACEABLE KINGDOM

PIONEERS

OF THE PEACEABLE KINGDOM

BY PETER BROCK

PRINCETON, NEW JERSEY
PRINCETON UNIVERSITY PRESS

TO CARMEN

The chapters of the present volume
are reprinted from a more extensive
book: *Pacifism in the United States:
From the Colonial Era to the First
World War* (Princeton University
Press, 1968). Whereas in the text I
have taken the opportunity to make
a few minor corrections and additions,
I have left the bibliography substantially as it appears in the full version.
I would again like to express my
thanks to the Friends Historical Library at Swarthmore College, particularly to Frederick B. Tolles and
Dorothy G. Harris for their help while
I was preparing the chapters included
in the present book. Most of the original work for these chapters was done
in this Library.

PETER BROCK

*Toronto, Ontario, Canada
7 November 1969*

Contents

Contents

On the North American continent pacifism, the renunciation of war by the individual, represented at first a transplantation into these new and open territories of an attitude that had originated among religious groups in the European homeland. Antimilitarism and the refusal to participate personally in any warlike activity formed, as it were, part of the intellectual baggage brought over the ocean by emigrants from their midst. The attempt to maintain these ideas, the transmutations and accretions that resulted from life in a new and often strange environment, and the eventual widening of the ideal of peace held by these sects to embrace members of other denominations constitute the content of the history of pacifism as it developed in North America.

The major pacifist sects that were transplanted to America had begun as outgrowths of the great religious movements that transformed the intellectual climate of large parts of northern and central Europe in the sixteenth and seventeenth centuries. Mennonitism and its offshoots formed the radical wing of the Protestant Reformation, which at the beginning was collectively known as Anabaptism, and the Quaker Society of Friends, for all the differences that set it apart from the parent movement, was a genuine child of mid-seventeenth-century English Puritanism.

The first of the European pacifist sects to send emigrants to North America in any large numbers was not the Mennonites, however, but the British Quakers, the origins of whose Society date back to the middle of the seventeenth century. For early Friends, it was not the legalistic injunction "Resist not evil" but rather an intuitional view of the wrongness of war and violence when held up to the Inner Light of Christ which shone within all men that became the source of their refusal to fight. Yet belief in the inadmissibility of war was only gradually arrived at, belief in the permissibility of fighting in a righteous cause only slowly abandoned. The final crystallization of the Quaker peace testimony may be dated to their declaration of January 1661 against taking up arms, either on behalf of an earthly kingdom or to inaugurate the kingdom of Christ. By this time the Commonwealth era, which had seen the birth and early expansion of Quakerism under the leadership of George Fox (1624-1691), was at an end. The restored Stuart monarchy was soon to begin a period of renewed persecution of Quakers and other religious nonconformists, when the Clarendon Code was enacted against all who dissented from the established Church of England.

The faith of the early Quakers was experiential, enthusiastic, and perfectionist. The pioneers of the movement were filled with an apocalyptic belief in the imminence of a new age of history, which would commence with their own victory in the "Lamb's War" (a phrase early Quaker writers liked to use to denote the struggle against sin and the "world"). For, unlike Anabaptists and Mennonites, the early Quakers did not expect the true church to remain always, to the end of time, a small and outcast minority in this world. Instead, they believed in the transforming power of the Holy Spirit, a power that would enable them to convert and remold the peoples of the whole earth. Theirs was to be a total victory. And their rapid spread during the 1650's, despite fierce persecution by the English government, seemed to confirm their optimism. It was only in the last decade of the century, after religious toleration had been granted by the English Parliament in 1689, that the Lamb's War was finally abandoned; only then was the attempt to conquer the world by the power of the Spirit replaced by the desire to maintain righteousness within the Quaker community.

A second point at which the Quaker *Weltanschauung* from the beginning diverged from that of the Anabaptist-Mennonite was in the Quaker's attitude toward the state. Unlike the Anabaptists and Mennonites, Quakers never regarded the state as at best merely a necessary evil and rulers as men who must by the very nature of their office stand outside the pale of the true Christian community. For Quakers, the godly ruler was no contradiction in terms. Rulers also could be guided by the Spirit. The role of the state had its positive aspect as well as the purely negative one of maintaining order among the ungodly; some measure of force in upholding righteousness in the community did not deprive the authorities of their Christian character. Early Friends, however, did not attempt to relate too closely the role of the Christian magistrate wielding the sword to suppress evil and unrighteousness within the state and their own abandonment of carnal weapons to withstand the external aggressor or the personal assailant. In fact, in Britain, it was not until the nineteenth century that the law permitted a Quaker to take an active role in politics or government. The problem of the pacifist magistrate was faced by Friends only in the New World—in Pennsylvania and, to a lesser degree, in Rhode Island, too.

Although Friends were always ready to quote scripture, particularly the New Testament, in support of their repudiation of armed force, as in defense of all their beliefs, and although their pacifism was certainly to some extent an attempt at restitution of what they believed was the practice of primitive Christianity, the Quaker peace testimony at the outset did not stem from any "notions" (to use the Quaker term). It derived essentially from their view that, in the grand crusade against evil they had been called by God to wage, only inner spiritual weapons were consistent with the leadings of the Spirit. Unrighteousness must be cast down, but not with the weapons of unrighteousness. The Quakers, indeed, may be described as nonviolent resisters rather than as nonresisters in the Mennonite style.

Later, humanitarian and even economic arguments were used by Quaker writers in pleading their case against war. Nonetheless, pragmatic considerations of this kind were considered as supplements, rather than as substitutions for the fundamental principle derived from the guidance of the Inner Light that had to be followed regardless of the cost. For Quakers, peace came to mean following the way of love that begins in the hearts of individuals and through them leavens society until all men are won.

The apocalyptic visions of the "First Publishers of Truth" were, however, replaced by a growing emphasis on gradualism. Thus, we find Robert Barclay (1648-1690) in his famous *Apology for the True Christian Divinity*, which from its first publication in 1676 remained for over a century and a half the most systematic and the most generally accepted statement of Quaker faith, putting forward in his treatment of peace contained in Proposition XV (Sections XIII-XV) a conditional justification of war for non-Quaker Christians, whose political ethic remained sub-Christian, as well as for non-Christians. And a little later William Penn (1644-1718) and John Bellers (1654-1725) elaborated schemes for establishing concord between the nations without requiring them to accept the lofty ideals of the Quakers.

Thus, the original testimony of Friends against war—which, like their other testimonies in such matters as the refusal to swear judicial oaths or to pay tithes, simplicity of attire and plainness of speech, and denial of hat honor and maintenance of strict honesty in business, had at first been regarded as part and parcel of their general strategy in the Lamb's War against sin throughout the world—then became the distinguishing mark of a sect, of a body, which, in spite of having now won toleration and even respect from society at large, did not expect that its peculiarities would gain universal acceptance in the world, much less that this world would ever come to embrace Quakerism. This devotional quietism that blanketed the early eighteenth-century Society of Friends was matched by an equally inward-looking witness for peace, which entailed personal renunciation of violence on the part of every Quaker but which lacked a more positive approach toward peace.

Early Friends in Britain had been, for the most part, country folk: farmers, shepherds, mechanics of one kind or another. A few of the well-to-do, even some gentlemen, had joined the movement. But its rural character, and especially its North-country origins (it was from the ranks of seekers and separatists in this area that Fox recruited his first adherents in the early 1650's), gave its stamp to emergent Quakerism, which to this day has remained a lay movement. But, by the end of the seventeenth century, its social composition had been transformed. Though a rural element continued within the Society, it was now the prosperous bourgeoisie that set the tone, even before townsmen had come to form a majority of the membership.

In Fox's own lifetime—and largely due to his efforts and organizational skill—a loose association of Friends was transformed into a Quaker Society with its established pattern of silent worship, written discipline, and formal membership. Birthright membership was not finally accepted until 1737, but by the late 1660's and early 1670's Fox had succeeded in setting up a Quaker organization for administration and for religious worship by establishing for these purposes a hierarchy of "meetings," from the monthly meetings at the bottom through quarterly meetings up to London Yearly Meeting at the top. The so-called Meeting for Sufferings, set up in 1676 during a period of acute persecution, eventually developed into an executive committee for the English Society as a whole. Much of this organizational framework had, in fact, come into existence during the previous decades. But by establishing it on a permanent footing, by, so to speak, institutionalizing the religion of the Spirit, Fox put an end to the threat of anarchy that had dogged Quakers from the outset. In most respects, the new organization became a model for the transplanted Quakerism of British North America and the West Indian islands.

The same institutionalization that created a Society of Friends was applied, also, to the Quaker repudiation of war. The peace testimony became a branch of the Society's discipline. As the old Quaker warriors in the Lamb's War died off, they were succeeded by a new generation for whom pacifism had become part of a traditional faith, albeit a faith that was often cherished with a genuine devotion. Anyone who deviated from the peace testimony by supporting military activities was now promptly disowned. However, in Britain, Quaker "sufferings" on account of refusal of militia or army service were never severe, although Friends in coastal areas encountered periodic trouble from attempts to impress them into the Royal Navy. In 1693, London Yearly Meeting passed the first of a series of resolutions condemning the arming of vessels owned or captained by Quakers (a prohibition not always obeyed, as minutes of local meetings had to acknowledge "sorrowfully" over the course of the succeeding century). In regard to taxes, though the position was not in all respects clear, almost every Quaker willingly rendered taxes "in the mixture," that is, where only an indeterminate proportion went to support war; and many eminent British Friends urged payment even when the money would be allocated wholly for military purposes, since this allocation might be construed as being solely Caesar's responsibility.

In the course of the eighteenth century, American Quakerism outstripped the British Society in numbers. It had originated in the efforts of missionaries who, beginning in the mid-1650's, crossed the ocean to publish the "Truth" in the struggling little settlements on the new continent. It grew thereafter with the influx of Quaker immigrants, who left their native land either to escape the religious persecution that lasted until the Glorious Revolution of 1688 or to seek better economic conditions in the New World, and it grew, too, with the conversion of colonists. The American Society of Friends remained, however, closely bound to Quakers in the British Isles, even after the overwhelming majority of Friends were American-born. Whereas ties between the immigrant Mennonites and Amish and their coreligionists in Europe became increasingly tenuous as time passed, it was not until the nineteenth century—when the great westward movement placed Friends in the same frontier conditions that had served to isolate the rural German peace sectaries earlier and when the American Quaker schisms shattered the unity of the Society—that the close Anglo-American Quaker connection was relaxed for a time.

Apart from the continuous and massive Quaker migration that continued for half a century and more (greatly augmented, of course, after Penn had acquired his province in 1682), it was the institution of traveling ministers that did more than anything else to cement ties between the two branches of Quakerism. By the end of the seventeenth century the exchanges had become two-way, for not only did Friends from the British Isles come to visit and encourage the struggling Quaker communities in the New World, but now the latter had grown strong enough to send their own concerned members for pastoral work in Britain. On the roster of ministers visiting America we find, besides George Fox, the names of many other leading British Friends. The itinerant Quaker minister may, indeed, be reckoned as one of the most effective builders of the spiritual empire of Friends.

Unity among Friends was also reinforced by other agencies. There was, for instance, the voluminous and often intimate correspondence between London Yearly Meeting and the various yearly meetings on the American continent, as well as between individual Friends on different sides of the ocean. Trade relations were usually close between British and American Quaker merchants, who often wielded an influence in their respective societies commensurate with their wealth rather than with their numerical strength. In addition, British and American Friends enjoyed a common religious culture and read the same devotional books and pamphlets. They came to share, too, from early in the eighteenth century on in joint humanitarian endeavors: such concerns as antislavery, penal reform, and the relief of material suffering exercised the conscience and imagination of the more sensitive spirits among Friends equally on both continents. Above all, London Yearly Meeting retained its position as a center of Quakerism as much for American as for British Friends, a position that it continued to enjoy even after the American colonies had established their independence. London's decisions, as we shall see later, were often accepted without argument by American yearly meetings and incorporated into their books of discipline.

The stout English and Welsh yeomen who made up the early generations of Quaker immigrants and, later, their descendants stressed proudly their rights as freeborn English citizens and were ready, in spite of their belief in nonviolence, to assert them even against their fellow Quaker, Proprietor William Penn. This was a quite different attitude from that displayed by the otherworldly German-speaking peasants and craftsmen from whom were drawn the members of the Mennonite communities of North America. After Friends, like other Americans, became citizens of the new Republic, they went on trying to leaven the world rather than to withdraw from it. Their continued quest for peace has represented one facet of this endeavor.

PIONEERS OF THE PEACEABLE KINGDOM

KEY TO ABBREVIATIONS
(*in footnotes and bibliography*)

AHR	*American Historical Review*
BFHA	*Bulletin of Friends' Historical Association*
C.O.	conscientious objector
EHR	*English Historical Review*
F.H.L.S.C.	Friends Historical Library, Swarthmore College
H.C.Q.C.	Haverford College Quaker Collection
M. M.	Monthly Meeting (Quaker)
MQR	*Mennonite Quarterly Review* (Goshen, Ind.)
NEQ	*New England Quarterly*
PMHB	*Pennsylvania Magazine of History and Biography* (Philadelphia)
Q. M.	Quarterly Meeting (Quaker)
Y. M.	Yearly Meeting (Quaker)

Chapter 1

The Society of Friends
in the Colonial Period outside
Pennsylvania

The peace testimony of the colonial Quakers was, we have seen, as much an outgrowth of the parent society in Britain as were the other elements of the faith, which the "First Publishers of Truth" brought with them on their journey across the ocean. This Anglo-American Quaker connection remained lively and close well into the nineteenth century. Yet, despite the manifold similarities in belief and practice, the peace witness of the colonial Quakers was never an exact reflection of that of Friends back in Britain, for in this New World the Quaker pioneers, like their fellow citizens of other faiths, had to face a complex of factors—geographical, political, economic, and religious—differing in many important respects from that existing back home. For the Quakers, a greater share in affairs of state (and this not only in Pennsylvania) and also, in many cases, greater insecurity in daily life introduced new problems in their attempt to create a fellowship of men and women dedicated to the achievement of a society without violence.

Quakerism was brought to the New World in the second half of the 1650's. Within a few decades adherents of the "Truth" (as its followers boldly called their faith) were to be found organized in compact meetings in most of the Atlantic coast colonies as well as in a number of the islands of the British West Indies. Important Quaker settlements soon arose in the existing colonies of Massachusetts, Plymouth, New Hampshire, Rhode Island, New York (then New Netherlands), Maryland, Virginia, and the Carolinas and also, with their opening to colonization, in New Jersey and Pennsylvania (along with Delaware). In the eighteenth century small Quaker groups came into being in Georgia as well as in Maine, to which Friends had found their way in the previous century. Only in Connecticut did Quakerism meet with scarcely any response during this period. Indeed, "by the middle of the eighteenth century there were more Quakers in the Western hemisphere than in Great Britain,"[1] even though by this date the early

---

[1] Rufus M. Jones, *The Quakers in the American Colonies*, p. xv. At the end of the colonial period there were probably about 50,000 Quakers on the American continent out of a total population of approximately 2,500,000.

missionary vigor that had aimed at bringing the whole world speedily into the spirit of Christian truth had given way to the cultivation of a narrower sectarian ethos, which sought to preserve intact the virtues of a "peculiar people."

Among the colonial Quakers, as in Britain, strict adherence to the peace testimony was maintained by the imposition of sanctions against those who deviated from it. Those members who strayed and would not express regret for their offense were dealt with in the same way as those who transgressed other precepts of the discipline, expulsion from the Society being the final step against any who remained impervious to admonition and exhortation. At this time there were still very few Friends who urged that, although pacifism should remain a collective witness of the Society, it would be better for the individual to decide exactly what stand he should take in regard to military service or self-defense. A nonpacifist Quaker like Penn's secretary, James Logan, or Anthony Benezet, the pacifist expatriate Frenchman who favored a relaxation of the discipline in regard to the peace testimony, remained isolated figures, and it was not until the twentieth century that the Society finally came to adopt their position (at least unofficially).

The main issue dominating the history of the Quaker peace testimony in colonial America was, of course, military service. Outside Pennsylvania, conscription for the local militia was in force in all the provinces for almost the whole period. Only in Rhode Island did the law give Friends complete exemption. Elsewhere, exemption, where provided for, was granted only on terms that were usually unacceptable to them, for Quakers would neither pay the required fine in commutation of service which they believed to be wrong in itself nor hire another man to perform it in their stead, as the law also sometimes permitted.[2] Obduracy of this kind often brought distraint of property—frequently far in excess of the amount of the fine—and sometimes imprisonment. However, there existed considerable variation in the rigor with which the law was enforced. In times of peace, and in small communities where the sincerity of Quaker objections

---

[2] Of course, Friends did not always live up to their principles in this as in other respects. To give just one example, in 1760 we find New England Y. M. lamenting: "We are sorrowfully affected, by the answers to the queries, that some Friends have failed in the maintenance of our Christian testimony against wars and fighting, by joining with others to hire substitutes, and by the payment of money to exempt themselves from personal service in the militia. . . . Let therefore the care of Friends, in their several monthly-meetings, be exerted to prevent any contributions for hiring substitutes, or other methods of exempting themselves from the militia, inconsistent with our well-known testimony" (*The Book of Discipline* [1785], p. 148).

4

was well known to their neighbors, law enforcement was mild, and delinquents often escaped without penalty. Indeed, the drills of the militia were at times more social than martial affairs. But, when a war scare occurred or when actual fighting had broken out, the Quakers often suffered considerable hardship as a result of their refusal to fight; and such occasions were not rare in seventeenth- and eighteenth-century America, for, with the Indian border not too far from any of the settlements and with the long coastline and the Caribbean islands open to attack from Britain's European enemies, whether Dutch or Spanish or French, and from marauding privateers who were also active in periods of nominal peace, war conditions were present most of the time. On such occasions, too, men of military age might be called out by special decree to participate in expeditions against the enemy outside their province.

Periodic musterings of the local militia and occasional summonses to active service at a distance did not exhaust the military demands that might be made of young Quaker males. They could also be required to take their turn in armed watches to guard against foreign invaders or indigenous marauders and could be called up for labor in building fortifications and military encampments. Moreover, in the New England coastal areas Quakers, especially those who had chosen the sea as their career, were sometimes subjected to impressment into the royal navy. Occasionally, too, cases are recorded where soldiers, coming under the influence of Quaker ideas while in the service, developed a conscientious objection to further military duties.[3]

---

[3] One of the most curious instances of this kind is contained in the memoirs of the eighteenth-century English-born Friend, Elizabeth Ashbridge (1713-1775), printed in the next century in *The Friends' Library*, vol. IV. She had emigrated to America as an indentured servant and had there married a young schoolmaster, who proved to be a hard drinker, an irreligionist, and a frequenter of bad company. The couple eventually settled in New Jersey, where she was converted to Quakerism and was recognized as a minister in the Society. Her religious views were, however, very unpopular with her husband, who ridiculed them and subjected his wife to blows and oaths on their account. Her attempts to reform him proved unavailing, and her efforts to interest him in Friends appeared at the time to be without effect. At last, in 1741 during a drinking bout in Burlington, her husband enlisted as a common soldier to fight in the expedition against Spanish-held Cuba. The rest of the story may be told in Elizabeth's own words: "I have since had cause to believe that he was benefited by the rash act, as in the army, he did what he could not at home; he suffered for the testimony of Truth. When they came to prepare for an engagement, he refused to fight; he was whipped and brought before the general, who asked him why he enlisted if he would not fight. 'I did it,' said he, 'in a drunken frolic, when the devil had the better of me; but now my judgment is convinced I ought not to fight, neither will I, whatever I suffer. I have but one life, and you may take that if you please, for I'll never take up arms.' He adhered to this resolution. By their cruel usage of him in consequence, he was

Quakers who were not liable to direct military service also had to face problems in adjusting their pacifist beliefs to the demands of Caesar. Here, perhaps, taxation was the most trying issue.[4] From the beginning, as we have seen, most Friends had felt that there was nothing inconsistent with their peace testimony in paying what they called taxes "in the mixture," that is, taxes of which only a part went for the support of war. They dutifully paid ordinary taxes to the government in time of war, too. There was less unanimity, however, in the case of special war taxes, where it was known that the whole sum paid would be used to carry on war. "George Fox himself paid war taxes," and so did a number of other leading Friends in the early days. Others refused. (And, of course, payment of any kind of assessment that could be at all construed as an alternative to direct military service was forbidden to Friends.[5]) The tax issue in its relation to the peace testimony was, as we shall see, to be vigorously debated among colonial Friends, some of whom advocated nonpayment not only of war taxes but of mixed ones, too. Finally, in the American Revolution, nonpayment of most taxes to an administration engaged in waging war against the traditionally established government became the official policy of the whole Society.

In their businesses many Friends took great care to avoid all support of warmaking, although there were still others whose laxness in this regard became a matter of concern to the Quaker meetings and had to be dealt with by them. The chief offenses were the manufacturing and trading of articles of war, the arming of vessels, either owned by members of the Society or used for shipping Quaker goods, and involvement in privateering.

Behavior in consonance with the peaceful principles to which the Society laid claim was demanded of every individual member. Naturally, since American Quakerism was a society made up of ordinary human beings, and not saints (although it did, indeed, produce several saints of the caliber of John Woolman), harmony among its members and between members and nonmembers was not always maintained. But members of the Society were expected to show an example of nonviolence in their daily lives, even if lapses from this high

---

so much disabled that the general sent him to Chelsea Hospital, near London. Within nine months afterwards he died at this place, and I hope made a good end" (p. 22).

[4] See Ernest R. Bromley, "Did Early Friends Pay War Taxes?" *Friends Intelligencer*, 16 Oct. 1948, pp. 591-93.

[5] See, e.g., a minute of New England Y. M. in 1762, *The Book of Discipline* (1785), p. 148.

standard would inevitably occur.[6] And, if the dispute were one between fellow members, Friends were forbidden to go to law until every attempt had been made to settle the affair by arbitration.

However, at least during this period, Quaker pacifism differed from the Anabaptist-Mennonite variety in its positive attitude toward the nonmilitary functions of the state. Not merely in Pennsylvania during the years of Quaker rule, but in Rhode Island, and much more briefly in New Jersey, Maryland, and the Carolinas, Friends participated in the government and legislature. In this sphere the practice of the Society in America during this period differed radically from that of its parent Society in Britain, which, as a body of religious dissenters, was by the law of the land effectively excluded from all part in government. But politics meant compromise, and we shall find, both in Pennsylvania and in the other colonies where Friends had access to power, that their peace testimony became to some extent adjusted to the demands of expediency. Still, they continued as a body to bear witness to a nonviolent way of life.

Throughout the colonial period the question of self-defense against Indian attack, especially where Quakers were settled in frontier districts, constituted not merely an academic exercise in pacifist dialectic but an issue that all might be called upon to face at some moment in their lives. The same was true for the Caribbean islands, where the sometimes more bloodthirsty pirate or privateer took the place of the marauding Indian. The history of Quaker Indian policy falls outside the scope of the present study except insofar as it bears directly on their pacifism.[7] The essence of this policy, both as carried out by individual Friends and as expressed in the actions of the Quaker regime in Pennsylvania, lay in their desire to deal justly with the Indian peoples, giving a fair price for their lands and settling only with their prior assent, dealing equitably with them in trade, and refraining from corrupting them by the sale of hard liquor. When Pennsylvania de-

---

[6] See, e.g., the following declaration made to his meeting by a Rhode Island Friend in 1767: "A man came to me in my field and tho' I desired him to keep off, yet [he] made an attempt to beat or abuse me. To prevent which I suddenly and with too much warmth pushed him from me with the rake I was leaning on, which act of mine as it did not manifest to that Christian patience and example in suffering trials becoming my profession I therefore freely condemn it and desire that I may be enabled for the future to suffer patiently any abuse or whatever else I may be tried with and also desire Friends to continue their watchful care over me." Caroline Hazard, *The Narrangansett Friends' Meeting in the XVIII Century*, p. 101.

[7] See Rayner Wickersham Kelsey, *Friends and the Indians 1655-1917*, pp. 19-24, 27-29, 38-47, 51, 52, 55-62, 70-74, for Quaker-Indian relations outside Pennsylvania during the period up to 1775.

parted from this policy (against the wishes of its Quaker legislators), bitter warfare eventually followed.

The American Indians with whom colonial Friends came into contact apparently remained unmoved by the Quaker message, despite occasional attempts by men like William Penn and John Woolman to reach them. Although there were Indians who showed some understanding of the indwelling God of the Quakers ("the good Spirit"), no converts were made. At times Quakers not only attempted to let their actions toward the Indians explain the nature of Quaker pacifism without the intermediacy of words, but tried also to expound the nature of the Society's nonviolent faith to them. A moving example of this latter approach is recorded in the autobiography of Samuel Bownas (1676-1753), a traveling minister, who in 1702 found himself in jail on Long Island (N.Y.) for speaking out against the Church of England. During his incarceration he was visited by "an Indian King" and three of his chiefs, who were able to converse in English. When the king inquired of Bownas what the differences were between Quakers and other Christians, Bownas sought among other things to elucidate the Quaker peace testimony. Christians outside the Society, he told his inquirers,

... held it *lawful* to kill and destroy their enemies; but we cannot think that good and right in us; but rather endeavour to overcome our enemies with courteous and friendly offices and kindness, and to assuage their wrath by mildness and persuasion, and bring them to consider the injury they are doing to such as can't in conscience revenge themselves again. He assented, *that this was good: but who can do it?* said he; *when my enemies seek my life, how can I do other than use my endeavour to destroy them in my own defence?* My answer was, That unless we were under the government of a better spirit than our enemies, we could not do it; but if we are under the government of the good Spirit, which seeks not to destroy men's lives, but to save them, and teaches us to do good for evil and to forgive injuries, then we can submit to *Providence*, putting our trust in the great God to save us from the violence and wrath of our enemies. The King said, *Indeed this is very good; but do you do thus when provoked by your enemies?* I said, sundry of our Friends had done so, and been saved from the rage of their enemies, who have confessed our Friends to be good men. Ay, said he, *they are good indeed; for if all came into this way, there would then be no more need of war, nor killing one the other to enlarge their kingdoms, nor one nation want to overcome another.* I then asked him, if this was not a right principle; and what would much add to the happiness of mankind? They all four said, *it was very good indeed; but feared few would embrace this doctrine.* I said, all things have their beginnings; and 'tis now our duty to embrace this truth, hoping that others by this example may do the same. They lifted up their eyes as a token of their assent, shewing by their words their desire that this good spirit might prevail in the world: *Then,* said they, *Things will go well.*[8]

The records of the period contain plentiful illustrations of the kind of nonviolent approach to personal defense that Bownas describes here as being the practice of members of his Society. Far more frequently than his coreligionists back in Britain, the American Friend was to find himself in situations of potential violence that would test this belief.[9]

Quaker pacifists at their best, whether in America or in Europe, bore witness to their beliefs in both a negative and a positive fashion—in the one case, by an uncompromising refusal to meet the military demands of Caesar and, in the other, by an outflow of love for their fellowmen, whether heathen Indians or Christians belonging to "enemy" nations. This witness remained circumscribed in its dimensions, however. There was little attempt, until the arrival of John Woolman and a handful of Friends who shared his outlook, to think through the social aspects of the peace testimony, to understand how Friends' protest against war and their refusal to resist attack by violence were related to shortcomings in the existing political and social order, in particular to the evil of slavery and to inequalities in wealth. With the exception of the practical experiment in peaceable government carried out in Pennsylvania, the American Quaker communities of the colonial period failed to examine the possibilities of creating a peaceful international order; no works were produced on this continent to parallel the schemes for international peace of the English Quakers, William Penn and John Bellers. In neither Britain nor America at this time had thinking within the Society matured to the point of exploring ways and means of setting up a nonviolent technique of dealing with aggression, whether inside society or from outside invasion.

Sources for the history of Quaker pacifism in the colonial period are

---

[8] *An Account of the Life and Ministry of Samuel Bownas,* pp. 79-81.

[9] The journals of visiting ministers from Britain (e.g., those of Thomas Story and Thomas Chalkley, who traveled in the West Indies and on the American continent during the first half of the eighteenth century, which have been used extensively in this chapter) also provide examples of a courageous upholding of Quaker nonviolence in situations of conflict.

plentiful enough, but (except for those relating to the Pennsylvania experiment) they do not easily lend themselves to a chronological treatment, nor can they readily be used to give an overall picture of the colonial scene. Each colony, after all, enjoyed a completely autonomous existence, dependent only upon the mother country; each had its own separate constitution and political and religious institutions, though derived from the same British roots; each moved to a large extent along separate lines of historical and economic evolution. Yet common factors there certainly were, factors which, developing in the course of the eighteenth century, led eventually with the war as catalyst to the creation of a united Republic out of these disparate provinces. In colonial Quakerism, likewise, there were common threads present which knit the Society throughout the different colonies into a community with, in this case, virtually one mode of worship and similar ways of life. On the other hand, here also the divergence in development, which dominated the overall American picture, was mirrored in the life of the Society of Friends. Autonomous organizations sprang up in New England, New York, Pennsylvania (together with Delaware and New Jersey), Maryland, Virginia, and North Carolina. In these areas the peace witness of Friends, though it followed roughly the same pattern in each, can best be illustrated by separate treatment. This, therefore, will be the method adopted in the more detailed account given below.

I

Probably the first Quakers to reach the American continent were two English women missionaries, Mary Fisher and Ann Austin, who landed in Boston on 11 July 1656. The alarmed magistrates drove them from the town within a month after their arrival. But on 7 August, a couple of days after their expulsion, eight more Quakers from England succeeded in making a landing. Despite the passing, soon after, of the first of a series of anti-Quaker laws of mounting severity that the Massachusetts colony (followed by its sister colony, Plymouth) directed against the "cursed sect," converts began to be made among the local people. Spreading also to unorthodox Rhode Island in the following year, the vigorous new faith, strong in its belief that it held the truth that would soon peaceably conquer the whole world, continued to gather new adherents in the Puritans' New England stronghold until "by the year 1660 . . . the whole southern part . . . was . . . honeycombed with Quakerism."[10] Neither the heavy fines, whippings of men

[10] Jones, *The Quakers*, p. 62.

and women stripped to the waist, ear croppings and tongue borings, nor even the death penalty imposed by law in 1658, which took the lives of three men and one woman in the course of the subsequent two years, were effective in stemming the tide of conversion. The year 1661 marked the foundation of New England Yearly Meeting, which still exists today. In that year, too, the most savage phase of persecution came to an end with an order procured by Quakers in England from King Charles II preventing any further executions for professing Quakerism (though it did not stop the passing of the barbarous "Cart and Whip Acts" of 1661 and 1662). Apart from a brief resuscitation of persecution in the years 1675-1677, the Quakers in Massachusetts won virtual toleration after the death of Governor John Endecott in 1665; and in the early 1670's, stimulated by the visit of George Fox and several other leading English Friends to this continent in 1672, Quakerism underwent considerable expansion throughout all of New England (except in Connecticut, which proved infertile soil for the new sect).

In Massachusetts the Puritan theocracy, at least in the beginning, successfully excluded the nonelect from all share in government. Thus, even after the cessation of persecution, Quakers there were never faced, as they were to be in neighboring Rhode Island and later in Pennsylvania, with the problems involved in squaring Christian pacifism with the requirements of Christian magistracy. Only remotely, by some vague and confused association of Quakerism with subversive Anabaptism in the minds of populace, priesthood, and magistracy alike, had their pacifism been responsible for the ferocious legislation that the civil authorities erected against them at the beginning in their unsuccessful attempt to exclude the sect altogether from the Bay colony. The roots of persecution lay elsewhere, above all in the challenge which early Quakerism presented to the church establishment in the colony.

After the fires of persecution had died down and the ardent enthusiasm of the first missionary effort had ebbed, the Massachusetts Quakers, who numbered over 3,000 in the first half of the eighteenth century, were content to pursue their way of life as a "peculiar people," worshipping God in their own fashion and living quiet lives apart from affairs of state. Compulsory service in the militia seems to have presented a serious problem only in wartime or during an invasion scare; at other times Friends usually either paid the comparatively small sums imposed as fines for nonattendance at drills or allowed their property to be distrained for failure to pay these fines (for among most New England Friends payment of commutation money was regarded as a dereliction of duty). Thus, in August 1675 during King Philip's War when an Indian attack on Boston was feared, we read, for instance, of "several men, some whereof are Quakers, [who] will not go out on command, and for their disobedience thereunto, are forced to run the gauntlet."[11] A second period of crisis came early in the next century after the outbreak of the War of the Spanish Succession, when preparations were on foot for an invasion of Canada from New England. A law was passed by the commonwealth of Massachusetts imposing a term of imprisonment on any who refused to bear arms and who were also unwilling to pay a fine in lieu of service; in addition, the law provided that delinquents were subsequently to be bound out to work for such time as was necessary to cover the cost of fine and imprisonment.

One of those Quakers who suffered under the law has left an account of his experiences. John Smith was born of Quaker parents in Dartmouth, Bristol County (Mass.), in 1681. In June 1703, then aged 22, Smith received a summons to join the militia, which he refused. At first, no action was taken against him. But in January of the following year, a year of intense Indian warfare, when the Massachusetts clergy were proclaiming the Indian atrocities to be God's way of punishing the colony's inhabitants for suffering Quakers to live in their midst—when, therefore, hostility toward the still unpopular sect was widespread—John Smith and a second young objector, Thomas Maccomber, were tried and fined at Bristol. Upon their refusal to pay this fine, the magistrate first attempted, unsuccessfully, to hire them out for up to four years in order to cover the cost and then sentenced them to hard labor in the fort at Boston for as long as would be necessary for them to work off the fine and incidental expenses.

While in prison at Bristol, the two men were visited by the weighty traveling minister from Britain, Thomas Story (1662-1742), and another Friend from Rhode Island. Story attempted to intervene on their behalf with the judge, Colonel Nathaniel Byfield. The judge proved not unfriendly, although he felt that only "ignorance, and a perverse nature," could lead anyone to refuse to fight against such dangerous enemies as the French and Indians had proved themselves to be. At the trial Story spoke on behalf of the two Friends. In reply to Colonel Byfield's query why Friends who willingly paid ordinary taxes

---

[11] *Narratives of the Indian Wars 1675-1699*, 1952 edn., p. 44. "Running the gauntlet" was a form of punishment frequently used by the Indians, in the course of which a man could actually be beaten to death. The quotation is from a contemporary eyewitness account, "The Present State of New-England with Respect to the Indian War."

could not pay in this instance, Story drew a distinction between a "general tax," which Christ had required his followers to pay regardless of the fact that Caesar might apply a part for war purposes, and a tax imposed in lieu of personal military service, an activity which Quakers believed to be contrary to their Christian profession. For their part, the young men stated that "'it was not obstinacy, but duty to God, according to their consciences, and religious persuasions, which prevailed with them to refuse to bear arms, or learn war.'"

Soon after arriving at Boston, Smith and Maccomber were sent to the fort, where they were supposed "to work as pioneers." Despite their unwillingness to perform labor of a military nature, they were on the whole treated well as prisoners: "the people behaved civilly towards me," Smith writes, "as believing I acted from a religious principle."

Story had followed the two men to Boston, and shortly after his arrival he paid a visit, along with two other Friends, to the governor of Massachusetts. To him he endeavored to explain the basis of Friends' objections to war. The governor was sympathetic, but he told Story "'that he was no disputant about religion; . . . to tell you the truth, said he, seeing the judges have given such a judgment, I cannot tell how to dispense with it; especially now in time of war, when every body thinks there is both so much need of help, and just cause of war.'" When Story mentioned the prophecy concerning the time when swords would be beaten into plowshares, the governor replied: "'That day . . . is not come; for you see many nations are at war at this time.'" In any event, he continued, if he were to release the young men before their time was up, he would set the whole community against him. If the judge had erred in sentencing them, then recourse should be had to the law to rectify the mistake. But we are poor people, Story now insisted, and cannot afford the costly process of appeal; we believe that you do possess the authority to release them if you wish. To this objection the governor responded as before, "'that the country would be about his ears if he should do that; but, said he, it is a harmless thing to work at the castle; they need not fight there.'" Story protested, "'that is an erection for war, and we cannot be active in such works as may be thought necessary there.'" Unfortunately, neither these arguments nor the petition Story later composed asking for the prisoners' release succeeded in gaining their object. The men remained in the fort for four months more until the governor finally relented and ordered them to be sent home.[12]

[12] John Smith, *A Narrative of Some Sufferings for His Christian Peaceable Testi-*

Thanks to young Smith's own narrative and the journal of the older Friend, Thomas Story, we can follow the details of the debate between Quaker conscience and the military establishment. Normally, as Henry J. Cadbury has written, "while today we are kept carefully informed of Friends in prison for refusal of military service, cases of the same sort two centuries ago existed uncollected and unlisted. A mere accident brings now one or another to our attention."[13] One such case, uncovered by Professor Cadbury himself, is that of Hatsell O'Kelley, a "husbandman" from the village of Yarmouth on Cape Cod who in 1748, at the end of the War of the Austrian Succession, was drafted for military service. However, the captain "by whose warrant he was impressed" was unable to "find any estate of the said Hatsell O'Kelley's whereby to make distress upon for said ten pounds," which was the penalty imposed for his refusal to serve. O'Kelley was therefore sentenced to six months' imprisonment in the Barnstable County jail and assessed the costs of prosecution. Nevertheless, O'Kelley did not have to languish for long in prison, for the monthly meeting at Sandwich raised the necessary funds to obtain his release. This meeting, at least in this period, apparently had no scruples about the payment of fines in lieu of service.

Quakers in the seacoast districts of New England, who often chose the sea rather than the farm as their source of livelihood, were subject to the danger of impressment into the British navy, as well as to the other perils of the seafaring life of that day. In time of war the chances of impressment occurring were, of course, greatly increased. Again, it is the young Quaker, John Smith, who provides us with a fully authenticated example of the impressment of a Quaker into the royal navy. Smith, after being released from his Boston prison, joined the crew of a ship bound for London that was owned by a well-to-do New England Quaker merchant. All went well on the voyage until

---

mony, pp. 6-10; A Journal of the Life of Thomas Story, pp. 264-70, 309-12, 339. Jones (The Quakers, p. 150) cites details from the minutes of New England Y. M. for 1712 concerning four young Massachusetts Quakers who were imprisoned for refusing to serve in the expedition to Canada of the previous year. Two of the men were well treated, but two, who had been imprisoned in Boston fort, were given such "hard usage" after they had been "thence conveyed by force on board transport under ye command of Major Roberton" that, as a result, one of them, John Terry, died "within twenty-four hours after their return to Boston." During the Seven Years War, in 1759 (the year the British captured Quebec), an act was passed by the Massachusetts assembly "for the speedy levying of soldiers for an intended expedition against Canada," in which Quakers were specifically exempted by name from the draft. They were, however, to be additionally taxed in a rather roundabout manner for the privilege of such exemption.

[13] Friends Intelligencer, 23 July 1949, p. 409 ("Letter from the Past—102" by "Now and Then").

April 1704 when, on arrival at Plymouth (England), they were met by British men-of-war who seized Smith and a second young Quaker sailor, Thomas Anthony, for service in the royal fleet. Several days later the vessel to which they were assigned met with a French ship. "When they were going to engage," Smith writes, "they placed us to a gun, and commanded us to fight, but we told them we could not, for Christ and the apostles spoke to the contrary; but they not regarding what we said, hauled us about deck to make us work, but we signified we could not on any such account." Realizing that they might inadvertently be trapped into some seemingly innocent but compromising action, the two Quaker seamen were careful not to do anything that might be construed as compliance with the fighting. Their conduct soon earned them the anger of one of the lieutenants, who ordered that they be given the "cat." As they were being whipped in this barbarous fashion, which was customary in the British navy during the eighteenth century, Smith prayed for his persecutors. Later, a rough but kindly boatswain's mate remarked to them concerning their punishment: "You have been beat enough to kill an ox." Their trials, however, were by no means over, for, all the while the ship was involved in further engagements, the captain and officers continued their endeavors to make the Quakers work. "They sent for us to make points for reefing the sails," Smith relates in one place, "which I refusing to do, some mocked and scoffed, while others filled with envy and malice, could scarce keep their hands from me." The two men were not released from the ship until over a year later when the captain, allowing them to go ashore at Plymouth, made it clear that he never wanted to see his two recalcitrant tars back on board again. English Friends cared for the young men, who needed time to recuperate after their thirteen months of rough treatment in Her Majesty's navy. In London, which they visited before returning to America, they lodged with old Thomas Lurting, the former fighting sailor turned Quaker.[14]

We do not know how many other Quaker John Smiths over the years were seized on board ship and taken off to serve in the royal navy, nor whether some yielded to threats and ill-treatment and others remained firm in upholding their Society's peaceable testimony. That impressment, at least in wartime, remained a peril for the Quaker sailors of New England is certain. One writer has unearthed nineteen certificates of membership issued by local meetings during the Seven Years War to Friends "bound on a whale voyage" in an attempt to protect them against impressment or at least to provide them,

[14] Smith, A Narrative, pp. 10-18.

if taken, with evidence to show that their protest against fighting was a genuine one.[15]

The onus of opposing military requirements and naval impressments was carried by the younger men. But all Quakers might at some moment of their lives have to face the issue of war taxes or have to decide what stand they should take in case of Indian attack on themselves and their families. In regard to special war taxes, whether intended for raising troops and war equipment or for paying for the erection of fortifications, no unanimity existed among New England Friends. There were certainly some who refused to pay and as a consequence had their property distrained or, if this were insufficient to cover the amount demanded, were thrown into jail. But many more, it would seem, paid in good conscience (the matter was finally left undecided by yearly meeting), and the example of such weighty English visitors as Thomas Story, who urged Friends to pay without compunction, must have exercised an influence in the direction of compliance.

In 1702 during the sessions of New England Yearly Meeting, discussion at one point turned to a minute concerning "what Friends might do, in case there should be a lay or tax laid upon the inhabitants for building some fortifications, and to provide men and arms for the security of the island [of Rhode Island]." A British visitor, John Richardson (1666-1753), found himself appealed to by Friends present to explain how the Society in England dealt with this knotty problem. New England Friends, one of them said (according to Richardson's account), "looked upon themselves but as the daughter, and Friends . . . in old England as their mother, and they were willing to act consistent with us as far as they could, and would know how we did there in that matter, whether we could pay to that tax which was for carrying on a vigorous war against France?" Despite Richardson's obvious reluctance to get involved in the debate, Friends remained insistent on hearing his views, refusing to proceed further with the discussion until he had spoken. "At last," Richardson goes on, "when I could not well do otherwise, I signified to that large Meeting, that I had heard the matter debated both in superior and inferior meetings, and privately, and the most general result was this; Friends did not see an effectual door opened to avoid the thing, that tax being mixed [i.e., in England] with other taxes; although many Friends are not so easy as they could desire." However, he added, "there is a great disparity between our circumstances and yours here." Above all, in Rhode Island at least, he told them, "you have . . . a great share in the

15 Robert J. Leach, "Nantucket Quakerism 1661-1763" (MS in F.H.L.S.C.), chap. XIII.

government" and may thus be able in this part of the country to prevent the imposition of a tax of the kind now being discussed. Finally, he concluded by warning American Friends not to be overeager to look to the parent society for a pattern of behavior, which might actually not be applicable in the transatlantic environment; instead, he advised them, "mind your own way in the Truth, and look not out."[16]

For the problem of Indian defense, indeed, the practice of British Friends could offer little that was immediately relevant, except in the way of general principle. Living as a small minority among the hardheaded Puritan settlers, Quakers in New England became enmeshed in the Puritans' often unfair and harsh policies toward the indigenous population, the unhappy results of which constituted a negation of Friends' methods in dealing with these peoples. When the Indians in retaliation went on the warpath and proceeded to burn outlying settlements and massacre their inhabitants, threatening as well the less accessible towns and villages, Quakers in these areas were as much exposed to atrocities as their non-Quaker fellow settlers. This Indian danger lessened as the eighteenth century passed by, but in earlier days Indian attacks occurred periodically. So far as the somewhat exiguous record indicates, Friends—with a few exceptions—remained loyal to their peace testimony despite the temptation to resort to arms in self-defense, and their peaceable demeanor seems on most occasions to have been recognized by the Indians, who left them alone. During King Philip's War (1675-1676), for instance, we hear of the visiting minister, William Edmundson (1627-1712), traveling without weapons up and down the country, which was then infested by hostile Indians on the warpath. Despite frequent scalpings of whites and the burning of homesteads, the unarmed Quakers whom he visited were apparently not harmed.[17]

We know more about the situation of Friends during the Indian troubles of 1704 because two English-born Friends, Thomas Chalkley (1675-1741) and Thomas Story, were traveling in the area at this time. "It was a dismal time indeed in those parts," writes Story, "for no man knew, in an ordinary way . . . on lying down to sleep, but his first waking might be in eternity, by a salutation in the face with a hatchet, or a bullet from the gun of a merciless savage." Most of the white settlers went on about their business during the day with their guns cocked ready for immediate use, and at night they took refuge within the fortified garrisons established up and down the country. "And some professing truth [i.e., Quakers] also went into the same

16 An Account of the Life of John Richardson, pp. 128, 129.
17 A Journal of the Life of William Edmundson, sec. IX.

with their guns, and some without them." The matter was debated in meetings: "the unfaithful," records Story, "not being content in their unfaithfulness, nor satisfied in their forts and guns, sought to justify themselves in that unworthy practice, condemning the faithful as wilful and presumptuous." But on the whole, according to the testimony of the two visiting Friends, their coreligionists refused to resort to arms in their defense and were left untouched by the Indians. One of the Friends whom Chalkley visited at this time told him of his own experiences.

As he was at work in his field the Indians saw, and called him, and he went to them. They told him, that they had no quarrel with the Quakers, for they were a quiet, peaceable people and hurt nobody, and that therefore none should hurt them. But they said, that the Presbyterians in these parts had taken away their lands, and some of their lives, and would now, if they could, destroy all the Indians.

On the other hand, we hear of another Quaker living nearby, who had decided to carry a gun, being shot and killed by Indians as he went to his work along with a second Quaker, who was unarmed and unharmed by them. "When they knew that the young man they had killed was a Friend," writes Story, "they seemed to be sorry for it, but blamed him for carrying a gun: for they knew the Quakers would not fight, nor do them any harm; and therefore, by carrying a gun, they took him for an enemy."[18]

The most striking incident which took place among the Massachusetts Quakers at this time was that involving the Doe (or Dowe) family. Mary and Henry Doe lived, together with their small children and Mary's widowed mother, in an isolated farmstead in the forest not far from the town of Salisbury, "a place of as much seeming danger as any: being within pistol-shot of a great swamp, and thicket, where Indians formerly inhabited." All three were Friends. At first, they refrained from seeking shelter at night in the nearest fortified place, as their non-Quaker neighbors were doing. But after a while the old lady became increasingly nervous and eventually persuaded the young couple, who apparently were only partially convinced of the rightness of this step, to accompany her to spend the nights in the stockade

[18] Chalkley relates a similar story of two Quaker farmers who for a long time refused to follow the example of their neighbors and arm themselves when they went to work in the fields. Finally, yielding to fear, they decided to take guns with them. "And the Indians, who had seen them several times without them, and let them alone, saying, 'They were peaceable men, and hurt nobody, therefore they would not hurt them,'" now took alarm and killed both men.

under protection. One day, according to Mary Doe's own account, her mother decided to visit a friend outside the fort, but she was ambushed and killed on the way by "the bloody cruel Indians." This event, regarded as a judgment by God, convinced first the daughter and then (somewhat reluctantly) her husband that they should return home for good and "stand in a testimony for truth, and trust in the name of the Lord." Although their non-Quaker neighbors considered their action deluded and certain to end in disaster for the whole family, they stayed on in their lonely homestead "when the Indians were at our doors and windows," the children being left alone in the house when the parents went to meeting.[19]

Massachusetts Friends seem thus to have been able successfully to dissociate themselves in the eyes of the Indians from the Indian policy of the colonial government. In Rhode Island for many decades government was largely in the hands of the Quakers, who eventually came to form a considerable section of the colony's population.[20] This oasis of religious toleration in the harsh environment of Puritan New England had come into being toward the end of the 1630's as a refuge for the "Antinomian" opponents of Massachusetts theocracy, who had gathered around Mrs. Anne Hutchinson. In some ways forerunners of Quakerism, the members of the group—at least some of them— seem to have held pacifist beliefs. John Winthrop wrote that "divers of them . . . would not wear any arms," and, according to an entry in the colonial records of Rhode Island, Nicholas Easton (1593-1675), a later convert to Quakerism who was to hold the office of governor of the colony, in 1639 "was fined five shillings . . . for coming to meeting without his weapons."[21]

Within a few years after the arrival of the Quaker missionaries in New England in 1656, a number of the colony's leading citizens joined the movement, and almost immediately the colonial capital of Newport became the center of New England Quakerism. The colony's tolerant policy toward religious unorthodoxy, as well as the similarity in belief between its founding fathers and the newcomers, led Rhode Island to provide shelter to the sect that was being so fiercely persecuted in the neighboring colonies. Thus, when in the autumn of 1657

[19] *A Journal of the Life of Thomas Chalkley*, pp. 40-45; Story, *Journal*, pp. 315, 316, 318; *John Farmer's First American Journey 1711-1714* (ed. H. J. Cadbury), pp. 7, 8. These three accounts, although they vary slightly in detail, are in substantial agreement with each other.
[20] The best study of Quaker government in Rhode Island is to be found in Jones, *The Quakers*, bk. I, chap. VIII.
[21] Jones, *The Quakers*, p. 23.

the commissioners of the United Colonies wrote from Boston requesting the authorities in Rhode Island to take steps to prevent the spread of Quakerism within its boundaries, the latter, while being careful to state their dislike of Quaker tenets, sent back a polite refusal. In the following spring the commissioners tried their hand at persuading the General Assembly of the Providence Plantations (which eventually joined Rhode Island) to expel all Quakers from their midst—again without success. The fellow citizens of Roger Williams (who, however, was no friend to Quaker doctrines) answered the request by stating that freedom of conscience was a fundamental tenet of their charter. They noted, too, that the sect was allowed to exist in peace in England itself. In their colony, however, Quakers would be required to fulfill all their civil obligations according to the law. "And in case they the said Quakers which are here, or who shall arise or come among us, do refuse to subject themselves to all duties aforesaid, as training, watching, and such other engagements, as other members of civil societies, for the preservation of the same in justice and peace," they will consult the English government as to "how to carry ourselves in any further respect towards these people so, that therewithall there may be no damage, or infringement of that chief principle in our charter concerning freedom of conscience."[22]

Quaker participation in governing Rhode Island commenced at the end of the Commonwealth period with the acceptance of the faith of Friends by many of its leading men. From 1663 (the date of the Rhode Island charter) until 1714, Quakers were almost uninterruptedly in control of the colony, and even thereafter, until the eve of the American Revolution, Quakers were still to be found in high office, although their influence on politics was less. The first phase of Quaker rule in particular, which came to an end with the death in 1714 of that Quaker stalwart in government, Walter Clarke (ca. 1638-1714), was a period of incessant warfare: the two Dutch wars of 1664-1667 and 1672-1674, King Philip's War of 1675-1676, and the French and Indian wars during the reigns of William and Mary and of Anne, paralleling the great struggles which were taking place on the European continent, all brought the little seacoast colony into the orbit of the fighting. The behavior of the Quaker politicians in Rhode Island, however, is in striking contrast to that of their brethren who ruled Pennsylvania during roughly the same period. Despite certain tacit compromises and rather devious devices, Penn's colony, as we shall see later in this story, attempted to steer clear of all direct military commitments; the Quaker rulers of Rhode Island, on the other hand, while

[22] *Records of the Colony of Rhode Island and Providence Plantations*, I, 374-80.

following a general policy of peace, took measures of a military character in their administrative capacity. "Cette conduite," writes a French historian of early American Quakerism, "n'était pas d'une exacte orthodoxie et d'une parfaite limpidité."[23] Yet it was never censured by any of the meetings or by George Fox or the other leading Friends who visited Rhode Island during this period.

The explanation of this apparent inconsistency actually seems to be fairly simple. Pennsylvania, in the eyes of Friends, was the "Holy Experiment," where—so far as its position as a possession of the British Crown would allow—Quaker pacifism could be worked out as a practical policy, as an example to the nations in peaceable living. True, Quakers were soon outnumbered there by men of different faiths. But the province owed its origin and long continued to draw its general tone from the religious Society which dominated its political life. The situation was different in Rhode Island, to which Quakerism had come as a guest and where Friends, though numerous,[24] never came to possess the special position that they held in Pennsylvania. If there were to be Quaker magistrates in Rhode Island—and, as we know, most Quakers rejected the Anabaptist view of the state—Friends could lay no claim to the colony as a fitting place for carrying out an experiment in their own "peculiar" views on the use of violence. Love, they believed, is the sole weapon that, in consonance with Christ's commands, his disciples ("a holy nation," Thomas Story calls them) may use in dealing with their fellowmen. In civilized society the awe in which the magistrate's office is held should be sufficient to maintain peace and order. Nevertheless, since in their view law functions under the old dispensation and not the new, they also believed that in extreme circumstances (to use Story's words) "force may be allowed . . . in the hand of a proper officer, whose business and duty it is to apprehend and bring to justice furious and incorrigible transgressors of righteous laws and ordinances of men, for the just rule of countries and nations."[25] Thus, the Quaker officers of Rhode Island felt it their

[23] Pierre Brodin, Les Quakers en Amérique au dix-septième siècle et au début du dix-huitième, p. 153. Cf. Thomas G. Sanders, Protestant Concepts of Church and State, p. 133: "The Quaker leadership in Rhode Island did not absolutize the principle of pacifism, but saw in public office an opportunity for Christian vocation and felt that some dimensions of political life by their very nature required coercion."

[24] Around 1700, for instance, half the population of Newport was Quaker. Half the population of the country districts of the South Narragansett shore during the first half of the eighteenth century was Quaker, too.

[25] See Story, Journal, pp. 364-67, for an exposition of this standpoint, which he presented in an argument with a Baptist preacher during his travels in New England in 1704. Such views were common among early Friends in Britain.

duty in their role as magistrates of a non-Quaker polity to take on occasion forcible measures against those who threatened the internal or external security of the little colony, whether they be Indians, French, or Dutch.

In 1667, for instance, Nicholas Easton (the same Nicholas Easton who had refused to carry arms in 1639) when deputy-governor acted as chairman of a committee appointed to levy a tax for the defense of Newport. Again, in 1671, Easton, now governor, assisted by a council that was predominantly Quaker, took steps to put the colony in a posture of defense against expected attack. Further military measures received the approval of governor and council in the course of this second Anglo-Dutch war. The Quaker administration did its utmost, however, to avert the bloodthirsty struggle with the Indians known as King Philip's War, which broke out on the mainland in 1675, largely owing to the aggressive policy of the colonial government of Massachusetts. Just prior to hostilities, the Rhode Island leaders attempted to prevent bloodshed by direct negotiations with the Indian leader; going unarmed to the latter's headquarters, they proposed that arbitration of grievances be substituted for fighting. But war came—an unnecessary war in the eyes of the Rhode Island's rulers—and the colony's mainland settlements were exposed to attack and destruction.

The Quaker politicians were now faced with their most acute dilemma since their access to power: involvement in a war that was neither one that they sought nor one that they could feel was just, even under the old dispensation.[26] William Edmundson, visiting Rhode Island around this time, speaks of the "great troubles" attending Friends "by reason of the wars" raging outside the colony between Indians and white settlers. "The people, that were not Friends, were outrageous to fight; but the Governor being a Friend, (one Walter Clarke) could not give commissions to kill and destroy men."[27] True, despite strong pressure for increasing military commitment from the non-Quaker inhabitants on the exposed mainland and from the other New England colonies, the Quaker-dominated administration and legislature did their best to avoid direct involvement in fighting the Indians. But—Edmundson's assertion to the contrary—they did once again sanction military preparedness, though in a rather halfhearted manner. On 12 April 1676, Clarke, on the eve of his election as governor to succeed the old pioneer of Rhode Island Quakerism, William Coddington (1601-1678), wrote to the Providence authorities: "We well

[26] Jones, *The Quakers*, pp. 173-79, 181-84.
[27] Edmundson, *Journal*, p. 81.

approve your advice and willingness to maintain a garrison, and have agreed to bear the charge of ten men upon the colony's account." The general assembly, which Quakers also dominated, had resolved that "there appears absolute necessity for the defence and safety of this colony" and therefore "for the orderly managings of the militia this Assembly do agree to choose a major to be chief captain of all the colony forces." Although naturally a non-Quaker was appointed to this post, his commission summoning him to do his utmost "to kill, expulse, expel, take and destroy all and every the enemies of this His Majesty's colony" was signed by Coddington, the Quaker governor. And, what is more, the two emissaries that the assembly had dispatched forthwith to Providence with instructions "to determine whether a garrison or garrisons shall be kept there at the charge of the colony and the place or places where they shall be kept and whether at all" were also Quakers.[28]

Clarke and a number of the other Quaker politicians took a leading part in the life of their meeting, serving as ministers and in other responsible functions. For a long period there is little evidence that either they or their fellow Quakers saw any inconsistency between their governmental activities and their profession as Friends (though it is interesting to note that they apparently stood aside when capital punishment was inflicted in court). Individual Friends had been exempted in 1673 from the military service that continued to be obligatory in the colony even after the Quakers came into virtual control of its government. (This was, incidentally, the first piece of legislation in America granting the right of conscientious objection to war.) The terms of the act were generous, for not merely did it exempt all who had genuine religious scruples against bearing arms but in peacetime demanded no alternative in the way of fine or civilian service from those who became conscientious objectors. In time of danger, however,

When any enemy shall approach or assault the colony or any place thereof, . . . then it shall be lawful for the civil officers for the time being, as civil officers (and not as martial or military) to require such said persons as are of sufficient able body and of strength (though exempt from arming and fighting), to conduct or convey out of the danger of the enemy, weak and aged impotent persons, women and children, goods and cattle, by which the common weal may be the better maintained, and works of mercy manifested to distressed, weak persons; and shall be required to watch to inform

[28] Jones, *The Quakers*, pp. 184-89. See also Douglas Edward Leach, *Flintlock and Tomahawk*, pp. 196, 197.

of danger (but without arms in martial manner and matters), and to perform any other civil service by order of the civil officers for the good of the colony, and inhabitants thereof.[29]

Thus, apart from a brief anti-Quaker reaction in 1676 after King Philip's War when exemption was withdrawn, Friends in Rhode Island, like their brethren in colonial Pennsylvania, remained untroubled by the problem of militia service, which on occasion proved so bothersome in the other provinces where the Society was established.

In the French and Indian conflict during William and Mary's reign, successive Quaker governors excused themselves under various pretexts from sending, in the shape of men and military supplies, the aid that the governor of New York was demanding. Although their peaceable principles may have contributed to their reluctance in the matter, these principles did not appear among the ostensible reasons given in their correspondence. The struggle around this time to prevent Massachusetts from gaining control over the colony's militia did not arise from pacifist scruples; it was rather the result of the Quaker politicians' ardent local patriotism, which had shown itself earlier in their championship of local autonomy against James II's attempt to convert Rhode Island into a royal colony.

Quaker participation in Rhode Island politics was less evident in the eighteenth century. But the leading Quaker family of this period, the Wantons, whose prominence in the Society was not unconnected with the fortune they had derived from their shipbuilding activities, contributed several outstanding local politicians. Like their predecessors, they too had to face the difficult task of squaring political necessity with their Quaker conscience. This dilemma is illustrated by the case of John Wanton (1672-1742). In his younger days he had, along with his elder brother, revolted against his father's Quakerism (the father Edward had been among the early converts in Boston) and had taken up amateur soldiering. In this pursuit John had acquired the rank of colonel of the militia. In 1712, however, having reached

[29] *Records of Rhode Island*, II, 495-99. In late 1675 a number of the wounded colonial troops were sent to Rhode Island to be nursed. A contemporary account relates: "Governor William Coddington received the wounded soldiers kindly, though some churlish Quakers were not free to entertain them until compelled by the Governor." Coddington would appear to have been acting within the rights accorded the governor by this act of 1673, which required pacifists in wartime "to perform any other civil service" that the nonmilitary authorities deemed beneficial. Jones (*The Quakers*, p. 186) makes an apt comment: "These Quakers believed the war thoroughly unjust, and desired to withhold from all acts which might seem like taking part in the war, though in declining to nurse wounded soldiers they were surely pushing their scruples too far."

the age of 40, he regained his Quaker faith and became an active and respected minister in Newport Meeting. An English Friend who visited the town in that year writes: "This John Wanton had been a valiant colonel: But now has ceased from carnal wars and is employed in Christ's service against the devil and his works."[30]

John's accession to Quakerism not only brought out his talents as a preacher but eventually opened the way to a political career in the province. From 1729 until his death in 1742, he served uninterruptedly first as deputy-governor and then, from 1733, as governor of the province. When, toward the end of his career, war with Spain (which developed subsequently into war with France) led the legislature, now no longer predominantly Quaker, to pass in 1740 an act providing for the defense of the colony and for dispatching volunteers to fight in the West Indies, the responsibility for the execution of these measures lay with the governor—John Wanton, the Quaker minister. Wanton continued to fulfill the duties of his office, despite strong criticism from his meeting, and defended himself vigorously against charges of inconsistency and violation of his obligations as a Friend. Times had evidently changed. Although John Wanton's conduct as an executive officer of the colony followed exactly in the pattern of a whole line of Quaker predecessors back to the days of George Fox, feeling in the Society at large had grown more sensitive (as it was also beginning to do on the question of slavery) to the implications of the peace testimony in public as well as in private life, and on this occasion a meeting committee was appointed to interview their friend, the governor. Even so, Wanton successfully asserted his right to behave as he was doing before his meeting, and there were several more Quakers in high office in the colony before the conclusion of the colonial period. John's nephew Gideon Wanton, who was governor in the mid-1740's, for instance, was responsible for sending reinforcements to serve in the expedition against Cape Breton Island in 1745. True, Stephen Hopkins was no longer a Friend when he signed the Declaration of Independence. But he was only disowned in 1774, and for an offense against the discipline unconnected with his disregard in public life for his Society's peace testimony. Altogether, indeed, the record of the political Quakers of Rhode Island makes an interesting contrast to the role played by their counterparts in Pennsylvania.[31]

Public life was not the only sphere in which Rhode Island Friends showed a certain ambivalence in their attitude toward their peace

[30] John Farmer's First American Journey, pp. 8, 18, 19.

[31] Jones, The Quakers, pp. 202-5, 207-12; John Russell Bartlett, History of the Wanton Family, pp. 53-55, 69-76.

testimony. Not infrequently during the eighteenth century, members in good standing—including scions of such prominent Quaker families as the Wantons, Pitts, and Hazards, to name a few—were implicated in privateering activities.[32] (In the early decades of the century some Friends on the little island of Nantucket belonging to Massachusetts, an island whose population at this time was largely Quaker, had also engaged in privateering.) In this case, however, public duty could scarcely be pleaded in exoneration of action that was so obviously in contradiction with Quaker pacifism: the arming of Quaker-owned or Quaker-captained vessels had been strongly condemned by the parent society in Britain as well as by Pennsylvania Friends. In 1774, New England Yearly Meeting renewed its disapproval of such conduct in an official minute. "Some professing to be of our Society," it stated sorrowfully, "have of late slighted and neglected this our ancient and Christian testimony to that degree as to be concerned in privateering, or as owners in ships going with letters of marque, which is a flagrant and lamentable departure from our peaceable principle." The minute then went on to call for the disownment of all who continued their connection with privateering after being summoned by their meetings to mend their ways.[33]

Nevertheless, despite the solemn ban on this activity, there is evidence that some of the Quaker merchants of Rhode Island (as well as some in England and a few in Philadelphia) had engaged in privateering during the Seven Years War, too, when Quaker-owned vessels were sometimes armed for protection against attack. That individual Friends put profit before precept is not surprising, but that, despite the official policy of yearly meeting, their local meetings apparently took no action against them sheds an interesting light on the state of the peace testimony at this date—particularly in view of the alacrity with which what seem to us today minor infringements of the discipline were punished by disownment.

Newport not only became the center of New England Quakerism but was also in the 1670's the birthplace of the small sect of Rogerenes (a movement that had broken away from the Baptists) whose religious doctrines and practice were shaped to a considerable degree under Quaker influence. Their pacifism, too, probably derived from the inspiration of Friends. We hear of "divers persons [in Rhode Island] of several societies, who are one in that point of conscience, of not training and not fighting to kill" (to quote the words of the colony's

[32] A. T. Gary [Pannell], "The Political and Economic Relations of English and American Quakers (1750-1785)," D.Phil. thesis, Oxford (1935), pp. 112-14.

[33] New England Y. M. ms Discipline, in the H.C.Q.C., pp. 116, 117.

militia act of 1673).[34] This may be a reference to Rogerenes as well as Quakers. The sect's founder, John Rogers, Sr. (d. 1721), was a prosperous and well-educated farmer and tradesman, who gained his first adherents among well-to-do townsmen and country folk. Fiercely persecuted for many decades outside tolerant Rhode Island, they eventually became centered in Connecticut around New London where, as a slowly dwindling group, they survived to the end of the nineteenth century, remaining throughout firmly devoted to their pacifist witness.[35] At the beginning of the eighteenth century Samuel Bownas had written of them: "They bore a noble testimony against fighting, swearing, vain compliments and the superstitious observation of days."[36] They protested, too, against slavery and, considering their very small numbers, remained remarkably active to the end in their advocacy of humanitarian causes.

Their founder, however, had preached an otherworldly nonresistance that was perhaps more akin to the Anabaptist-Mennonite tradition than to the Quaker position (with which the Rogerenes differed also in regard to their views on baptism and the sacraments). "We are of another kingdom," he told his followers, "and therefore are not to be concerned in the kingdom we do not belong to, either to sit in judgment with them, or to fight and kill under their kingdom," being ready however "to pay them tribute for the carrying on the affairs of their kingdom and government" according to Christ's and the apostles' precepts. His disciples, he said, must stand aside from the work of government, which is tainted with blood, refusing not only to bear arms but to serve as "governor, judge, executioner or juryman, or to be active in the making any laws which may be useful in the body of the kingdoms of this world."[37]

II

Across the sound from the Rogerene settlements in Connecticut lies Long Island, where Quakerism had already taken root among English colonists before the Dutch lost it in 1664. In fact, "the first Quaker in the American colonies" was probably a Long Island resident, Richard Smith, who had been converted during a visit to England in 1654.[38] Later, Quakerism spread to the mainland of the province of New York,

---

[34] Records of Rhode Island, II, 496.
[35] See Ellen Starr Brinton, "The Rogerenes," NEQ, XVI, no. 1 (March 1943), 3-19.
[36] An Account of the Life of Samuel Bownas, p. 85.
[37] Quoted in John R. Bolles and Anna B. Williams, The Rogerenes, pp. 349-51.
[38] Jones, The Quakers, p. 219.

first to Westchester County and Manhattan and then slowly up the left bank of the Hudson. Apart from the Quaker merchants, tradesmen, and artisans of New York City, Friends in the province during the colonial period consisted mainly of farming folk and village craftsmen.

Under Dutch rule at the beginning there was a short period of persecution, but thereafter the Quakers were left more or less in peace. As New York Yearly Meeting wrote in an epistle, dated 1701, to London Yearly Meeting: "The government is kind to Friends and we enjoy our liberty."[39] Occasionally, however, there were clashes over the question of military duties. In 1672, for instance, at the outset of the second Anglo-Dutch war (in which the Dutch succeeded in regaining control of the province for a brief period), Friends, along with their fellow citizens, were asked to contribute "voluntarily" toward the repair of the fortifications of New York. Eight members of Flushing Monthly Meeting thereupon sent a letter of explanation to the English governor, in which they wrote:

It is not unknown to the Governor how willing and ready we have been to pay our customs, county rates, etc., needful town charges, etc., how we have behaved ourselves peaceably and quietly amongst our neighbors, and are ready to be serviceable in any thing which doth not infringe upon our tender consciences. But being in measure redeemed out of wars and strifes we cannot for consciencesake be concerned in upholding things of that nature. As you yourselves well know it hath not been our practice in old England or elsewhere since we were a people. And this in meakness we declare in behalf of ourselves, and our Friends, having love, and goodwill to thee, and to all men.[40]

Although on this occasion the administration appears to have been satisfied (at least no further steps were taken to enforce payment), Friends continued to suffer some hardship for their stand as conscientious objectors. The case of young John Underhill, son of the well-known English soldier of fortune of the same name, is typical of the experiences of young Friends at that date. Underhill, who had emigrated from England, settled eventually at Oyster Bay where he and his whole family became Quakers. In 1676 we find him being put in prison for refusing either "to train in the militia" or "to work on the

---

[39] *Ibid.*, p. 252.
[40] John Cox, Jr., *Quakerism in the City of New York*, pp. 70-72. The letter is also quoted in Jones, *The Quakers*, pp. 249, 250, in a slightly different version dated 10 October. Cox's volume is based directly on the New York meeting records.

fort."[41] A number of other Friends suffered distraint of goods for such offenses.[42] Despite the protests of the Quaker communities of the province that this action was contrary to the guarantee of religious liberty enjoyed by all the colony's inhabitants, the governor and his council refused to relent. To a Quaker petition asking for exemption from compulsory militia training, delivered in February 1686, the reply was given, "That no man can be exempted from that obligation and that such as make failure therein, let their pretence be what they will, must submit to the undergoing such penalties as by the said act is provided." From an account that Friends drew up in the following year, we learn that property valued at anything between 6s. and £15, and even higher, was seized for nonpayment of militia fines. The goods taken included not only sheep, cattle, and swine, but articles of farm equipment, household utensils, bed linen, and clothing.[43] The leading New York Friend of the period, John Bowne (1628-1695) of Flushing, originally an immigrant from England, was among those who were thus penalized: "Taken from John Bowne for his son Samuel not training, two sheep by John Harrison, the 3rd of the 7th month, 1687, worth £1.0.0.," runs the record, a typical entry for the late seventeenth century.[44] In the eighteenth century the same routine of fining Quakers for their failure to attend militia musterings and subsequently distraining the goods of the delinquents continued, though in a somewhat more moderate form.

Throughout the colonial period Quakers in New York, small in numbers and humble in station, were consistently excluded from political office.[45] The situation was different in the neighboring Jerseys where Friends were in political control until 1702, when the two parts were handed over to become a united colony under the Crown, and where, in West Jersey, they had been thickly settled from its beginnings in 1675. (In East Jersey, even though William Penn and a group of

[41] Quoted in Anna Davis Hallowell, *James and Lucretia Mott*, p. 8. (The Underhills were ancestors of the Motts.)

[42] Brodin, *Les Quakers en Amérique*, pp. 268, 269.

[43] XV. *Papers relating to Quakers and Moravians*, pp. 1003-7.

[44] Quoted in *Bulletin of Friends' Historical Society of Philadelphia*, vol. 9, no. 1 (1919), p. 42.

[45] The visiting English minister, James Dickinson (1659-1741), records in his *Journal*, p. 106, the convincement on Long Island in the year 1696 of "a captain in the army, and a justice of the peace, who were afterwards called before the Governor of New York, and because they could neither swear nor fight any longer, they laid down their commissions, having received the truth in the love of it." A Quaker could, without being inconsistent, serve as a justice of the peace in colonies like Pennsylvania, however, where office was not directly associated with oathtaking and armed force.

Friends obtained possession as proprietors in 1681, Quaker influence and settlement were on a considerably smaller scale.) In the late seventeenth century, especially in the western province, we find Friends filling the office of governor and sitting in the councils and in the assemblies. Many became wealthy men as planters, merchants, and shipowners. In the eighteenth century they often succeeded in adding culture to wealth; the Quaker gentlemen of New Jersey were the match of the Quaker grandees of Philadelphia across the river, with whom, indeed, they were united not only by the fact that New Jersey Friends shared the same yearly meeting (established in 1681) with those of Pennsylvania but also by close ties of marriage and social intercourse.

Nevertheless, the overwhelming majority of Quakers in New Jersey, as in the other colonies, were countryfolk, simple farmers and artisans for the most part, who did not always easily find a common language with the cultured and wealthy upper crust of their Society. When the colony passed into the possession of the Crown, it was the rank-and-file Quakers who had to face (what was a new issue for them) the question of militia conscription. Although Friends were guaranteed under the new order both freedom of worship and the right to make an affirmation in place of an official oath, they became liable for training in the militia and for service with it in time of war or danger of invasion. As in most of the other colonies, the authorities here, too, considered it quite sufficient for assuaging Quaker consciences to allow bona fide members of the Society the privilege of paying a fine in lieu of drilling or of hiring a substitute if the militia were mobilized for active service. The meeting records, therefore, begin to show from that point on a long series of distraints on property that parallels the story in other provinces. Perhaps because of the Quaker origins of the colony, however, Friends rarely appear to have been subjected to imprisonment for nonpayment. We hear, too, on occasion of reluctance on the part of the local constables to enforce distraint upon Quaker neighbors.[46]

---

[46] Brodin, *Les Quakers en Amérique*, p. 294. The records of Burlington M. M. contain the following rather involved entry for 1706: "It was ordered by this meeting, that there should be persons appointed out of each particular meeting belonging to this meeting, to speak to every Friend belonging to their respective meetings, to bring in an account to the next monthly meeting, of the goods strained from them for refusing to pay to the upholding of the militia" (Ezra Michener [ed.], *A Retrospect of Early Quakerism*, p. 372). There is a record of an amusing case in the next decade involving a member of Newtown M. M. who was disciplined by this meeting for threatening the constable who had come to distrain his property for an unpaid militia fine. The unruly Friend pledged himself in the future "not to give such occasion of offense but to make orderly as becoming his profession" (quoted in John E. Pomfret, "West New Jersey: A Quaker Society

But in wartime, as always, Friends' difficulties increased. In 1740, for instance, Governor Lewis Morris, who estimated the number of Quakers in West Jersey at that time to be as high as a third of the total population,[47] wrote somewhat testily of the negative response of members of the Society to his efforts to raise troops for the newly begun war: Friends were, he complains, "generally a laborious, honest and industrious people, but want not their share of craft; and they are unaccountable [sic] obstinate and tenacious."[48]

During the next round in the great Anglo-French contest of the eighteenth century, in 1757, a special call was made, first, for 1,000 and, then, for 3,000 militiamen "to go off as soldiers, to the relief of the English at Fort William Henry" in the province of New York. Among those chosen were a number of young Quakers from Burlington County. Of them John Woolman writes in his *Journal*:

> Some [of those drafted] were at that time in great distress, and had occasion to consider that their lives had been too little conformable to the purity and spirituality of that religion which we profess, and found themselves too little acquainted with that inward humility, in which true fortitude to endure hardness for the truth's sake is experienced. Many parents were concerned for their children, and in that time of trial were led to consider, that their care to get outward treasure for them, had been greater than their care for their settlement in that religion which crucifieth to the world, and enableth to bear a clear testimony to the peaceable government of the Messiah.

1675-1775," *William and Mary Quarterly*, 3rd ser., VIII, no. 4 [Oct. 1951], 510). A later case of un-Quakerlike belligerency in dealing with a military officer making a distraint is cited in Lois V. Given, "Burlington County Friends in the American Revolution," *Proceedings of the New Jersey Historical Society*, vol. 69, no. 3 (July 1951), p. 202. In 1782 a member of Evesham M. M. in that county was disowned for striking the officer with a stick. In this case the man's acknowledgment of error was not accepted by his meeting. We also find occasional record of New Jersey Friends being disciplined for having taken up arms especially during an emergency. After an invasion scare in 1704, for instance, four young members of Burlington M. M. submitted an acknowledgment of error to their meeting for having done so. "It seemed best," they said ingenuously in extenuation of their conduct, "for those that had guns [presumably, for the purpose of hunting], to take them, not with a design to hurt, much less to kill, man, woman or child; but we thought that if we could meet these runaways [who had escaped from an enemy vessel], the sight of the guns might fear them" (quoted in Amelia Mott Gummere, *Friends in Burlington*, p. 38; see also pp. 38-41, 44).

[47] Jones, *The Quakers*, p. xvi, gives an estimate of nearly 6,000 Quakers in New Jersey by 1775.

[48] Pomfret, "West New Jersey," p. 494.

A few of the Quaker conscripts expressed their willingness to march or to provide substitutes. Several more slipped away across the borders of the province to wait until the emergency had passed. Others decided to stand by their church's position and went to the militia captain, telling him the reasons for their refusal either to serve themselves or to get a substitute to go in their stead and stating at the same time that they would not try to run away. The captain, who was probably well acquainted with the Quaker attitude toward war, agreed to allow them to return home, warning them that they were still liable to be called up if the need arose. As things turned out, they were left in peace.[49] (One of those who refused to serve on this occasion later recorded in his journal: "Although my part might appear but as a drop in the ocean, yet the ocean, I considered, was made up of many drops.")[50] Earlier in the year, however, Quaker draftees in other parts of the province do not appear to have been quite so lucky. Woolman relates that "in some places they were [drafted], and such who stood true to their principles though they were taken away and nearly tried I have not heard that the officers were inclining to severity."[51]

Where fines had been imposed for failure to muster and distraint of property followed on nonpayment of fine, Friends in New Jersey had been warned by Yearly Meeting in 1755 not to accept money returned by kindly officers as "the overplus," that is, the difference between the amount of the fine and the proceeds of the sale of the delinquent's goods. Acceptance of such a sum would, it was felt, diminish "our peaceable testimony in its primitive authority and purity."[52]

Among those who were most concerned to reinvigorate the languishing peace testimony of Philadelphia Yearly Meeting (in which New Jersey Friends were included) was the Quaker tailor of Mount Holly, John Woolman (1720-1772), whose *Journal*—from which we have already quoted—was to become a religious classic. Love, the love of all created things, was the overriding emotion which inspired this naturally rather timid and sensitive man to courageous and outspoken defense of all God's creatures—"all animal sensible creatures"—suffering in one form or another from injustice or cruelty or oppression, whether they were African slaves or American Indians

[49] *The Journal and Essays of John Woolman* (ed. A. M. Gummere), pp. 211, 212, 224, 225.

[50] *A Journal of Joshua Evans*, p. 19.

[51] Letter from John Woolman to Abraham Farrington, dated 1 Oct. 1757, in *PMHB*, XVII (1893), no. 3, 371.

[52] Minutes of the Y. M. of Friends at Philadelphia for 1749-1779, pp. 77, 78 (printed in part in *Rules of Discipline* [1797], p. 131).

or English postboys, or the dumb animals who had few champions in those times.[53] "I rejoice, that I feel love unfeigned toward my fellow-creatures," he wrote to his wife.[54] He saw a natural harmony in the universe as the only possible condition for a creation emanating from an all-loving God. War, therefore, whether among civilized nations or between the more advanced and the less advanced peoples of the world, was an overturning of God's order. Woolman, therefore, put special value on the Quaker peace testimony and strove to keep his fellow Friends faithful to it, as fervently as he did in leading them to renounce their legal rights to property in men. But for him pacifism meant far more than a refusal to fight: it was part and parcel of a non-violent philosophy of life which, drawing its inspiration from Christian belief, sought to relate all man's activities in a coordinated whole. Thus Woolman, almost alone among eighteenth-century Quakers, attempted—one might say—to socialize the Society's peace testimony. This witness, he believed, was inadequate if Friends did not also try to remove the causes of war that lay concealed in the economic system, in such social institutions as the slave system, and in political relations with their Indian neighbors.

Basic to Woolman's economic theory was the idea of trusteeship: wealth is a trust with which a man is endowed by God, and he is responsible for using it to forward God's purposes. Desire to amass riches is wrong because in it—"like a chain in which the end of one link encloseth the end of another"—lies strife and, ultimately, war. In a striking passage in the essay which he significantly entitled "A Plea for the Poor" (which was published after his death as *A Word of Caution and Remembrance to the Rich*), he writes:

Wealth is attended with power, by which bargains and proceedings contrary to universal righteousness are supported; and here oppression, carried on with worldly policy and order, clothes itself with the name of justice, and becomes like a seed of discord in the soul: and as this spirit which wanders from the pure habitation prevails, so the seed of war swells and sprouts and grows and becomes strong till much fruit are ripened. Then cometh the harvest . . . Oh! that we who declare against wars, and acknowledge our trust to be in God only, may walk in the light, and therein examine our foundation and motives in holding great estates. May we look upon our treasures, the furniture of our houses, and our garments in which

[53] A good instance of Woolman's sensitivity to animal suffering is provided by H. J. Cadbury in "Some Anecdotes of John Woolman: Recorded by John Cox," *Journal of the Friends Historical Society* (London), XXXVI (1946), 49, 50.
[54] Woolman, *Journal*, p. 232. See also pp. 156, 157.

we array ourselves, and try whether the seeds of war have nourishment in these our possessions, or not.[55]

This doctrine was strong meat indeed for the Quaker grandees of Philadelphia and the Jersey shore (as, in fact, it has since remained also for the more modestly affluent). Woolman himself always strove to testify in his own daily life to a simple way of existence, one in which the seeds of war could not easily take root, and examined carefully all that he did in an effort to rid himself of anything that might possibly contribute, even remotely, to fostering war. It was this self-scrutiny that led him to abandon his career as a successful shopkeeper, for in that business he found it difficult to prevent himself from becoming prosperous. Later we find him giving up wearing dyed clothing and hats—at the risk of seeming eccentric—because (although his reasoning here appears rather devious) their use appeared to him an unnecessary luxury.[56]

His concern for the fair treatment of Negroes and Indians and for the recognition of their human dignity on the part of white Americans is a story that has often been told and need not be repeated here, except insofar as it bears directly on Quaker pacifism. Whereas Friends from the beginning had attempted to carry out a policy of justice and goodwill toward the Indians with whom they came in contact, an awareness of inconsistency between Friends' principles and the practice of slaveholding only ripened slowly (unlike the obligation to treat their Negroes kindly, which was always insisted upon). Woolman was one of those most responsible for bringing about the abolition of slaveholding among Friends and for launching the Society on its antislavery career. In all his contacts with his fellow members up and down the country, and in his public ministry, he was always careful to point out —gently, but insistently—the implicit hypocrisy of asserting the wrongfulness of all wars and at the same time holding in bondage fellowmen whose subjection was the result of armed force. As he told Virginia Yearly Meeting during one of his visits to that colony—by no means pleasing all those present who heard him—"as purchasing any merchandise taken by the sword, was always allowed to be inconsistent with our principles, negroes being captives of war, or taken by stealth, those circumstances make it inconsistent with our testimony to buy them; and their being our fellow-creatures, who are sold as slaves, adds greatly to the [difficulty]."[57]

The same painstaking exploration of all implications of the Quaker

---

[55] *Ibid.*, p. 419.   [56] *Ibid.*, p. 246.
[57] *Ibid.*, p. 195. See also pp. 255, 256.

objection to war, in order to discover where, in actions that previously had gone unnoticed, a possible source of conflict might be hidden, can be seen in Woolman's reactions to calls to pay war taxes or to billet soldiers in his house. In 1758, when an officer came to place one of his soldiers in Woolman's house, Woolman, after thinking the matter over, decided to submit without complaint "in a passive obedience to authority" but to refuse the legal compensation for this service, for reasons that he explained to the officer.[58] The question of taxation and its relation to the peace testimony exercised Woolman's thoughts, too, especially after the outbreak of the French and Indian War had made the matter once again topical. He was aware that (as we have already seen) both in the past and in his own day many weighty Friends on both sides of the Atlantic, men whose opinions he respected, had paid not only taxes "in the mixture" but also those that were specifically imposed to subsidize warlike measures. Yet, he writes, "[I] could not see that their example was a sufficient reason for me to do so," for the circumstances in which early Friends in Britain had found themselves, separated as they were from all participation in government, were quite different. However unpleasant it might be to run counter to the accepted view of the Society, this stand was still preferable to one which went against the voice of conscience within. "The spirit of truth required of me as an individual to suffer patiently the distress of goods, rather than pay actively." In December 1755, with the cooperation of a small group of Friends of Philadelphia Yearly Meeting whom he found to his surprise—after believing at first that his was a quite isolated opinion—to be of like mind, Woolman was instrumental in getting an unofficial declaration issued advising against the payment of war taxes, even though in their views on this point Friends were by no means unanimous.[59]

The danger that Woolman and his colleagues detected in Friends' acquiescence in this matter was twofold. In the first place, they feared that the easy circumstances in which Friends in the two provinces lived (especially in Pennsylvania, where there was no militia conscription), with persecution for any tenet of their religion a matter of past history, had bred an insensitivity to the call of conscience when obedience to it threatened to bring material loss—"a carnal mind" Woolman calls it in his *Journal*. Secondly, with Friends still holding the reins of political power in Pennsylvania and impelled by their position toward increasing compromise with the exigencies of power, these early Quaker absolutists felt the need, more acutely than most of their brethren, to

---

[58] *Ibid.*, pp. 81, 82. See Janet Whitney, *John Woolman*, pp. 225-30.
[59] See below, chap. 3.

reassert the compelling force of Friends' belief in nonviolence in order to override the demands of political expediency whenever the two should clash. Moreover, they asked, how could the Friends in office be expected to express Quaker principles in the commonwealth's policy if the Society at large failed to take a clear stand on the issue of contributions to war? The danger here was—to quote the *Journal* once more—that "by small degrees, there might be an approach toward that of fighting, till we came so near it, as that the distinction would be little else but the name of a peaceable people."

Woolman in this instance—as, indeed, in all that he said and did that relates to peace—stood for a renewal of the Society's witness for a nonviolent world. He was not content to follow unthinkingly in the footsteps of earlier generations or to repeat their precepts mechanically in a changed situation that called for new methods of action if the testimony were to remain a live one. The points where he took issue with the opinion prevailing among Quakers sometimes appear forced or extreme. But it is really not so much the form of his protest that is important as its spirit, the spirit that reneweth. The fervor of Woolman's advocacy of a peaceable creation, his all-embracing concept of peace as a total way of life instead of a specialized Quaker profession, stands out in contrast to the often arid and negative pacifism of eighteenth-century Quakerism. The essence of Woolman's pacifism is summed up in one passage from his *Journal*:

> It requires great self-denial and resignation of ourselves to God to attain that state wherein we can freely cease from fighting when wrongfully invaded, if by our fighting there were a probability of overcoming the invaders. Whoever rightly attains to it, does in some degree feel that spirit in which our Redeemer gave his life for us, . . . Many [Quakers] . . . having their religion chiefly by education, and not being enough acquainted with that cross which crucifies to the world, do manifest a temper distinguishable from that of an entire trust in God.[60]

Woolman, the apostle of antislavery within his Society, often felt called to journey into the Southern colonies to take his message to the small groups of Friends there. His reception, though usually polite,

---

[60] Woolman, *Journal*, pp. 204-10. Cf. the epistle composed by Woolman in 1772 just before leaving for England (*Journal*, p. 486): "The principle of peace, in which our trust is only on the Lord, and our minds weaned from a dependence on the strength of armies, to me hath appeared very precious; and I often feel strong desires that we who profess this principle may so walk as to give just cause for none of our fellow-creatures to be offended at us, and that our lives may evidently manifest that we are redeemed from that spirit in which wars are."

was not always too cordial; for a hard core of Quaker slaveholders in both North and South did not take kindly to the idea of emancipation, and it required many decades of quiet but firm insistence on the part of Woolman and other concerned Friends, as well as some disowning in the last resort, to finally eradicate this "seed of war" from the life of the Society. In their profession of the peace testimony, however, the Southern meetings showed the same degree of faithfulness as their Northern brethren: the pattern of war resistance, its achievements and defects, were roughly similar in both sections of colonial America.

III

The earliest cases recorded of Quakers on the American continent being penalized for their stand as conscientious objectors to service in the militia come from the province of Maryland, where the first Quaker, Elizabeth Harris, arrived in late 1655 (or in 1656), shortly before (or just after) Mary Fisher and Ann Austin landed in Boston. Elizabeth Harris and the early Maryland missionaries soon gathered converts.[61] As early as 1658 we read of one "Richard Keene, refusing to be trained as a soldier had taken from him the sum of 6l.15s. and was abused by the sheriff, who drew his cutlass, and therewith made a pass at the breast of the said Richard, and struck him on the shoulders, saying *You dog, I could find in my heart to split your brains.*" Fines in money or in tobacco continued to be imposed on Friends not only for their refusal to train in the militia but, in addition, for their objection to taking oaths. The poorer members of the Society suffered considerable hardship on this account. In the early times, before this usually tolerant colony had come to regard Quakers as a respectable if somewhat peculiar sect, severer penalties were sometimes imposed. Edward Coppedge, for instance, not only had property distrained to the value of £5.7.0 for his refusal to train or to pay fines in lieu thereof, but he "was also whipped by order of the military officers." In 1662 a number of Quaker objectors were given two months in prison for not paying a fine of "five hundred pounds of cask-tobacco."[62] One John Everitt is reported as having run "from his colors when pressed to go to the Susquehanna Fort, pleading that he could not bear arms for conscience's sake," for which offense he was ordered to be "kept in chains

[61] Among these converts were a sprinkling of men who remained active in political life (although by the end of the seventeenth century Friends had ceased to play an active role in this sphere). The beginnings of what became Baltimore Y. M. arose out of a visit George Fox paid to the area in 1672.

[62] Joseph Besse, *A Collection of the Sufferings of the People called Quakers,* II, 378-82.

and [to] bake his own bread" until such time as his trial could be arranged.[63]

After the first few years Quakers in Maryland seem to have suffered few disabilities for their pacifist beliefs. In time a routine came to be established: as each young Friend reached military age, his local meeting would supply him with a certificate of membership to show to the militia authorities. Then, upon refusal to pay the small statutory fine, the property of the objector or his family was distrained: probably, at least in peacetime, this penalty did not amount to much and was not a serious inconvenience to those concerned. From time to time a young man would break with family tradition and attend muster. His monthly meeting in that case would appoint some trusted Friends to labor with him to bring him to see the error of his ways. Sometimes they succeeded. To take just one case out of many hundreds: Henry Pratt from Third Haven Monthly Meeting in Talbot County, records an early eighteenth-century minute, "hath of late gone to training" despite the attempts of Friends to dissuade him. A committee of four members of the meeting was appointed, and after some time their efforts were crowned with success. "They dealt with him," they were able to report finally, "in the love of God as from the meeting, letting him know how inconsistent it is with the universal testimony of truth to go to training, which he acknowledged and said he kindly accepted of Friends' love and care towards him and that he was really convinced he ought not to go to training and for the time to come hoped he should stand clear of it."[64] Sometimes, however, Friends had to admit failure, the young man remaining adamant in his decision even when faced with the inevitable disownment, which would entail a difficult break with the family faith and often bring sadness to his parents and relatives, too.

If the question of militia service among Maryland Friends, as throughout the whole community of Friends in America, remained a fairly straightforward one—a consistent Quaker must neither serve himself, nor hire a substitute, nor send his servant in his place, nor pay the fine imposed for refusal to train—there were other questions

[63] Quoted in Jones, *The Quakers*, p. 279. Kenneth L. Carroll ("Persecution of Quakers in Early Maryland [1658-1661]," *Quaker History*, vol. 53, no. 2 [Autumn 1964], p. 75) quotes an order issued by governor and council in 1659 against Quaker missionaries—"vagabonds and idle persons"—who had been attempting to dissuade settlers both "from giving testimony or becoming jurors" and "from complying with the military discipline in this time of danger." The justices were told to have them "apprehended and whipped from constable to constable until they shall be sent out of the province."

[64] Carroll, "Talbot County Quakerism in the Colonial Period," *Maryland Historical Magazine*, vol. 53, no. 4 (Dec. 1958), p. 345.

where the connection with the military was not so clear. In the middle of the eighteenth century during the French and Indian War, when war came directly to many of the provinces, Friends did not always find it easy to know where to draw the line—or perhaps they were under greater temptation or stronger pressures to connive at some semi-military activity. In 1759, for instance, a minute of East Nottingham Preparative Meeting notes:

> That divers members thereof have some time ago, inadvertently or otherwise, been concerned in contributing to the furnishing (in some measure) of wagons, horses and provisions for conveying military stores for the use of the army. Such a contribution being declared by the last Yearly Meeting to be a military service and by our last quarterly meeting enjoined on each monthly meeting to report for the same, is taken notice of and cleared up (they having been respectively spoken to on the subject).

A couple of years later, Little Britain Preparative Meeting disowned a couple of young apprentices who had consented to work under military direction on the fort at frontier Pittsburgh, along with their master, who was not a Friend.[65]

The seven years and more of the French and Indian War, as we shall soon see, were also to bring their trials to the Friends in neighboring Virginia, where by the end of the colonial period there were nearly 5,000 Quakers scattered in meetings over a wide area, a figure somewhat larger than the estimated 3,000 Friends in Maryland at this date. Quakerism came to Virginia in 1657, barely a year after its commencement in Maryland and New England. In Virginia, however, where government throughout the colonial period continued to be controlled mainly by members of the established Anglican church, Friends took little part in affairs of state. Yet some of them in the course of time became quite affluent as owners of large plantations (like the Pleasants family at Curles) and owners of many slaves, too—until eventually the ferment generated by Woolman and his like led to the abandonment of slaveholding within the Society.[66]

[65] *Bi-Centennial of Brick Meeting-House, Calvert, Cecil County, Maryland, 1701-1901*, pp. 53, 54. (Little Britain is in Pennsylvania, but the meeting came to be associated with East Nottingham Q. M. in Maryland.)

[66] Among those who followed in Woolman's footsteps was Robert Pleasants, who after his conversion to abolition freed all his slaves at considerable financial loss and thenceforward devoted much of his energies to the antislavery cause. "We as a people are principled against fighting," he wrote in May 1775 at the commencement of the Revolutionary War in a passage reminiscent of the writing of Woolman

In 1666 the Virginia legislature made provision for having a fine of 100 pounds of tobacco (which passed as currency in the province) imposed for each time a person refused to attend militia musters. Although not mentioning them specifically by name, the legislators undoubtedly had Quakers in mind when drafting this clause.[67] For more than a century afterward, with minor variations in the nature of the fines demanded for refusal of service, there was a long record of heavy distresses levied upon Quaker conscientious objectors. There were even occasional cases of arrest and imprisonment, although as usual the degree of severity with which the law was implemented varied from one period to another and from district to district. Gradually, however, the earlier antagonism toward Quakers died down, so that at the beginning of the new century, in 1702, Virginia Yearly Meeting could write to London: "Friends doth here keep our meetings peacefully and quietly, blessed be the Lord for it, but Friends are generally fined for not bearing arms and that grand oppression of priests' wages, though the magistrates are pretty moderate at present and truth gains ground."[68]

A serious crisis arose for Friends in 1711, during the War of the Spanish Succession, when, upon hearing a rumor that the French were about to invade the province by sea from the West Indies, Governor Alexander Spotswood prevailed on the assembly to order an emergency mobilization of the militia for labor service on the coastal fortifications. The governor's pleasure at his success in persuading the colonial legislators to take action was, however, marred by one setback: the resistance of the little community of Quakers to what must have appeared to him to be the quite legitimate demands of national defense against impending enemy attack. As he wrote home to Lord Dartmouth in a letter dated 15 October 1711:

> I have been mightily embarrassed by a set of Quakers who broach doctrines so monstrous as their brethren in England never owned, nor, indeed, can be suffered in any government. They have not only refused to work themselves, or suffer any of their servants to be employed in the fortifications, but affirm that their consciences will not permit them to contribute in any manner of way to the defence of the country even so much as trusting the government with

---

himself. "Should we not be equally concerned to remove the cause of it?" (Quoted in Adair P. Archer, "The Quaker's Attitude Towards the Revolution," *William and Mary Quarterly*, 2nd ser., I, no. 3 [July 1921], 175.)

[67] Stephen B. Weeks, *Southern Quakers and Slavery*, p. 171.

[68] Quoted in *Encyclopedia of Quaker Genealogy*, VI: *Virginia*, ed. W. W. Hinshaw *et al.*, 94.

provisions to support those that do the work, tho' at the same time they say that being obliged by their religion to feed the enemies, if the French should come hither and want provisions, they must in conscience, supply them. As this opinion is quite different from practice in Carolina, where they were most active in taking arms to pull down the government,[69] tho' they now fly again to the pretence of conscience to be excused from assisting against the Indians, I have thought it necessary to put the laws of this country in execution against this sect of people, which empowered me to employ all persons as I shall see fit for the defence of the country in times of danger, and impose fines and penalties upon their disobedience.

Angrily, the governor went on to say that he expected loud protests from the Quakers because of his brusque treatment of them, as well as attacks on himself from the Society in England. "But I'm persuaded I shall not incur my sovereign's displeasure so long as I act by the rule of law, and it is absolutely necessary to discourage such dangerous opinions as would render the safety of the government precarious." Moreover, he added, if members of the Society were to be granted exemption from their duties as citizens, all the lazy and cowardly of the province would soon be found under cover of the Quaker name.[70]

Among those with whom the governor had taken counsel "concerning what should be done with obstinate Quakers" was William Byrd, the wealthy owner of Westover plantation on the James River and a justice of the peace. When earlier in the same month in which Governor Spotswood had written to London several Quakers appeared before Squire Byrd in court, along with other militia delinquents, they were fined. "I spoke gently to the Quakers," wrote the squire in his diary, "which gave them a good opinion of me and several of them seemed doubtful whether they would be arrested or not for the future. I told them that they would certainly be fined five times in a year if they did not do as their fellow subjects did."[71] In fact, some Quakers were kept in prison for periods of ten days for nonpayment of fines.[72] Others, however, cooperated, according to the yearly meeting records —either because they feared the consequences of not obeying the authorities or because they did not see anything contrary to Quaker

[69] For the Cary Rebellion of 1711, see below, p. 47.
[70] *The Official Letters of Alexander Spotswood*, I, 120, 121. See also pp. 85, 95, 100, 101, 108, for assertions by Spotswood that the North Carolina Quakers had taken up arms against the government in the Cary Rebellion.
[71] *The Secret Diary of William Byrd*, pp. 409, 415, 416.
[72] *John Farmer's First American Journey*, p. 6.

principles in doing so (in which view they might, indeed, have found some support in the writings of earlier Friends). These Quakers consented to carry out the labor assigned them, or else hired someone to work in their stead, or paid the fine imposed by the court—and thus had to be dealt with later by their meetings.[73]

The imposition of fines, distraints, and imprisonment continued even after the conclusion of the great struggle against France in 1713 and the inauguration of several decades of peace. In 1742, after the British empire had once again become involved in war, Virginia Quakers reported on their situation: "The men in military power act toward us in several counties with as much lenity and forbearance as we can reasonably expect, as they are ministers of the law; tho' in some places they are not so favourable." Indeed, as usual, several young Quakers were in jail as conscientious objectors at the time this report was written.[74]

The outbreak of the French and Indian War—"the commencement of a war with a most barbarous and savage enemy in this our late peaceful colony"—began a period of renewed trials for Virginia Quakers, as it did for some of their brethren in other provinces, as well as for members of the German peace sects. One settlement of Friends (at Goose Creek) was abandoned on account of the constant threat of Indian attack, but most Quakers living in the exposed frontier areas held their ground, though appearing "to the outward eye to be in imminent danger" (again, to use the words of the yearly meeting's epistle to London in 1758).[75] No Friend is known to have been attacked or killed by the Indian raiders. On the other hand, some members of the Society collaborated with the military in defense measures, either by helping with the construction of fortifications or by carrying weapons themselves for use against attack. Of Providence Preparative Meeting it was afterward reported: "All of them have been concerned in building a fortification and dwelling therein for defence against the Indian enemy." This constituted one of the reasons for later discontinuing this meeting; its members having departed so gravely from Friends' peaceable witness, its further existence appeared to many to cast a slur on the sincerity of the Quaker peace testimony.[76] And, of course, all who participated in military measures of

[73] Hinshaw, *Encyclopedia*, VI, 94; Weeks, *Southern Quakers*, pp. 173, 174.
[74] Margaret E. Hirst, *The Quakers in Peace and War*, pp. 348, 349; Weeks, *Southern Quakers*, p. 174; Jones, *The Quakers*, p. 319. Jones cites the case of a slave worth £9 being taken for nonpayment of militia fines from a Quaker named Thomas Ellyson.
[75] Hinshaw, *Encyclopedia*, VI, 292.
[76] *Hopewell Friends History 1734-1934*, p. 58.

this kind were subsequently dealt with and disowned, unless they displayed suitable contrition.

However, perhaps because a greater backsliding from the rigid position usually required by Quaker pacifism seems then to have taken place, greater leniency was apparently shown to those who were liable to be called up under a special militia act passed on 1 May 1756. According to the terms of this act, a ballot was to be held to choose one out of every twenty men for active service with the forces defending the province's frontiers. A representative meeting of Friends gathered immediately and decided against Friends' participation in the ballot or, in case any were chosen to serve without their consent, against payment of fine or the hiring of a substitute (these last two procedures, of course, having always been contrary to Quaker practice). Yet, despite this decision, the older members of the Society in fact mostly advised compliance, "under an apprehension of the consequence which might ensue to our young men, who by a refusal would be liable to be taken away as soldiers and either compelled to act in that station, or be made great sufferers in bearing a faithful testimony against it." As a result, many drew lots along with non-Quakers and, if the ballot went against them, acquiesced in the fine that was imposed on those unwilling to march.

Only seven young men had the courage to resist: five from Henrico County and two from New Kent County in the area around Richmond. They soon found themselves under arrest. After a week in jail, they were brought before the court. While refusing to make the required affirmation of allegiance or to take off their hats before the justices— actions which hardly won the favor of the court—they asserted their readiness to comply with the laws in all things not against their conscience. But, they said, "to bear arms or fight we could not." Thereupon one of the judges told them: "Then . . . you must work at the forts." Naturally, they refused to obey this order, too, and were sent back to prison. On the following day they were dispatched under escort to Fredericksburg and from there to Winchester, then a frontier post under the command of young Colonel George Washington. The journey lasted over four days, a long and weary tramp under trying conditions. The seven men suffered severely from hunger, due not to the harshness of their guards but rather to the meticulousness of their Quaker consciences: "For as we could not do any service, we had not freedom to eat of the king's victuals and having depended in a great measure on buying on the road where provisions proved so scarce, and the demand from our company so great that we being under some restraint had not an equal chance, so was [sic] obliged sometimes to go with hungry stomachs." Their refusal to answer their names at roll call, which took place thrice daily—since answering might be construed as an acknowledgement of their status as soldiers—so infuriated the captain in charge of the company that he threatened to take one of the youths and have him whipped as an example to the rest. The sentence would have been carried out but for the protest of one of the soldiers (who were, indeed, becoming increasingly well disposed toward their prisoners) at the idea of punishing a man for his religious scruples. After this incident the Quakers informed the captain "that if he called us on any other occasion we were ready and willing to answer but not as soldiers, which we could not submit to be."

After arriving finally at Winchester, the Quakers were placed in the guardhouse along with a number of deserters and petty offenders, "a parcel of dirty lousy wicked and profane creatures." They were kept there for five weeks. Although the soldiers guarding them proved friendly and allowed them various minor privileges, the officers continually attempted—sometimes by persuasion, at other times by threats of whipping to the measure of 500 strokes each—to get them to accept service, if only to work on the fortifications. A short while later, a Quaker minister and leader in the Virginia community of Friends, Edward Stabler, arrived in Winchester with greetings and encouragement from the brethren. Stabler was able to get an interview with Colonel Washington, who had just returned from a tour of inspection on the frontier. Not overly friendly on this occasion, Washington told Stabler that he had received orders from Governor Robert Dinwiddie to whip the men until they agreed to work on the fort. He intended, he said, to carry out these instructions shortly, unless the men changed their minds. However, impressed perhaps by the Quakers' unwillingness to compromise their principles, Washington subsequently relented and agreed to release them from the guardhouse on parole, allowing them to lodge in the town with local Friends. Since Governor Dinwiddie refused to sanction their release before their legal term of service had expired, the men remained at Winchester until near the end of the year. Before their departure they went to thank Washington for his generous treatment of them. Wishing them "a good journey home," the colonel in answer to their expressions of thanks "told them they were welcome, and all he asked of them in return was that if ever he should fall as much into their power as they had been in his, they would treat him with equal kindness."[77]

[77] See my article "Colonel Washington and the Quaker Conscientious Objectors," *Quaker History*, 53, no. 1 (Spring 1964), 12-26. [Quotations from this article made here are reprinted by permission of *Quaker History*.] There I have printed

Barely a decade before the Revolutionary War, Friends in Virginia at last obtained temporary relief from the century-long round of distraints and imprisonments (as well as from the occasional backslidings, as in 1756, when, in spite of the Society's official testimony against this practice, fines were paid by so many that no disciplinary action appears to have been taken against the offenders). In 1766, after the yearly meeting had petitioned the assembly in the matter, this body passed a new law exempting bona fide Quakers in peace time (though not in time of war) from all obligations connected with militia training. Although on some occasions colonial Quakers objected to the necessity of having to produce certificates of membership in order to obtain exemption from militia service, the Virginia Quakers, feeling perhaps that they had already proved their sincerity in the cause of peace by a century and more of sporadic suffering, do not appear to have balked at this requirement under the present act. Rufus Jones cites a typical entry from meeting records:

At our monthly meeting held at the Western branch in Isle of Wight County in Virginia the 27th of the 6 month 1767: The overseers of each meeting are desired to collect the names of each of their members that are liable by a late act of assembly to be enlisted in the militia against our next monthly meeting, that a list may be given to the colonel or chief commanding officer of each county as by act of assembly directed; and have the indulgence granted by the same.[78]

The most southerly province in which Quakers were represented in any considerable numbers during the colonial period was North Carolina.[79] The establishment of Quakerism there dates back to 1671; in subsequent decades, in the absence of any serious competition from other denominations until the end of the seventeenth century, a large number of the unchurched in this still rather wild frontier area were

---

an account of their experiences by one of the men entitled "A Brief Narrative of the Conduct and Sufferings of Friends in Virginia, respecting an Act of Assembly passed the 1st day of the 5th month 1756 for drafting the Militia" from the manuscript in the H.C.Q.C. Woolman records in his *Journal*, p. 193: "I lodged at James Standley's, father of William Standley, one of the young men who suffered imprisonment at Winchester last summer on account of their testimony against fighting, and I had some satisfactory conversation with him concerning it."

[78] Jones, *The Quakers*, p. 320.

[79] In the eighteenth century small Quaker groups were formed in South Carolina and Georgia. But Quakerism in these provinces remained very weak; no provision for conscientious objection existed there, nor apparently is anything known about local Quakers who may have successfully or unsuccessfully maintained a pacifist stand.

gathered into the Society of Friends. By the end of the colonial period there were nearly 5,000 Quakers in the province.

The first recorded collision between Quakers and authority resulting from their conscientious objection to war occurred in the spring of 1680. In that year, to quote from a Quaker manuscript, "the government made a law that all that would not bear arms in the musterfield, should be at the pleasure of the court fined." Therefore, it goes on, "Friends not bearing arms in the field; they had several Friends before the Court, and they fined them, he that had a good estate a great sum and the rest according to their estates; and cast them into prison, and when they were in prison, they levied their fines upon their estates." Nine men in all suffered in this manner, and they were kept in jail for about six months. Weeks considers that this treatment, unusually harsh for North Carolina, was due to the resentment of the popular antiproprietary party then in power at the earlier opposition Quakers displayed against them at the time of the Culpepper Rebellion in 1677. Several of the Friends imprisoned in 1680 had signed a protest three years before against what was considered the seditious conduct of the popular party at that time. Anyhow, for the rest of the colonial period the North Carolina Quakers were treated leniently by the authorities. True, distresses on their property for nonpayment of militia fines and war taxes (such as the ones imposed in 1740 to cover the cost of erecting powder magazines in each county and to buy provisions for the troops)[80] were levied, but these were usually small in amount and were only imposed sporadically. The penalty of imprisonment appears to have been administered more rarely than in neighboring Virginia.[81]

Indeed, for a time Quakers were virtually exempt altogether from any obligations in regard to militia service. This circumstance resulted from the appointment in 1694 of a fellow Quaker, the English squire from Wycombe in Buckinghamshire, John Archdale (1642-1717), to the post of governor of the Carolinas. As governor—and at the

[80] In the French and Indian War apparently almost all Quakers in the province paid war taxes. Woolman in his *Journal* (pp. 200, 201) relates how, when journeying through North Carolina in 1757, he met a Friend, a minister and a working farmer possessing no slaves, who had refused to pay a recently imposed war tax, preferring to have his goods distrained rather than contribute in this way to an activity he believed inconsistent with Quaker ways. "And as he was the only person who refused it in those parts, and knew not that any one else was in the like circumstance, he signified that it had been a heavy trial upon him, and the more so, for that some of his brethren had been uneasy with his conduct in that case."

[81] Weeks, *Southern Quakers*, pp. 172, 173. See also Francis Charles Anscombe, *I have Called You Friends*, pp. 149-51.

same time "admiral, captain general and commander-in-chief of all the forces raised . . . both by sea and land within our said province" (to give the exact wording of the proprietors' letter of appointment)[82]— Archdale had the responsibility for enforcing conscription into the militia. However, in 1696 he was successful in getting the assembly to pass an act exempting from service all Friends whom the governor should certify as being motivated in their refusal to bear arms by genuine religious scruples. Archdale, unfortunately, returned to England in the same year, and a few years later, in 1703 during the governorship of Sir Nathaniel Johnson, the existing generous exemption was withdrawn. Quakers once again became liable to the old alternatives of service or fines. During the same period, as a result of the imposition of an oath of allegiance on all public servants, Friends were gradually removed both from the assembly and from all responsible offices within the province, which during Archdale's term they had largely controlled.

This change from the previously tolerant policy that had prevailed in the province resulted from efforts of the Anglican establishment to gain the upper hand there, efforts that were backed both by the Crown and by a majority of the proprietors. Once again, an antiproprietary party was formed, and this time it enjoyed a great deal of support from the Quakers—at least until 1711, when its leaders resorted to arms in order to turn the tide. The acting governor, Robert Cary, who headed the rebellion, was Archdale's son-in-law but was not himself a Friend. Several Quakers did join it as individuals, including Emmanuel Lowe, another son-in-law of Archdale's. The revolt, however, was easily suppressed. Lowe's case—his "stirring up a parcel of men in arms and going to Pamlico and from there to Chowan in a barkentine with men and force of arms contrary to our holy principles"—came up before North Carolina Yearly Meeting shortly afterward. As a result, Lowe was removed from the yearly meeting's executive committee for "having acted diverse things contrary to our ways and principles." But, presumably because he expressed suitable regret for his actions and promised to refrain from warlike behavior in the future, he was not disowned by the Society.[83]

Conscription for the provincial militia continued in force during the decades that followed. The French and Indian War, which began in 1755, was the only period when the colony was immediately threatened by enemy attack, however. In 1757 the yearly meeting, which was unsuccessful in its attempts at this time to obtain relief from its

[82] Quoted in Jones, *The Quakers*, p. 344.
[83] Weeks, *Southern Quakers*, pp. 165, 166.

militia obligations, appointed a standing committee to assist those who became entangled with the military, and in the following year two Friends were delegated in each of the counties where Quakers were settled to attend court martials "there to give the reason for our non-appearance as required by law."[84] But no Friends in North Carolina appear to have been called out on active service, as they were in Virginia.

The Regulator Movement—led by a former Quaker, Hermon Husband—which expressed the grievances of the underrepresented back counties over excessive taxation and official corruption, disturbed the peace of the Carolinas between 1766 and 1771. Although the view, sometimes put forward, that the Society backed the "regulators" is without foundation, several Friends were later dealt with by their meetings for complicity in the movement. Demands were made from time to time by the government's forces for provisions and equipment. "The people commonly called Quakers living in Rocky River and Cane Creek and thereabouts in Orange River," for instance, were required by Governor Tryon "to furnish for His Majesty's troops now marching under my command six wagonloads of flour . . . and also six able wagons and teams with sufficient drivers to attend the troops with the said flour." Although the governor promised that "the wagons and teams will be returned when the service is over," it is doubtful if the Friends in question complied—at least voluntarily—with the order.[85] In 1771, after these disturbances had ended, the legislature at last gave the Quakers in North Carolina the same status vis-à-vis the militia as Virginia had given its Quakers half a decade earlier: provided they could produce a certificate of membership in good standing, Friends in the colony were now granted complete exemption.[86]

IV

No account of American pacifism in the colonial period would be complete without a brief survey of the Quaker communities established in the British islands of the West Indies, which during that pe-

---

[84] Julia S. White, "The Peace Testimony of North Carolina Friends prior to 1860," *BFHA*, vol. 16, no. 2 (1927), p. 61.

[85] *Ibid.*, p. 62.

[86] Lists of members were compiled by local meetings in this connection. See, e.g., M. P. Littrell, M. E. Outland, J. O. Sams, *A History of Rich Square Monthly Meeting of Friends*, p. 21. But cf. the opposite practice recommended by Philadelphia Y. M. in 1742 in regard to certificates of exemption from compulsory militia service in the Three Lower Counties (see *Rules of Discipline of the Yearly Meeting of Friends for Pennsylvania and New Jersey* [1797], p. 130).

riod enjoyed close trading relations with the American mainland.[87] Here, in an area where sorties by Great Britain's European enemies (France, Spain, and Holland were all near neighbors in the Caribbean), semi-official privateering and raids by common pirates, and attacks by the aboriginal inhabitants or by revolting Negro slaves were not infrequent occurrences, Quaker pacifists faced some of their most trying experiences and difficult dilemmas. It is not surprising, therefore, that the local authorities occasionally lost patience with Quaker objectors and dealt harshly with them for their resistance to accepting a share in the common defense. Sometimes, however, the powers that be seemed to understand their position and were reluctant to force men to act contrary to religious scruples they might have against bearing arms. This fact, surely, must be placed in the balance alongside the severity and even cruelty that were often meted out, especially in the early days, to Quaker objectors.[88]

Quakerism came to the British West Indies in the second half of the 1650's, and soon meetings were established in a number of islands as a result of the work of the Quaker evangelists among their white inhabitants. Quakers eventually numbered several thousand in Barbados, and even more in Jamaica. Small communities existed also on Antigua, Nevis, and Montserrat in the Leeward islands and on "the remote Bermudas" out in the Atlantic far to the north of the Caribbean islands. Finally, at a time when Quakerism was already beginning to decline elsewhere in the West Indies, the seed was transplanted in the late 1720's to the very small island of Tortola in the Virgin Islands.

It was Barbados that, in George Fox's schemes to found a missionary empire across the Atlantic, provided the link between the continental

[87] A good account of the Quaker peace testimony as practiced by Friends in the British West Indies is given in Hirst, *The Quakers in Peace and War*, chap. XII. This chapter is based largely on manuscripts in the Public Record Office (London) and in the collections of London Y. M.

[88] An interesting illustration of the above remarks is to be found in a conversation related by Story in his *Journal* (p. 444) between himself and a high-ranking naval officer, Charles Wager, Rear Admiral of the Blue, which took place in April 1709 during the Quaker's visit to Jamaica. The admiral, whom Story describes as "a person of a calm, sedate temper, naturally courteous, and no way elevated," received his unusual visitor politely. "As he is a man of war," Story goes on, "we discoursed on that subject; and as I am a man of peace, we conversed religiously, and not martially; he for the punishment of privateers and pirates, as dogs, wolves, lions, bears and tigers; and invaders and breakers of the peace, and robbers; but I was rather for saving the life, that poor sinners might have time to repent and be saved: though what passed between us, was with the greatest civility and temper; the meekness of Christianity being more apparent in his deportment, than any martial harshness."

settlements and those on the islands of the southern sea. The "island of Barbados," writes Rufus Jones, "was, during the seventeenth century, the great port of entry to the colonies in the western world, and it was during the last half of that century, a veritable 'hive' of Quakerism. Friends wishing to reach any part of the American coast, sailed most frequently for Barbados and then reshipped for their definite locality. They generally spent some weeks, or even months, propagating their doctrines in 'the island' and ordinarily paying visits to Jamaica and often to Antigua, Nevis and Bermuda." A Quaker missionary in 1661 called Barbados "the nursery of truth."[89]

In 1660 the council, worried at the effect that the growth of Quaker doctrines among the islanders might have on the state of military preparedness, passed an act punishing refusal of service in the militia with a fine of "five hundred pounds of sugar for the first offence," to be raised to a thousand pounds for each subsequent failure to muster. The objector was to be confined to prison until the fine was paid. The rate of fining gradually increased over the following decades as a result both of a decline in the price of sugar and a rise in the frequency of militia musterings. Quakers now had to face a number of problems. As freemen, they were required to attend musterings in person and to take up arms when there was an alarm, and they were liable, if owners of landed property, to provide a certain number of foot soldiers and horsemen, depending upon the size of their property. In addition, Quakers (including men not otherwise liable for military service and women, too) encountered trouble for their refusal to permit the authorities to requisition either their Negro slaves or their horses for labor service on the island's fortifications, although these were sometimes taken off by force against their master's wishes. Petitioning by the Society failed to move the administration to abandon its policies of distraining the property of the well-to-do (which usually resulted in the confiscation of goods of considerably more value than the amount of the fine) and of putting those who had little on which to levy a distress in prison for periods lasting from a few days to over a year. Besse gives details of a number of cases of hardship from this period. William Piersehouse, for instance, was sentenced to four months' "hard imprisonment, to the great impairing of his health," for refusing to send any of his "servants" to work on the fortifications. Thomas Hunt, Sr., was fined 360 pounds of sugar "for not appearing in arms, though his age might reasonably have excused him." Most of those who were punished by fines or imprisonment or both, however, were young men, who were most liable to be called to train.

[89] Jones, *The Quakers*, pp. 26, 41.

A not unusual experience for Barbados Quakers of military age at this time was that which befell John Gittings in the years 1668-1669. Besse tells the story:

John Gittings, in the year 1668. Then taken from him by John Higginbotham Lieutenant-Colonel, one iron pot, for not bearing arms, worth 100 lb. of sugar. Afterward the aforesaid Gittings was sent for into the field by a file of musquetiers, by order of the said Higginbotham, who made his *mittimus* and sent him to gaol from constable to constable, where he remained twelve days, but was then set at liberty by Daniel Searl, Governor at that time. Ferdinando Bushel, Captain of Foot, sent a drummer with soldiers, and took from him a fat hog, for not serving in arms, which was worth 500 lb. of sugar. Nathaniel Trevanyan, Captain, sent a soldier with a Sergeant, and took from him a sow worth 250 lb. of sugar. Ferdinando Bushel, Captain of Horse, sent Thomas Perry, his Deputy-Marshal, who demanded of the said Gittings 2000 lb. of sugar for not trooping, for which he took away his horse, and never returned any thing again, which horse was worth 4000 lb. By order of a court of war he was committed to prison for a year and one day for not appearing at an alarm. The said Ferdinando Bushel, Major, sent Samuel Buckley, Marshal, to him the said Gittings, who demanded of him 630 lb. of sugar for not trooping, for which he took away a mare-colt appraised at 1500 lb. and returned no overplus. John Jennings, William Goodall, and other commissioners for the fortifications, sent Matthew Pinket, Constable, who took away from him in cotton to the value of 840 lb. of sugar, for not sending seven negroes one week to help him build forts.

On the 26th of the eighth month 1669. Then Joshua Chapell, Deputy-Marshal to Samuel Buckley, together with George Maggs and William Clark, took from him three sheep, for not trooping, worth 500 lb. of sugar. Taken from him in all to the value of 7690 lb.

The comparatively mild treatment accorded Gittings in 1669 was clearly attributable to the fact that he spent most of that year in jail.

In 1675 the penalties for conscientious objection were made more rigorous as a result of complaints from governor and council that Quaker noncombatancy was having an adverse effect on the efficiency of the militia. Three years later an 18-year-old Quaker apprentice, Richard Andrews, died as a result of ill-treatment while in the hands of the military, when on several occasions he was "tied neck and heels so straight that he could hardly speak."

The new governor, Sir Jonathan Atkins, was particularly vehement in his dislike of the Quakers. As he told the Committee for Trade and Plantations in London in 1680, Quakers "to the great discontent of the people, to their own great ease and advantage, . . . neither will serve upon juries, find arms, or send to the militia nor bear any office, shifting it off with their constant tricks 'they cannot swear,' when profit is the end they aim at." In the same year Sir Jonathan, forwarding a map of the island to the commissioners, was forced to explain that it was not entirely accurate with regard to detail since the mapmaker, being a Quaker, had omitted to mark on it either the churches or the fortifications!

At first, the reign of the Catholic King James II, William Penn's friend, brought an even severer militia act, passed in 1685. The continuing drop in the price of sugar led the authorities to seek another medium in which to measure their militia fines. Now, the Quakers complained, "they levy their execution upon our most serviceable negroes, both men, women and children, taking away, parting and selling husbands, wives, and children one from another, to the great grief, lamentation and distraction of our negro families." Seizure of valuable cattle and horses and the extension of the liability for militia service in a household to include the apprentice as well as the master added to the Quakers' distress. As a result, "the young people go off the island to their own hurt and parents' grief." At last, however, owing to the intervention of London Meeting for Sufferings with the king, probably through Penn's contacts at court, the government in London instructed the island authorities to show greater leniency in dealing with Quakers who had scruples against bearing arms. Some relaxation ensued, but it was followed again by bouts of severity, including further occasions on which recalcitrant Quakers were tied "neck and heels" for their objection against war, a practice that continued into the reign of William and Mary. The situation eased during the eighteenth century. But by the third quarter of the century Quakerism had died out entirely on the island.

A complicating factor in the situation here as in the other Caribbean islands was the possession of slaves by Quaker planters, many of them men of affluence. Although the movement for emancipation within the Society had scarcely got under way before Quakerism disappeared from the area, good treatment of their bond servants was a fundamental point of Quaker practice that George Fox and ministering Friends had insisted upon since the earliest days. The fact of their owning slaves, of course, involved the planters to a considerable degree in the support of a system based upon force and terror. We have just seen, too, that their conscientious scruples against war sometimes led to misery for their slaves rather than to personal hardship for themselves, apart from the loss of their Negroes' labor. At the same time their humanitarianism aroused the ire of the authorities as well as the anger of their fellow planters, who were afraid that the Quakers' attitude might incite the Negroes to revolt. Fear of an armed Negro uprising seems to have been ever present in the minds of the islanders, both within the administration and among the ordinary white citizenry. Thus, we find Friends doing all they could to show that, in fact, they had no ill designs in this respect. In their "Representation" of 1675 they point to "our readiness and diligence in watching, and warding, and patrolling in our persons and horses which for some time was accepted, since the late wicked contrivance of the Negroes, which the Lord by his witness in the heart made known for the preservation of the island and inhabitants." However, the willingness of Friends on the island to perform part of their duties, if allowed to do so unarmed, evidently failed to persuade the authorities to relax either their requirements or the penalties consequent upon disobedience.[90]

The story in Jamaica, where Quakers were considerably more numerous than elsewhere in the British West Indies, followed much the same pattern of distraints and imprisonments as in Barbados. Although a proclamation of 1662 granted Quakers personal exemption from bearing arms "provided they shall contribute for the same," subsequent legislation withdrew this concession until 1670, when the governor and council, baffled by the passive resistance offered by the Quakers, once again granted them conditional exemption; the alternative offered was to contribute a sum sufficient to furnish three substitutes in place of each Quaker objector. The imposition of fines and distresses continued unabated. According to Margaret Hirst, however, "the fines cannot have been very strictly enforced."[91] One case of cruel treatment is reported. This took place in 1687 when a young man, Peter Dashwood, was twice forced "to ride the wooden horse with a musket at each leg" for his refusal to train in arms.

In the Leeward islands Quaker communities grew up on Antigua and Nevis. Several prominent citizens were converted to the new faith, and there seems to have been the same kind of apprehension on the

[90] Hirst, *The Quaker in Peace and War*, pp. 309-14; Besse, *Sufferings*, II, 278-95, 314-18, 322, 330-33, 337-40, 342-49; Charles D. Sturge, "Friends in Barbados," *Friends Quarterly Examiner*, XXVI, no. 104 (Oct. 1892), 493.

[91] Hirst, *The Quakers in Peace and War*, pp. 314, 315. See also Besse, *Sufferings*, II, 388-91; H. J. Cadbury, "History of Quakers in Jamaica" (MS in microfilm, F.H.L.S.C.), pp. 72-83.

part of the authorities here, as in Barbados and elsewhere, that the spread of Quakerism would mean a serious depletion of the islands' military potential. So, in 1671, after William Edmundson and another traveling Friend were refused permission to land on Nevis, the governor of neighboring Montserrat, who visited their ship, told Edmundson: "We hear since your coming to the Carribee-Islands [i.e., the Leewards], there are seven hundred of our militia turned Quakers, and the Quakers will not fight, and we have need of men to fight, being surrounded with enemies, and that is the very reason why Governor Wheeler [of Nevis] will not suffer you to come on shore."[92]

Nevis had first received the Quaker message between the years 1656 and 1658. Thereafter a number of cases were recorded concerning Friends who were in prison for failing to appear at musters or on guard duty, "for not appearing in arms at an alarum," or "for refusing to go with their men to assist in making trenches and bulwarks to fortify the island." In some cases the punishment was repeated many times. There were instances, too, of the application of the familiar "neck and heels" treatment to recalcitrants. In 1674 the governor received a petition from ten Quaker objectors which had been smuggled out of prison. The men had been confined in different parts of the fort in order (so the authorities hoped) to prevent communication between them. In it they state:

> It is now twelve days since we were confined here, and there are some of us who have wives and children, and have nothing to maintain them but our labours. Now, General, the reason why we are thus imprisoned we do not well understand, unless for keeping the commandment of Christ, which we dare not disobey. . . . We desire that He would order thy heart that thou mightest discern betwixt us, who are in scorn called Quakers, a peaceable people, who fear God and make conscience of our ways, and those who run wilfully on their own heads and disobey thee.[93]

This forthright declaration had its effect, for the governor ordered the men to be released.

In the following year a new crisis occurred as a result of the Nevis Quakers' efforts to practice Christian pacifism in the lawless environment of those danger-infested seas. Previously, as in Barbados, the governor had permitted Friends to perform their statutory duty of watching for enemies, pirates, and other marauders, without carrying arms as the other white inhabitants on the island were obliged to do.

[92] Edmundson, *Journal*, p. 55.
[93] Besse, *Sufferings*, II, 352-54, 360, 366.

Now some members of the Society began to have reservations as to whether this practice was in fact consistent with a strict observance of the Quaker peace testimony, considering the close connection such an activity, though noncombatant, had with the all-pervading atmosphere of war on the island. Word of these doubts reached the ears of George Fox, who in November 1675 dispatched an epistle from his home at Swarthmore Hall in Lancashire "to Friends at Nevis and the Carribbee Islands concerning Watching." In it he upheld the views of those who believed it right to comply with the order to watch, pointing out that it was "a very civil thing, and to be taken notice of" that the governor had allowed them to perform this service unarmed and that, in addition, this was a privilege that Friends in Jamaica and Barbados (where it had been granted for only a brief period when a slave uprising threatened) would have been only too glad to obtain. Ordinarily, he went on, Friends in both town and country took precautions not to be surprised by bandits and housebreakers, as Quakers who owned sailing vessels did to guard against attack by pirates or enemy warships, and they were ready to have recourse to the magistrate if they suffered damage from the enemies of society. Watching without arms, therefore, in no way compromised Friends' testimony against all wars.

It seems that Fox's advice did not find acceptance with the majority of the Nevis meeting, for a little later we find the governor reporting home concerning its members: "They will neither watch nor ward, not so much as against the Carib Indians, whose secret, treacherous and most barbarous inroads, committing murders, rapes and all other enormities, discourages the planters in the Leeward Islands more than any one thing, knowing how they have been made use of in the last war by our neighbours."

So unpopular in fact did the Quakers now become with the islanders that in July 1677 the assembly passed a law imposing a heavy fine on anyone privy to the entry into the island of a Quaker and providing for that Quaker to be forthwith expelled. The reason alleged for this severity was that the Quakers had become a subversive element because they persuaded people to refuse to bear arms in defense of king and native soil. As soon as this act had been passed, Friends on the island drew up a statement declaring the assertions contained in it to be untrue. Pledging their loyalty to the Crown, they maintained that their sole object was to turn men toward the light of Christ, which takes away the need for defense by carnal weapons and for all killing. "If any are convicted by the Spirit of God in their own hearts, that fighting with any carnal weapon to the destroying of any man, although their greatest enemy, be sin, then to him it is sin, if he do it."[94]

Turning from Nevis, where (so far as the surviving records show) the authorities apparently began from the end of the 1670's to regard Friends' noncombatancy more leniently, we need not linger in surveying the Quaker settlement on the neighboring island of Antigua over the by now familiar story of distraints and imprisonments, which were the lot of the male Quakers eligible for military duties from the first conversions around 1660 until near the end of the century.[95] Two incidents involving the peace witness of Antigua Friends are, however, worth brief mention. The first took place in 1664 when the island came briefly into the possession of the French. The commander of the fleet which had captured the island allowed any of its male inhabitants who took an oath of allegiance to the King of France to remain on the island; the rest were to be removed as prisoners of war. Fear concerning the fate of their families, who, left without assistance, would be exposed to the attacks of hostile Indians after the French had withdrawn, led all but four of the menfolk to take the oath. These four were the heads of the four families which then made up the little Quaker community on the island. The English governor, who had himself sworn allegiance (although he later went back on his oath, adds Besse), tried to persuade the men to conform by pointing out the dire consequences of refusal. After they had explained to the French commander that their religion prevented them from taking an oath, he told them that he was willing to accept their word alone that they would not fight against the French King for the remainder of the war. Then one of the Quakers replied: "We desire to be rightly understood in this our promise, for we can freely promise not to fight against the King of France, nor for him, nor indeed against the King of England, nor for him; for we can act no more for the one than the other in matter of war; only as the King of England is our natural prince, we must owe allegiance to him."[96] This display of loyalty to the English crown did not, however, protect the Quakers on the island from being continually harried for their pacifist scruples after the English had regained possession.

[94] Hirst, *The Quakers in Peace and War*, pp. 316-18, 323.

[95] Besse, *Sufferings*, II, 370-74, 376-78. In the seventies and eighties, under the command of a certain Major Thomas Mallet, physical manhandling of Quaker objectors by other militiamen was not infrequent on the island. Mallet, however, not long afterward came to a sudden and bad end according to Besse, who is fond of pointing out (see, e.g., pp. 344-49) that those who persecuted Friends for their peaceable principles—as well as on other grounds—were frequently struck down by God's vengeance!

[96] *Ibid.*, II, 371.

The second incident concerned the controversy which split Antigua Friends beginning in the year 1705, which, though it involved only one or two dozen persons at the most, provides a vivid illustration of the problems facing Quakers in these exposed islands. In 1705, when a French fleet appeared in the area and ravaged the neighboring islands of Nevis and St. Kitts, emergency defense measures were taken on Antigua. The authorities permitted Friends to make their contribution in the form of noncombatant auxiliary service, and they were not obliged to carry arms. Duties included "building of watch-houses, clearing common roads, making bridges, digging ponds," carrying "messages from place to place in the island, in case of danger by an enemy," as well as appearing at the place of muster without weapons. A difference of opinion soon arose between the older members, including the clerk of the little meeting, who found the compromise acceptable (perhaps, as Margaret Hirst suggests, because they could recall the stringent measures applied against Quaker objectors in former days), and the younger men, who regarded it as an impermissible watering down of their peace testimony and, indeed, as "all one" with the performance of directly military duties. By 1708 the conflict had grown so sharp that both parties proceeded to write to London Yearly Meeting for its opinion both on this matter and in regard to the payment of church rates, which was also in dispute between the two groups.

In the statement they submitted, the older men cited in their support George Fox's epistle written in 1675 to Friends in Nevis, who had faced a similar problem some thirty years earlier (as discussed above). The young men, in turn, declared in their letter:

> Whereas it is often ordered by the Government that fortifications are to be built, for the accomplishments whereof ponds for holding water (for the use of these persons who defend these places and inhabit them) are also to be dug, now the same Friends do think that if the Government will excuse them from carrying of great guns to these places, and digging of trenches, building of bulwarks, and such warlike things, and instead thereof employ them in digging these ponds, building of bridges, repairing of highways, building of guard-houses, and such things, they can freely do them, yet we do think that in such a case to dig ponds or the like to be excused from carrying of guns, etc., is not bearing a faithful testimony against such things, but below the nobility of that holy principle whereof we make profession, and (at best) but doing a lawful thing upon an unlawful account and bottom. Yet we are very will-

ing to dig ponds, repair highways, and build bridges, or such convenient things when they are done for the general service of the island and other people at work therein equal with us, and not to balance those things which for conscience' sake we cannot do. . . . And as concerning alarms or invasion of an enemy, we are free to give notice to the magistrate of an approaching danger or be serviceable as far as we can at such times, in going to see what vessels may be off or giving them information in such things, though as to carrying of permits for vessels of war "quietly to pass" such and such forts, when we are sensible their commissions are to kill, sink, burn, and destroy the enemy, we are scrupulous and not free in that case. And as concerning watching, we are free to do it in our own way [that is to say, by appearing without weapons].

But to appear on the musterfield, even without weapons, would be totally inconsistent with their peace witness, a view which, they added, the monthly meeting had finally come to share with them.

Margaret Hirst has rightly described the reply to these two epistles sent by London Meeting for Sufferings in the following year as "a temporizing document . . . instinct with that spirit of timidity and caution, combined with a genuine loyalty to the tolerant English Government, which marked Quaker leadership in the first half of the eighteenth century." Among its signatories were George Whitehead (after Penn perhaps the most influential figure in the Society of Friends) and Fox's son-in-law, Thomas Lower. This document went even further than the Antigua elders had done in urging compliance with the "intentions of love and favour granted by the magistrates" of the island. "As for digging ditches and trenches and making walls," it went on, "they are of like use with doors, locks, bolts and pales, to keep out bloody wicked and destructive men and beasts; and to give warning and to awake our neighbours by messengers or otherwise to prevent their being destroyed, robbed or burnt, doubtless is as we would desire should in the like nature be done and performed to us." The London Friends warned their overseas brethren against appearing to the authorities "a self-willed and stubborn people." Their definition of what action was "not an evil in its own nature, but service and benefit to our neighbours," ran directly counter, however, to that given by the young men in their letter. Unfortunately, there is a break in the record, so that it is not known what effect the missive from London had on the opposition group in the Antigua meeting. Within a couple of decades Quakerism had ceased to exist on the island.[97]

[97] Hirst, *The Quakers in Peace and War*, pp. 322-26.

Even more remote than this "dark and barren island" was Bermuda, far out in the Atlantic, where in 1660 two Quaker preachers began to spread their message among its sparse inhabitants. A small meeting was set up in a private house, as was so often done in the early days of transatlantic Quakerism. The new converts do not appear to have encountered difficulties vis-à-vis the militia until 1665, when a certain Captain Dorrell with a troop of eight militiamen broke into the house where Friends were holding a meeting, dragged two of its members out by force, and carried them off to the musterfield. There the captain charged one of the two whom he had arrested, Francis Estlake, "with neglect of duty in not appearing among them in arms, and under that pretence tied him neck and heels together, which punishment the said Captain Dorrell threatened to inflict on him and others of his persuasion as often as they should neglect what he called their duty." However, instead of further tortures of this nature, the worst that was in fact inflicted on Friends in the future was either a fine of one shilling for each failure to muster or to appear in arms on an alarm or distress for nonpayment thereof, that was the outcome of a law passed in the following year.[98] Still, Quakerism never took deep root in Bermuda; by the early years of the next century there were only two Friends left on the island.

Indeed, the fact that the severity practiced against Quakers on account of their conscientious objection to military service[99] on the whole grew less from the turn of the century on may in part have been due to the declining numbers and vigor of the little societies lodged so precariously in this uncongenial soil. Not only on Bermuda but also on Antigua and Nevis, Friends practically disappeared in the course of the first two decades of the eighteenth century; and on Jamaica, too, the downward trend had already begun. Only on Barbados did the Society continue to flourish for a time.

Nevertheless, West Indian Quakerism did expand to one new area in the eighteenth century: the tiny island of Tortola in the Virgin Islands, which measured only about twenty-four square miles. Tortola was first settled as late as 1720. At the outset its inhabitants numbered a mere 100 persons, a figure which rose to around 5,000, the majority of whom were Negro slaves, before the disappearance of Quakerism from the island. Quakerism was implanted on Tortola in 1727

---

[98] Besse, *Sufferings*, II, 366, 367.

[99] The Quakers' opposition to taking oaths or to paying tithes—the two other major points at which Quaker practice on the islands clashed with authority—was a further cause of their ill-treatment by the latter.

as the result of a brief visit of a London merchant and traveling minister, Joshua Fielding. Among those who soon joined the Society of Friends was the lieutenant-governor of the island, John Pickering, whose father had been a Quaker, although Pickering himself had lapsed from the faith. During the 1730's a meeting was held regularly in the governor's house, and eventually as many as five meetinghouses were established on the island. Most of those who joined were slave-owning planters; Pickering himself possessed over 500 Negroes at his death in 1768. Pickering's conversion to Quakerism soon created difficulties for him, since in his capacity as governor he was in charge of the island's defense, holding the rank of major in its militia. As he wrote to a Quaker acquaintance in London of the first few years after becoming a Friend, when he still could not quite accept a fully pacifist position for himself:

> The thing soon made a great noise that I had turned Quaker, and was soon buzzed in the General's ear,[100] on which he wrote me, he heard that I had turned Quaker and if so, he thought me not a proper person to govern an island: In answer to which I wrote him, that it was a religion or Society I owned and loved above all others, and that I was endeavouring with God's assistance to live up to, tho' I had not yet got over or seen beyond that of self preservation or defending my country or interest in a just cause . . . and that if he did not like my holding the commission on these terms, he might give it to whom he pleased, for I should not alter my opinion or religion for all the honours he could confer on me nor all he could take away.

To this letter Governor Matthew gave a most friendly reply, confirming him in his position and even going so far as to say "that he believed a good Quaker bid fairer for Heaven than a wicked Protestant of his own religion."[101]

But with the coming of the wars of mid-century, when the island was in constant danger of attack from enemy ships, first Spanish and then French, and from these nations' privateers, and with the ripening of his own views into a full-fledged acceptance of Quaker pacifism, Pickering's position became untenable, and in June 1742—undoubtedly much to Pickering's relief—Governor Matthew finally relieved him of his office.

---

[100] A reference to Governor-General William Matthew of the Leeward Islands, under whose command Tortola lay.

[101] Charles F. Jenkins, *Tortola: A Quaker Experiment of Long Ago in the Tropics*, pp. 7-9, 51.

A year earlier the well-known English-born Quaker minister, Thomas Chalkley, had come to Tortola on a pastoral visit from his Philadelphia home. Shortly before his sudden and unexpected death on the island, he wrote home to his wife in a letter dated 16 August 1741: "The governor, his wife and her sister are dear tender hearted Friends, and he seems to be better satisfied as to defence since I came than he was before."[102] He notes with satisfaction—"to the mortification of all the great swordsmen"—Governor Matthew's continued confidence in Pickering, despite the latter's growing pacifist proclivities. And, indeed, for a while Matthew appears to have been willing to allow the overwhelmingly Quaker population (that is, if we leave the Negro majority out of account) to remain in a state of disarmedness. For Chalkley reports: "The General hath sent for the warlike arms here, saying if the people were Quakers they would have no need of them, that he should want them at Antigua. . . . If they could trust Providence with their interest, they had a right to do what they would with their own."

The arrival on the island of a new, non-Quaker governor signified that, in fact, the regional authorities were unwilling to risk the loss of the island to the enemy as a result of Quaker defenselessness. In 1748, Friends reported on the likelihood of their incurring penalties for disobeying both a recent requirement that all islanders keep firearms in their homes in readiness for use in case of alarm and an order from the governor to contribute money to build forts and protective turrets around the island. But, unlike their brethren on the other islands, neither in this case nor in regard to their unwillingness to serve with the island's miniature militia do Tortola Friends seem to have come into any serious collision with the authorities over their noncombatancy.[103] The reason probably lies in the preponderant influence Quak-

[102] In his *Journal* (p. 207) Chalkley describes the hesitation—likewise finally overcome—of an earlier convert to Quakerism in Barbados (called "P. M." in Chalkley's account) in accepting the pacifist element in Friends' message. In a conversation with this man, Chalkley had reminded him of the injunctions contained in the Sermon on the Mount: nonresistance to evil, turning the other cheek, loving enemies, going the second mile, etc. "After I had used these arguments," Chalkley goes on, "he asked me, *If one came to kill me, would I not rather kill than be killed?* I told him, No; so far as I know my own heart, I had rather be killed than kill. He said, *That was strange, and desired to know what reason I could give for it.* I told him, That I being innocent, if I was killed in my body, my soul might be happy; but if I killed him, he dying in his wickedness, would, consequently, be unhappy; and if I was killed, he might live to repent; but if I killed him, he would have no time to repent; so that if he killed me, I should have much the better, both in respect to myself and to him." The argument set forth here by Chalkley is typical of those used by early Friends and some later non-Quaker pacifists discussed in this book.

[103] Jenkins, *Tortola*, pp. 19, 38, 85, 89.

ers wielded in the island's affairs, even after their leader Pickering had been replaced as governor.

"Things are yet young and tender here," wrote Chalkley in 1741.[104] And, indeed, Quakerism on Tortola, to an even greater degree than in the other West Indian islands, was a tender plant which fairly soon succumbed to its harsh and unfriendly environment. The isolated little Quaker group, even though it had gained fellowship for a time from the existence of a second community of Friends settled on the nearby island of Jost Van Dyke, began to decline in the 1760's, especially after Pickering's death, and it vanished altogether in the next decade.

Quakerism in the West Indies, like the Society of Friends on the American mainland, was at the beginning a manifestation of the dynamic missionary outreach of early English Quakerism. The new faith, however, failed to take permanent root on the Caribbean islands: its uncompromising pacifism, one cannot help feeling, was probably among the main factors accounting for the disappearance of Quakerism from this area within a century or so of its promising beginning.

On the American continent, too, the peace testimony brought its dilemmas and its hardships to the Quaker communities scattered along the coastal areas from Maine to Georgia and sometimes gave rise to conflict between the colonial authorities and these stubborn sectaries. But here the loyalty of the Quakers to their principles did not, after the first few decades of fierce persecution that greeted them in some areas had passed, prevent the acceptance of the Society into the texture of American life. In most provinces, indeed, Quakers were content to remain to a large extent a people apart, a community set off both from the state church and from the unchurched by the character of the severe discipline which the Society imposed on its members. In one province, however, the province of Pennsylvania, Quakers long held a position of authority, owing to the circumstances of its founding, and were for many decades leaders in political, social, and economic life. Thus, though Pennsylvania Quakerism exercised an influence on the remaining societies of colonial America second only to that wielded by the parent body in England, it differed in many important respects from these other branches of overseas Quakerism. We must now turn, then, to a consideration of the "Holy Experiment" and its aftermath.

[104] *Ibid.*, p. 85.

Chapter 2

The Pacifist as Magistrate:
The Holy Experiment in Quaker Pennsylvania

I

William Penn's colony on the banks of the Delaware was intended to be a "Holy Experiment" in the wilderness, a Quaker Eden almost, set down in the forests of a new and scarcely explored continent. Hopes were high at the beginning that here at last God's children, after fighting valiantly in the Lamb's War back in the Old World, might establish a peaceable kingdom where Friends could dwell in amity with each other and with the rest of the world. And that world too, it was still believed, would eventually be won over to the Quaker faith. Pennsylvania, as the colony was called in honor of its founder's father, Admiral Sir William Penn, would in its internal institutions and its external relations constitute, as it were, a blueprint of a world to come, a new society from which war would be banished and where physical force would be contained within the limits of police action. For such a commonwealth of peace and justice, as Penn expressed it, "the nations want a precedent."[1]

Quaker control of Pennsylvania lasted seventy-four years. Yet long before this period had run out, the Holy Experiment was seen to have failed. The reasons for its failure and, even more, the conclusions to be drawn concerning the viability of pacifism as practical politics have been keenly debated ever since by historians and political scientists. This chapter is not intended as a study of Quaker Pennsylvania in all its manifold aspects: it will confine itself solely to discussing the relationship of Quaker pacifism to the domestic and external policies of the province.

The enormous expanse of forest land that was to become the province of Pennsylvania (along with Delaware formed from the three Lower Counties within Penn's grant), which until then was very

---

[1] Quoted in Guy F. Hershberger, "The Pennsylvania Quaker Experiment in Politics, 1682-1756," *MQR*, X, no. 4 (Oct. 1936), 197. I am extremely grateful to Professor Hershberger for allowing me to read a typescript draft of his forthcoming monograph on pacifism in Quaker Pennsylvania (referred to below in the notes to this and the succeeding chapter as "MS book"). This is based on a wide array of sources in both printed and manuscript form and will undoubtedly constitute the standard work on the subject for many years to come.

sparsely inhabited except for the indigenous Indian tribes, had been assigned to William Penn by King Charles II probably, at least in part, as repayment of an old debt owed by the Crown to the late Admiral Penn. Penn and other English Quakers, as we have seen, had already been involved in the founding of the Jerseys, and Quaker immigration to America already went back almost three decades. The most important factor in Penn's plans for the new colony now was his desire to create a refuge for his persecuted coreligionists: Pennsylvania would prove to a skeptical world what Quakers could achieve in a primitive but friendly environment. True, Penn also hoped with the profits accruing from his overseas landholding to restore his financial stability, which was already declining in large part because of his generous support of the Quaker cause; but this was a factor of secondary importance for his scheme.[2] Finally, in his negotiations with the Crown, Penn had also urged the advantages that England would gain from the expansion of British settlement in this area.

Penn arrived in his new province in October 1682, seven months after the issue of the royal charter granting him his title to the land. His first sojourn in the New World lasted only two years; his departure earlier than he had expected was necessitated by his affairs in England. On returning home, he reported with satisfaction to a leading English Quaker, Stephen Crisp, that there was "not one soldier, or arms borne, or militia man seen, since I was first in Pennsylvania."[3]

The practice of nonviolence in the relations of man with man, whether savage or civilized, was as much a part of Penn's personal philosophy as it was a central tenet of the Quaker religious faith. Although some writers have concluded from certain of his utterances that Penn's condemnation of international war admitted of exceptions, that his pacifism was relativist, this claim surely is a misconception.

[2] E.C.O. Beatty, *William Penn as Social Philosopher*, pp. 43, 45, 46, 83, 175.
[3] Quoted in Catherine Owens Peare, *William Penn*, p. 283. An attempt by the mystically minded near-Quaker Thomas Tryon (1634-1703), pacifist, health reformer, and teetotaler, to persuade Quaker immigrants to adopt vegetarianism in their new homeland obviously failed. In his *Planter's Speech to his Neighbours & Country-Men of Pennsylvania* Tryon urged the Quakers to banish all lethal weapons from their settlements, even if used only to obtain food. For him, the animal kingdom was included in the precepts of Christian nonviolence. "Does not bounteous Mother Earth furnish us with all sorts of food necessary for life?" he inquired. "Though you will not fight with, and kill those of your own species, yet I must be bold to tell you, that these lesser violences (as you call them) do proceed from the same root of wrath and bitterness, as the greater do." He warned the Quaker settlers that, if they brought up their children to kill animals for food, they might become so accustomed to handling weapons that they would finally be reluctant to renounce their use against their fellow men (see pp. 17-28). Tryon did not himself visit the American continent.

Admittedly, in his famous *Essay towards the Present and Future Peace of Europe* (1693) he included (presumably) military sanctions as a last resort against a country that refused to accept the arbitration of the European diet of nations which his peace scheme postulated. It is true, too, that in the plan for intercolonial union that he propounded in 1696 provision was made for military defense. But these proposals applied only to the non-Quaker world: they represented interim recommendations that were necessary for the time being until the Quaker remnant had transformed the world. The New Testament and the Inner Light revealed to Penn as much as to the other Friends of this age a higher path, a condition of being difficult to attain yet to be prayerfully sought after, where the wearing of a sword became impossible. Penn, observes Henry J. Cadbury, "repudiated . . . any reliance upon the methods of war" in framing the government of Pennsylvania.[4] Although the establishment of religious toleration and constitutional government was the main goal of the province's founder, the creation there of a weaponless state "in accordance with the peace principles enunciated in . . . [the] sermon on the mount"[5] was also among his objectives.

The elevation of what was a personal, almost vocational pacifism into a political policy was, however, fraught with danger. Here, indeed, lay the seeds of later misfortune. For built into the very foundation of the Quaker commonwealth was the element of dependency on a higher authority that had by no means renounced the use of force in international relations, that was, moreover, soon to become engaged with its French imperial rival in a long drawn out, if intermittent, struggle which was to outlast Quaker government in Pennsylvania. Pennsylvania remained a colony of the English Crown; Quaker rule always had to function within this limitation. After Penn's death in 1718 and the conversion of his children to the Church of England, the proprietorship, too, slipped from Quaker hands. Thenceforward, the home authorities, the Penn proprietors, and increasing numbers of the inhabitants of the province that had hospitably opened its doors to the hosts of non-Quaker immigrants seeking admittance (who already began to outnumber members of the Society there by around the turn of the century) were all to a greater or less degree out of sympathy with the pacifist ideals of the Society of Friends.

At the very outset Penn had to accept titular military rank in his province, even though he did not intend to institute defensive meas-

[4] H. J. Cadbury, "Penn as a Pacifist," *Friends Intelligencer*, 21 Oct. 1944.
[5] Samuel M. Janney, *Peace Principles exemplified in the Early History of Pennsylvania*, p. 162.

ures within its borders—the military provisions of the royal charter of 4 March 1682 being to some extent a device to make English claims over the territory legally secure.[6] The charter, indeed, contained the following clause:

> And because in so remote a country, and situate near many barbarous nations, the incursions as well of the savages themselves, as of other enemies, pirates and robbers, may probably be feared. Therefore, we have given and for us, our heirs and successors, do give power by these presents unto the said William Penn, his heirs and assigns, by themselves or their captains or other, their officers, to levy, muster and train all sorts of men, of what condition, or wheresoever born, in the said province of Pennsylvania, for the time being, and to make war and pursue the enemies and robbers aforesaid, as well by sea as by land, yea, even without the limits of the said province, and by God's assistance to vanquish and take them, and being taken, to put them to death by the law of war, or to save them at their pleasure, and to do all and every other act and thing, which to the charge and office of a Captain-General of an army, belongeth or hath accustomed to belong, as fully and freely as any Captain-General of an army, hath ever had the same.[7]

As a result, we find "Captain-General" Penn during the greater part of his prolonged absences from the province delegating his military duties to a series of deputy- or lieutenant-governors who, some being soldiers by profession, did not share the Quaker scruples concerning war.[8]

At first, Penn had experimented with the appointment of prominent local Quakers to head the administration while he was away; "Quaker deputies, however, found it difficult to deal with the exigencies of government."[9] As Penn himself wrote in 1688 upon appointing the English Civil War veteran, Captain John Blackwell, as his deputy: "Being not a Friend, [he] could deal with those that were not and stop their mouths, and be stiff with neighbors upon occasion. This was my motive to have him."[10] Ever present in the background of Penn's thought must have been the possibility of the Crown's depriving him

[6] E. Dingwall and E. A. Heard, *Pennsylvania 1681-1756: The State without an Army*, p. 25.

[7] *Charter to William Penn and Laws of the Province of Pennsylvania*, p. 88.

[8] Cf. Charles P. Keith, *Chronicles of Pennsylvania . . . 1688-1748*, I, 156; II, 418.

[9] Hershberger, "Quaker Pacifism and the Provincial Government of Pennsylvania, 1682-1756," *University of Iowa Studies: Studies in the Social Sciences*, X, no. 4 (1937), 9.

[10] Hershberger, *MQR*, p. 198.

of his province if he were unable—or unwilling—to provide for its defense in time of war or threat of invasion. This possibility was in fact realized in 1692 when administration of the province was placed in the hands of Governor Benjamin Fletcher of New York.[11]

Although Penn regained possession two years later, he did so only at the price of a seeming renunciation of the pacifist position on his part. Promising to transmit to the provincial council and assembly all requests from the Crown in respect to defense measures, Penn told the Committee of Trade and Plantations: "He doubts not but they will at all times dutifully comply with and yield obedience thereunto." Even Sharpless, who tends to give a somewhat idealized picture of Quaker rule, is forced to describe Penn's words as "disingenuous." "For," he goes on, "he must have known that these Quaker bodies would do nothing of the kind."[12] True, Penn had not explicitly committed his own individual conscience; but he had compromised the Quaker reputation for straightforward dealing. Hershberger, while sympathetically describing the hard choice Penn had to face between probable extinction of all his hopes for the Quaker province and the possibility of regaining control at the cost of a compromise on principle, rightly speaks here of "a certain flirting with deception, which does not quite fit in with the ethical standard of a pious and spiritual Quaker."[13] Yet, in extenuation of Penn's action, it should be said that Penn's promise was probably adopted by the two parties as a face-

[11] Joseph E. Illick, *William Penn the Politician*, p. 117. See also pp. 125, 127, 128.

[12] Isaac Sharpless, *A Quaker Experiment in Government*, I, 191, 192. Margaret E. Hirst describes this incident as "the least satisfactory moment of Penn's career" (*The Quakers in Peace and War*, p. 359).

[13] Hershberger, *MQR*, p. 200. Cf. the story told to Benjamin Franklin (*Autobiography*, 1964 edn., p. 188) by the nonpacifist Quaker James Logan, who as a young man had accompanied Penn in the capacity of private secretary on the latter's second journey to Pennsylvania in 1699. "It was war time," Franklin relates, "and their ship was chased by an armed vessel supposed to be an enemy. Their captain prepared for defence, but told William Penn and his company of Quakers, that he did not expect their assistance, and they might retire into the cabin; which they did, except James Logan, who chose to stay upon deck, and was quartered to a gun. The supposed enemy proved to be a friend; so there was no fighting. But when the secretary went down to communicate the intelligence, William Penn rebuked him severely for staying upon deck and undertaking to assist in defending the vessel, contrary to the principles of Friends, especially as it had not been required by the Captain. This reproof being before all the company, piqued the secretary, who answered, *I being thy servant, why did thee not order me to come down: but thee was willing enough that I should stay and help to fight the ship when thee thought there was danger.*" Logan's most recent biographer, Frederick B. Tolles, states that Franklin's account, though possibly inaccurate in some details, may be regarded as substantially correct (*James Logan and the Culture of Provincial America*, p. 13).

saving formula, for the home authorities must surely have been well acquainted with the intransigent pacifism of the Quaker sect. The recovery of the province from the dangers which Crown rule posed for the continued existence of the Holy Experiment perhaps seemed to Penn worth a merely verbal concession. As he told his Pennsylvania Friends: "Things are not just now . . . as you may reasonably desire. . . . Accept this part of the goodness of God, and wait for the rest. We must creep where we cannot go, and it is as necessary for us, in the things of life, to be wise as to be innocent."[14]

Thus, in the relationship of Quaker pacifism to both the domestic government and the external affairs of the Quaker province, Penn and his fellow Friends strove to maintain a nicely adjusted balance between relativist "wisdom" and absolutist "innocence." The attempt frequently ran into difficulties and was finally abandoned in the middle of the next century. Let us begin our examination of the history of the Holy Experiment by considering the problem of the maintenance of internal order by a government whose members were almost all pledged by their religious belief to uphold nonviolent policies.

Unlike the nonresistant Mennonites who were soon to come out from Central Europe to settle in the Quaker colony, the Society of Friends from its inception had adopted a positive attitude toward civil government. Friends made a clear distinction between the waging of war by the state against an external enemy and the state's function of law enforcement against the domestic lawbreaker. Although they repudiated all participation in armies and the organization of military defense and practiced nonresistance in personal relations, Quakers were active in politics and in the magistracy and, moreover, became increasingly vocal in their new home in maintaining the rights belonging, as they believed, to true born Englishmen.[15] They did not share the pessimistic *Weltanschauung* of those reared in the Anabaptist tradition, the conviction that the godly would always constitute a small remnant on this earth. For Quakers, the Inner Light illumined all men, to however small a degree; all mankind, therefore, might sooner or later be reached by the redeeming spirit. "The result," writes Hershberger, "was an optimistic hope for the imminent Christianization of the social order."[16]

Although this underlying optimism led Quakers to undertake the establishment of a Christian commonwealth, they also shared with the

[14] Hershberger, *MQR*, p. 199.
[15] "We are Englishmen ourselves, and freeborn, although in scorn called Quakers," stated Maryland Friends in 1681 (Rufus M. Jones, *The Quakers in the American Colonies*, p. 333).
[16] Hershberger, *MQR*, p. 193.

rest of the Christian church a belief in the depravity of human nature in general when not restrained by government, a condition that had existed since the Fall when God had instituted civil government to suppress the evildoer and the impious as well as to promote the welfare of society. Penn, the friend of Algernon Sidney, would have included as well among the most important functions of the state the securing of liberty (though not egalitarian democracy), property, and religious toleration. These were the principles that animated Pennsylvania's founder and successive generations of its Quaker rulers.

In his preface to the final draft of the first Frame of Government which Penn issued as the province's constitution in April 1682 before his departure for America, the duties of magistrate and subject are clearly set forth: the former is exhorted "to terrify evil-doers . . . to cherish those that do well," while the latter is enjoined to render willing obedience "not only for wrath, but for conscience sake." "Government," wrote Penn, "seems to me a part of religion itself, a thing sacred in its institutions and end." It must not merely wield "coercive or compulsive means"; correction of evildoers is only "the coarsest part of it." "Kindness, goodness and charity" must be the methods employed to further the material and moral welfare of the community under its care.[17]

Pennsylvania's Quaker rulers, whether in the assembly and the executive council (which in the seventeenth century shared the legislative power) or in the lower magistracy, had no compunction in administering a police force and in imposing on malefactors the penalties laid down in the law. However, Penn and his people were successful in ameliorating some of the harshness and cruelty of the contemporary English penal code. Prisons were set up, but (at least in theory) these were to have a redemptive purpose. We read, for instance, in the "Laws agreed upon in England" in 1682 before the colony was formally established: "That all prisons shall be workhouses for felons, vagrants and loose and idle persons; whereof one shall be in every county."[18] At this date, an attitude of this kind was indeed a revolutionary advance in penology. Brandings and earcroppings are mentioned from time to time in the court records in the next century, but from the beginning "the favorite method of punishing was by whipping" and imprisonment,[19] with fines employed for less grave of-

---

[17] *Charter to William Penn etc.*, pp. 91, 92.
[18] *Ibid.*, p. 100.
[19] Pennsylvania, its founder states in a letter of 1701 (quoted in Beatty, *William Penn*, p. 231), had been "at great charge to build strong prisons, with high brick walls, grates, bolts, chains, etc., and one to watch and ward as well as" to seize dangerous malefactors. For Penn's zeal in urging the suppression in Pennsylvania

fenses.[20] "Some of these punishments," writes Lawrence H. Gipson, "may seem to our generation extreme and harsh, nevertheless, the Great Law [of 1682] was remarkable for its humaneness, especially as it existed side by side with codes loaded down with atrocious sanctions."[21] In many instances, the harsher penalties inscribed on the statute books seem to have been inflicted only infrequently. Apparently, however, neither Penn nor his fellow Quakers at this time held a testimony against capital punishment. At the beginning in Pennsylvania, in contrast to the mother country where according to English law a multitude of offenses were punishable by death, this penalty was retained for only two offenses: murder and treason. Although it is doubtful whether the Crown would have given its approval to the establishment of the Quaker colony if any punishment less than death had been made the penalty for these two crimes, its retention passed apparently without protest from any member of the Society. In a letter written from England in September 1688, for example, we find Penn directing his deputy-governor, Blackwell, "that the murderous woman's sentence should proceed, the case being notorious and barbarous."[22]

In the early decades of the eighteenth century we can observe a stiffening of the provincial penal code, a widening of the range of offenses for which harsh penalties were inflicted. In the so-called New Castle Code of 1700, "multilation and branding stand out among the new sanctions." "There was little of redemption in these punishments."[23] The climax in this process came in 1718 when the provincial assembly passed a law extending the death penalty to twelve more felonies, which were punished in this way in English law. In this case the abandonment to a large degree of the Quaker province's more enlightened attitude resulted from political maneuverings which had been going on for a number of years. The Quakers' enemies had

---

of pirates and of interlopers in respect to the English navigation laws, see *ibid.*, pp. 84, 217-27, 230, 231.

[20] H.W.K. Fitzroy, "The Punishment of Crime in Provincial Pennsylvania," *PMHB*, LX, no. 3 (July 1936), 260-64.

[21] Lawrence H. Gipson, "Crime and Its Punishment in Provincial Pennsylvania," *Pennsylvania History*, II, no. 1 (Jan. 1935), 6.

[22] *Pennsylvania Colonial Records*, I, 252. This, however, seems to be the only case of capital punishment inflicted in the province before 1700. It is interesting to note that Penn's more radical contemporary, the vegetarian pacifist Thomas Tryon, also did not disapprove of capital punishment. In his *Planter's Speech* (p. 31) he writes: "And if any wilfully commit man-slaughter, then let such perish by the same sword or weapon."

[23] Gipson, "Crime and Its Punishment," p. 9; Fitzroy, "The Punishment of Crime," p. 249.

been attempting to deprive them of their political predominance by forcing an oath on holders of judicial and administrative office within the province. These officials would then have been required to take a test oath themselves and to administer one to others. In order to prevent the consummation of their opponents' designs and to maintain their right to make an affirmation in place of an oath, the Quaker assembly finally agreed in a kind of bargain with the home government to a measure which would approximate the Pennsylvania penal code to that prevailing back in England. The Quaker bench acquiesced without a murmur in the law's increased stringency. In January 1730, we find David Lloyd (1656-1731), the former leader of the country party among Friends and an ardent upholder of the Quaker peace testimony insofar as it related to attack from without the state, supporting the execution of a convicted burglar. He "justly deserves to die," he then wrote, "and it may be of ill consequence to spare him."[24]

However, since harsher measures had begun to be introduced much earlier, the deeper reasons for this development must be sought elsewhere. During the time when almost all the inhabitants still belonged to the Society of Friends, few problems had arisen in connection with law enforcement. Those were the days when it was enough for Thomas Lloyd (1640-1694), when acting as chief executive of the province, to go out into the streets at night and deal out religious admonishment to any roisterous character he met with there. "Philadelphia became under his control the most decorous of cities."[25] But the influx of non-Quaker immigrants that began toward the end of the seventeenth century made the maintenance of law and order an increasingly complex problem. The preamble to an act of 1698 states that "many dissolute persons, notwithstanding the said laws [i.e., already on the statute book], have committed divers thefts and robberies within this government."[26] The idyllic conditions of the early days, when the strong arm of the law was only rarely needed to reinforce the meeting discipline of the religious Society to which most citizens belonged, soon passed, and the need grew for more effective police control, as did the clamor from the side of the non-Quaker settlers for more forcible action. In the case of moral offenses, the Puritan strain in Quakerism generated an impetus of its own in legislating against such things as profanity, drunkenness, and sexual

[24] Roy N. Lokken, *David Lloyd*, pp. 198, 237; Sharpless, *Political Leaders of Provincial Pennsylvania*, p. 103.
[25] Sharpless, *A Quaker Experiment*, I, 69.
[26] Fitzroy, "The Punishment of Crime," pp. 248, 249.

irregularity. "I recommend to you," Penn told Quaker officials in Pennsylvania in a letter dated 21 October 1687, "the vigorous suppression of vice, and that without respect to persons or persuasions. Let not foolish pity rob justice of its due and the people of proper examples."[27] And in 1727, for instance, we find that stalwart Quaker pacifist, Thomas Chalkley, reproving the largely Quaker magistracy for their alleged laxness in enforcing the law in this respect. "The Lord," he relates in his *Journal*, "was angry with the magistrates . . . because they use not their power as they might do, in order to suppress wickedness; and do not so much as they ought, put the laws already made in execution against profaneness and immorality: and the Lord is angry with the representatives of the people of the land, because they take not so much care to suppress vice and wickedness, . . . as they ought to do."[28]

For all its strictness, however, the Pennsylvania legal code throughout the period of Quaker rule undoubtedly continued to temper justice with mercy to a greater extent than other contemporary systems of law.[29] In civil disputes between members of the Society of Friends the parties were required to settle the affair by arbitration within the Society; recourse to courts of law was permitted only if arbitration were refused by one party, who would then suffer disownment for failure to abide by the discipline. Law suits involving a Friend and a non-Friend, however, could be settled in an ordinary court of law without endangering the member's status within the Society.[30] Thus, conciliation was combined with a relatively mild system of law enforcement in an effort to produce a commonwealth that was governed, be it only approximately, in the spirit of the Sermon on the Mount.

Church and state were formally separate. Nonetheless, despite the

---

[27] Beatty, *William Penn*, p. 35. See also pp. 290-92.

[28] Chalkley, *Journal*, 1754 edn., p. 203.

[29] Gipson, "Crime and Its Punishment," p. 16.

[30] See Appendix B in Tolles, *Meeting House and Counting House*. Complaints sometimes made about inconsistency between the Quakers' disapproval of taking their own disputes to the provincial courts and their willingness at the same time to serve as magistrates in these courts do not appear to me justified, especially in view of the fact that as early as 1683 (*Charter to William Penn etc.*, p. 128) provision was made (although apparently rarely put into effect subsequently) for appointing "common peacemakers" "in every precinct," the results of whose arbitration were given the force of law. Thus, not only was there no objection in principle to recourse on the part of Friends to the state machinery of justice; but, on the contrary, this machinery as framed by the province's Quaker rulers contained means of arbitration and extrajudicial conciliation open to all citizens, Friend and non-Friend alike. Of course, it is possible to argue that the Christian pacifism to which Quakers adhered is incompatible with participation in state affairs, including its judicial side. But this is a different question.

fact that the Society of Friends was granted no special privileges not possessed by other denominations, a close link existed between the government and the Quaker community. The same men who sat in the assembly (and at first in the council, too)—where, beginning as early as the mid-1680's, some of the Quaker representatives in fact from time to time displayed more heat than charity in the pursuit of their political goals—often took a prominent part also, at least during the early decades, in the deliberations of the yearly meeting, which until 1760 was held alternately in Philadelphia and Burlington (it has always included parts of New Jersey as well as strictly Pennsylvania territory). Weighty Quakers occupied most of the high judicial offices in the province, and the administration of justice in town and country was to a large extent carried out by members of the Society. A minute of Philadelphia Monthly Meeting in 1685 well illustrates the Quaker character of the state in practice:

> John Eckley and James Claypoole are appointed by this Meeting to request the magistracy of the county that they will please to keep their court on the first 5th day of every month, which, if they please to grant, then the weekly meeting, which hath hitherto been on the 5th day, shall be on the 4th day, that so the court and the meeting may not be on the same day.[31]

It was not always easy for the Quaker administrators to draw the line between police action, which could be carried out with a minimum of physical force, and measures where a degree of force that was scarcely consistent with a nonviolent philosophy appeared necessary. An incident of this latter type occurred in 1691 and aroused strong criticism—not from orthodox Friends but from a small dissident group that was to break away from the Society in the following year under the leadership of the Scotsman George Keith (1638-1716). The causes of the Keithite schism, however, were unconnected with pacifism or government: they stemmed from Keith's attempt to play down the doctrinal importance of the Inner Light in contrast to the authority of the Bible and the historic Jesus.

Early in 1691 a man named Babbitt and some associates stole a vessel from the harbor in Philadelphia and proceeded to commit a number of robberies on the river traffic. Upon receiving information of Babbitt's depredations, three magistrates—including a leading Quaker, Samuel Jenings—issued a warrant "in the nature of a hue and cry"[32]

[31] Quoted in Sharpless, *Quakerism and Politics*, p. 82.
[32] Samuel Smith, "The History of the Province of Pennsylvania," *The Register of Pennsylvania*, VI (1830), no. 16, 242. See also no. 18.

to apprehend the miscreants. Armed with this authority, and possibly (the accounts are contradictory) with no weapons more lethal than this, several young Quakers succeeded in capturing Babbitt's gang and bringing them to justice. The affair caused quite a stir, and it was their seizure and punishment that led Keith and his Christian Quakers (as his followers now called themselves) to denounce the Quaker magistracy for what they alleged was a dereliction of the Society's peace testimony.

In several tracts the Keithites now argued the inconsistency of Quaker participation in government. In their view, a Friend should refuse appointment as assemblyman or provincial councillor, justice of the peace or sheriff, constable or juryman, if their duties of office involved "the taking away of life or any other corporal punishment." In fact, they said, the magistracy was scarcely conceivable without the use of the sword "as the executive part of . . . office cannot in any ordinary way (and without miracles) be done without it." The application of force for police purposes within the state scarcely differed in principle from, or was in any way less reprehensible in a follower of Christian nonviolence than, the use of deadly weapons against an enemy from outside. "A pair of stocks, whipping post and gallows, are carnal weapons, as really as sword or gun, and so is a constable's staff, when used, as [it] hath been by some, to beat and knock down the bodies of some obstinate persons." If a constable might use physical violence against a domestic wrongdoer so as to lead to his death, why—asked the Keithites—was it unchristian to employ lethal weapons against an outside aggressor such as the French or Indians? Would not the Quaker magistrates eventually be brought to sanction the use of force against armed invaders? "For it is not the number being great or small that makes a thing to be right or wrong." The Keithites, like the Anabaptists and Mennonites, did not deny the divine sanction or practical need for the state to curb evildoers—even to the extent of waging defensive war. But the Quaker, the Christian, must have no part in such action.

To the arguments that Quakers in government could help to assuage its harshness and that their withdrawal would probably mean their replacement by cruel and evil rulers, the Keithites sternly replied that it could never be right to do evil that good might come and, moreover, that good and just men were to be found among non-Quakers, and even among the heathen, who would administer the state according to their natural lights. Let all who are convinced of the Truth, they advised, retire from the magistracy and leave government to those who have not yet reached a full awareness of the meaning of Christian nonviolence.[33]

The Keithites, however, went beyond a general criticism of Quaker involvement in running the state. Seizing upon the Babbitt affair, they accused Samuel Jenings, and those members of the Society who had aided and approved his forcible suppression of piracy, both of transgressing Friends' testimony against fighting and of undermining the position of Quakers in Britain, the American colonies, and the West Indian islands who at this very time were suffering for their refusal to accept service in the militia. "Is not their practice here," wrote Keith and his five colleagues in *An Appeal* which they drew up in the late summer of 1692 concerning the stance of Pennsylvania Quakerdom, "an evil precedent, if any change of government happen in this place, to bring sufferings on faithful Friends that for conscience sake refuse to contribute to the militia? And how can they justly refuse to do that under another's government, which they have done, or allowed to be done under their own?" They poured scorn on the Quaker magistrates "preaching one day, *Not to take an eye for an eye, Matt. 5.28*" in their capacity as Friends' ministers and on the next reversing their position "by taking life for life" in consequence of their obligations on the bench.[34]

Official Quakerdom, already irritated by the acrimonious dispute with Keith over theological matters, quickly struck back. The first edition of the *Appeal* was seized as a seditious publication tending to bring the magistracy—a predominantly Quaker magistracy—into disrepute, and its printer, the Keithite William Bradford, was arrested. Together with Keith and one other "Christian Quaker" who had signed the tract, he was then tried and found guilty. The penalty for Keith and his colleague was merely a £5 fine, which was not in fact collected from them.[35] But the spectacle of men, until recently prominent and respected members of the Friends' community, being arraigned and punished by Quaker judges for, among other offenses, propounding—in a manner, it is true, that these judges deemed offensive to the magistrate's office—what, in the Keithites' view, were true Quaker peace principles,[36] was extremely unedifying. Although the

[33] *A Testimony and Caution to such as do make a Profession of Truth, who are in scorn called Quakers*, pp. 1-10. This anonymous pamphlet was issued by the Keithite M. M. in Philadelphia on 28 December 1692.

[34] George Keith *et al.*, *An Appeal from the Twenty Eight Judges to the Spirit of Truth & true Judgement in all faithful Friends*, pp. 7, 8.

[35] Ethyn Williams Kirby, *George Keith*, pp. 57-59, 72, 73, 81-85.

[36] In 1693 Keith wrote that he and his friends had been harried "by fines and imprisonment, for asserting the Quakers' principles against the use of the outward sword" (quoted in Kirby, *Keith*, p. 85).

Keithites obviously welcomed the opportunity that the Babbitt affair offered to add yet one more argument in their controversy with their opponents, there does not appear to be any reason to doubt the sincerity of their rigorist interpretation of Friends' peace testimony. In 1700, Keith, who had meanwhile returned to England, joined the established church, becoming an Anglican priest not long afterward, and his Christian Quaker group as a result soon dissolved. Whether the fervent episcopalian and still more rabid anti-Quaker that Keith now became retained anything of his Anabaptist views on war and government is not known.

Along with their uncompromising pacifism, Keith's Christian Quakers, it may be noted, adopted a critical attitude in regard to Quaker slaveholding. Though not explicitly urging the abolition of slavery within the province by law, the Keithites charged the Society of Friends with inconsistency in permitting ownership of slaves among its own members. This, argued the Keithite *An Exhortation and Caution to Friends Concerning Buying or Keeping of Negroes*, which William Bradford issued in August 1693 at his New York print shop, contravened the ban on "prize goods" which the Society maintained; for enslavement of Negroes resulted as much from "war, violence, and oppression; and theft and robbery of the highest nature," as did the seizure of property resulting from directly warlike actions.[37]

The Keithites, however, were not the first American Quakers to attack slaveholding by Friends for, among other reasons, its connection with war. The earliest protest of this kind had come five years before; its authors were members of the Germantown Friends meeting drawn from Dutch- and German-speaking Quakers who had joined the Society before their migration to the New World. Though mostly Nether-

[37] Thomas E. Drake, *Quakers and Slavery in America*, pp. 14, 15. Drake points out that this identification of the acquisition of prize goods and of slaves as both flowing from the same source, war, was common among Quaker antislavery advocates in the eighteenth century. They did not realize, of course, that the first to use this argument in their community had been the dissident Keithites. Cf. Sydney V. James, *A People Among Peoples*, pp. 127-29, 136, for the use made by American Quaker antislavery advocates in the first half of the eighteenth century of the general argument that slavery was incompatible with the Society's peace testimony. At first, many of these men encountered strong resistance from their meetings. Among the most devoted of the early abolitionists was the French-born Quaker Anthony Benezet, who in 1754 told Philadelphia Y. M.: "How can we, who have been concerned to publish the gospel of universal love and peace among mankind, be so inconsistent with ourselves as to purchase such who are prisoners of war, and thereby encourage this unchristian practice . . . ?" (George S. Brookes, *Friend Anthony Benezet*, pp. 80, 81, 475, 476). By this date the cause had made considerable headway among Friends and the buying, if not yet the keeping, of slaves was frowned on by the Society.

landers in origin, they had come out a few years before from the west German towns of Krefeld and Krisheim, where they had been converted from the Mennonite faith. The reasons for their emigration were mixed, economic and religious motives each having played a role.[38] The protest against slavery was signed on the meeting's behalf by four of their number, including the intellectual leader of the Germantown settlement, Francis Daniel Pastorius (1651-1719).[39] Its authors declared the impossibility of maintaining slavery except through the threat of physical force: slavery's origins and its fruits were violence. Slaveholding in Quaker Pennsylvania was gaining Friends a bad reputation on the European continent. What would Friends do if their slaves combined together and revolted?

> If once these slaves . . . should join themselves, fight for their freedom, and handle their masters and mistresses as they did handle them before; will these masters and mistresses take the sword and war against these poor slaves, like, we are able to believe, some will not refuse to do? Or have these negroes not as much right to fight for their freedom, as you have to keep them slaves?[40]

The protest was premature. Forwarded up through monthly, quarterly, and yearly meeting in Pennsylvania, it was finally pigeonholed by London Yearly Meeting without any action having been taken. However, the ferment did not subside altogether, and the antislavery movement among American Friends slowly increased in strength during the course of the following decades.

Whereas an awareness of the seeds of war that lay within the institution of Negro slavery only matured among Pennsylvania Quakers slowly and painfully, the sensibility they displayed in their treatment of the indigenous inhabitants of the province was greater right from the beginning. It is not the purpose of this chapter to enter into a detailed study of Quaker relations with the Indians during the period

---

[38] See William I. Hull, *William Penn and the Dutch Quaker Migration to Pennsylvania*, chap. IV. Among the causes of their departure from Germany were difficulties encountered in connection with their objection to military duties. See pp. 237, 266, 289.

[39] One of the signatories, Abraham op den Graff, seems to have been of a rather obstreperous character. In December 1703, for instance, it was recorded that he "did mightily abuse the bailiff [Arent Klinken, also a Quaker, who in 1697 had provided stocks for punishing minor offenders and whose house in 1697 became a temporary prison] in open court wherefore he was brought out of it to answer for the same at the next Court of Record." Sometime after 1708 Op den Graff returned to the Mennonites. See C. Henry Smith, *The Mennonite Immigration to Pennsylvania in the Eighteenth Century*, pp. 113, 115.

[40] The protest is printed in full in Hirst, *Quakers in Peace and War*, Appendix E. See also Drake, *Quakers and Slavery*, pp. 11-14.

of Quaker rule.[41] Suffice it to say that from the start Friends strove to deal justly with the native inhabitants, to protect them from the corrupting influences in European civilization, and to live beside them in peacefulness. At the outset Penn made it a principle that all land should be purchased at a just price, and later deviations from fair practice in this respect which took place after Penn's death (and for which Quakers as a whole were not, in fact, responsible) were among the factors leading ultimately to a deterioration in relations with the Indians.

There was certainly an element of benevolent patriarchalism in the attitude of Brother Onas (as the Indians called Penn) toward the native inhabitants, unspoilt children of nature in the view of Penn and many of his contemporaries (as there was a similar element in Penn's relations with his own people in Pennsylvania). There was, too, some ambiguity in his treatment of the Indians as virtually sovereign owners of the land and in his simultaneous acceptance of his own monarch's claims to rule in the area. This ambiguity is revealed, for instance, in the famous letter he addressed to the Pennsylvania Indians in October 1681 when he was beginning preparations to visit his new patrimony across the waters. There is one all-powerful and all-loving God for all the peoples on earth, he told them. "Now this great God hath been pleased to make me concerned in your parts of the world; and the king of the country where I live hath given unto me a great province therein; but I desire to enjoy it with your love and consent, that we may always live together as neighbors and friends."[42] Whatever the theoretical implications of European settlement might have been, so long as the situation was not complicated by the intrusion of non-Quaker authorities and settlers, good relations were maintained between the Indians and the Quakers—even if the practice frequently followed by successive Quaker assemblies of appeasing the Indians with gifts may appear to us today of somewhat dubious value. As hunters primarily, the Indians were willing in principle, as Hershberger has pointed out, to coexist peacefully alongside the white-skinned cultivators of the soil. Although it has sometimes been asserted that the long peace was chiefly due to the unwarlike qualities of the Delawares and Shawnees, who were the tribes in closest contact with the Pennsylvania settlements, they were to give

---

[41] See Rayner Wickersham Kelsey, *Friends and the Indians 1655-1917*, pp. 24-27, 29-34, 47-57, 62-70, 74-83, for Pennsylvania Quakerdom's Indian policy up to the outbreak of the Revolution.

[42] Quoted in Peare, *Penn*, p. 223.

all too visible proof of their belligerence during the French and Indian War that ultimately brought Quaker rule to an end.

II

Although the Quaker government was fairly successful in bringing its Indian policy into line with the requirements of the Society's peace testimony, the problem of squaring the duties of administering the province within the framework of English imperial policy with a pacifist witness that would have at least some relevance in public life became increasingly difficult. In the far north and northwest the French were a potential menace even to the mid-Atlantic colonies, though the threat only became immediate toward the middle of the eighteenth century. In addition, the province was exposed to enemy attack by water and to the depredations of pirate and privateer. This situation gave rise to a running debate between successive Quaker-dominated assemblies and a long line of deputy-governors who, representing the absentee proprietors, had inherited the unenviable task of extracting support for war measures from the Quaker legislators. "Hosts of mosquitoes are worse than of armed men," said Captain John Blackwell, the first of these governors to attempt the task, in the course of the humid summer of 1689, "yet the men without arms worse than they."[43] His sentiments were to be echoed by his successors in similar circumstances. For, commingled with the straight pacifist issue, other factors were usually present to complicate the debate: obscure intrigues and countermaneuvers stemming from the assertion by provincial politicians of their constitutional rights against the claims of the proprietary interest or from the understandable reluctance, exhibited by the citizenry of all the colonies, to pay out money for purposes that seemed remote from their own concerns. As time passed and the pacifism of the Quaker-born politicians became more and more perfunctory, became in fact merely an inherited belief to which they made a formal bow of acknowledgement, political and economic opposition to defense measures began to predominate.

Pacifism became a public issue for the first time in the fall of 1689 soon after the outbreak of "King William's War" with his continental rival Louis XIV, which was to last until 1697 when the Treaty of Ryswick brought a short pause in the long Anglo-French struggle. At the beginning of November, Governor Blackwell came before the council with a request from the English government for defensive measures

---

[43] *Ibid.*, p. 312. See also Hershberger, MS book, chap. 4: "Worldly Power *versus* Christian Love," n. 28.

in the colony. At first, the Quaker members of the council hedged, alleging that such steps were in fact not needed. Said John Simcock: "I see no danger but from the bears and wolves. We are well, and in peace and quiet: let us keep ourselves so." However, one Quaker councillor, Griffith Jones, went so far as to urge qualified support of the governor's request. "Every one that will may provide his arms," he said. "My opinion is that it be left to the discretion of the governor to do what he shall judge necessary." These words brought Samuel Carpenter to his feet. Carpenter, a man of considerable spiritual stature whose growing affluence gave additional weight to his utterances, had suffered heavy distraints on his property for refusal of service in the militia earlier while a resident in Barbados.[44] He now spoke out plainly concerning the Quaker objection to war. "I am not against those that will put themselves into defense," he told the governor, "but it being contrary to the judgement of a great part of the people, and my own too, I cannot advise to the thing, nor express my liking it. The King of England knows the judgement of Quakers in this case before Governor Penn had his patent. But if we must be forced to it, I suppose we shall rather choose to suffer than to do it, as we have done formerly." This affirmation of willingness to suffer rather than compromise on principle, reminiscent of the earlier "heroic" age of Quakerism, was one that was only rarely to be heard in the official utterances of Quaker politicians in the decades to come. Much more frequent, as we shall see, were the attempts to ward off contributions for military purposes by appeals to expediency of various kinds.

On this occasion, however, Carpenter's example seems to have injected boldness into some of his colleagues. When the discussion was resumed two days later, we find John Simcock stating forthrightly: "We can neither offensively nor defensively take arms." At the same time, the Quaker councillors expressed their unwillingness "to tie others' hands" (to quote Simcock again) if they did not share Quaker scruples on this question. And they repeatedly stressed their loyalty to the Crown and their readiness to act as dutiful subjects in all matters which did not go against conscience. Finally, the five Quaker councillors, who formed a majority at that session, withdrew to consult among themselves. Their decision, which Blackwell's arguments were unable to shake, was to refuse active support to measures involving military preparedness, while at the same time giving the governor carte blanche (but with no money attached) to take on his own such defensive measures as he thought fit.[45] This was, indeed, about the

---

[44] Hirst, *Quakers in Peace and War*, p. 357.
[45] *Pa. Col. Records*, I, 306-11.

furthest that Quaker administrators of Pennsylvania could go in opposition to the warlike activities of the realm of which they still remained an integral part.[46]

In the following year the council approved the organization of an *ad hoc* militia within the province against possible French and Indian attack, provided that it was undertaken by private initiative without financial or other aid from the administration.[47] But such tepid support for preparedness did little to assuage the hostility of those who were pressing for the inclusion of Pennsylvania within the scheme of imperial defense. The governors of the other colonies, some of which were more exposed to enemy attack than Pennsylvania, were among the most severe critics of Quaker rule in Pennsylvania. In addition, Penn's friendship with the Catholic James II had brought suspicions of Jacobite sympathies down on his head after the Glorious Revolution of 1688; and, as we have seen, these doubts, along with fears of the military consequences of Quaker pacifism, were instrumental in bringing about the temporary conversion of Pennsylvania into a Crown colony under the authority of Governor Fletcher of New York in May 1692.[48]

The Quaker politicians, however, proved no more amenable to the Crown's representative, Governor Fletcher, than they had been earlier to Quaker William Penn's deputy, Governor Blackwell. We find Fletcher reporting to the Lords of Trade back home on his sojourn in the Quaker province:

> I have spent some weeks there but never yet found so much self-conceit. They will rather die than resist with carnal weapons, nay they would persuade me their province was in no danger of being lost from the crown, though they have neither arms or ammunition, nor would they suffer those few to be trained who were free for it, their minutes of council and assembly which we are now transcribing for you, will appear a farce.[49]

In 1693 the assembly was, in the end, persuaded to grant the sum of £760—but only after the governor, who attempted to convince the legislators that present defensive measures were analogous to such means

[46] Hershberger's remark, *MQR*, pp. 203, 204—"Their conscience still forbade military action, but they preferred not to use the moral argument against it if another could conveniently be found"—does not appear too stringent a comment on the Quaker contribution to debates on military measures on this and on subsequent occasions.

[47] Edwin B. Bronner, *William Penn's "Holy Experiment,"* p. 138.

[48] Winifred Trexler Root, *The Relations of Pennsylvania with the British Government*, pp. 261, 262.

[49] Quoted in Robert L.D. Davidson, *War Comes to Quaker Pennsylvania 1682-1756*, p. 13.

of protection as high walls, locked doors, and watchdogs that even Quakers used to guard their personal property, finally agreed to confirm their laws and privileges. The governor had at the same time offered a sop to the Quaker conscience by giving a somewhat vague assurance that money contributed by war objectors "shall not be dipt in blood." Yet it was clear that even if it would not be spent directly on the purchase of arms and ammunition, the appropriation was to be used for such scarcely less military purposes as the payment of officers' salaries.[50]

In the following year the assembly, now under the leadership of that ebullient Quaker constitutionalist, David Lloyd, expressed its willingness to vote money to purchase food and clothing for the Iroquois, who might otherwise go over to the side of the French.[51] Although the humanitarian guise of the request—"to feed the hungry and clothe the naked"—scarcely veiled the underlying military implications of the appropriation, the Quaker assemblymen were on this occasion prepared to swallow the pill when sugared in this way. After the province had been returned to Penn, further grants of money were passed by the assembly in 1695 and 1696 "to be made use of as he [the king] pleased." In 1696, Penn himself had intervened, urging David Lloyd and leading Pennsylvania Quaker politicians like Samuel Carpenter to use their influence in favor of a positive response to the Crown's requests for money. Refusal, Penn claimed, might endanger the existence of Quaker rule. At this date a further and extremely cogent reason for compromise lay in the desire of Lloyd and the Quaker politicians to obtain a revision of the second Frame of Government of 1683 in favor of an extension of the rights of the colonists. Penn's deputy, Governor Markham, finally acceded to their demands in November 1696, whereupon the assembly made their appropriation.[52]

Harmony on this issue was not of long duration, however. For in May 1697 the assembly turned down a request for at least £2000 to maintain Pennsylvania's quota of 80 men for colonial defense, which Governor Fletcher of New York had transmitted through Captain Markham's mediacy. The matter had been discussed at a joint meeting of council and assembly. The grounds given for rejection were, however, nonpacifist. "Considering the infancy and poverty of this government, which also lieth under other considerable debts," they felt that the province could not at this stage afford expenditure on such a

---

[50] *Pa. Col. Records*, I, 400.
[51] Roy N. Lokken, *David Lloyd*, pp. 56, 64-66. The bill was not accepted in the end by Governor Fletcher, because he had other objections to it.
[52] *Pa. Col. Records*, I, 490-92; Lokken, *David Lloyd*, pp. 70, 71.

scale. At the same time, they expressed their "readiness to observe the King's further commands, according to [their] religious persuasions and abilities."[53]

By the end of King William's War, it had become clear that the "religious persuasions" of the Quaker politicians concerning the inadmissibility of Christian participation in war of any kind, though undoubtedly genuine, were somewhat elastic. They might be stretched on occasion to meet the exigencies of practical politics: hope for a political concession, perhaps, if the legislators proved amenable, or anxiety over the possible curtailment of their rights if they remained adamant in refusing all compromise. During this period—and, indeed, virtually up to 1756—a saving clause or a significant vagueness in phraseology was used to cushion the full impact of such action on the continued validity of their peace testimony.

Certainly, critics like Guy F. Hershberger are right in pointing out the subtle but corrupting influence that Quaker involvement in the game of political power exerted on the Society's politicians and, indeed, on the Society as a whole. Parliamentary practice usually demands a certain give-and-take: "the Quakers found it very hard to reconcile their two ideals of representative government and pacifism."[54] Moreover, the maintenance of a Holy Experiment in living became increasingly identified with—indeed, slowly came to be replaced by —the political supremacy of the Quaker party in the province; it seemed worthwhile to guarantee this supremacy at the price of sacrificing some of the content, if not the form, of the Society's peace testimony. "The more they fought for power the more did they weaken their peaceful testimony. But to the political Quakers the struggle for power meant more than the cause of peace."[55]

Yet Quaker policy in the matter of war appropriations was by no means devoid of a certain logic, granted its basic premises. Friends' belief that a society patterned on the principles of the Sermon on the Mount was still achievable short of the millennium gave the original impulse to the creation of the Holy Experiment. Obedience to the powers that be, another central principle of Quakerism's political philosophy, meant in the context of colonial Pennsylvania not only obedience to the provincial Quaker authorities but to the Crown back in England. "And let none use their liberty by abusing of it," the New Jersey-Pennsylvania Yearly Meeting instructed its members, especially

[53] *Votes and Proceedings of the House of Representatives of the Province of Pennsylvania (Pennsylvania Archives,* 8th ser.), I, 195-97.

[54] Hershberger, "Quaker Pacifism and the Provincial Government of Pennsylvania, 1682-1756," Ph.D. diss., U. of Iowa (1935), p. 64.

[55] *Ibid.,* pp. 91-94.

the young people of its meetings, in 1694; they would be abusing it, among other ways, "by refusing to render to the government its lawful demands of tributes or assessments, for, according to scripture, we are to be subject to every ordinance of man for the Lord's sake."[56] If Caesar used this tribute for war, that was his concern; as we have seen, there does not appear to have been a testimony among early Friends against paying war taxes, let alone those "in the mixture." True, decade after decade we find the Quaker legislators displaying obvious reluctance to sanction the raising of money for war, a hesitation which did not stem solely from the pragmatic reasons, whether justified or not, that were alleged for refusal of requests of this kind. For it was one thing for English Friends excluded from Parliament and administration to pay whatever sums were demanded by their government willingly; it was quite another thing—even if in theory the distinction was somewhat unclear—for Quakers in the seat of government to take responsibility for raising taxation that would be spent on war. That the direct responsibility for expending the money was delegated to others and that the money was voted "for the use of" the Crown served, however, to veil the reality of Quaker complicity in the direction of military preparations, if only intermediately. From this practice flowed some of the ambiguities of Quaker "defense" policy in Pennsylvania. Nevertheless, although the assembly was not always able to prevent its nonpacifist fellow citizens from forming some kind of military association for defense, it did consistently refuse official consent to the organization of a militia on even a voluntary basis until a few months before the end of Quaker rule in the province. Here it did not seem possible to construct a viable bridge between civil obligation and religious conscience.

The conclusion of peace in 1697 did not mean an end to the military demands that the Quaker legislators had to face. The Atlantic seaboard colonies formed one long extended frontier where warfare was endemic on both land and sea. If Pennsylvania was relatively secure by virtue of her geographical position and the peaceful Indian policy of her rulers, other provinces continued to face danger and to demand defensive measures, too, in time of nominal peace. Thus, in June 1701 we find King William III requesting Penn, who was then in Pennsylvania, for £350 to be dispatched as his province's allocation of the costs of erecting fortifications on the New York frontier. In explanation of their refusal to grant this sum, the assembly, to whom the governor had passed on the royal demand, pleaded both the poverty

[56] "A General Testimony against all Looseness and Vanity" (1694), MS in F.H.L.S.C., typescript p. 18.

of a young colony already overburdened with taxes and quitrents and the tardiness of neighboring provinces to contribute their share to the common defense. Let His Majesty be assured, they told Penn, "of our readiness (according to our abilities) to acquiesce with, and answer his commands, so far as our religious persuasions shall permit, as becomes loyal and faithful subjects so to do." There was only a hint here of any conscientious scruples against contributing to military measures. However, Quaker views on war were well known in official circles. Yet why provoke royal anger by emphasizing the provincial rulers' unorthodoxy on this point if the requisition could be turned down on less controversial grounds? Writing home to his son in the following November, the governor told him:

> If they say, But you will not fight? I answer, King Charles, King James and King William knew that we are a Quaker colony, it was so intended . . . let us not be persecuted in our country when our consciences are tender, that came so far and have endured and spent so much that we might enjoy them with more ease than at home.[57]

Penn had stubbornly resisted growing pressure to set up a militia in the province. But he did give his approval at this time to the establishment at the entrance to the Delaware Bay of an armed watch against pirates and other possible invaders. In refutation of the complaints lodged at home against the province's alleged defenseless condition by the Anglican Colonel Robert Quarry, judge of the independent Vice-Admiralty Court in Pennsylvania and leader of the anti-Quaker faction there, Penn had asked what good a militia would be in the province "since by land there is none to annoy it"; "by sea, the position of the country and the manner of our settlements considered, . . . a small vessel of war would, under God's providence, be the best security."[58]

The Quaker political community faced the outbreak of Queen Anne's War in 1702 with its pristine idealism somewhat dimmed. In the previous year Penn's generous Charter of Privileges had vested all

[57] *Votes and Proceedings*, I, 278, 280, 289, 290; *Pa. Archives*, 2nd ser., VII, 12. See also Illick, *Penn the Politician*, pp. 187-89; Mary Maples Dunn, *William Penn*, pp. 180, 181.

[58] *Correspondence between William Penn and James Logan*, I, 27. See also Beatty, *William Penn*, pp. 113, 114; Bronner, *Penn's "Holy Experiment,"* pp. 209, 211; Root, *Relations of Pennsylvania with the British Government*, pp. 274-79. At the conclusion of chap. 3, "William Penn and the Holy Experiment," MS book, Hershberger discusses another example, taken from the year 1710, of Penn's support of armed action by the English government against enemy attack on sea and river traffic.

legislative power in a unicameral legislative body based on a fairly wide electoral franchise and subject only to his deputy's veto, thereby reducing the provincial council to a merely advisory status.[59] Friends, although rapidly becoming a minority of the population, continued as before to dominate provincial politics through their heavy concentration in the geographical areas and in the social groups most liberally represented in the assembly, as well as through the high regard in which they were held by some of the new immigrants who gave them their political support. Yet Quakers on the whole showed little gratitude to Penn for his liberal attitude, quite exceptional at that date, and accepted what he had granted as simply the minimum rights and privileges due true-born Englishmen.

Indeed, Friends in politics had not shown themselves free from bitter factional strife. Slowly an antiproprietary party had coalesced under the leadership of the Welsh lawyer, David Lloyd, with its supporters drawn chiefly from the country Quakers. Against these country Friends were pitted the Quaker conservatives, small in numbers but eager to defend the proprietor against what they considered the "villainy" of Friend Lloyd and anxious to establish a stable society in which the increasingly affluent Quaker merchants of Philadelphia would exercise the same deserved authority within the province as they wielded in the counsels of Philadelphia Monthly Meeting. The acrimonious debates that took place during the last decade of the seventeenth century and during the first two of the eighteenth, both within the assembly and outside it, may have represented an important step in the evolution of American constitutional rights, but they were not an entirely edifying spectacle within a Society dedicated to the pursuit of brotherly love.

The place occupied by the peace testimony, although it still formed a vital part of the religious belief of almost all Pennsylvania Friends, became more and more anomalous. The political element, the argument from expediency, played an ever increasing role in the Quaker assembly's opposition to military measures. A recent Quaker historian states—perhaps a little too severely—that, by the time of Penn's final departure for England in 1701, already "the 'holy experiment' was nearly forgotten." But, as he admits, "a residue remained from the idealism of the early years, a residue that leavened the society as well

---

[59] By the second Frame of Government of 1683 the number of seats in the council had been reduced from (a theoretical) 72 to 18 and in the assembly from (a theoretical) 200 to 26. This size was retained for the two bodies in the Charter of 1701. By 1752 the number of assemblymen had been raised by stages to 36.

as the government of Pennsylvania during the remainder of the colonial period."[60] The history of the Quaker peace testimony, like many other aspects of the Society, over these years is to a large extent the story of the interplay between political expediency and the residual idealism that eventually became one of the factors leading to Quaker withdrawal from politics.

Quaker readiness within certain limits "to contribute for support of government,"[61] even if the use made of the money granted was for military purposes, usually provided a possible modus vivendi between assembly and home government (in the person of the proprietor's deputy) so long as the deputy-governor behaved with a modicum of tact. But in 1703, owing to a misjudgment of character that unfortunately was neither the first nor the last in his career, Penn appointed that rather foolish young man, John Evans, as his deputy (with instructions, incidentally, to see that "nothing may lie at my door in reference to the defence of the country").[62] The results were disastrous. In March 1706, for instance, believing with "the inexperience and assuming of youth," as an eighteenth-century Quaker historian expressed it,[63] that their pacifism was but a tender plant that could easily be uprooted, Evans attempted to panic the Quakers into approving the organization of a militia and other defensive measures by raising an alarm of a French invasion by sea threatening Philadelphia. Apparently Friends in the city almost to a man remained calm and did not budge in their determination to avoid taking any step that might compromise their peaceable principles. When the alarm proved false, relations between Evans and the assembly (even though the house was temporarily in control of the conservative party among the Quakers) became extremely strained. Tension increased when further acts of provocation from Evans's side followed within a few months.[64] As Hershberger aptly remarks: "The alarm did not cause the pacifism of the Quakers to break down. The break-down came when they learned the alarm was false. . . . What had been preserved of the spirit of love during the false alarm was now lost in the fight with the governor"

---

[60] Bronner, *Penn's "Holy Experiment,"* p. 2.

[61] *Votes and Proceedings,* I, 477.

[62] Illick, *Penn the Politician,* p. 224. But Penn also instructed Evans that Quakers and other religious pacifists must not be "compelled in person or purse" in connection with defense measures. See Dunn, *William Penn,* p. 174.

[63] Robert Proud, *The History of Pennsylvania,* I, 468.

[64] Hirst, *Quakers in Peace and War,* p. 362. See also *Pa. Col. Records,* II, 243, where a minute of the council speaks of the proof that the assemblymen, who were all (with one exception) Friends, had given of their pacifist convictions "in the late alarm in not joining at all with the rest in bearing arms."

that became increasingly vehement after the victory of the Lloyd party in the October elections.[65]

Continued rumors of impending attack from enemy privateers during the summer months of 1706 were regarded skeptically by both council and assembly, and Governor Evans's requests for measures to meet the danger were received coldly. In September the assembly in a "Humble Address" to the governor turned down his requests categorically, pleading in extenuation of their refusal the poverty of the province and the tardiness of neighboring colonies to erect fortifications. Above all, however, they argued that in fact the menace was chimerical. "We hope," the Quaker politicians told Evans, "we are not in much danger of the enemy, considering our remoteness from the sea, and difficulty of access."[66] Once again in a situation of this kind, it was considered more prudent to make no mention of Friends' conscientious scruples against war.

The pacifist issue was certainly a delicate one for the Quaker rulers of an English colony. James Logan (1674-1751), who almost alone among the prominent Friends of this period did not share his sect's belief in nonviolence, was perhaps for this very reason acutely aware of the precarious nature of the existing compromise. "Friends can scarcely bear up under the difficulties they are oppressed with," he told Penn in 1703. If the Crown should insist that the province make an effective contribution to the war effort, "our government will be soon broken or miserably exposed." Logan's advice to his master was to rid himself, and Friends, of the burden of government, a load too heavy to bear in a world that was obviously not yet prepared to follow their peaceable example. "For my own part," he confided, "I am weary of government affairs as they must be managed."[67]

Penn, too, was evidently growing weary of his responsibilities in the New World since pressing business at home prevented his settling among his people across the waters and since, with each year, his lengthening absence from Pennsylvania widened still further the gap between the founder-proprietor and his independent-minded Quaker subjects and coreligionists. But it was his financial misfortunes, in part undeserved and in part due to his incompetence in money matters, that led Penn from 1703 on to begin negotiations with the Crown for the eventual surrender of his province. Penn naturally insisted on safeguards for the political rights of the provincials and for the special religious testimonies of his Friends. They would have to continue free

---

[65] Hershberger, Ph.D. diss., p. 106.
[66] *Votes and Proceedings*, I, 573-76.
[67] *Penn-Logan Correspondence*, I, 233-35.

from the obligation of taking oaths or of rendering military service or paying fines in lieu thereof. Agreement was at last reached in 1712, but Penn's sudden stroke which to a large extent deprived him of his mental powers put an end to the transaction before the final papers had been signed.

Chief among those who supported Penn's design was, of course, his former secretary Logan. In May 1708, for instance, we find Logan reporting to Penn, with the declared intent of proving the impossibility of combining pacifist beliefs and governmental responsibilities, that the depredations of enemy privateers on coastal traffic had recently become so severe that vessels were venturing out from the Delaware River only "under convoy of a small man of war from New York who comes round on purpose." Presumably, Philadelphia Quaker merchants were among those who took advantage of this paramilitary protection, though perhaps they may have regarded this as essentially police action. But the Friends' dilemma was a real one. As Logan went on: "This last business of the privateers upon our coasts infesting us above others, because unarmed, has brought Friends to a pretty general confession that a due administration of government, (especially in a time of war), under an English constitution is irreconcilable with our principles."[68]

In August, when the governor called a special meeting of the assembly to present a request for money to provide the wherewithal for eradicating enemy privateering, he compared such action to the forcible suppression of disorder within the state by the police, a not ineffective analogy in view of the Quaker support for government in this respect. "We have laws against thieves and robbers," he said, "and we have officers to put those laws into execution; if they resist, they are taken by force, and by force, when occasion, are obliged to submit to the last extremity; and without this there would be no such thing as government." It it were right to use physical force on the domestic wrongdoer even to the ultimate point of inflicting death, then were not similar measures justified against those who now aimed to destroy the whole state?

The argument was certainly plausible (it had Quaker Logan's agreement).[69] Yet it was not entirely convincing, for there were, indeed,

---

[68] Amelia M. Gummere, "Two Logan Letters," *Journal of the Friends' Historical Society*, IX, no. 2 (April 1912), 87-89.

[69] In the first half of 1709, when a French privateer had made a landing on the lower reaches of the Delaware and rumors of imminent invasion by a French fleet were rife, Logan was to tell Penn: "That a private murderer or robber should be taken and hanged, and yet public ones should be suffered to proceed without any resistance, is made the subject of so much banter and scorn, that 'tis very uneasy

significant differences between force to back law and war measures flowing from the absence of international law, differences that were to be urged by Quakers both within the assembly and outside it, as we shall see. But there was no hint of this line of argument in the reply drawn up by the assembly two days later in answer to Governor Evans's speech. Giving vent to indignation that trade should have been thus disrupted without Her Majesty's navy being able to take adequate steps to prevent it and, at the same time, setting out in review the financial support that the people of Pennsylvania had given the government in recent years "according to their abilities and circumstances," the assembly limited itself to a vague expression of willingness to grant money if it could really be proved that previous appropriations were insufficient to cover the present need. "For, as we partake of the Queen's gracious protection to all her subjects," the address (signed by David Lloyd, as speaker of the house) concluded, "so we hold ourselves obliged, in duty, to give supplies for supporting this government, according to the powers granted by the royal charter . . . altho' we do not pretend to direct the way and manner that the Governor . . . should dispose of those supplies."[70]

In the following year the incompetent Evans was replaced as Penn's deputy by Charles Gookin. A war atmosphere prevailed: threats of direct invasion by sea and talk of more distant conflict with the French on the northern frontiers disturbed the province's calm. Thus, one of the first actions of the new governor was to approach the assembly early in June 1709 with a request for the sum of at least £4,000, which would cover the cost of Pennsylvania's share in equipping its quota of men to the number of 150 in the proposed expedition against Canada. On the recommendation of a number of leading Quaker councillors and assemblymen, the request was refused as incompatible with the pacifist views of the overwhelming majority in the province's ruling bodies. Instead, as a gesture of goodwill insisted on by the more conservative councillors who had been drawn into the discussion, the assembly voted the Queen a mere £500 as "a present." This gift was disdainfully turned down by Governor Gookin, probably not least of all because of the proviso attached that the money should be paid out only when the legislature was quite sure that it would not be used for war purposes. Although the plea of poverty was not omitted on this occasion either as an explanation of the smallness of the sum voted, conscientious objection to war was now

---

to those concerned." He adds: "Those who differ from us in persuasion, as one half of Philadelphia does, are full of complaints, and Friends so uneasy under them" (*Penn-Logan Correspondence*, II, 344, 345; see also pp. 347, 348).
[70] *Votes and Prcoeedings*, II, 804-8.

given the most prominent place in the assembly's explanations.[71] The uncompromising character of this apologia for the assembly's conduct may have stemmed from the fact that the appropriation was being requested for an offensive campaign rather than for allegedly defensive, quasi-police action, assistance to which could be cloaked in suitably vague terminology. Two years later, however, Quaker consent was readily obtained for an expedition against Canada of an almost identical kind. The reason for this otherwise surprising change of attitude must be sought in the development of domestic politics in Pennsylvania.

In the elections of 1710 the Lloyd party was overwhelmingly defeated, and the Quaker conservatives gained complete control of the assembly. Their victory at the polls had been due largely to support given them by Philadelphia Yearly Meeting, where the well-to-do elements, who were alarmed at the vehemence with which the country party pressed their attacks against the proprietary interest, exercised great influence. These conservative Friends remained loyal to the Quaker peace testimony, although some among them—the elder Isaac Norris (1671-1735), for instance—seem to have entertained serious doubts about its compatibility with participation in government. All felt that their political opponents within the Society, driven on by their desire to assert provincial rights, had lost sight of the equally important testimony of rendering obedience to the powers that be. Thus, in July 1711 when Governor Gookin placed before the assembly a request from Her Majesty for £2,000 to help equip another expedition against the French in Canada, its consent was quickly given. Its address stated:

> That the majority of the inhabitants of this province being of the people called Quakers, religiously persuaded against war, and therefore cannot be active therein; yet are as fully persuaded, and believe it to be their bounden duty to pay tribute, and yield obedience to the powers God has set over them in all things, as far as their religious persuasions can permit; and therefore we take this occasion to express our duty, loyalty, and faithful obedience to our rightful and gracious Queen Anne.

The money being voted on this occasion "for the Queen's use" would, the assembly hoped, be considered "as a token of our duty" toward the Crown.[72]

As Isaac Norris had foreseen, the vote aroused "clamours and un-

---

[71] *Ibid.*, II, 860; *Pa. Col. Records*, II, 459-64. See also Tolles, *James Logan*, p. 49; Sharpless, *A Quaker Experiment*, I, 196-200.
[72] *Votes and Proceedings*, II, 990, 991.

easiness" among Friends in the province, who were now being required by their political and spiritual leaders (in this case, one and the same persons) to subsidize a military expedition. In fact, as we have seen, the policy and the motives behind it were not new: what was more novel perhaps was the unconcealed military purpose of the whole appropriation. But Norris argued that Friends had no business to be concerned with the use the Queen might make of the tax now to be paid by the province, "*that* being not our part, but hers."[73]

Among those who were most active in drumming up support for the tax among members of the Society was the English-born Thomas Story, a member of the provincial council at this time who, as we have already seen, was both a courageous exponent of Quaker pacifism and a proponent of rendering all war taxes to Caesar. In his sermons Story now exhorted Friends to pay the recent imposition willingly and with a clear conscience. In the Anglo-Dutch wars of the previous century, Dutch Friends, he told them, had contributed their share of the tribute demanded to carry on military operations, while Quakers in England at the same time had paid taxes to King Charles II to support his war effort against the Dutch. Friends in the two countries were not guilty of each other's blood because they had fulfilled their Christ-imposed duty of rendering tribute to Caesar. "The application," in Story's view, "is the business of kings and not of subjects" —words that echo those of his colleague, Isaac Norris.[74]

On the whole, apparently, Friends did pay the war tax of 1711; whether they did so as willingly as the conservatives hoped is not clear from the surviving sources. Indeed, we do hear of distraint being levied on the property of Quakers in Bucks County and in Chester County by order of the magistrates (who were also Friends, of course) for refusal, presumably on conscientious grounds, to pay the tax voted by the Quaker assembly. Moreover, several Friends were put in prison and at least one disowned by the Society for resistance to the tax. Thomas Story was himself strongly attacked in an anonymous pamphlet. The author, who described himself in the preface as "a plain rustic," approved payment of ordinary taxation but dissented from rendering straight war levies of the sort demanded in 1711. "Philalethes," which was the pseudonym the author adopted, may have been an adherent of the Lloyd party, which, in fact, returned to

[73] *Penn-Logan Correspondence*, II, 436. Story was later to claim that the money then voted would be spent on "bread and flour" for the troops; but that its allocation for such directly nonlethal purposes was in the minds of the Quaker assemblymen when the appropriation was made is far from clear.

[74] Emily E. Moore, *Travelling with Thomas Story*, pp. 124-27.

power in 1714; this connection is implied by Story in the rebuttal he drew up against the tract of his opponent, whom he identifies with a certain "turbulent" Quaker, William Rakestraw. Yet the doubts "Philalethes" cast on the compatibility of participation in the civil magistracy with maintenance of the Quaker peace testimony seem to disprove too close an association with the constitutionalist party.[75] At any rate, "Philalethes" in many ways appears as a forerunner of the radical peace men who were to bring great weight to bear on the Society in Pennsylvania early in the second half of the century.

III

A long period of peace and increasing prosperity for Pennsylvania followed the signing of the Treaty of Utrecht in 1713. The war issue did not crop up again in an acute form until the autumn of 1739 after the outbreak of war with Spain. But, during this quarter of a century of peace, tendencies already present in the development of the province's Quaker community were to grow in strength and to prove of fundamental importance in the trying decades of mid-century.[76]

In the first place, we find that increasing wealth among the Quaker bourgeoisie centered in Philadelphia considerably diminished the earlier idealism. As Frederick B. Tolles has shown, the countinghouse became a serious rival to the meetinghouse in the devotion of many Philadelphia Friends. Moreover, riches combined with political authority and the increasingly hereditary character of membership in the Society lessened the hold of Quaker pacifism on many members of the Society engaged at one or another level in the public affairs of the province.

[75] *Tribute to Caesar, How paid by the Best Christians, And to What Purpose*, preface and pp. 11-15, 26, 27. The tract bears no date of publication; however, it probably appeared between 1713 and 1715. Convincing evidence of Rakestraw's authorship is given by Hershberger in MS book, chap. 4. Rakestraw appears to have been disowned by Philadelphia M. M. in late 1713 for his campaign against Story. Story's reply (entitled "Treason against Caesar") to Rakestraw's pamphlet remained in manuscript. Emily Moore has published extracts from the copy deposited in the Quaker collections at Friends House (London), and it is discussed in Hershberger, MS book. See also Hershberger, MQR, pp. 207-9.

[76] This period is dealt with in two chapters of Hershberger, MS book: chap. 5, "Power, Prosperity, and Complacency," and part of chap. 6, "Unquakerly Indian Relations." Concerning the spiritual aspects of Pennsylvania Quaker development, Thomas G. Sanders has this to say: "In the early years of Quakerism it was assumed that a conversion underlay an individual's living a changed life, whereas in Pennsylvania it was believed that men have a natural inclination or capacity to conduct themselves in the way of the kingdom . . . the original eschatological element changed from a kingdom oriented to the will of God and guided by God's prophets to an essentially ethical realm of brotherhood, peace, and love" (*Protestant Concepts of Church and State*, p. 137).

Secondly, just as the Quaker virtues of sobriety and thrift had brought both the reward of material well-being and the danger of spiritual decay, so the Quaker tolerance which had led William Penn to open the doors of his province to all comers both "established a situation of cultural pluralism and thereby created the conditions for cultural growth," to use Tolles's words,[77] and at the same time exposed the Society to eventual engulfment in a sea of immigrants whose religious and political views were often quite alien to the Quaker ethos. True, the Germans for the most part, especially the small body of Mennonites and allied sects, proved reliable political allies of the Quaker interest. But the tough and restless "Scotch-Irish," as these northern Irish Presbyterian immigrants came to be called, remained almost wholly out of sympathy with Quaker ideals even though they proved to be enterprising pioneers. In conjunction with the adherents of the Episcopalian church, they provided the backbone of the anti-Quaker faction. But for a long time the frontier districts where the Scotch-Irish chiefly settled were underrepresented in the assembly: in 1752 they still had only 10 out of 36 seats. Along with the votes of the Germans, who looked on the Quakers as their benefactors for granting them a refuge in Pennsylvania and as their protectors against involvement in foreign war and oppressive conscription such as had blighted their lives back in Europe, this underrepresentation of the Scotch-Irish population served to shore up Quaker rule against the day when their position as a minority would make their continued political predominance impossible. Although under the Quakers restriction of the franchise was certainly no worse, indeed was considerably less illiberal, than in the mother country, the very conditions of colonial life made it inevitable that politically underprivileged elements would eventually demand political equality. And, in the struggle to achieve this equality, Quaker peace principles became an important issue, although in fact most of the Quaker politicians had virtually ceased before mid-century to regard pacifism as of relevance in the political realm.

A third area where, during the years of peace, changes beneath the surface of public life brought about conditions less favorable to a political witness of Quaker pacifism, lay in the sphere of Indian relations. These relations remained outwardly friendly, but such incidents as the notorious "Walking Purchase" of 1737, whereby Indians were deprived quasi-legally of considerable areas that they believed to be rightfully theirs, stored up trouble for administration and people in the years ahead when the French came into a position to utilize the

[77] *Quakers and the Atlantic Culture*, p. 131.

smoldering grievances of the Pennsylvania Indians. Although it is true that James Logan was involved in this shady transaction, it is also true that neither the Society as a whole nor the Quaker-dominated assembly was responsible in this instance for the bad faith of the province's proprietors, the former Quaker and now Episcopalian Penns. Yet this was, in fact, only one incident in a chain of events that originated in the deep conflict of interest between indigenous Indian and European settler over rights to the land. Quakers had consistently tried to resolve this conflict by fair practice in obtaining land. But the non-Quaker immigrants who began to stream into the province in increasing numbers as the eighteenth century advanced were not so particular as Friends were about the methods they used in their dealings with the Indians.[78] And the Quakers found it as difficult to control them as they had, in the case of the Walking Purchase, to prevent Crown or proprietary interest from doing things which ran counter to their own Indian policy. Gradually and almost imperceptibly, the tender plant of conciliation between Indian and white inhabitants of the Quaker colony that had sprung from the seed sown so hopefully by Penn and his early Friends was trodden under foot.

However, when war came to Pennsylvania again in the fall of 1739, it was not an Indian war, nor one that brought direct attack from internal or external enemies; as earlier, it meant only indirect involvement in the great imperial conflict that was shaping up between those old rivals, Great Britain and the Bourbon powers of France and Spain. The whole world was to become a battlefield now; eventually the struggle got entangled in the complicated rivalries of Central Europe, as well as in such distant spots as the Indian subcontinent. Pennsylvania's Quakers were thus caught up unwillingly in a long and bitter conflict of global dimensions.[79] However, their opposition to war, which for many Quakers active in politics on both the provincial and local level was by now somewhat lukewarm, was complicated by the fact that the provincial assembly was simultaneously engaged in a vehement contest with the proprietors of Pennsylvania. Thus, the issue over the decade and a half to come was rarely a straightforward one between simple adherence to the Society's traditional peace testi-

[78] See Sherman P. Uhler, *Pennsylvania's Indian Relations to 1754*, pp. 88ff., 108, 109, 111ff.

[79] Herbert L. Osgood writes of this period: "Quaker principles as to war became a question of large significance in general colonial politics, for the frontier and the struggle to maintain and defend it had now so far developed that Pennsylvania had become in a true sense a keystone of the structure" (*The American Colonies in the Eighteenth Century*, IV, 49). And general colonial politics, it may be added, formed only a part of the global policies of the major West European powers.

mony and wholehearted support for the war effort. Instead, party politics, the political power game, was subtly intermixed with considerations of Christian principle and absolute morality.

In October 1739, upon receiving news of the outbreak of war with Spain, Deputy-Governor George Thomas came before the assembly with a request to put the province in a condition of defense—in other words, to raise and equip a militia, erect fortifications, and provide the funds necessary for measures of this kind. If these measures were not taken, he told the Quaker legislators, their towns might be sacked and the colony ravaged by invaders.[80] However, the house showed no anxiety to discuss the matter and postponed its consideration to the end of the year. Then, on 5 January 1740, it drew up its reply in the traditional form of a "Humble Address," an answer that in fact was a straight refusal to comply with the governor's recommendations. They reminded him that liberty of conscience, the free exercise of religious scruple, had been by charter guaranteed to the inhabitants of the province by its founder and that his people, the Quakers, had always been "principled against bearing of arms in any case whatsoever." (During the previous autumn, in fact, Pennsylvania Yearly Meeting had issued a strongly worded call to its members to remain "vigilant" in upholding Friends' peace testimony and in keeping free from complicity in "warlike preparations, offensive or defensive.")[81] True, there were now many in the province who did not share Quaker principles concerning war, who "for ought we know" might think it necessary to take up arms in defense of country and hearth and who, should therefore be permitted to act as their consciences prompted them. Still, there could be no compulsion exercised in the matter. For, on one hand, to make conscription for militia service universal would not only be a violation of the colonial constitution but would also entail persecution of the numerous conscientious objectors in the province; while, on the other hand, the exemption of the latter from the working of the law would make an unfair distinction between members of the same commonwealth. In any event, no matter how its provisions were framed, the imposition of a militia law would constitute "an inconsistency" on the part of a body almost all of whose members were convinced pacifists. Let the governor take whatever steps he wished (although how he would find the money to implement his designs the address ignored), since he was legally entitled to institute military measures. "Morally speaking," the home government was chiefly responsible for seeing that the province was preserved "from the in-

[80] *Votes and Proceedings*, III, 2512, 2513.
[81] Ezra Michener, *A Retrospect of Early Quakerism*, p. 295.

sults of our enemies." Their trust, the assemblymen piously concluded, lay in the Almighty's arm, "which not only calms the raging waves of the sea, but sets limits beyond which they cannot pass."

A debate on the viability of pacifism as provincial policy ensued between the adroit governor and the assembly, which was now being led by the equally dexterous new speaker of the house, John Kinsey (1693-1750). This confrontation brought out the basic difference of viewpoint between the two sides. Governor Thomas's first reaction to the address of 5 January had been one of indignation. The very same day he wrote to the proprietors, exclaiming angrily: "Those who profess conscience, will not allow others to act agreeable to theirs, that is, to make use of the strength and courage God has given them to defend all that can be dear to a man in this world."[82] Behind the scenes he began to work for exclusion of the Quakers from the assembly by means of a test oath—a scheme that came to nothing owing to the influence of the Quaker parliamentary lobby in England and to the eventual granting by the assembly of money that could be employed for war purposes. However, in his exchanges with the assembly the governor spoke moderately, expressing consideration for Quaker scruples. His views were presented in two communications dated 10 and 23 January 1740 respectively.

Thomas in the first place stressed his desire to preserve constitutional freedoms and to avoid penalizing conscience. "I have always been a professed advocate for liberty, both civil and religious, as the only rational foundation of society," he stated. He agreed that there should be no attempt to coerce Quakers and other nonresistants to bear arms. Yet, in his view, a compulsory militia for nonpacifists was essential if the province was to protect itself effectively. The latter, indeed, formed the majority of the inhabitants of the province. And this fact led Thomas to make a second point, that the assembly, being "the representatives of the whole body of the people," should reflect, too, the needs and desires of the whole people, and not merely of the Society of Friends, to which almost all the assemblymen happened to be affiliated religiously. Thirdly, Thomas cleverly utilized Quaker approval of civil government and the mobilization of physical force behind the law, even to the point of inflicting the death penalty on thieves and murderers, in order to draw a parallel between this practice and the repulsion of the external enemies of society by force of arms. "You yourselves," he told the assembly, "have seen the necessity of acting in civil affairs as jurymen and judges, to convict and condemn such

[82] Quoted in Root, *Relations of Pennsylvania with the British Government,* p. 280.

little rogues to death as break into your houses, and acting in other offices where force must necessarily be used for the preservation of the public peace."

The governor appealed to Quaker precedent, too, in arguing his case for the assembly's support. He reminded them of the example of their English brethren dutifully paying taxes "for carrying on a war against the public enemy." He cited the minutes of the provincial council in the case of the military appropriation of 1711 (discussed above). Was not this tax imposed for the purpose of a military expedition against the French in Canada? The circumstance that the money was in fact misapplied by the governor at the time (as the assembly now asserted in reply) did not alter the principle. Thomas even attempted to prove that Penn, their founder, could have been only a very lukewarm pacifist since he had accepted the title of captain-general from the king and was known to have issued a commission—"which I have under his own handwriting"—for the officer in command of a fort at New Castle. Finally, the governor stated his opinion that God means for us to make provision to protect ourselves. Goodness and goodwill were not sufficient to ward off enemies. Moreover—and whatever the Quaker politicians might argue to the contrary—the safety of the province was endangered now that Pennsylvania was exposed to imminent attack both by land and by sea.

The Quaker assembly replied point by point to the governor's arguments and persuasion in messages dated 19 and 26 January. The assemblymen contended that there was in fact no need for the kind of measures the governor demanded. There was no war yet with the French, and they hoped there would not be one in the foreseeable future. By reason of its natural situation and its many inhabitants who, except for the Quakers, were willing to take to arms should an enemy invasion by ill chance occur, Pennsylvania was safe from danger. They believed their present peaceful policy, the governor's assertions notwithstanding, had the support of a large majority of Pennsylvania citizens, including many who did not in theory hold Quaker views on war. "Otherwise, why do they need to be compelled [i.e., to join a militia] who think it necessary for their common safety?" Again, the assembly reiterated its trust in divine protection for those who strove after righteousness, "even as the world is at present circumstanced." God, they told the governor, "for the sake of ten righteous persons, would have spared even the cities of Sodom and Gomorrah." They rejected Thomas's analogy between fighting and killing in war on one hand and police action and judicial execution on the other. To kill a soldier was to destroy a human being whose sole crime, per-

haps, was "obedience to the commands of his sovereign . . . who may
. . . think himself in the discharge of his duty"; whereas to execute
"a burglar who broke into our houses, plundered us of our goods, and
perhaps would have murdered too, if he could not otherwise have accomplished his ends," was simply to apply the known judicial penalty
for violating "laws human and divine."[83]

With some indignation the assembly sought to rebut the interpretation Thomas attempted to put on past Quaker actions. "The payment
of taxes in carrying on a war by our Friends in England," they said,
"is not parallel to the case under consideration." ("But as you have not
been pleased to shew the difference, I must still conclude that there
is not any," countered the governor.) The 1711 appropriation was
granted simply as tribute to Caesar, as a token of their respect for Her
Majesty the Queen, and not as approval of a military campaign.
And as for the alleged belligerence of Penn himself, the assembly could
only presume that the governor had not consulted his writings, for
there he would have discovered that Penn "not only professed himself
a Quaker and wrote in their favour, *but particularly against wars and
fighting*, in which he has said so much and so well for himself . . . we
need say little for him." His supposed approval of warlike measures
stemmed solely from his recognition that some elements of the province's population did not subscribe to Quaker nonviolence. Surely,
Friends' principles concerning war had for several generations been
well enough known at home to both Crown and administration for
there to be little need now of an elaborate defense.[84]

The discussion dragged on during the following months without
much that was new being added to the argument. Although the Quakers' case was certainly weakened by approval of capital punishment,
which watered down the consistency of its nonviolent witness, the distinction that they made between war and police action possessed
greater validity than the governor was prepared to recognize. In his
eyes, Quaker opposition to war was sufficient to incapacitate them for
all part in public affairs. He asked them indignantly:

[83] This distinction is, indeed, a fundamental one in the Quaker position. Cf.,
e.g., Philadelphia Y. M.'s *The Ancient Testimony of the People called Quakers,
reviv'd.* of 1722, where a sharp contrast is drawn between "the material or carnal
sword, invented by men to execute their wrath and revenge upon their fellow-
creatures," on one hand and "the sword of justice 'ordained of God for punishment of evil doers, and praise of them that do well'" on the other (p. 23).

[84] *Pa. Col. Records*, IV, 366-75, 380-84, 387, 388. For this whole controversy
between Governor Thomas and the assembly, see also Sharpless, *Quakerism and
Politics*, pp. 111-27; Osgood, *The American Colonies in the Eighteenth Century*,
IV, 54-60; Brent E. Barksdale, *Pacifism and Democracy in Colonial Pennsylvania*,
pp. 11-16, 44, 57.

If your principles will not allow you to pass a bill for establishing a militia, if they will not allow you to secure the navigation of the river by building a fort, if they will not allow you to raise men for His Majesty's service, and on His Majesty's affectionate application to you for distressing an insolent enemy, if they will not allow you to raise and appropriate money to the uses recommended by His Majesty, is it a calumny to say that your principles are inconsistent with the ends of government at a time when His Majesty is obliged to have recourse to arms . . . ?[85]

In the summer of 1740 the debate became involved with an extraneous issue, when in the middle of the harvest season the administration began to recruit indentured servants for service with the military. This action aroused the angry protests of Quaker merchants and farmers, who regarded it as an attack on the sanctity of contract. But, although the assembly remained adamant in refusing to sanction a militia and still continued to reiterate its repugnance to voting money for the purpose of killing, it did tentatively agree to make a grant ("a tribute to Caesar," as they put it) of £3,000 "for the king's use," provided these "redemptioners" were released from service and allowed to return to their masters.[86]

Meanwhile, no less a person than the distinguished Quaker minister, Thomas Chalkley, had come forward to defend the Friends' viewpoint and to strengthen assemblymen and other members of the Society in their passive resistance to the governor. Until then, he told them, the Lord had preserved the province from harm because his people had trusted in him and had renounced the ways of war. "Yet I would not be understood to be against the magistrates exercising the power committed to them, according to just law," Chalkley was careful to add, "but national wars, woeful experience teacheth, are destructive to the peaceable religion of Jesus, to trade, wealth, health and happiness." He warned them in prophetic strain that, if they were to backslide and sanction violence now, their enemies would overrun the country. Let them not excuse themselves by pleading the influx of non-Quakers, nonpacifists, into the province. The king had bestowed the land upon Penn as a refuge for Friends. Why, he demanded of those who disagreed with their views on war, "did they come among us, if they could not trust themselves with our principles, which they knew or might have known, if they would?"[87]

[85] *Pa. Col. Records*, IV, 465. Cf. p. 442.
[86] *Ibid.*, pp. 425, 435, 436, 441.
[87] Chalkley, *Journal*, 1754 edn., pp. 317, 318.

The assembly's appropriation of 1740 had been turned down by the governor because of the strings attached to it. And so the trial of strength between the Quaker assembly and the military-minded governor continued. An English Friend, who was a careful observer of American affairs, wrote now of his coreligionists in Pennsylvania: "Your cause is undoubtedly good, but I am afraid you discover a little more warmth than is quite consistent with the moderation we profess." He chided their representatives in the legislature for the "acrimony" of their debates which, despite undoubted provocation on the governor's part, was unseemly in men of their religious profession.[88]

More critical of the assembly's stance was William Penn's former secretary, James Logan, who was still a prominent, if not particularly popular, member of the Society. Logan, indeed, seems at first to have given Governor Thomas support in his efforts to extract money from the assembly, for Logan, as we know, had always been out of sympathy with Friends' views on war, although out of loyalty to his people he had not publicly expressed his dissent. In fact, he tells us, he had refrained from taking a more active part in the Society's affairs because of his disagreement on this important article of faith. Early in his career he had even been disciplined by Philadelphia Monthly Meeting for accompanying the sheriff and an armed posse in an attempt to dislodge squatters from an island in the Delaware River and had been forced to present a somewhat grudging "acknowledgment" of error.[89] Logan has, in fact, been called "too good an imperialist to be a good Quaker."[90] His unscrupulous dealings in the fur trade—buying at a low price, selling at an exorbitantly high price, and trafficking in rum with the Indians—and the undefined yet undoubted role he played in the Walking Purchase of 1737 were certainly out of tune with the ethos of his first patron, William Penn, and of his Quaker coreligionists. In 1718, for instance, we find him working behind the scenes to establish a garrison settlement on the Indian frontier near Conestoga manned by pugnacious Scotch-Irish immigrants, and he continued to urge firm military measures on the frontier. Nevertheless, Logan claimed to regard offensive war as unchristian. A war of defense, however, was another matter (and, somewhat illogically, Logan regarded the imperialist conflicts of his time in this light). This type of war, in his view, was but an extension of police action, of which all Friends approved.

Thus, in September 1741, we find Logan composing a long letter for presentation at Yearly Meeting then convening in Philadelphia.

88 R. Hingston Fox, *Dr. John Fothergill and His Friends*, p. 301.
89 Printed in *Friends' Review*, XVI, no. 18 (3 Jan. 1863), 276.
90 Tolles, *James Logan*, p. 157.

In it he urged Friends, in view of the threatening situation on the province's western frontiers along the Ohio River valley, where the French were already—in his opinion—a potential menace to security, to follow Governor Thomas's advice and withdraw from government, since they were obviously unwilling to shoulder its responsibilities. The dilemma of combining pacifist convictions and the duties of the magistracy, Logan reminded them, had troubled Penn to such an extent that he had concluded that his continued governorship was possible only by acting through a non-Quaker deputy. This dilemma, Logan claimed, echoing Thomas's arguments of the previous year, stemmed from the fact that "there is no difference, in the last resort, between civil and military government; and . . . the distinction that some affect to make, between the lawfulness of the one and of the other, is altogether groundless." Since Penn's day, now that Friends numbered at most a mere third of the province's inhabitants and its growing wealth offered a tempting prey to England's enemies, the situation had become even more untenable for a Quaker magistracy. Even though some of the newcomers might support Quaker defenselessness because it spared their pockets, those who had no religious scruples against it should be required to contribute to the defense of their land, either in their own persons or from their property. Moreover, contrary to what some now claimed (Logan must have been referring to Chalkley, although he did not mention him by name), Penn had never intended his colony to remain an exclusively Quaker dominion. Therefore, he entreated all Friends "who for conscience-sake cannot join in any law for self-defence" to recognize reality and, after the manner of their British brethren, who eschewed public positions "above those of the respective parishes where they live," to withdraw from government before they were driven out—or the enemy took over.

Logan, feeling perhaps that his presence at Yearly Meeting under the circumstances would be unwelcome, gave his epistle to his son William—the future provincial councillor—to deliver to Friends. A committee of five, which was thereupon appointed to advise "whether it contained matters which were fit for the meeting to take into consideration," decided in the negative, claiming that its contents were chiefly "of a military and geographical nature" and therefore unsuitable for a religious gathering. Only one dissenting voice was raised when the committee reported: the well-to-do Philadelphia merchant, Robert Strettell (disowned a few years later for refusing to remove the armaments he placed on a vessel he owned), pleaded that Logan's letter be read before the assembly. However—so the story runs—the

Friend sitting beside him plucked at his coat, saying peremptorily: "Sit thee down, Robert, thou art single in that opinion."[91]

Robert Strettell and James Logan were certainly not alone among Pennsylvania Friends in their rejection of Quaker pacifism. Among the politically inclined Quakers who filled the seats in the legislature and occupied the justices' bench in the civil courts, there must have been an increasing number of at least nominal Friends who (if the later record may be taken as presumptive evidence) had ceased to accept this tenet of their traditional faith. Not for another generation was the actual size of the minority opinion to be revealed, however, for with no compulsory militia—indeed, for most of the time with no militia at all—there was rarely an occasion when the Society's discipline had to be applied to deviants from its peace testimony. Then, too, the Revolution was to show that the bulk of members remained loyal to the pacifist position.

Every now and then, however, some particularly ebullient and vocal Friend, less discreet than the politic Logan, found himself at odds with his Society for some public disregard of the Quaker stance on war. Such a one, for instance, was Samuel Chew (1693-1743), chief justice of the Lower Counties and a member of Duck Creek Monthly Meeting near Dover (Delaware). On 21 November 1741, two months less a day after James Logan had penned his antipacifist letter, Mr. Justice Chew addressed a speech from the bench to the grand jury of the county of New Castle, which Benjamin Franklin published soon afterward. In his speech Chew, with rather un-Quakerly vehemence, launched a broadside not merely against the Pennsylvania assembly's recent opposition to the governor's policy of preparedness but against the basic concepts of his denomination's peace testimony.[92] He came down unequivocally in favor of "the lawfulness of defence against an armed enemy."[93] Pacifism he described as a doctrine without foundation either in human reason or in divine revelation, the consequences of

91 "James Logan on Defensive War," *PMHB*, VI, no. 4 (1882), 402-11. See also Tolles, *James Logan*, pp. 27, 28, 39, 90, 153-56, 178-83, 218, 219. Logan, annoyed at the rejection of his epistle by Yearly Meeting, had thirty copies printed by Franklin under the title *To Robert Jordan, and other Friends of the Yearly Meeting for Business, now conven'd in Philadelphia*, but he was dissuaded from distributing them by his wife and prominent Friends in Philadelphia. A parallel effort to convince the German-speaking peace sects of the need for a complete divorce of religious pacifism from political activity was made by Conrad Weiser: his endeavors were as unsuccessful as Logan's, partly owing to the opposition of Christopher Saur, Sr., who urged continued support for the Quakers at the polls.
92 Living up to this peace testimony was made more difficult in the three Lower Counties by the establishment of compulsory militia service.
93 This was the title given to the speech when it was reprinted as an 8-page pamphlet "by desire of several gentlemen" in 1775 after Samuel Chew's death.

which were both "pernicious to society, and entirely inconsistent with, and destructive of all civil government," which would prove impossible if armed force were not the ultimate sanction for the enforcement of the law. And, pointing a finger at his fellow Quaker magistrates, Chew went on:

> We see that these very people who assert the unlawfulness of all manner of defence, willingly serve in the legislature, consent to the enacting sanguinary and other penal laws, act as sheriffs, serve upon juries, sit in courts of judicature, and there try and condemn men to death. Is it not amazing, that any men should take it into their heads that it is lawful for one Christian forcibly to put another to death, after his hands are tied behind him, and yet think it unlawful to bind him by force, or even to kill him, in his unlawful resistance?

If constables in a Quaker province may use staves in an emergency to quell a riot even though death may result from a broken head, why, Chew asked, may not more lethal weapons be employed to oppose a more dangerous assailant? If some should be surprised to hear a Quaker argue in this fashion, said Chew, he "would have such to believe" that it was because he placed truth and the good of his country and of mankind above uniformity of religious belief or the interests of any one particular sect, even his own if it were mistaken. War, a "just and necessary war" with a dangerous enemy, had commenced, and, in his view, the behavior of the Quaker legislature in refusing full support to the country's war effort had transformed what before was merely an error of private judgment into public policy endangering the commonwealth.[94]

Judge Chew could scarcely have believed that, after this frontal attack on so central an element in the Quaker creed, he would escape censure by the Society. He probably did not care. The public nature of his statement, unlike the criticisms of Logan which were confided in proper form to the executive organ of the Society, constituted a challenge, which Friends did not hesitate to take up. After consideration of his case had commenced in his meeting, he launched a further attack on Quaker policy in Pennsylvania in August 1742, again equating it with a threat to the state and contrasting it with that of "the sensible Quakers in England." And now, he went on angrily, for speaking in the august capacity of one of His Majesty's judges he was being called to account by "a paltry ecclesiastical jurisdiction that calls it-

[94] *The Speech of Samuel Chew, Esq.; . . . Nov. 21. 1741*, pp. 3-16.

self a Monthly Meeting . . . of the people called Quakers." He complained of "insolent" behavior toward him, threats to expel him from
the Society unless he withdrew what he had said. "An amazing instance this, of the intoxicating nature of power, and of the voracious
unbridled appetite these meek self-denying Christians have after it."
To this unwarrantable intervention in the affairs of justice, to this almost Romish tyranny, he had no intention of submitting. And, he
added, he personally knew others in the Society (here we have no
reason to doubt the veracity of Chew's statement) who shared his disagreement with the pacifist position and his conviction concerning
the unfitness of Quaker pacifists to act as lawmakers and administrators.[95] It should hardly be surprising that shortly afterward the
Quakers of Duck Creek proceeded to the final step of disowning their
refractory member.

The validity of the case urged by both Logan and Chew against
the Quaker position rested basically on their assertion that there was
no real distinction between the force behind law and the violence
stemming from international war. A difference in the degree and purpose of the force applied could not, they held, constitute a difference
in kind; correcting a child by spanking was, in their view, essentially
of one nature with killing an enemy soldier in battle.[96] To us today it is
also clear that Quaker politicians, who at this time were becoming more
and more deeply implicated in questionable compromises regarding
war measures, did not envisage any techniques of nonviolent defense
beyond sometimes expressing a vague readiness to conquer by suffering (an affirmation belied by the middle-class prosperity which was
taking them even further from the spiritual atmosphere of the period
of Quaker martyrdom) and that, in order to cover over an objection
of principle that many of them no longer shared, they had come increasingly to rely on arguments drawn from expediency and from the
party disputes in which they had become engaged in defending what
they deemed their political rights.

Franklin, in an illuminating—and, in this instance, veracious—passage in his *Autobiography* concerning Pennsylvania's Quaker politicians, speaks of the "embarrassment" with which at this time they
approached each request from the Crown or sister colony for a military
appropriation. They were torn between two desires: on the one hand,
to avoid provoking the government into retaliation by a clear refusal

[95] *The Speech of Samuel Chew, Esq.; . . . Aug. 20. 1742*, esp. pp. 8-13. See
also Burton Alva Konkle, *Benjamin Chew 1722-1810*, pp. 31-35.
[96] Cf. Fothergill's comment on Logan's views quoted in Fox, *Dr. John Father-
gill*, p. 301.

of aid—especially now that the proprietors, the governor, and influential sections of public opinion in the province had broached the possibility of removing Quakers from the assembly by a legal enactment; and, on the other, to escape an open repudiation of their denomination's peace testimony by an unqualified acceptance of the need for war. "Hence," Franklin writes, they employed "a variety of evasions to avoid complying, and modes of disguising when it became unavoidable."[97]

The evasiveness of the Quaker politicians in voting money usually, of course, took the form of resorting to the phrase "for the king's use"—an old device that dated back many decades. Thus, in October 1741, soon after Logan had made his unsuccessful attempt at pressuring the Society to withdraw from politics, the assembly voted the sum of £3,000 "to be applied to such uses as he [the king], in his royal wisdom, shall think fit to direct and appoint."[98] This offer was rejected by the governor. At last, however, after the elections in the following year, the two sides reached an accommodation on the various points at issue between them. Governor Thomas nevertheless could not refrain from venting his sarcasm at the assembly's changed attitude in his message of 17 August 1742:

> To declare their consciences could not allow them to raise or apply money for victualling and transporting soldiers, and yet to determine to give £4,000 to the king's use, that is, for victualling and transporting soldiers can, in my opinion, no otherways be accounted for, consistent with a good conscience, than upon a supposition of a new revelation intervening between the positive refusal and the determination to give.[99]

At the time of the Cape Breton expedition, in July 1745, when it was clear that the money the Crown was requesting would be used for purposes of war, the assembly in voting the sum of £4,000 added the proviso that the governor lay out the part allocated directly to him for the needs of the troops "in the purchase of bread, beef, pork, flour, wheat or other grain."[100] According to Franklin, who was clerk of the assembly during that period, Governor Thomas, upon receiving news of the appropriation, commented: "I shall take the money, for I understand very well their meaning; *other grain*, is gunpowder."[101] If, in-

---

[97] Franklin, *Autobiography*, 1964 edn., pp. 188-90.
[98] *Votes and Proceedings*, IV, 2709.
[99] *Pa. Col. Records*, IV, 591, 592.
[100] *Ibid.*, p. 769. See also Hershberger, "Pacifism and the State in Colonial Pennsylvania," *Church History*, VIII, no. 1 (March 1939), 67.
[101] *Autobiography*, p. 189.

deed, Thomas was correct in placing this interpretation on the phrase —and in his favor, as Franklin points out, stands the fact that the assembly, usually so quick to defend its privileges, raised no questions when the governor proceeded to act on this assumption—the assembly cannot be acquitted of a measure of hypocrisy; for, at the same time as they had voted this grant, they had informed the governor that "the peaceable principles professed by divers members of the present Assembly do not permit them to join in raising of men or providing arms and ammunition."[102] On the other hand, no positive proof of such double-talk on the part of the assembly has ever been discovered.

Whether or not Franklin erred on this occasion, it is indeed difficult to detect thenceforward any consistent and determined effort on the part of Quaker assemblymen (if, indeed, there really had ever been any such effort) to see that war taxes, when voted, would be used for some semi-noncombatant, rather than directly warlike, purpose. It is true that there was still to be frequent opposition to appropriations, either on the grounds that they were not in fact necessary for the safety of the province or because of the political squabbling between the assembly and the proprietary interest represented by the deputy-governor. In June 1746 we find the assembly expressing its readiness to donate money to buy presents for friendly Indians who might otherwise turn to the French, and at the same time stating "that men of our peaceable principles, cannot consistently therewith, join in persuading the Indians to engage in the war." Yet two months later the same body voted money to the amount of £5,000, which the governor at once laid out in raising and equipping "four companies of men, for an expedition against Canada." And no word of protest was raised.[103] The setting up of a compulsory provincial militia under the authority of the legislature was virtually the only military measure that the assembly balked at in principle.

During the invasion scare of 1747-1748 the establishment of a voluntary militia was once again tacitly approved. Rumors that the French and Spanish were about to descend on the province from its seaward side, backed by actual incursions of their privateers on the shores of

---

[102] *Pa. Col. Records*, p. 769. Additional evidence in favor of Franklin's assertion can be seen in the fact that the two commissioners appointed by the assembly to supervise the governor's expenditure of the money voted—John Pole and John Mifflin—were both Friends, although Mifflin, at least, was not a pacifist. "The two," writes Keith in his *Chronicles of Pennsylvania* (II, 873), "may have allowed Thomas to make the purchases." They would scarcely have done so, however, if they had not been assured of the assembly's approval.

[103] *Votes and Proceedings*, IV, 3104-6, 3109. See also Sharpless, *Political Leaders of Colonial Pennsylvania*, pp. 175, 176. The actual expedition proved abortive.

Delaware Bay, grew in volume during the summer months of 1747; agitation increased to organize militarily and strengthen the almost nonexistent defenses. While Philadelphia Yearly Meeting in July exhorted Friends to be vigilant in seeing that their conduct matched their "peaceable principles" and to avoid "joining with such as may be for making warlike preparations, offensive, or defensive,"[104] and while the Quaker-dominated assembly continued to reject the governor's pleas for military measures, public leaders like Benjamin Franklin (1706-1790), who advocated an active policy of preparedness, began to take steps to provide the province with armaments and a body of men trained to resist attack. That Franklin had some support for this move among members of the Society of Friends is clear. As he relates in his *Autobiography*, his scheme to use the funds of his recently formed Union Fire Company to buy tickets in a lottery, the proceeds of which would cover the cost of erecting and arming a river battery to protect Philadelphia, obtained the open or tacit approval of almost all its Quaker members. Still, his calculation that at that date the ratio of genuine Quaker pacifists to those who favored some measure of defense was one to twenty-one was undoubtedly a gross exaggeration. Not only does the subsequent behavior of Friends in the successive war crises that beset Pennsylvania disprove it, but at that very same moment in another fire insurance company almost all the Quaker members voted against buying lottery tickets for the battery (a fact not mentioned by Franklin in his account).[105] It is probable that Franklin's Quakers, although still members in good standing with the Society (according to his recollection, at any rate), were representative of the younger elements who were finding the Society's discipline in regard to peace, as in other matters, increasingly irksome and constraining.

There was one prominent representative of an older generation, however, who backed Franklin's endeavors to the hilt. This was James Logan, who had donated a considerable sum for purchasing lottery tickets. When in November of the same year Franklin published (anonymously) in a pamphlet which he entitled *Plain Truth* a plea for the organization of at least a voluntary militia, Logan wrote him in enthusiastic support. "Ever since I have had the power of thinking," wrote the Quaker, "I have clearly seen that government without arms is an inconsistency. Our Friends spare no pains to get and accumulate estates, and are yet against defending them, though these

---

[104] MS Additions to Philadelphia Y. M. Discipline, July 1747, p. 113 (typescript in F.H.L.S.C.).

[105] *Autobiography*, pp. 182, 183, 186, 187.

very estates are in a great measure the sole cause of their being invaded.[106]

Franklin's little tract, which went into a second edition after the first 2,000 copies quickly sold out, displayed all its author's skill as a propagandist. In it he presented the danger to Pennsylvania, now that all the other British colonies had put themselves in a posture of defense, of its proving a magnet to attract the enemy both on account of the wealth of its leading city and because of its openness to attack. He warned against what he considered a false sense of security resulting from the long peace on the Indian frontier, a calm that the machinations of the French might now cause to be shattered at any moment. In vivid colors he depicted the horrors of a sacking that might soon be visited on the city of Philadelphia: fire, slaughter, rapine, robbery. The wealthy proprietary party had proved its unreadiness to make adequate financial sacrifices for defense. And if the Quaker majority in the assembly, on whom the main responsibility for providing means to protect the province rested, was unwilling on grounds of conscience to shoulder the burden, they should retire "for a season" and give way during the emergency to persons who did not share their scruples. In the meantime, he appealed to "the middling people"—the traders, shopkeepers, and farmers—to take upon themselves the task of defense that had been neglected by the legislators and the upper-class and to organize themselves in "an Association" for this purpose.[107]

Franklin's *Plain Truth* was a challenge that Friends could not afford to pass by.[108] Other attacks on the Quaker position were appearing in the Philadelphia press, too. First to enter the lists was the well-to-do New Jersey Quaker historian, Samuel Smith (1720-1776), who entitled his reply *Necessary Truth*. Smith, it is true, was unwilling to censure those who sincerely and after consideration of the pros and cons of the case had concluded that armed defense was compatible with Christianity. But he took great pains to defend his Society from charges of inconsistency for upholding suppression of the domestic criminal while refusing support to war as a method of removing the external aggressor.

The difference between them is manifestly this; the one, to wit,

---

[106] *The Papers of Benjamin Franklin*, vol. 3, p. 219.
[107] *Ibid.*, pp. 180-204, where the whole of *Plain Truth* is reprinted.
[108] After a German version of *Plain Truth* had appeared along with other anti-Quaker pamphlets in German, this challenge was also seen as a threat to the Quaker hold on the German vote, a threat which might even cause some of the German peace sectaries to waver in their political allegiance. Christopher Saur, therefore, took up his pen in defense of Quaker pacifism and issued three pamphlets in German in reply to Franklin.

government, is ordained of God, and magistrates are said to be his ministers. But the other, to wit, war, is more or less the offspring of lust. The magistrate, in the execution of his office is to be in all respects upright, to know no revenge or lust of any kind, a thing exceedingly difficult, if not altogether impracticable in the execution of military exploits. The one of these God has seen meet to ordain for the benefit of mankind; but the other forbidden, to prevent their destruction.[109]

Underlying Smith's arguments is the assumption that no essential difference exists in the case of international conflicts between wars of aggression and wars of national defense. If it was right to condemn the former, then the arguments put forward by Franklin and his associates in favor of the latter were likewise groundless.

Franklin, though a layman and freethinker, soon gained stout reinforcement for his position from a number of clergymen of different denominations. Among them was the Presbyterian minister, the Rev. Gilbert Tennent, a leading Philadelphia churchman and one of the foremost figures in the Great Awakening. On Christmas Eve, 1747, Tennent preached a sermon on the text "The Lord is a man of war" (Exodus 15:3), which, when it was published soon after, bore the title: *The Late Association for Defence, Encourag'd, or The Lawfulness of a Defensive War*. On 1 January 1748, the well-to-do and cultured young Quaker merchant, John Smith (1722-1771), brother to Samuel, intimate friend of John Woolman, and (somewhat surprisingly) soon to be James Logan's son-in-law, wrote in his diary: "Gilbert Tennent's Sermon on the Lawfulness of War came out today, and I was so moved at the deceit and quirks in it that I determined to essay an answer and accordingly began one." It was finished within eight days. Submitted for the perusal of several leading members of Yearly Meeting, it soon received the Society's approval for publication and appeared in an edition of 1,000 copies on 30 January.[110] In fact, writes Tolles, "John Smith spoke semiofficially for the Society of Friends." His pamphlet was eagerly gobbled up by a public that throve on controversy, especially if it embraced—as in this instance —both politics and theology.

John Smith's vindication of Quaker pacifism is the most important item written by a Pennsylvania Friend in defense of the peace testimony during the period of Quaker control of the province. For the

[109] Samuel Smith, *Necessary Truth*, pp. 9, 10, 12-14. Smith's work was published anonymously.
[110] *Hannah Logan's Courtship*, pp. 139-41.

modern reader it appears, with its copious citing of scriptural texts and its attempt to answer Tennent point by point, to be a rather tedious and sterile compilation. Yet, to quote Tolles again, what to us seem defects "undoubtedly enhanced the effectiveness of Smith's reply in the minds of contemporaries." Its underlying sincerity is unmistakable.[111]

Smith centers most of his 56 pages on disproving Tennent's contention that war finds approval in the gospels (though he concedes that it had on occasion received divine sanction in the case of the Jews under the old dispensation). He uses the history of the early church to back up his argument for the pacifist nature of Christ's message and stresses the positive character of Christian pacifism—love of enemies and nonretaliation. At the same time, however, he points out that God's concern for his followers will not necessarily spare them persecution, loss of possessions, and even death itself. He defends Quakers against the charge of cowardice by citing their past record of courageous endurance of suffering for a righteous cause ("when many of the same profession with this sermon-writer hid themselves") and asserts their often impugned consistency in acting as magistrates[112] while refusing to participate in war. Finally, "in the present unhappy state of human affairs," he points to the unwillingness of Friends "to condemn [their] superiors engaging in war" if the latter felt it necessary. "We rather think it probable that as they have shewn a noble and Christian disposition, in granting liberty and protection to such as are of tender consciences, it may please God to bless their arms with success, and reward them for their kindness to his people, who desire to live in obedience to the inward appearance of his spirit.[113]

The Quaker politicians in the assembly were, indeed, prepared to give their unofficial blessing to the Voluntary Association of the People, as Franklin's organization was called.[114] It provided a convenient channel to drain off the energies of the more belligerent sections of the population, which might otherwise have proved dangerous to the administration; it quieted for the time being the demand for a compulsory militia bill which, even with a conscience clause at-

[111] Tolles, "A Literary Quaker: John Smith of Burlington and Philadelphia," *PMHB*, LXV, no. 3 (July 1941), 306.

[112] Smith himself was a justice of the peace and had participated in proceedings leading to the imposition of the death penalty.

[113] John Smith, *The Doctrine of Christianity*, esp. pp. iii, 3-6, 10, 12, 19-22, 32, 33, 40-45, 49-54. Tennent, among others, later published a lengthy reply to Smith.

[114] See Davidson, *War Comes to Quaker Pennsylvania*, chap. IV; Theodore Thayer, *Pennsylvania Politics and the Growth of Democracy*, pp. 20-23; Hershberger, MS book, chap. 9 ("The Voluntary Militia").

tached, was still unacceptable to the Quaker legislators; and it some-what eased relations with the new deputy-governor, Anthony Palmer (who now bore the official title of President of Council). Of course, it was not expected that Quakers would join the Association; indeed, if they did, they could expect to be excluded from the Society for dis-regarding its discipline. As another Quaker pamphlet, written anony-mously in answer to Franklin and Tennent, stated concerning such disownments: "Here is fully applied that saying of Scripture, *They that went out from us, because they were not of us."* These deviants from the peace testimony had made their choice: there was no in-justice in cutting them off.[115] Yearly Meeting and its subordinate bodies were, in fact, ready to take disciplinary action against such persons.[116]

In the spring of 1748 renewed fear of imminent invasion by an en-emy fleet arose. A voluntary militia was now in existence, and batteries had been set up at suitable points along the river—all, however, at private expense, for, as the governor complained in a letter dated 5 March asking the British commander-in-chief at Cape Breton for the loan of some cannon, "we have the misfortune to have an Assembly consisting chiefly of Quakers." In reality, the assembly's stand was somewhat ambivalent. In a message sent in May to President

[115] *A Treatise shewing the Need we have to rely upon God as Sole Protector of this Province,* p. 20. The author's main argument against the Voluntary Associa-tion was that military preparations were both unnecessary and extremely costly to the province. He attempted to rebut Franklin's contention that Quakers whose consciences prevented them from providing for defense should resign during the war emergency: first, by asserting that it was not logical that they should "relin-quish their power for a season, in order that others might act in that in which their conscience forbad them"; and, secondly, by pointing out that, if they did so, it was unrealistic to imagine that it would ever be possible for them to resume power after the emergency had passed. See pp. 18-22. The anonymous author also severely criticized the ill-treatment of Indians by neighboring provinces, com-paring it unfavorably with Quaker policy in Pennsylvania (p. 15).

[116] Although Philadelphia merchants provided a better example in regard to arming their own ships than did their English brethren, they appear at this period to have practiced—and got away with—at least one other, rather less serious infraction of the peace testimony: permitting their vessels to travel under armed convoy of British men-of-war or privateers. Even a stout pacifist like Israel Pem-berton II (1715-1779), who for fifteen years beginning in 1750 was clerk of Philadelphia Y. M., urged the necessity of this practice, since insurance rates would otherwise have been almost prohibitive. He added, somewhat sanctimoniously, "for my own part [I] confess I put little confidence in such help and protection." See Thayer, *Israel Pemberton,* pp. 18, 19. However, in his *Pennsylvania Politics* (pp. 22, 23) Thayer mentions that some Quakers who in 1747 had contributed toward financing a Pennsylvania privateer, the *Warren,* were disciplined by their meetings. Hershberger, MS book, also has illuminating sections in chap. 8 ("Quak-ers take stock") on "the privateering problem" during this period and on the policy followed by Philadelphia Y. M. of regularly disowning members who per-sisted in privateering and arming of their ships.

Anthony Palmer and his council, the assembly, having stated the difficulty it found in expressing its sentiments on the subject, reiterated the personal objection of most members, and many of their constituents, to bearing arms under any circumstances and their desire at the same time to leave others free to do their duty as they conceived it. In view of the fact that a large proportion of Pennsylvanians did not share their peace principles, the assemblymen did not hesitate to express their gratitude both to the British navy for its protection of commerce and to the governor of New York for his military aid, "as . . . it may have quieted the minds of divers of our inhabitants, tho' it is a favour we could not have asked, [being] intended for such a mode of defence in which we do not place our confidence."[117]

The dilemma confronting the assembly was twofold: it represented a minority opinion in the province on an issue of such vital importance as defense had now become, while within its own ideology Quakerism gave qualified support to the magistrate's sword. Quite apart from the need for circumspection in dealing with the demands of a superior authority at home, the theory of representative government and the Quaker view of the state created, therefore, a duality in the administration of Pennsylvania, two policies that were constantly in danger of cancelling each other out. The province was no longer an unarmed state relying on its very defenselessness and the accompanying goodwill, and the power of the Lord, to give it protection; forts and armaments were at hand, and a militia existed—albeit on a semi-voluntary basis. Yet, if we take the legislature to be its guiding force (and if we exclude the occasional sum voted "for the king's use"), Pennsylvania was still trying officially to follow in the footsteps of its founding fathers, who came to this land to tread the path of nonviolence toward all men, Europeans and Indians alike.

In this same summer of 1748, for instance, we find a radical country Quaker like John Churchman (1705-1775) exhorting the Quaker patricians of the assembly—to Speaker John Kinsey's alarm—to stand firm in their opposition to "carnal weapons and fortifications," remembering that God had preserved the province "in peace and tranquillity

---

[117] *Pa. Col. Records*, V, 204, 207, 208, 236. Even the strict pacifist John Smith, supported by James Pemberton (1723-1809), proposed at one point that a voluntary subscription be raised among Friends to reimburse councillors for expenses incurred in connection with the emergency defense measures, although he soon withdrew his approval after suffering pangs of conscience that he had acted without due consideration and in an un-Quakerly spirit. Pemberton also withdrew from the scheme, and other Quakers whom Smith had approached in the matter all indicated their disapproval. This incident is discussed in Hershberger, MS book, chap. 9, on the basis of Smith's manuscript diary.

for more than fifty years," and at the same time reminding the mayor of Philadelphia (an office frequently held by Quakers) of his obligations as an executant of God's wrath. He was, Churchman tells us in his journal,

> . . . engaged to lay before him the nature of his office as a magistrate, and exhorted him to take care that he bore not the sword in vain, but put the laws in execution against evil doers, such as drunkards, profane swearers, etc. and to be, in his authority, a terror to the wicked, and an encourager to them that do well.[118]

True, in this case "terror to the wicked" did not include waging war against an external "enemy." But we see the assembly, too, speaking of the president and the by now largely non-Quaker council as of "those whose duty it is to protect men in the enjoyment of their religious and civil liberties."[119] They had the duty, then, of extending such protection in the manner that answered their consciences. Let each tolerate the other, pleaded the assembly, which now denied any intention of restricting the military preparations of those without Quaker scruples in the matter. The actual outcome was confusion. Pennsylvania was living neither disarmed by the spirit that knows no evil nor strong according to the wisdom of this world.

Peace returned in October 1748 with the signing of the Treaty of Aix-la-Chapelle. Thus, the final crisis that was to end Quaker rule in Pennsylvania, and to resolve the dilemma created by the attempt of a (nominally) pacifist colonial administration to work within the framework of the imperial power politics of the mother country, was averted for a few years.

---

[118] *An Account of the Gospel Labours of John Churchman*, pp. 68-73. Churchman, like Chalkley a little earlier, argued that the non-Quaker settlers should accept Quaker pacifism as official policy, since its establishment in the province was known to them when they came over to Pennsylvania.

[119] *Pa. Col. Records*, V, 336.

Chapter 3

Quaker Pennsylvania: The Crisis of 1756 and Its Aftermath

The death in 1750 of John Kinsey—clerk of Philadelphia Yearly Meeting for the previous twenty years, speaker of the Pennsylvania assembly since 1739, and chief justice of the provincial supreme court after 1743—symbolized the passing of an epoch: the era of close integration of the affairs of meetinghouse and political assembly. True, Kinsey had engaged in some rather dubious financial transactions during his lifetime, including misappropriation of public funds[1] (conduct that was, indeed, not at all uncommon for a British politician reared in the age of Walpole yet was extremely unseemly for a Quaker dignitary). Nevertheless, Kinsey was, as Sharpless correctly states, "the last great Quaker political leader."[2] His successor as speaker of the assembly, Isaac Norris II (1701-1766), was also a Friend. However, Norris, who belonged to one of the leading Philadelphia Quaker families and remained a member in good standing until his death, did not, like Kinsey, take a prominent part in the affairs of the Society. Nor did he share Kinsey's absolute pacifism, even though he defended the position in his official utterances so long as this was the policy of the assembly he represented. In October 1754, for instance, we find him stating: "I am satisfied the Law of Nature, and perhaps the Christian system leaves us a right to defend ourselves as well against the enemies who are within the reach of our laws, as those who owe no subjection to them."[3] By this date a number of his fellow Quakers in the legislature were equally, if not more unequivocally, supporters of defensive war.

Until well into the second quarter of the century most Quaker legislators still personally adhered to pacifism (we have no reason to believe insincerely) even though they were perfectly prepared, as Speaker Kinsey himself said in 1744, "to let no expense be wanting proper to put the country into a posture of defence, in such manner as their known principles would admit of."[4] But opinion in the legisla-

---

[1] These transactions were revealed, to the shocked surprise of his executors, only at his death.
[2] Isaac Sharpless, *Political Leaders of Provincial Pennsylvania*, p. 179.
[3] Frederick B. Tolles, *Meeting House and Counting House*, p. 25.
[4] Theodore Thayer, *Israel Pemberton*, p. 50.

ture on this matter was gradually changing, so that eventually the house's Quaker majority for the most part came to share the standpoint of the younger Norris (which, indeed, was also that of his father-in-law, James Logan). When exactly this transition occurred is not clear, but it must have been around mid-century.

Its accomplishment did not, however, signify the end of the assembly's resistance to making regular appropriations for military purposes. For, even before this time, there had been a second factor responsible for generating resistance that was often more powerful than pacifism—the staunch antiproprietary attitude of the Whiggish Quaker party. This party, which had coalesced in the 1730's out of the former radical and conservative groupings of the early decades of the century after a long period when political allegiances were in a state of flux, remained unyieldingly opposed to the Tory and Anglican circles which now formed the Penn interest. Although very far from being social revolutionaries, these Quaker Whigs strove to defend the privileges of the assembly and of the well-to-do elements represented in it—which they tended to identify with the interests of the whole province—against what they considered the encroachments of the proprietors and their deputy, the governor. In this respect they were being true to one strand in their Quaker inheritance. Had not William Penn himself proudly told Governor Fletcher of New York in 1692 after the Crown had entrusted Pennsylvania to the latter: "I thought fit to caution thee that I am an Englishman"?[5] Pride in being Englishmen and in participating in the heritage of England's liberties was shared equally by Penn's Quaker settlers and their descendants, who cherished their "birthright as *English* subjects" even if, as their *Ancient Testimony* of 1722 stated, they eschewed "the protection by gun and sword which others make the terms of their allegiance."[6] The Quaker assemblymen of the early 1750's continued to stand up for their rights as Englishmen even after they had lost all but a nominal interest in injecting a Quaker flavoring into their resolutions on military measures.

Besides the paper currency problem, the great issue dividing assembly and proprietors during this period was the former's proposal to tax the estates of the latter, hitherto exempt, on an equal footing with property of ordinary citizens in the province. This dispute rendered nugatory the assembly's appropriation in 1754 of as large a sum as £15,000 to meet the impending danger to the western frontier from the French advance in the Ohio River valley and from hostile Indian attacks. Even now the assembly refused point-blank to impose com-

[5] E.C.O. Beatty, *William Penn as Social Philosopher*, p. 82.
[6] *The Ancient Testimony of the People called Quakers, reviv'd*, pp. 18, 19.

pulsory militia service on those not having a conscientious objection to fighting. And the old vague formula still appeared in the debates of the chamber, as in this citation from February 1754:

It is well known the Assemblies of this province are generally composed of a majority who are conscientiously principled against war, and represent a well-meaning peaceable people, deeply sensible of the great favours, protection and privileges they enjoy under the present royal family, and therefore ready and willing to demonstrate their duty and loyalty, by giving such sums of money to the King's use, upon all suitable occasions as may consist with our circumstances, or can be reasonably expected from so young a colony.[7]

The failure to reach accommodation on this occasion resulted from disagreement on an issue entirely unconnected with the peace principles of the Society of Friends. Isaac Norris in a letter to his brother Charles, dated 31 May 1754, summed up the situation in the following extremely revealing passage:

And indeed whatever difficulties our Assemblies may have in appropriating money to warlike purposes, when there is a good harmony and confidence in their governor, what they give may be made very effectual by leaving the disposition of it wholly to himself, and can be pretty easily obtained . . . on all suitable occasions, but when that confidence is lost the difficulties attending the granting money in that manner are very considerable with those who have otherwise a good influence in our house.[8]

The same crisis of confidence rather than any basic scruples of conscience on the assembly's part was responsible for the failure of the governor's efforts to obtain money in the course of the first half of the following year; for the bill to raise £50,000 for the king's use, which the assembly finally passed in July 1755, had a proviso attached stipulating that the proprietary lands should be taxable along with the

[7] Votes and Proceedings, V, 3654. "As I am well acquainted with their religious scruples," wrote Governor James Hamilton to Governor Dinwiddie of Virginia on 13 March 1754 (Pa. Col. Records, VI, 2), "I never expected they would appropriate money for the purpose of war or warlike preparations, but thought they might have been brought to make a handsome grant to the King's use, and have left the disposition of it to me, as they have done upon other occasions of the like nature." Did Hamilton, then, not realize the true complexion of the majority's views now on war? Or—as he had been in office since 1748 and should have been well informed on provincial politics—was this only a pretense to drum up feeling against the antiproprietary party?

[8] Quoted in William S. Hanna, Benjamin Franklin and Pennsylvania Politics, p. 66.

rest. A little earlier in the same month, General Braddock's disastrous defeat by the French near Fort Duquesne ushered in a period of Indian warfare on the frontier: Penn's old friends, the Delawares and Shawnees, had now become Pennsylvania's enemies. "The roots of the conflict," Tolles writes, "lay . . . in the harsh facts of imperial power, French expansionism and the land-hunger of Virginia planters and London merchants."[9]

The annual assembly elections of October 1755 coincided with the first Indian attacks on the frontier settlements. As usual, the Quaker party without difficulty won an overwhelming majority—owing in some measure to the inequitable franchise that underrepresented the frontier districts. "Quakers were only about a fifth of the total population of Pennsylvania, but they held two-thirds of the seats in the legislature."[10] As Indian marauders advanced into the more settled areas, attacking outlying farmsteads and killing their inhabitants, feeling rose against Friends. A correspondent from Reading reported: "The people exclaim against the Quakers, and some are scarce restrained from burning the houses of those few who are in this town."[11] Animosity was apparently directed more against members of the Society as such, where a new and more rigorous pacifist spirit was blowing, than against the politicians in the assembly who, though they bore the name of Friends, were now mostly out of touch with these vital currents that were infusing fresh life into an increasingly moribund Society.

Yearly Meeting, which was gathered at this time in Philadelphia, exhorted Friends to remain unmoved by "the commotions and stirrings of the earth . . . near us" and, instead, to put their trust "in the munition of that rock that all these shakings shall not move."[12] Men like John Woolman, Anthony Benezet, John Churchman, and John Pemberton (1727-1795)[13] were the most active here. These Friends from Pennsyl-

[9] "The Twilight of the Holy Experiment: A Contemporary View," *BFHA*, vol. 45, no. 1 (1956), pp. 30, 31. Tolles points out here that one of the chief figures in promoting the Ohio Company, the activities of which were in part responsible for exacerbating the Anglo-French conflict in the Ohio River valley, was none other than the English Quaker merchant, John Hanbury, a leading member of London Meeting for Sufferings. For Hanbury's role in this regard, see the detailed evidence marshalled in Hershberger, MS book, chap. 10: "John Hanbury, the Ohio Company, and the Beginning of the French and Indian War." See also Sherman P. Uhler, *Pennsylvania's Indian Relations to 1754*, chap. XIII.

[10] Brent E. Barksdale, *Pacifism and Democracy in Colonial Pennsylvania*, p. 16.
[11] *Pa. Col. Records*, VI, 705.
[12] Ezra Michener, *A Retrospect of Early Quakerism*, p. 297.
[13] He and his brothers—Israel, the merchant grandee, and James, the most politically inclined of the three—stood halfway between the old Quaker political past and the movement of Quaker renewal, of purification from worldliness, that,

vania and neighboring New Jersey were assisted in their efforts by visitors from England—Samuel Fothergill (1715-1772), Catherine Payton (later Phillips; 1727-1794), and Mary Peisley (1717-1757)—who were likewise zealously stirring their fellow members to a revived interest in the peace testimony. This tenet, they told Friends, was an essential part of their Quaker faith; if they abandoned it, they would lose a vital element of their religion and become indistinguishable from the mass of quasi-Christians. They spoke out against those Friends who now wished to approve of "defensive" war, and they warned sternly against repetition of the kind of compromises that had been made in the past by the Quaker politicians.[14]

Already in August the new governor, Robert Hunter Morris, had become alarmed at the activities of what may be described as the peace party within the Society of Friends. He complained about the pacifist sermons being preached by Quaker ministers and about the efforts of committees belonging to local meetings to instill loyalty to the peace testimony in their members. He feared the influence such a stand would have both upon the morale of the people at large and "even upon the Assembly, a great majority of which are Quakers." According to Morris, the Quaker pacifists had attributed Braddock's defeat to "a just judgment" of God "upon our forces."[15] The religious Society of Friends, if not yet the Quaker politicians, was on the way to being branded as a subversive element in the commonwealth that their ancestors had founded.

The events of the autumn revealed the widening chasm that existed between the outlook of the nominal Quakers who sat in the provincial assembly—even if they were still anxious to remove Indian grievances responsible for the conflict—and the new spiritual leaders whose influence in favor of nonviolent approaches was rising within the Society and who had been responsible for the insistently pacifist tone of Yearly Meeting's utterances that fall. The situation of the Society was indeed serious. As James Pemberton confided to his Quaker friend in England, Dr. John Fothergill (1712-1780), recent happenings had "produced a greater and more fatal change both with respect to the state of our affairs in general and among us as a Society than seventy preceding years."[16] Two measures of the assembly

---

gathering strength first among Friends of Pennsylvania Yearly Meeting, was eventually to embrace the whole Society in America.

[14] *Memoirs of the Life of Catherine Phillips*, pp. 131, 139, 140; Tolles, "The Twilight of the Holy Experiment," p. 37.

[15] *Pa. Archives*, 4th ser., II, 478, 489, 490.

[16] John J. Zimmerman, "Benjamin Franklin and the Quaker Party, 1755-1756," *William and Mary Quarterly*, 3rd ser., XVII, no. 3 (July 1960), 293.

in particular, both passed in November 1755, aroused strong opposition among Quaker peace men: the appropriation, after an uneasy accommodation had been reached concerning taxation of the proprietary lands, of the large sum of £60,000 "for the king's use" (which, of course, everyone knew meant military expenditure); and the establishment at last of a provincial militia. Resistance appeared even in the assembly. Seven Quakers voted against the supplies bill, and, even though a broadly framed conscience clause was included in the militia bill, placing that force, though now officially supported, on a virtually voluntary basis, there were four dissenters who voted against that bill, too—James Pemberton, Joshua Morris, Joseph Trotter, and Peter Worral.[17] The militia bill, which on account of its mildness was described by Governor Morris as "intended to answer no purpose but to amuse the people,"[18] was eventually quashed by the home government in the following July as unconstitutional. But the raising of a tax to implement the grant made for carrying on the undeclared war soon commenced.

While the tax measure was being debated in the assembly, twenty prominent personalities from Yearly Meeting—including members of well-to-do Philadelphia families like Israel and John Pemberton, John Reynell, John Smith, and Mordecai Yarnall and concerned ministers like Anthony Benezet, John Churchman, and Daniel Stanton—presented a strongly worded address to that body, protesting against "raising sums of money and putting them into the hands of committees who may apply them to purposes inconsistent with the peaceable testimony, we profess and have born to the world," and warning the house that many Friends would feel obliged in protest to refuse payment of such a tax that was in fact, they maintained, an infringement of religious liberty. The petitioners were careful to point out their approval of paying taxes for peaceful purposes "judged necessary towards the exigencies of government."[19] Yet they were actually reversing the long accepted practice of Pennsylvania Friends, who, whatever their particular political complexion, had not balked at paying tribute money that they knew would be applied in large measure to military ends, provided the transaction was cloaked (as, indeed, it still was in the present instance) with the threadbare phrase "for the king's use."

The assembly, with four members dissenting (one of whom was James Pemberton, brother to two of the signatories to the address),

---

[17] *Votes and Proceedings*, V, 4132.

[18] Winfred Trexler Root, *The Relations of Pennsylvania with the British Government*, p. 308.

[19] *Pa. Archives*, 1st ser., II, 487, 488. See also *An Account of the Gospel Labours of John Churchman*, pp. 169-71.

replied somewhat curtly to their coreligionists' plea, evidently regarding it as an uncalled-for intervention in what was none of their business. The address, they said,

> . . . appears to us (however decent the language may be in respect to the house) assuming a greater right than they were invested with, and an indication that they had not duly considered what has been heretofore transacted in the Assemblies of this province, particularly in relation to the act for granting *two thousand pounds* for the Queen's use, passed in the year 1711, and is therefore an unadvised and indiscreet application to the house at this time.[20]

While their reference to the war appropriation of 1711 was a skillful move and the Quaker assemblymen could rightly fear the use the governor might make against them of the implied threat in the address to boycott war taxation if imposed,[21] the assembly's reply underlines the degree to which most of its Quaker members had drifted away from the Quaker views on war that were undergoing a revival in Yearly Meeting as a whole. Concerning this growing divergence between the assembly and Yearly Meeting, the proprietors' secretary, the Rev. Richard Peters, was correct when he wrote at this time: "Tho' the majority of them [i.e., the Quaker assemblymen] have been stiff in opposition against proprietor and government . . . they are for defence." And Israel Pemberton, who sternly criticized them from a standpoint exactly opposite to that of Peters, lamented the influence that these respected members of society and the Society might have on some of the weaker brethren. For him, the passing of a militia act was the last straw, the point of no return: "Their entering into these measures," he wrote, was "a manifest inconsistency and not to be reconciled to the profession" of the Society to which they belonged.[22]

The taxation now to be levied on the inhabitants of the province to provide the sinews of war—a war that would be waged on Pennsylvania territory rather than in some more distant spot outside its boundaries—also proved a landmark in the developing crisis. It created great uneasiness among Friends at large. Grave doubts arose, reports Israel Pemberton, "whether we could individually give our approbation to this measure by freely paying our assessments."[23]

---

[20] *Votes and Proceedings*, V, 4173, 4174.

[21] In fact, in a letter to the proprietor, Thomas Penn, dated 22 November, Morris attempts to discredit the assembly's good faith vis-à-vis defense measures by citing the address (*Pa. Col. Records*, VI, 739).

[22] Thayer, *Israel Pemberton*, pp. 88, 89.

[23] *Ibid.*, p. 90. Among those who shared such feelings was Israel Pemberton himself. Although some opponents of the Quakers, like Richard Peters, for instance,

The *spiritus movens* behind this opposition was undoubtedly John Woolman (whose thoughts on the subject of taxation have been touched on in the first chapter). Indeed, it was Woolman, supported by kindred spirits like John Churchman, Anthony Benezet, and Samuel Fothergill, who organized a protest against the new tax soon after it had been passed by the assembly. They raised the question in mid-December at a joint meeting in Philadelphia of two standing committees that had been appointed at the recent yearly meeting to deal with the current emergency. The conference was held at a moment of intense excitement in the city. As Woolman recorded in his *Journal*: "While these committees sat, the corpse of one . . . slain [by the Indians on the frontier] was brought in a wagon, and taken through the streets of the city, in his bloody garments, to alarm the people, and rouse them up to war." To Woolman and those who thought like him, this incident appeared as a symbol of the method of violence toward which members of the Society were now being required to contribute; moreover, this was a contribution that had been imposed by men who bore the name of Friends. Not all his colleagues, it is true, saw the matter quite in this light. "To refuse an active payment at such a time," they argued, "might be an act of disloyalty, and appeared likely to displease the rulers, not only here but in England." "Still there was a scruple so fastened upon the minds of many Friends, that nothing moved it." Therefore, after much discussion and prayer and several adjournments to give time for further thought, a group of those most concerned about the issue, numbering twenty-one, attached their signatures to a document whose chief author had been Woolman. It was entitled "An Epistle of Tender Love and Caution to Friends in Pennsylvania," and it bore the date 16 December 1755.

The epistle, which was not issued as an official declaration of the Society as a whole although the prominence of its signatories ensured it a respectful hearing by members, was a forthright declaration. It expressed pain at finding the assembly voting a sum of such magnitude almost exclusively for military uses, "for purposes inconsistent with our peaceable testimony." True, a small portion might be destined

---

attempted to cast doubt on Pemberton's sincerity in this case, insinuating that his reluctance to pay was due to the heavy assessment that would be made on his property, there is no reason to doubt the genuineness of his scruples, especially since he was prepared to endure burdensome distraints for nonpayment. (In 1740, Israel Pemberton had been among the "young fry of Quakers" whose strongly antiwar stand had aroused the anger of this same Peters; see Thayer, *Pennsylvania Politics and the Growth of Democracy*, p. 13). Some prominent English Friends opposed tax refusal as imprudent (Thayer, *Israel Pemberton*, pp. 114, 115).

for innocuous ends, for conciliating the Indians, for instance, or for relieving war sufferers. "We could most cheerfully contribute to those purposes if they were not so mixed" with the support of war. Therefore, its authors intimated their intention of refusing payment of the tax on grounds of conscience, "though suffering be the consequence of our refusal." This, if it should come, "we hope to be enabled to bear with patience."[24]

It is doubtful whether most of the substantial Quaker bourgeois who signed the document realized its novel implications, although they were apparent to such religious radicals as Woolman and Churchman. For the epistle reversed previous Quaker practice in sanctioning payment at least of taxes "in the mixture," if there was some doubt about direct military imposts. It now said in effect that, where any considerable portion of the money was destined for war, tax objection was the only consistent policy for Friends to follow, just as they had refused payment of tithes to an established church where these were demanded from them. But apprehension about the effect that the quasi-military policy of a nominally Quaker assembly might have on the integrity of the Society as a whole probably served to hide from some of the signatories the radical nature of the policy now being recommended in their epistle.

The early months of 1756 saw an intensification of the political crisis. The tax boycott now being threatened, added to the traditional Quaker pacifism, provided plentiful ammunition for use by the Quaker party's political opponents of the proprietary group in an effort to dislodge their rivals from their position of supremacy in the assembly. "Pacifism was not the real reason, of course, for removing the Quakers from the Assembly,"[25] because most of the nominal Quakers in that body were not pacifists; those few who were for the most part interpreted their pacifism as a purely individual credo that should not preclude approving war measures in their public capacity. But the pacifism professed by the Society as a whole provided an excellent excuse for getting rid of the core of the antiproprietary party. And a convenient lever lay ready to hand for the anti-Quaker group to effect this ejection: impose a test oath on all candidates for office, including seats in the assembly, and their political enemies would be broken (or so they expected, at least). This scheme was, as we have seen, over half a century old and had been contemplated at intervals when the policies of the Quaker-dominated assembly clashed with the interests

[24] *The Journal of John Woolman* (ed. A. M. Gummere), pp. 205-10. See also Janet Whitney, *John Woolman*, pp. 207-12, 219.
[25] Hanna, *Franklin and Pennsylvania Politics*, p. 95.

of proprietors, home government, or adherents of the Anglican church. The threat of its implementation had been responsible, at least earlier, for the various compromises devised by Quaker politicians in respect to war and the penal code, in particular.

The first to raise this proposal during the present crisis seems to have been the doughty Dr. William Smith (1727-1803), provost of the College of Philadelphia and a leading Episcopalian, in a pamphlet he had published as early as February 1755 called *A Brief State of the Province of Pennsylvania.* In it he accused Quakers in the assembly and outside it of being responsible—rather from self-interest than conscientious scruples in the case of the Quaker legislators—for the unprotected state of the province, for its defenselessness in face of the French and Indian menace. "It is very plain," he wrote, "they have no mind to give a single shilling for the King's use, unless they can thereby increase their own power." He therefore called for the imposition on all assemblymen of a test oath together with a declaration of readiness to defend the country militarily, as well as for the disfranchisement of the Pennsylvania Germans, whom Smith depicted as a potential fifth column on account of their support of Quaker policies, and the curtailment of their cultural rights.[26] Smith's arguments appear to have won little favor with the Pennsylvania electorate, which had as usual returned the Quaker party to power in the autumn elections. But in London, where his pamphlet was printed, the idea made a greater impression and was taken up with enthusiasm a little later by Proprietor Thomas Penn.[27]

In the early months of 1756 it really seemed likely that the British Parliament would be persuaded to enact legislation requiring a test oath in Pennsylvania. However, the Quaker lobby and a number of prominent English Quakers at once took steps to prevent passage of such a measure. In close cooperation with the Lord President of the Council, Earl Granville, in particular, they were able to hammer out a compromise solution that averted the danger of a test oath, while at the same time promising in exchange a temporary withdrawal of Pennsylvania Friends from the political scene for the duration of

[26] William Smith, *A Brief State of the Province of Pennsylvania,* pp. 11-17, 22, 23, 26-42.

[27] Francis Jennings, "Thomas Penn's Loyalty Oath," *American Journal of Legal History,* vol. 8, no. 4 (Oct. 1964), pp. 303-13. See also Thayer, *Pennsylvania Politics,* pp. 39-41. On p. 24, Thayer writes: "Quaker government in the eyes of the people was synonymous with good government, freedom, and low taxes." It was in these virtues, and not in any sympathy with pacifism as such, that the attraction of Quaker rule for the non-Quaker electorate lay.

the war emergency.[28] That this was planned as "a strategic retreat"[29] rather than as a permanent withdrawal is obvious, if only from the pains that were taken to ensure the possibility of eventual return.

But what Hanna aptly calls "the exclusion crisis" was not so easily overcome. The stumbling block was the resistance of many Pennsylvania Friends to accepting the decision made by their London brethren.[30] The certainty expressed, for instance, by the London Quaker merchant, Robert Plumsted, who had both strong commercial ties with, and family relations in, Philadelphia, "that those who are really Quakers will be very glad to withdraw from the present scene of action"[31] was overoptimistic. True, the influential Philadelphia Quarterly Meeting, in the defense of its members' participation in affairs of state ("some allowance must . . . be made for human imperfections," it pleaded) which it addressed to London Meeting for Sufferings in April 1755, had hinted at the possibility of a general withdrawal from politics "whenever it may appear impracticable for us [otherwise] to preserve . . . those principles" of peace that Quakers had always held. The epistle mentioned, moreover, that some had already taken that step, believing that only in this way could they maintain "our Christian testimony in all its branches." But Philadelphia Friends went on to explain the reason for continuing Quaker participation in government: the lack of capable men to defend the liberties and constitutional rights of the province against the ever present threat of arbitrary power from the side of the proprietary interest. Until this obstacle was overcome, "we cannot after the most deliberate consideration judge we should be faithful to [the province], to ourselves, or to our posterity, to desert our stations and relinquish the share we have in the legislation."[32]

There, indeed, lay the rub. Abandoning political power appeared to many sincere Quakers as an abandonment of political responsibility. But to retain political power, at least while war was raging on Pennsylvania soil, came increasingly to mean a repudiation in practice, if not

[28] See Zimmerman, "Franklin and the Quaker Party," pp. 307-12; Hanna, *Franklin and Pennsylvania Politics*, pp. 97-99.

[29] Jennings, "Thomas Penn's Loyalty Oath," p. 304.

[30] As Hershberger points out (MS book, chap. 11), it was not primarily pacifism but concern for their "imperialistic interests" that accounts for the anxiousness of some leading lights in London Y. M., like John Hanbury, to see the Quaker pacifists withdraw from politics.

[31] C.A.J. Skeel, "The Letter-book of a Quaker Merchant, 1756-8," *EHR*, XXXI, no. 121 (Jan. 1916), 141.

[32] This epistle is given in full in Sharpless, *A Quaker Experiment in Government*, I, 234-40.

in name, of Friends' witness for a peaceful world. To say that the issue was simply political and economic power is to disregard the genuine dilemma in which politically minded Quakers, including many who were genuinely attached to the peace testimony, found themselves in this period of crisis.

One such political pacifist was James Pemberton, who provided a link between the movement of renewal within Yearly Meeting and the Quaker politicians in the assembly. It was to him, in particular, that Dr. John Fothergill addressed the appeals of London Friends. "You accept of a public trust, which at the same time you acknowledge you cannot discharge," Fothergill told him. "You owe the people protection, and yet withhold them from protecting themselves. Will not all the blood that is spilt be at your doors?"[33] The same question was being asked angrily and ever more insistently by men who, unlike the Quaker Fothergill, thereby sought to discredit the Society and all its works. Early in 1756 Provost Smith published a sequel to his pamphlet of the previous year. Demanding still more effective defense measures from the assembly, he accused the Quaker pacifists outside it —"infatuated enthusiasts," he called them—of responsibility for the rising tide of Indian atrocities and denounced (not altogether without justification) the backstage influence of Yearly Meeting and its subordinate bodies—"degenerated into political cabals"[34]—on the politics of the province. Meanwhile, for several months there had been circulating petitions and tracts of similar content. Addresses of this kind were being directed to the home government in London, to the Crown, and to the Lords of Trade, who were immediately responsible for relations with Pennsylvania.[35] All this material was eagerly seized upon by Thomas Penn and his cronies for use in their political maneuvers against the dominant party in the assembly. Although pure Quaker pacifism was probably widely unpopular at this juncture, the degree of opposition that existed in regard to the Quaker party which, as is clear, no longer objected to military preparations was undoubtedly grossly exaggerated in the propaganda of its enemies, as is shown by the hold that the party continued to exert on the (admittedly restricted) electorate over the years to come.

The back counties, of course, were suffering most severely from Indian sorties; therefore, the back inhabitants, particularly the Scotch-

[33] Letter dated 16 March 1756, R. Hingston Fox, *Dr. John Fothergill and His Friends*, p. 308.
[34] William Smith, *A Brief View of the Conduct of Pennsylvania, for the Year 1755*, pp. 21, 23, 72-81.
[35] See Charles J. Stillé (ed.), "The Attitude of the Quakers in the Provincial Wars," *PMHB*, X, no. 3 (1886), 294ff.

Irish frontiersmen, were most virulent in denouncing the Quakers and the Quaker assembly, which was supposedly following a Quaker policy.[36] In fact, during the winter months the province was being placed on a war footing, so that in May, shortly after the official declaration of war against the Delawares and Shawnees made by the governor and council on 12 April,[37] the assembly could claim that the province was militarily prepared, even if the organization of the militia left something to be desired ("we have indeed had little experience of a militia in this province, and a law for regulating it was a new thing to us," they pleaded in extenuation). "By the care of the Governor and the commissioners for disposing of the sixty thousand pounds by us granted for His Majesty's service," they stated, "the frontier of this province is now in a better state of defence than that of any other colony on the continent, being guarded by a line of forts at no great distance from each other, all strongly garrisoned."[38] There was no qualification now in the assembly's support of the war effort. Gone was the pretense that the disposition of funds granted "for the king's use" was no business of theirs, for here we see the assembly through its special commissioners directly supervising the expenditure of the military appropriation and taking responsibility for recruiting soldiers and for the organization of militia. And this was an assembly 28 of whose 36 members were at least nominally members of the Society of Friends.

It is not surprising, then, that on the eve of the declaration of war we find Philadelphia Friends reaffirming in messages to the assembly and the governor their renunciation of all war and their continued belief in a nonviolent way of settling affairs with the Indians. They protested, too, at the savage proclamation that accompanied the declaration of war, offering a reward for the scalps of enemy Indians, regardless of age or sex.[39] These steps, indeed, constituted a challenge that could not be glossed over: the Quaker peace testimony was at

---

[36] Their opponents were quick to point out that there were few Quakers living in the exposed frontier districts (see, e.g., Stillé, p. 301). We do, however, hear of one presumed Quaker family falling victim of Indian attack at the beginning of the year. In a letter dated 5 Feb. 1756, a clergyman reports: "One Sherridan, a Quaker, his wife, three children and a servant, were killed and scalped" (quoted in *The Journals and Papers of David Schultze*, I, 163). Cf. Barksdale, *Pacifism and Democracy*, p. 27. See also Churchman, *An Account*, p. 175, for the rising unpopularity of Quakers, even in Philadelphia, as knowledge of frontier atrocities spread during the early months of 1756.

[37] The declaration was approved with only one dissenting vote, which was cast by Quaker William Logan (1718-1776), son of James, who, although not an absolute pacifist, stood closer to the Quaker position than his father had.

[38] *Votes and Proceedings*, V, 4234, 4235.

[39] *Ibid.*, V, 4216-20; *Pa. Col. Records*, VII, 83-86.

stake. Twelve days later Benezet reported to an English Quaker: "Many of our Friends begin to rouse from that lethargy in which they have too long been plunged, thro' a love of this world, an endeavour to reconcile those two contrarities—the world and heaven." They were awakening to a realization of the incompatibility of the Quaker witness for peace with the politics of a state at war.[40] And this message was being effectively brought home to Friends throughout the province by the endeavors of Benezet himself, the visiting English ministers, and American Quaker preachers like Woolman, Churchman, and John Pemberton. The results of their efforts with the Quaker assemblymen were meager: among some assemblymen, as we have seen, they were simply regarded as an unwarranted intervention in matters that were not their concern.

"If the potsherds of the earth clash together, let them clash!" declared Samuel Fothergill.[41] Friends must now stand clear of all involvement in warlike activities. This message was reinforced by the repeated advice emanating from London Yearly Meeting that Friends must retire for a time at least from provincial politics, by the insistence of English Quakers that their own reputation would be tarnished if they failed to implement their pledge to the home government of Friends' withdrawal from the assembly for a season. London Yearly Meeting did not always find it easy to understand the obvious reluctance with which Pennsylvania Friends contemplated shedding the burden of direct political power, and it was, besides, genuinely concerned not merely with the threatened enactment of a test oath but with the integrity of the Society's peace witness in the Quaker province. The pressure it brought to bear on Friends in Pennsylvania, combined as it was with an increasing feeling of discomfort at their own position in the assembly, finally led to the resignation on 7 June of six of the most concerned Friends sitting in that body, headed by James Pemberton.[42] "Many of our constituents," they stated in their letter of resignation, "seem of opinion that the present situation of public affairs call upon us for services in a military way, which, from a conviction of judgment, after mature deliberation, we cannot comply

[40] George S. Brookes, *Friend Anthony Benezet*, p. 220.
[41] George Crosfield, *Memoirs of Samuel Fothergill*, p. 261.
[42] For a detailed account of English Friends' influence on their brethren during the 1755-1756 crisis, see A. T. Gary [Pannell], "The Political and Economic Relations of English and American Quakers (1750-1785)," D.Phil. thesis, Oxford (1935), pp. 85-101. See also Sharpless, *A Quaker Experiment*, I, 250-254; Barksdale, *Pacifism and Democracy*, pp. 30-35, 37, 39, 40. There is also much material on this subject in Hershberger MS book.

with." Their withdrawal would both be "conducive to the peace of our own minds, and the reputation of our religious profession."[43]

The resignations of 7 June symbolized the end of Quaker rule in Pennsylvania. They marked the point when the last fragile remnants of a Holy Experiment disintegrated. As Franklin wrote ironically a week later: "All the stiff rump except one that would be suspected of opposing the [military] service from religious motives have voluntarily quitted the Assembly."[44] These resignations did not, of course, eliminate at one stroke the presence of members of the Society of Friends in the assembly, for the majority of Quaker representatives not sharing the pacifist scruples of their six colleagues still clung to their seats. Still less did it mean the destruction of the popular party's political ascendancy since, as we shall see, this continued under Franklin's leadership for almost another two decades, that is, under non-Quaker auspices but still with the old name of the "Quaker party" in use in popular parlance. Again, these resignations did not signify the ending of all hope of a Quaker return to power, of the reinauguration of a peaceable commonwealth within the confines of the Quaker colony. As has been aptly observed, "the object of the move from the standpoint of Quaker politicians . . . was the preservation of power, not its relinquishment." And this intention became evident in the elections of the following October.

Then, even though pressure was brought to bear by Friends' meetings to prevent members from standing for the assembly, the Quaker influence was placed as usual behind the popular so-called Quaker party, and its candidates swept the field once again. "Quaker influence in Pennsylvania," states a recent writer with a shade of exaggeration, "had never been more apparent."[45] But, instead of exerting it directly from within the assembly, the leaders of the Society now hoped to operate as a pressure group acting on both provincial politics and social life.

Nevertheless, the new policy did not prove acceptable to all the Friends active in politics. Three Quakers did indeed refuse to run as candidates, and four more after election were brought to give up their seats—somewhat reluctantly and, as they stated in their letter of resignation, because they understood "that the Ministry have requested

[43] *Votes and Proceedings*, V, 4246. See also *ibid.*, pp. 4245-50; *Pa. Col. Records*, VII, 148-51.
[44] Quoted in Thayer, *Pennsylvania Politics*, p. 56.
[45] Ralph L. Ketcham, "Conscience, War, and Politics in Pennsylvania, 1755-1757," *William and Mary Quarterly*, 3rd ser., XX, no. 3 (July 1963), 431, 432.

the Quakers . . . to suffer their seats, during the difficult situation of the affairs of the colonies, to be filled by members of other denominations, in such manner as to prepare, without any scruples, all such laws as may be necessary to be enacted for the defence of the province."[46] Yet twelve Quakers, either actual members of the Society or generally considered as such, remained in the new house—a proportion amounting to as much as a third of the whole. Isaac Norris II remained as speaker, despite the efforts of the two delegates of London Meeting for Sufferings, John Hunt and Christopher Wilson, who had just arrived from England, to persuade him of the need to retire as an example to others; thus his name continues to appear on the military measures sanctioned by the assembly.

In the months and years to come the Society took steps to convince their recalcitrant politicians of the need to conform, but Friends were obviously unwilling to cut them off altogether. We hear, for instance, of the monthly meeting in Chester County laboring with old George Ashbridge, a country Quaker who had sat in the assembly since 1743, and being bluntly told by him (in the words of the meeting minute): "He do [sic] not feel himself culpable."[47] And, indeed, Ashbridge continued to sit in the assembly until his death in 1773. Samuel Foulke, who accepted election for the first time in 1761, long after the stricter brethren had withdrawn and while the war was still on, remained clerk of his Richland Monthly Meeting and a respected Quaker elder in spite of his failure to follow official Quaker policy.[48] In this instance, not even a mild censuring appears to have been administered to the aspirant to political office. When peace came, the way appeared open for the Society to return to politics, and even James Pemberton in 1765 accepted reelection to the assembly.[49] But, in fact, as we shall see, such hopes were illusory. True, Friends remained an influential factor in politics up to the outbreak of the Revolution, and even Quaker pacifism was still palely reflected in provincial policy, which never imposed a throughgoing militia organization and retained something of the Quaker spirit in its relations with Indians.[50] But the so-called Quaker party was firmly in the grip of the pro-war Benjamin Franklin, while the pacifist element was uppermost now in the councils of Philadelphia Yearly Meeting and in the lower Quaker meetings.

[46] *Pa. Col. Records*, VII, 292, 293.
[47] Sharpless, *Political Leaders of Provincial Pennsylvania*, pp. 193, 194.
[48] Gummere's notes to Woolman's *Journal*, pp. 553, 554. Foulke was disowned during the American Revolution for having taken the "test."
[49] See Sharpless, *A Quaker Experiment*, I, 269.
[50] Ketcham, "Conscience, War, and Politics," pp. 435, 436; Hanna, *Franklin and Pennsylvania Politics*, pp. 99, 103-7, 228.

Moreover, after 1764, when the assembly petitioned the Crown to remove Pennsylvania from the hands of the Penn family and transform it into a Crown colony, some conservative Friends like Isaac Pemberton, fearing that Anglican domination would result from such a transference, switched over support to the proprietary interest.[51] As a new and revolutionary era approached and more radical elements began to group themselves to the left of the old popular party, ancient political alignments were beginning to break up.

If in 1756 Pennsylvania Friends had not yet given up hopes of an eventual return to the political *status quo ante* 1755, they had already begun to seek out extrapolitical channels through which they could express their concern for reestablishing peaceful conditions within the province and for proving their readiness to make material sacrifices to achieve this aim[52] and through which also, perhaps, they might be able to satisfy their less Quakerly desire to discredit what they considered the disastrous Indian policies of the proprietaries which the governor represented. Thus there came into existence in the summer of 1756 the Friendly Association for Regaining and Preserving Peace with the Indians by Pacific Means.[53] The Association was nominally independent of the Society of Friends but, in fact, was sponsored semi-officially by Philadelphia Yearly Meeting. "Unfortunately," writes Thayer, "from the outset, the activities of the Friendly Association were involved with provincial politics."[54] That the Association was to some extent a political maneuver is probably true; that it was also conceived as an instrument whereby the Quaker peace testimony

[51] Zimmerman, "Franklin and the Quaker Party," p. 291.

[52] An earlier example of this kind of motive for Quaker philanthropy is suggested by Tolles, *Meeting House and Counting House*, p. 229. At the beginning of the decade, when Governor Hamilton and the anti-Quaker interest were agitating for defense appropriations which the Quaker assembly stubbornly refused to pass, the very considerable support given by wealthy Quaker merchants and by the assembly itself to the founding of the Philadelphia Hospital in 1751 was most probably due, at least in part, to the desire to prove that Friends could be generous where no scruples of conscience intervened.

[53] The Association was founded in July but did not really get going until the following autumn. It acquired its full name in December 1756. See esp. Thayer, "The Friendly Association," *PMHB*, LXVII, no. 4 (Oct. 1943), 356-76, and his *Israel Pemberton*, chaps. VIII, XI-XIII. The most recent treatment of the Friendly Association is to be found in the penultimate chapter of Hershberger, MS book. Israel was in fact the moving spirit behind the Association's activities; among his chief associates were his brother John, Jonathan Mifflin, and John Reynell, all of whom made generous financial contributions to its work. The collaboration of the nonresistant Mennonites and Schwenkfelders was also enlisted by the promoters of the Association.

[54] "The Friendly Association," p. 356. Sydney V. James (*A People called Quakers*, p. 178) calls the Association "this grandiose adventure in pressure politics."

could find practical expression, whereby pacifism could be shown to yield positive results where the opposite policy of military action proved sterile, is also correct. Although the governor and council regarded it as meddlesome interference,[55] they were forced by the Association's initiative in this respect to enter into negotiations with the Indians. Peace was in fact reached with the Delawares in August 1757 and was extended to include other tribes in the conference at Easton in 1758. In addition, before the Association finally folded soon after the conclusion of peace in 1763, Quakers had succeeded to some degree in transferring blame for the bitter frontier warfare from their own shoulders, where many in the early years of the conflict had tended to place it, onto those of the proprietors and their agents. Whether considered as a farsighted endeavor to promote peaceful coexistence or as a narrow attempt to regain by other methods the political influence lost by the Quaker withdrawal, the Friendly Association deserves at least brief mention in any account of the development of Quaker pacifism in Pennsylvania.

For all their backstage political influence and their efforts to prove the practical efficacy of a peaceable political policy, the events of the winter of 1755-1756 ushered in a time of troubles for Pennsylvania Quakers. Their hardships, of course, were slight in comparison with those endured by earlier generations of Friends on both sides of the ocean or in later periods of war and stress, or even at the present time of conflict by Friends in other and less tolerant colonies—not to speak of the sufferings of their fellow provincials of other faiths in the exposed frontier districts. But it was with sadness that many Quakers saw war come to Penn's patrimony and military requisitions being made on his people by a legislature that still contained a number of professing Friends. In three areas the Quaker conscience found itself confronted with the requirements of a state at war: militia service (compulsion, however, was confined to the Three Lower Counties that were to become Delaware), war taxation, and demands for various auxiliary services with the army.

Already in 1756 the assembly of the Three Lower Counties, following the example of their Pennsylvania counterpart, had enacted a

[55] A view that has been held, too, by some recent historians, e.g., Daniel J. Boorstin, *The Americans: The Colonial Experience*, 1964 edn., p. 57, and Hanna, *Franklin and Pennsylvania Politics*, pp. 107-10. It should be noted that in a letter, dated 9 July 1754, the Quaker Meeting for Sufferings in London had strongly urged Pennsylvania Friends to pay all taxes "for the support of civil government." Payment, London Friends thought, was "agreeable to the several advices of the Yearly Meeting founded on the precept and example of our Saviour" (quoted in H. J. Cadbury, "Nonpayment of Provincial War Tax," *Friends Journal*, 1 Sept. 1966, p. 441).

new militia law—but in this case, as earlier in this area, service was obligatory and penalties were attached for failure to obey, "without any exemption of persons who conscientiously scruple to comply therewith." Soon Quakers began to be fined for failure to muster, and, in accordance with the pattern elsewhere, their goods were distrained for refusal to pay. Early next year we find Philadelphia Yearly Meeting, which had oversight over Delaware Friends, appealing to the new deputy-governor, William Denny, for redress. Their petition singled out for special criticism the conduct of one of the New Castle County justices, David Bush, who along with his underlings had acted in a particularly offensive fashion. Most of those who suffered at the hands of these officials were simple farming folk, for whom the confiscation of livestock or farm equipment or household goods meant serious hardship, as well as losses usually in very considerable excess of the original fine. In one instance the cradle in which the man's infant child lay dying was seized; other goods worth £2 in all were taken along with the cradle for a fine of merely 10s.[56]

In Pennsylvania proper, the most difficult issue that had to be faced was whether or not to pay the taxes that were being used to carry on a war of which Friends disapproved both on principle and on grounds of political expediency. Most paid; some refused, and, relates Woolman, "in many places, the collectors and constables being Friends, distress was made on their goods . . . by their fellow members." James Pemberton wrote to Samuel Fothergill in November 1756:

> Our situation is indeed such as affords cause of melancholy reflection that the first commencement of persecution in this province should arise from our brethren in profession, and that such darkness should prevail as that they should be instruments of oppressing tender consciences which hath been the case. The tax in this county [Philadelphia] being pretty generally collected and many in this city particularly suffered by distraint of their goods and some being near cast into jail.

This was a painful situation indeed—but one which Yearly Meeting was unable to resolve satisfactorily. In the fall of 1757, for instance, a committee appointed to consider the question concluded that, since it was clear that there existed a wide "diversity of sentiments" among members, those of one opinion censuring those who took an opposite view, the matter should not be discussed publicly by Friends,

[56] *Pa. Col. Records*, VII, 403, 404; *Pa. Archives*, 1st ser., III, 165-70. See also W. R. Gawthrop, "Retrospect of Wilmington Friends" in *Friends in Wilmington 1738-1938*, p. 35.

who were adjured "earnestly to have their minds covered with fervent charity towards one another."[57]

In the privacy of Quaker meetings, however, the merits and demerits of tax refusal continued to be debated. Thus we hear of Woolman arguing the question with a Pennsylvania Quaker justice in the summer of 1758. According to Woolman, although Friends must approve of the general purposes of civil government, they should not give active support to it if the particular governmental measure was one which they deplored, as was the case now with taxes for war. The proper conduct in such a situation was to refuse payment and endure meekly the hardships consequent on the inevitable distraints: "this joined with an upright uniform life may tend to put men athinking about their own public conduct." The justice demurred. Not refusal of payment, he contended, but quiet remonstrance with the authorities whom they believed to be acting wrongly was the correct response. For him, a tax boycott was an unjustifiable act of civil disobedience. But, countered Woolman, surely no government has a right to our unconditional acquiescence, and, where it was bound on a wrong course, "an active obedience in that case would be adding one evil to another." For a man to suffer quietly the legal penalties for refusing to consent to evil appeared to him "most virtuous."[58]

Only the coming of peace stilled, for the time being, the controversy generated among Friends on this issue. Less debatable was the question of the response to be made to the various demands for helping the war effort that was being waged on Pennsylvania soil. As early as 1756, in answer to a query from Shrewsbury Quarterly Meeting in New Jersey, Yearly Meeting declared participation in the watch to be "a military service . . . that no Friend should either in person, or by paying others, be concerned therein."[59] Thus, performance of the kind of noncombatant services alongside the militia that, according to a new—and stiffened—militia act projected in 1757, might be demanded in an emergency of Quakers and other sectaries who conscientiously objected to bearing arms would also appear to have been ruled out

[57] Woolman, *Journal*, p. 210; Sharpless, *A Quaker Experiment*, I, 249. See also Minutes of the Yearly Meeting of Friends at Philadelphia for 1749-1779 (Dept. of Records of Philadelphia Y. M.), p. 110. This epistle is signed not only by the more radical tax objectors like Woolman, Churchman, and John Pemberton but also by Councillor William Logan and Samuel Wetherill, future leader of the Free Quakers of the Revolutionary era, neither of whom were pacifists, of course, let alone tax radicals. The decision was clearly a compromise between the two divergent wings of Pennsylvania Quakerism.

[58] Woolman, *Journal*, pp. 214, 215.

[59] A Collection of Christian and Brotherly Advices (1762), MS in F.H.L.S.C., p. 402.

for a consistent Friend. But the bill was vetoed by the governor before it could become law. Friends, the majority of whom were still farmers living in the country areas of the province, did have to face frequent requests to furnish wagons and horses to assist the military, and the Quaker merchants of Philadelphia were often faced with the problem of importing war supplies on their ships. In June 1758 a minute of the Meeting for Sufferings, which Yearly Meeting had set up in 1756 on the model of the London body of the same name to deal with the new and trying situation in which Pennsylvania Friends found themselves, declared unequivocally that voluntary assistance "with ships, waggons, or other carriages for transporting implements of war or military stores" was a dereliction of Friends' discipline. Deviants in this respect were to be dealt with by their meetings "in order to convince them of their error."[60]

In this same year 1758, Yearly Meeting took a decisive step in their strategic retreat from the political arena, second in importance only to the withdrawal from the assembly two years earlier. For, although this withdrawal had encompassed almost all the Quaker assemblymen who remained close to the Society, there were still many devoted Friends in the subordinate magistracy, functioning as justices of the peace or as constables in the towns and in the country districts or participating in the various other lesser offices of government. Most of these men held to the Society's peace testimony, as they did to its other tenets. A few were even militant pacifists, like Justice Aaron Ashbridge (1712-1776), a prosperous farmer in Chester County, of whom complaint was made by the military early in 1757 that he "not only refused to attest his recruits, but discouraged the men that were brought to him for that purpose from entering into the king's service."[61] That Quaker magistrates, as this remark implies, were being required in their official capacity to administer oaths and collaborate in military matters—and thus deviate from two of Friends' most cherished testimonies—was placing the Society in an increasingly anomalous situation.

In 1758, therefore, under the compelling spiritual influence of John Woolman and his co-workers (for the purely political motives for withdrawal that had been apparent in regard to the assembly no longer

---

[60] Gummere's introduction to Woolman's *Journal*, p. 53; *Rules of Discipline of the Yearly Meeting of Friends of Pennsylvania and New Jersey* (1797), p. 131.

[61] Quoted in Gummere's notes to Woolman's *Journal*, p. 585. Aaron, surprisingly enough, was the son of George Ashbridge, who had stubbornly refused to resign his seat in the assembly in 1756. His second wife, who had died in 1755, was Elizabeth Ashbridge (whose first husband's strange story is told above in n. 3, chap. I). Aaron Ashbridge's term of office came to an end in 1757, perhaps as a result of his forthright antimilitarism.

applied to anything like the same degree), Yearly Meeting strongly advised members against continuance in, or acceptance of, civil offices where they would in any way be involved in "enjoining or enforcing the compliance of their brethren or others with any act which they conscientiously scruple to perform." (At the same time, the meeting also took the momentous step of excluding Friends who purchased slaves from holding positions of trust within the Society.) Members who, after being lovingly "labored with" by their meetings, refused to resign office should henceforward be debarred from sitting "in our meetings for discipline" or from employment "in the affairs of truth, until they are brought to a sense and acknowledgement of their error." Henceforth, the Quaker magistrate, though not actually disowned, would continue as a semi-outcast in the community of Friends.

Yet even this measure was not completely effective in drawing Friends out of the magistracy. In the following year, for instance, a traveling English minister, William Reckitt (1706-1769), after visiting Friends at Darby reported that "several had been meddling and concerning themselves" with military matters and that there was considerable confusion about how Friends should behave in respect to participation in administration. He complained generally of "a grievous refractory libertine spirit" among them. Even as late as 1763, the caution of 1758 was being repeated on account of "the painful occasion of uneasiness, which still continues to subsist in divers places," from members continuing to hold office; and in the following year Friends were warned not to be "accessory in promoting or electing any of our brethren to such offices."[62] Thus, in the lower magistracy, as in the central legislature, the Quaker withdrawal was carried through only slowly and painfully and with much soul-searching and hesitancy on each side. Although not brought to final completion before the end of the colonial period, the withdrawal nevertheless was widespread enough, when combined with the new religious currents in the Society, to transform Pennsylvania Quakerdom from a vitally important element in the political establishment into a group that lay merely on the periphery of provincial politics. The final stage in the process came only as a result of the Society's experiences in the Revolutionary War.

The settlement of 1763 brought twelve years of official peace to the American colonies. The growing colonial movement against the policies of the home government, in the early stages of which Pennsylvania

[62] Michener, A Retrospect, pp. 274, 275; Some Account of the Life and Gospel Labours of William Reckitt, pp. 143, 144.

Friends played an important part, introduced new problems for the Quaker peace witness, problems which were intensified as resistance deepened and relations between the colonies and the mother country deteriorated until finally they issued in open and armed conflict.

One incident in this period must be dealt with here, for in a way it provides a link between the crisis of Quaker pacifism in 1755-1756, when the alleged failure of Quaker government to provide for the province's defense was used to remove Quaker politicians from power, and the crisis which resulted from the outbreak of the American Revolution exactly two decades later, when the issue was the justifiability of armed opposition to allegedly tyrannous rule. This incident was the famous Paxton Riot of 1764,[63] which represented a reaction on the part of frontier elements in Pennsylvania to the Indian uprising further north known to history as Pontiac's Conspiracy (the Pennsylvania Indians were suspected by many frontiersmen of being in league with hostile Indians). In November the Moravians had the Indians under their care removed to Philadelphia since they felt that these Indians were not safe in the Bethlehem area. In the following month the government-protected Conestoga Indians, who lived not far from Lancaster, were massacred almost to the last man, woman, and child by groups of armed frontiersmen—many of them Scotch-Irish—who called themselves the "Paxton Boys"; and in February the Paxton Boys marched on Philadelphia, which thereupon put itself in a posture of defense. Among those elements most culpable in the eyes of the Paxton Boys and their supporters in promoting what they considered policies of appeasement toward the Indians were, of course, the Quakers, some of whose members still sat in the assembly and whose name was still given colloquially to the majority party in that body. Isaac Pemberton, not unnaturally, was their particular bête noire. As it happened, the whole affair soon petered out: on approaching Philadelphia, the Paxton Boys, instead of attacking, contented themselves with placing a list of grievances in the administration's hands and then returned home without further trouble.

In the excitement of the moment, however, and with the intention of protecting the Indian refugees in the city who, it was feared, might also be massacred by the irate Paxton Boys, some 200 young Philadelphia Quakers took up arms. To them the choice seemed to lie between passive acquiescence in "the progress of horrid murderers" and active resistance to their further advance. Even though few, if any, of the older members were involved, and even with due allowance

[63] For the incident's effect on Quakers, see Sharpless, *A Quaker Experiment*, vol. II, chap. III.

made for what James Pemberton described as "the instability of youth," still it constituted—in the words of Samuel Fothergill—"a sorrowful defection from our religious testimony."[64]

The Society's enemies seized upon the activities of these young enthusiasts in an effort to discredit the sincerity of Friends as a whole. We find the German Lutheran pastor in Philadelphia, the Rev. Henry Melchior Mühlenberg, commenting sarcastically: "What increased the wonder was, that the pious lambs in the long French, Spanish and Indians Wars had such tender consciences, and would sooner die than raise a hand in defence against these dangerous enemies, and now at once . . . rushing upon a handful of our poor distressed and ruined fellow citizens and inhabitants of the frontiers."[65] A whole series of pamphlets issued from the press during the following year arguing the case for or against both the Paxton Boys and their chief butt, the Quakers.[66] One of the anti-Quaker items—*The Conduct of the Paxton-Men, Impartially Represented*—even cites the Babbitt incident of 1691 (see above) to prove that Quakers had never in fact been principled against bearing arms. And today, the anonymous author went on, "did not your Philadelphia Quakers take up arms, and declare they would fight in one case, namely, in defence of Friend Indians?"[67]

This, of course, was a libel. But the care with which local meetings in Philadelphia for the next three years endeavored to bring their delinquent members to acknowledge the error of their recent conduct shows the concern felt in the Society lest this episode should cast doubt on the sincerity of its pacifism. They sternly rejected any attempt to equate the action of their young militants with quasi-police action, a legitimate exercise of force which might be squared with Friends' testimony against war. Success was achieved in most instances, but, it was reported, "some appear rather in a disposition to vindicate their conduct." A few did indeed remain recalcitrant, justifying the use of arms in defense, until the action was finally dropped in mid-1767. No one was disowned.[68]

The "war" Quakers of 1764 were forerunners of the Free Quakers of the American Revolution. However, the animus of their adversaries,

[64] Crosfield, *Samuel Fothergill*, p. 443.

[65] *The Paxton Papers* (ed. John R. Dunbar), p. 41.

[66] These tracts have been collected and published in the volume entitled *The Paxton Papers*, which also contains material on the Quakers' response during and after the emergency.

[67] *Ibid.*, pp. 275-77.

[68] Sharpless, *A Quaker Experiment*, II, 50-54. On the other hand, some who participated in the "Quaker" brigade of 1764 became firm pacifists in later years, among them its leader Edward Penington, who was one of the Virginia exiles in 1777.

the Paxton Boys, was directed mainly against the now vanishing political Quaker of an earlier age. For by this date, although neither Quaker nor non-Quaker was always aware of it, Quaker Pennsylvania had become a part of past history.

Quaker Pennsylvania, from the heyday of the Holy Experiment through the successive epochs of David Lloyd and John Kinsey up to the concluding phases of the rule of the Quaker party, has been evaluated in quite different ways by subsequent historians. For some writers it has seemed to be proof of the failure of a philosophy of nonviolence and of its fatuity, at least in the political arena. For others it has stood as a blueprint for a better and more peaceable world, an example of farsighted idealism to which future generations can look back for inspiration. Still others have regarded its record as illustrating, above all, the thoroughly inadequate expression given to the pacifism that its rulers professed, at least in theory; not doctrinaire pacifism, then, or "the curse of perfectionism,"[69] but lack of steady adherence to right principle and a tendency to compromise were the sources of its decline. On the other hand, the contradiction between Quaker law enforcement inside the state and Quaker noncombatancy in the face of external foes is held by some to have invalidated the whole experiment *ab initio*. That the idea of the Holy Experiment did become tarnished in the course of the years and with the growing affluence of the Society of Friends is a point on which almost all are in agreement, though there is no unanimity concerning the date when it effectually came to an end. It is also generally recognized that, apart from the moot question of defense policy, the Quaker legislators did achieve considerable success in such areas as civil and religious liberties, constitutional government, penal reform, Indian relations, and commercial development. An estimate of its relative success or failure cannot, therefore, be based on one facet of its policy alone.

In fact, it seems extremely doubtful whether Quaker Pennsylvania can be taken either to prove or disprove the validity of pacifism as a practical political policy, even if we consider only the earlier decades of its history before the idealism generated at its foundation had begun to wear thin. For from the very beginning its pacifist legislators, as we have seen, were not free agents in shaping the province's external relations; enmeshed in Britain's imperial strategy, they became increasingly unable to detach Pennsylvania from the worldwide ramifications of the power struggle among the great European states. This impotency was as potentially limiting in the early days as it was in

---

[69] Boorstin, *The Colonial Experience*, p. 63.

later decades, when the Quaker assembly's opposition to military measures in the colony was caused more by considerations relating to their own power struggle with internal political antagonists than by their ethico-religious scruples concerning war. Pennsylvania's pacifism, therefore, was always closely circumscribed by the mother country's dependence on military means to maintain its position in international politics.

Moreover, the failure of Quakerism to remain the majority creed and Friends' inability to impart their belief in nonviolence to any but a fraction of the non-Quaker immigrants who crowded into the province from the end of the seventeenth century presaged the final collapse of any attempt to impose a pacifist political policy on the colony. Quaker rule in the first half of the eighteenth century, hence, the continuation of Quaker policies on peace and war, came increasingly to depend on an inequitable electoral system.

Only if Pennsylvania had been as truly self-governing in its foreign policy as it actually was in its internal affairs, and only if it had remained a community which still shared for the most part Quaker views on war, could it have become a reliable testing ground for the political practicability of the pacifist precepts of the Sermon on the Mount.

Chapter 4

Quakers and the
American Revolution

I

For all but one of the English-speaking provinces of the North American mainland the Revolutionary War brought the transition from colonial status to independence. This change was at first opposed officially by the Society of Friends and by a considerable proportion of those who remained members. Their opposition was based upon two grounds. First, and most fundamental, was Friends' rejection of the method of war and their personal objection to taking part in it, which prevented them from giving support to a cause that was being pressed by resort to arms. All those who remained in the Society, after it had been purged of members who did not share its peace testimony, assented to this point of discipline, including a minority in the Society who sympathized with the aims and final goal of the Continental cause. In the second place, alongside and reinforcing the Christian pacifism that Quakers had upheld since their crystallization as a denomination in the mid-seventeenth century, there now entered into their thinking and practice a political element (that was, however, still religiously inspired). Loyalty to the powers that be, a peaceable demeanor toward the rightful ruler of the land, had become as much part of the makeup of eighteenth-century Quakerism as it was of the churches which derived from the labors of the sixteenth-century Dutchman, Menno Simons. This, it was believed, was the pure doctrine inculcated by the teachings of the gospels and in the writings of Paul the apostle. In addition, as a factor buttressing sentiments of loyalty there arose a consciousness among many Friends of the manifold advantages to the Society on both sides of the Atlantic that had flowed from the British Crown over the past century and more.

Thus it came about that, in—and even before—the armed struggle that ensued from 1775 on, a church that was religiously pacifist took up a position that, politically, swung from attempted neutrality to a stance that at times was so close to loyalism that it was understandably mistaken for such by the great majority of the Quakers' fellow citizens. Among the immediate causes that led many Friends throughout the continent to mingle their pacifism with hostility, veiled or open, to the new governments that were ultimately set up in the former colonies by those who espoused, first, military resistance to the demands of the mother country within the framework of the imperial connection and, then, not many months after the first clashes at Lexington and Concord, a complete separation from the British monarchy, was the great prestige wielded in the whole American Quaker Society by Philadelphia Yearly Meeting. At the outbreak of the Revolutionary War this meeting, in fact, included over half the total number of Friends on the American continent. The various yearly meetings were autonomous bodies, but Friends everywhere, from Maine to Georgia, looked to the deliberations and decisions of the Quaker city for a lead in the policies they should adopt themselves.

During the decade before 1775, when the seeds of the Revolution were slowly ripening, the outlook of prominent Philadelphia Friends, of those circles of wealthy Quaker merchants who often gave the tone to the pronouncements of their yearly meeting (despite occasional rumblings of opposition from country Quakers, who by no means saw eye to eye on all subjects with their city brethren), veered from a restrained opposition to the stringent policy against the American colonies that the Grenville ministry had initiated at the end of the Seven Years War to an increasing distaste for the American movement of opposition that the home government's measures aroused. In 1765 a number of leading Quaker merchants in Philadelphia had, indeed, supported opposition to the hated Stamp Act, while attempting to dampen the violent emotions that were already beginning to come to the surface among irate colonials. Prominent Quaker merchants, like Israel and James Pemberton, Henry and James Drinker, John Reynell, Thomas Wharton, Thomas Clifford, and some fifty more participated in the ensuing economic boycott of British goods by using American manufactures whenever possible and by signing the Philadelphia nonimportation resolutions of that year.[1] The objectionable Townshend Acts of 1767, which marked a further step in Britain's attempt to raise taxes in the colonies for revenue purposes while not allowing the Americans to participate in framing legislation, likewise aroused opposition among Philadelphia Quakers. But, as the colonial movement gradually veered from a constitutional opposition that relied mainly on peaceful means to action that contained implications of violence, many Friends, like some other future "Tories" who had previously been sympathetic to the movement, began to draw back. And opinion among influential circles in Philadelphia Yearly Meeting became increasingly

---

[1] Among these Quaker "nonimporters" were nine who were in the party of allegedly pro-British Quakers deported to Virginia in 1777 (see below).

suspicious of the rightness of Friends' participation in the movement. As early as 1765, at the time of the Stamp Act crisis, the meeting's epistle to New England Yearly Meeting contained the significant warning: "May we be watchful to keep out of those things."[2] This feeling grew stronger at the beginning of the seventies when the smuggling of tea, the chief item still taxed after the repeal of the Townshend duties in 1770 which formed the background of the famous Boston Tea Party of December 1773, constituted a leading weapon in the armory of colonial resistance. Although it might be pleaded that such activities were nonviolent for the most part, still they were clearly un-Quakerly, for they amounted, in effect, to defrauding the king of his lawful revenue and were therefore contrary to the Quaker testimony of honest dealings in all business matters. Members of the Society who partook in such activities—and they were fairly numerous, it would seem, from the evidence of local meeting records—were called to account. As agitation in the country grew, feeling within the Society began to harden. Typical of this trend was the state of mind revealed at a general meeting of Philadelphia Friends called in mid-October 1773 to discuss the current situation. According to the report sent to English Friends by one of the leading participants, James Pemberton, who was later to play a vital role in Philadelphia Yearly Meeting during the Revolution:

Altho' we are not insensible of the incroachments of powers and of the value of civil rights, yet in matters contestable we can neither join with nor approve the measures which have been too often proposed by particular persons and adopted by others for asserting and defending them, and such is the agitation of those who are foremost in these matters it appears in vain to interfere.[3]

Noninterference in political affairs and official disapproval of those of its members who continued active in the movement of colonial opposition thenceforward marked the policy of the Society of Friends both in Pennsylvania and in the other five yearly meetings on the continent. Throughout the over eighty monthly meetings into which the Society was grouped, a uniformity of conduct was enforced by dis-

---

[2] Quoted in Arthur J. Mekeel, "The Quakers in the American Revolution," Ph.D. diss., Harvard U. (1939), p. 18. This monograph, unfortunately not published, gives a comprehensive account of the Society of Friends during the war years, based on a wide variety of sources: manuscript Quaker meeting records and the unpublished papers of prominent individual Friends, contemporary newspapers, and official government documents. Mekeel's work has proved most useful in the preparation of this chapter.

[3] Letter dated 30 Oct. 1773, quoted by Mekeel.

ciplinary measures against those who deviated, in intent as well as in deed, from the peaceable standard set up.

The First Continental Congress, which met in Philadelphia in early September 1774, was dominated by the patriots, and the Continental "Association" which it adopted on 20 October for the purpose of enforcing more effectively the boycott of British goods amounted to a declaration of economic war against the home government, although few among the Congress's members were yet in favor of a complete break with Britain. There were Friends, and some near Friends, among the members of the Congress; however, those who continued on the path which the patriots had begun to tread soon either found themselves disowned or of their own accord ceased their connection with the Society of Friends. For the Society thenceforward set its face firmly against colonial resistance, feeling that the steps already taken constituted an illegal opposition against the sovereign power and would, if pursued further, result in armed rebellion and a state of war—suspicions that were confirmed by the development of events in Massachusetts during the winter months.

In January 1775, therefore, Philadelphia Yearly Meeting issued two declarations summing up its position in view of the impending conflict. The first was drawn up on 5 January by the Meeting for Sufferings and was designed primarily for use within the Society, for it was addressed (as the style was in such cases) "to our friends and brethren in these and the adjacent provinces." The epistle opened with a phrase describing the Anglo-American conflict that was repeatedly to crop up even after open war had broken out: it spoke of "the troubles and commotions which have prevailed" (a state of confusion "in this once peaceful land" that in the ensuing years would never be dignified with the name of war in the eyes of the more loyalistically inclined Friends, for wars took place only between legally constituted governments). The main tenor of the document was to warn all those members who had become entangled in the politics of resistance to withdraw, recollecting in time "that to fear God, honour the king, and do good to all men, is our indispensable duty."[4] In fact, it called on Friends to

[4] Thomas Gilpin (ed.), *Exiles in Virginia*, pp. 284-87. A preliminary warning directed against Friends who had publicly supported the resolves of the Continental Congress was issued by Meeting for Sufferings on 15 Dec. 1774 (printed in Isaac Sharpless, *A Quaker Experiment in Government*, II: *The Quakers in the Revolution*, 107). Cf. John A. Woods (ed.), "The Correspondence of Benjamin Rush and Granville Sharp 1773-1809," *Journal of American Studies*, I, no. 1 (April 1967), 14 (Rush to Sharp, 1 Nov. 1774): "The colonies are determined to carry all the resolutions of our Congress into execution. We shall wait with impatience to hear of the proceedings of the Parliament. But we are preparing for the worst. A military spirit is kindled among us. We talk with less horror than formerly of a

take a further step on the path toward complete disengagement from public life that had commenced in 1756.

The second document issued officially by Friends during this month, and likewise signed by James Pemberton in his capacity as clerk, was entitled "The Testimony of the People called Quakers" and was in the nature of a public declaration of their position. It was given wide publicity both within and outside the Society, and it was even translated into German for distribution chiefly among the Mennonites, who had sent delegates to Philadelphia to confer with the Quakers on the crisis.[5] The "Testimony" was short but left little doubt about where Friends—at least those who wielded most weight in the affairs of Philadelphia Yearly Meeting—stood in the mounting dispute between Britain and her colonies. Quakers, its framers claimed, had a religious duty "to discountenance and avoid every measure tending to excite disaffection to the King, as supreme magistrate, or to the legal authority of his government." It declared its complete confidence, as a result of past goodwill shown by the monarchy, in peaceful and loyal remonstrances as an effective method of righting any justifiable grievances that the colonies might entertain in respect to the home government. "We deeply lament," the "Testimony" goes on, "that contrary modes of proceeding have been pursued, which have involved the colonies in confusion, appear likely to produce violence and bloodshed, and threaten the subversion of . . . constitutional government, and of . . . liberty of conscience." It ended by an unequivocal declaration of opposition to the exercise of authority that was already being practised in some areas by colonial patriots; this it branded as a "usurpation of power," and it went on to condemn "all combinations, insurrections, conspiracies, and illegal assemblies."[6] The lines were fairly drawn: the other yearly meetings followed the lead given by Philadelphia, and henceforth there could be little doubt where official Quakerism stood in relation to the takeover of power that would be effected by the colonial forces during the ensuing months.

True, many among even the conservative Friends of Philadelphia, New York, and New England still retained inner reservations concerning the policies pursued by the English government. Even as loyal a British American as James Pemberton could write as late as May 1775

---

civil war. In two or three months there will be forty thousand men completely armed and disciplined in the Prov[ince of] Pennsylvania—many of whom [will be] Quakers. Thus you see a lively sense [of] public injuries has destroyed the strongest prejudices of education and religion."

[5] Mekeel, "The Quakers," pp. 76, 77.
[6] *Exiles in Virginia*, pp. 282-84.

of the "mistaken policy" of Britain "in the management of this unhappy contest."[7] Moreover, his correspondent in this instance, the wise and energetic English Quaker, Dr. John Fothergill, along with other British Friends, like David Barclay, who were in close touch with events across the Atlantic, considered that their American brethren had gone too far in opposition to the colonial cause which, in their view, had so much of right on its side. Commenting on the January "Testimony" of Philadelphia Friends, Barclay gently chided them for not having confined themselves to restating Friends' opposition to all warlike actions ("there on that ground your best friends wish you to remain," he wrote) and for having launched, instead, into a semi-political declaration. And Fothergill—"more American than the conservative American Friends themselves," as Sharpless has described him—was upset to think that a document such as the "Testimony" might only serve to strengthen the resolution of the court to continue a policy of strength in regard to the colonies, a policy that English Friends were doing their best to counter in favor of conciliation.[8] So we find the doctor telling James Pemberton in March 1775: "Submission to the prevailing power must be your duty. The prevailing power is the general voice of America."[9]

For men like Pemberton, however, and for the many Friends in town and country meetings up and down the continent who seemingly followed their lead, the general voice of America stood opposed to the still voice of Quaker conscience, which commanded loyalty to the established power and an exacting neutrality in the turmoil of war that was coming to their country. The overturning of kings and governments was God's business and not that of a people apart, as Friends were. As an epistle of North Carolina declared in the following October, they must not meddle in such affairs, "nor . . . be busybodies in matters above our station."[10] Already, before hostilities had formally broken out, Friends were gaining unpopularity for their refusal to sign the "Association," the declaration to abide by the nonintercourse agreements that, in effect, signified allegiance to the new authority represented by the Continental Congress and the local revolutionary committees. Already they were being branded as "Tories" in the eyes of neighbors who could not—or did not want to—distinguish between passive neutrality and active aid to the British interest, when in fact, as Tolles remarks with particular reference to the Quaker merchants of

[7] Sharpless, *A Quaker Experiment*, II, 121.
[8] *Ibid.*, pp. 114, 118.
[9] Mekeel, "The Quakers," p. 81.
[10] Dorothy Gilbert Thorne, "North Carolina Friends and the Revolution," *North Carolina Historical Review*, XXXVIII, no. 3 (July 1961), 323.

Philadelphia who gave tone in many respects to the whole Society, "far from being Tories in the usual sense, [they] had stood for years as outspoken exponents of the Whig ideals of liberty and property."[11] In Virginia we find one quarterly meeting (Henrico) endeavoring to remove the stigma of disloyalty that was already being fixed on them by advising members to link their refusal to "associate" with the peace testimony: they were to explain to the new authorities that their religious principles prevented them from acting "in any matter which [might] have a tendency to the shedding of blood."[12]

In 1776, in two further statements of policy, Philadelphia Yearly Meeting, heedless of the sound advice given by Dr. Fothergill and his English associates, confirmed in even more categorical terms its previous negative attitude toward the new regime in the province. "The Ancient Testimony and Principles of the People called Quakers, renewed, with respect to the King and Government," which a representative meeting of Friends published on 20 January, was filled with nostalgia for the good old days under kingly rule and with lamentation at the unhappy changes in government which were taking place in the province and which the framers of the "Ancient Testimony" clearly hoped might be stemmed by a public protest of this kind on the part of such a highly influential group as Friends still were in Penn's commonwealth. "The inhabitants of these provinces [i.e., Pennsylvania and New Jersey] were long signally favoured with peace and plenty." In conclusion, Friends deplored—not unreasonably, it must be said—the impending break with Great Britain.

At the end of the year, after the Declaration of Independence had consummated the severing of ties between the colonies and mother country that Friends had so much feared and after Penn's constitution of 1701 had been swept away, Friends again appeared with an epistle, dated 20 December and directed this time "to our friends and brethren in religous profession, in these and the adjacent provinces." The letter was intended to strengthen the resolution of members in face of the rising hostility shown them—and all others who were suspected of friendly feelings toward the British cause—by the new authorities and the patriotic section of the community. It was also aimed at hardening their resistance to the various demands—for military service, special taxes, test oaths, etc.—that were being made on them. Its purpose, it said, was "to strengthen the weak, confirm the wavering, and warn and caution the unwary against being beguiled by the snares of the adversaries of truth and righteousness," lest "the fear of suffer-

---

[11] Frederick B. Tolles, *Meeting House and Counting House*, p. 28.
[12] Mekeel, "The Quakers," pp. 82, 83.

ing, either in person or in property, prevail on any to join with or promote any work or preparation for war." Friends were called upon to refuse obedience to these "arbitrary injunctions and ordinances of men, who assume to themselves the power of compelling others, either in person or by other assistance, to join in carrying on war," and to suffer the consequences of their disobedience to unlawful authority meekly.[13]

To the new regime, statements of this kind appeared as a challenge. Tom Paine (1737-1809), the Quaker-born rationalist, fulminated against what he called the "factional and fractional part" of Philadelphia Quakerdom responsible for its public utterances, accusing these persons of partiality to the British enemy and crypto-Toryism. Their pacifism, he contended, if it were genuine, should be able to distinguish between a commendable goal, independence, and the forcible means by which it was being achieved that would naturally incur their disapproval. "O! ye fallen, cringing, priest-and-Pemberton-ridden people!" he cried. "What more can we say of ye than that a religious Quaker is a valuable character, and a political Quaker a real Jesuit."[14]

The "Ancient Testimony" at the beginning of the year and Philadelphia Friends' epistle in December, combined with the momentous resolutions of their yearly meeting in September discussed below, were taken by the Second Continental Congress and by the radicals who were now in control of the provincial administration as a declaration of disloyalty to the new regime. In this belief they were, in fact, mistaken, for the statements expressed rather a traditional loyalty to the old order and passive, if unenthusiastic, obedience to the new. They did not represent a departure from the Quaker peace testimony but rather an extremely conservative interpretation of its implications. At its September sessions Yearly Meeting had enjoined Friends, among other things, to withdraw from all participation in the country's new political life and to refrain from paying fines or commutation in lieu of active service or from partaking in business activities connected with the war. These testimonies and resolutions, which were echoed in declarations of the other yearly meetings on the continent, formed the background both for the development of the Society during the remaining years of war and for the course of action pursued in regard to it by the various American authorities.

The discipline of the Society, which was exercised as vigilantly in wartime as in the previous years of peace, ensured "a fairly consistent

[13] *Exiles in Virginia*, pp. 287-93. See also p. 248.
[14] *The Writings of Thomas Paine*, I, 1894 edn., 126, 208. See also Robert P. Falk, "Thomas Paine and the Attitude of the Quakers to the American Revolution," *PMHB*, LXIII, no. 3 (July 1939), 306, 307.

and uniform conduct on the part of the Quakers throughout the continent."[15] Their peace witness during the Revolutionary War was collective and traditional; in some ways it lacked the stamp of individuality. There was little attempt on the part of private Friends to expound Quaker pacifism either by the published or the spoken word. In part this silence may be attributed to the difficulties always inherent in peace propaganda in wartime, in part, also, to the predominantly rural composition of a large section of the membership (although the Society did contain a highly cultured urban minority). But the main cause lay in the increasingly withdrawn character of Quaker pacifism, the pacifism now of a people apart—a transformation that was overtaking a number of its other traditional testimonies, too. A yearly meeting, as the mouthpiece of the Society, might need to publish from time to time a defense of its views on war for presentation to the authorities or before the general public in order to clear up the misunderstandings that were rife with regard to their position; such a body might feel called upon to restate its grounds for renouncing war in order to exhort its members to continued steadfastness in witnessing to this aspect of its faith or to bring support and comfort to Friends in other areas. But, unless we include a number of essays (most in manuscript form) devoted to the question of paying taxes in wartime and intended mainly for internal circulation among members of the Society, very few individual Friends felt called upon at this time, when one might have expected a crop of publications on the subject, to do battle in print for their peaceable principles.

Among the few, however, was Anthony Benezet (1713-1784), crusader against war, slavery, and spirituous liquors and a prolific pamphleteer on behalf of all these causes. Benjamin Rush describes in one of his essays an encounter he had with Benezet on a Philadelphia street corner. "In one hand," writes Rush, "he carried a subscription paper and a petition; in the other he carried a small pamphlet on the unlawfulness of the African slave-trade, and a letter directed to the King of Prussia upon the unlawfulness of war."[16] War and slavery, Benezet never ceased to insist, emanated from the same source: lust for wealth and for power over men, which constituted a direct contradiction of the Christian message. The fulfillment of the Christian message of peace was incumbent on nations as well as on individuals, "for a christian nation differs no otherwise from a christian person, than as the whole differs from one of the parts of which it essentially consists"—so he was telling his fellow Americans

---

[15] Mekeel, "The Quakers," p. 118.
[16] Quoted in George S. Brookes, *Friend Anthony Benezet*, p. 75.

in 1778.[17] And in the same year he published his "Serious Reflections affectionately recommended to the well-disposed of every religious denomination,"[18] in which in true Quaker fashion he advised his countrymen to look within themselves for the causes of the war rather than to seek them in the supposed faults of the enemy. "We fight against those we esteem our foes," he wrote, "and instead of labouring to overcome our sins, we basely yield to their temptations." Let us remember what Christianity means and pray for reconciliation with our enemies, he told both the contending sides.

Probably more effective in the long run than the kind of small-circulation pamphlet produced by the saintly, highly respected, but perhaps little heeded Benezet—and probably more telling, too, than the often platitudinous and uninspiring pronouncements of official Quakerism—were the efforts of simple men and women in the Society to argue with, and convince, neighbors and strangers concerning the validity of their views on war, which were so much out of line with those of the rest of the community, whether procolonial militants, dissident Tories, or even indifferent middle-of-the-roaders. Unfortunately, this kind of quiet propaganda for Quaker pacifism finds little reflection in surviving documents of the period: encounters of this sort passed for the most part unrecorded. Occasional insights do exist, however, in the Quaker journals. One of these is provided by the boyhood recollections of Henry Hull (1765-1834), who was then living in an isolated frontier area of upstate New York. A few Friends were settled there, and they had built themselves a small primitive log meetinghouse. In the absence of other places of religious worship in the neighborhood, services attracted non-Quakers, to whom many of the articles of Quaker belief—and especially, we might imagine, the Society's peace testimony—were new and sometimes strange at first. "The meeting was often attended," says Hull, "by a number of raw, rustic-looking people, most of whom were not Friends; and they would gather together near the house, before the meeting time, and engage in disputes about the war, sometimes with high words and angry looks." When time to go into meeting arrived, however, they quieted down. "There is good reason to believe," Hull goes on, "that

[17] Anthony Benezet, *Serious Considerations on Several Important Subjects*, pp. 2-12, 27. The section in the pamphlet devoted to war is, however, largely made up of extracts from *Address to the Clergy*, written by the early eighteenth-century Anglican clergyman William Law in 1760-1761, sections of which are directed against war and militarism.

[18] Reprinted in Brookes, *Benezet*, pp. 495-97. Benezet was also active in lobbying successive presidents of the Continental Congress, as well as other prominent personalities on both sides, on behalf of the Quaker peace testimony. See, e.g., Brookes, pp. 324, 325, 330, 331.

many of these persons were sincere-hearted, for some who were not then members of our Society, afterward joined in religious fellowship, and became united in bearing a Christian testimony against war, by patiently suffering the spoiling of their goods."[19] Thus, for all the occasional heated tempers and angry argument, and even in time of war when passions were aroused against talk of peace, we find these rough upcountry farmers, frontiersmen dwelling in the deep wilderness of the north, responding to the Quaker message of conciliation and love to all men.

A further instance of quiet and effective propaganda for peace occurs in the journal of another New York-born country Friend, Joseph Hoag (1762-1846). Around the year 1780 when still in his teens, Hoag while on a journey fell into conversation with a man who soon launched into a violent attack on Quakers because of their refusal to fight for the American cause. Embarrassed and tongue-tied at first and conscious of his shortcomings as a champion of his people, the boy finally plucked up courage. As he wrote later:

As I commenced all fear departed, words flowed rapidly, and I was enabled to . . . open to him our principles, give him our reasons for them, and to prove them by many Scripture passages; and finally, to show him it was impossible for a true Quaker, to be either whig or tory, for they implied opposite parties, and both believed in war, but Friends did not.

The man, visibly moved by the boy's eloquence and obvious sincerity, told him after he had concluded: "There must be great wisdom amongst the Quakers, for so young a man to know so much."[20]

A second positive expression of the Quaker witness for peace in wartime that can be put alongside the quiet working for peace of countless men like Benezet or Hoag whose names have not been recorded, and one that has become typical of the Society in this twentieth-century age of violence, is its relief work for the sufferers of war. One of the earliest examples of this Quaker humanitarianism was shown in the first years of the American Revolution. The work arose out of the British blockade of Boston in the second half of 1774 and the subsequent siege of the town by the American army after the outbreak of

[19] *Memoir of the Life and Religious Labours of Henry Hull*, pp. 25, 26.
[20] *A Journal of Joseph Hoag*, pp. 12, 13. (For the story of how, in 1777, Joseph's Quaker father, Elijah Hoag, found himself in the local jail because of his resistance to military orders, see pp. 17-21.) See also *Friends' Miscellany*, IX, no. 6 (Jan. 1837), 286, for the story of an encounter in Charleston in 1778 between the Lancaster Co. (Pa.) Quaker minister, Joshua Brown, and an Old Testament-minded South Carolina judge.

open hostilities in the following year. The organization of relief for those who were suffering as a result of warlike action was undertaken by the Meeting for Sufferings of Philadelphia Yearly Meeting, which grouped within its ranks a number of the most wealthy Quakers and which at that date had not yet come to feel the direct impact of the fighting. At first, assistance was limited to the small Quaker community in Boston, but the objective soon broadened to include—within the limits of Friends' resources—all who needed help, a pattern which was to become typical of later Quaker relief. When Washington, as commander of the army besieging the British in Boston, permitted only funds, and not Quaker personnel from outside the area, to pass through the lines, distribution became the responsibility of a group of New England Quakers, among the most active of whom was the famous Providence merchant, Moses Brown (1738-1836), a recent convert to Quakerism.[21] The British evacuated Boston in March 1776, and Quaker effort then turned to concentrate on the hapless refugees from the city and neighborhood scattered about the adjoining townships. Altogether over 3,000 families were aided, almost all of them non-Quakers, and over £4,000 was expended on relief, most of this money having been raised among members of Philadelphia Yearly Meeting. In its "Advices" issued at this time, we find it exhorting members, "and particularly . . . those who have received the increase of earthly possessions," to contribute liberally to the relief of the distressed by curtailing, if necessary, their outlay on themselves.[22]

Philadelphia Meeting for Sufferings noted, when the relief work drew to a close in the summer of 1776, that it had made "a good impression on the minds of some who have been prejudiced against Friends." In negotiations with Generals Washington and Howe, Friends had made it clear, not only that their help would be given "without distinction of sects or parties," but that their motives derived from the same source as their objection to war, that their action, indeed, reflected the positive side of this testimony. Relief, they stated to the contending generals, must be so administered "that our religious testimony against wars and fightings may be preserved pure."[23]

Quakers thereafter continued to aid the civilian victims of war, though only sporadically on a much smaller scale and with their own people primarily in view; help was given, for instance, to the desti-

---

[21] For Brown's part in the relief work, see Mack Thompson, *Moses Brown*, pp. 116-30.
[22] Sharpless, *A Quaker Experiment*, II, 140. See also p. 123.
[23] H. J. Cadbury, *Quaker Relief during the Siege of Boston*, p. 13.

tute islanders of Nantucket and in Virginia and Pennsylvania when war hit these provinces.[24] But for the most part, as was scarcely unavoidable in the circumstances of war when the Quakers formed a small and unpopular minority standing out, along with several even smaller and more obscure religious groups, against the tide of opinion on either side, their witness expressed itself in seemingly negative attitudes, in their refusal to participate in certain activities demanded of them by the public authorities or expected of them by public opinion. We must now survey in turn the various points at which the Quaker conscience clashed with a nation in arms and the disabilities they suffered as a result of their unwillingness to compromise. But first we should take a closer look at the machinery by which Friends supplemented the still small voice within by a discipline which assured the convinced, encouraged the fainthearted and the hesitant, and combed out those who failed, either through laxness or more often because of a different interpretation of what was right, to abide by the rules of the Society.

The main lines of Quaker policy were laid down by the various yearly meetings, primarily Philadelphia as we have seen; the implementation of policy was the responsibility of the local meetings, quarterly and monthly. Although quarterly meetings did act in a supervisory capacity, it was the monthly meetings that exercised direct control over members, and we find that most of these meetings were extremely active during the war period both in exhorting members to loyalty to "our Christian peaceable testimony" and in dealing with those who contravened it in some way. Most monthly meetings set up special committees of tried and trusted Friends whose business it was to visit all members who had strayed and to endeavor to bring them to a sense of error, in fact—to use the words of one such committee—"to strengthen the weak and confirm the wavering in this time of probation."[25] Varying success attended these efforts. A not untypical entry, taken from a Pennsylvania rural meeting, runs as follows: "They have gone through with respect to visiting their members, to inspect into their faithfulness, and . . . they had reason to believe divers have not been so upright in maintaining our testimony against military requisitions as becometh followers of Christ. But a considerable number they apprehend have en-

---

[24] See Mekeel, "The Quakers," chap. XIV, and Sydney V. James, *A People among Peoples*, pp. 258-64, for Quaker relief efforts during the Revolution. The best account of the Boston operation is given in H. J. Cadbury's pamphlet cited in the previous footnote.

[25] Radnor Monthly Meeting Minutes of Sufferings 1776-1779 (MS in F.H.L.S.C.), p. 21.

deavoured to be faithful therein so far as appeared."[26] Expulsion from the Society followed inexorably if no change could eventually be effected in a person being "dealt with," as, indeed, had always been the practice of the Society. A special committee was usually appointed, also, to collect details of Friends' "sufferings" on account of their opposition to the war: at its annual assembly in September 1776, Philadelphia Yearly Meeting, for instance, had required its constituent meetings to send up such accounts periodically to Meeting for Sufferings. These records, many of which have survived from all areas where Quakers were settled, provide much insight into the state of the Society during the Revolutionary period.

II

The strict control exercised by a local meeting over the conduct of its members brought with it the possibility of abuse, the ability of the Quaker community to impose an overall conformity by threat of cutting off a recalcitrant member and thus denying him the support of his Society if he were called up for military service. The outside world had (not unnaturally in this era) a stereotyped view of the Quaker and would give short shrift to any who did not fit this picture. The Pennsylvania "Dutchman," Jacob Ritter (1757-1841), who served in the Revolutionary War but later became a Quaker, tells an amusing story of the experiences of a "gay" young Friend at the hands of the military after he had been inducted into the Continental army. When the young man had explained his refusal to serve on the grounds that he was a Quaker,

> The presiding officer [Ritter used to relate in his Pennsylvania Dutch dialect] replied, "But you are no Quaker for you have not the 'cooterments'" (accoutrements). The young man then produced some written credentials by which he proved his right of membership. The officer now called for a shears that he might trim him; and so he cut off his capes and his lappels, and *sich a hair tail he had behind* (a cue), and then said to him, "now you may go, now you look more like a Quaker."[27]

The "gay" Quaker got off lightly in this instance because he had clear proof of membership. If his meeting had already dealt with him for his failure to conform to the Quaker norm of dress (or for marrying out or for dancing or for a dozen or more deviations in behavior that

[26] New Garden Monthly Meeting Committee on Sufferings, Minutes 1780-1782 (MS in F.H.L.S.C.), p. 17.
[27] Joseph Foulke, *Memoirs of Jacob Ritter*, p. 48.

—at least theoretically—might not exclude a perfectly genuine objection to war), the army would certainly not have released him so easily. Of course, at that date Quaker pacifism was much more an integral and indissoluble part of the whole Quaker religious ethos than it is today when there are Quaker nonpacifists and non-Quaker and unaffiliated pacifists. In many instances, those who then broke with custom on one issue broke with it on a number of others, and the pressure of community thought forged a quite genuine belief among most Quakers that conformity in cut of dress or style of hair or manner of speech was essential to a truly conscientious objection to war. Yet, even so, it is hard to believe that there were not some nonconformists in regard to Quaker externals (many of which have since been altogether abandoned)—whether they merely nursed their dissent in private or manifested it openly, suffering the penalty of disownment for daring to do so—who at the same time held as a result of their upbringing among Friends a quite sincere objection to war. One may suppose, moreover, that, since some in that century who were disowned for support of warlike activities still continued to worship with Friends thereafter and to associate themselves with the other points of their discipline apart from the matter of war, there would also be those who assented in regard to the peace testimony while dissenting on some other item then regarded as binding on all members. The records have little to say on the subject. We do hear, however, of a North Carolina man, Joseph Newby, who had been a member of the Society until his disownment for marrying out, objecting at the end of 1778 to the draft, which was ordered in connection with the British offensive in South Carolina. He was joined by nine other Quaker conscientious objectors, who were, however, more fortunate in being able to produce proof of membership. But after some discussion Newby, too, was finally released along with the rest.[28]

Proof of membership, then, was an extremely important matter for

[28] Mekeel, "The Quakers," pp. 231, 232. Two related cases from the same yearly meeting are discussed in Thorne, "North Carolina Friends and the Revolution," p. 329. The first is taken from Pasquotank M. M. where in 1782 one William Price, a young man of military age, "joined himself in marriage with a woman not of our Society." "As he hath lately obtained a certificate from this meeting," the minute continues, "in order to clear him from military services, Friends think it necessary to order a paper of denial against him." The second case is that of Caleb Goodwin of Perquimans M. M., a former soldier who had been admitted as a member in 1780 when he was given "a few lines setting forth that he is in unity" by his meeting in order to shield him from being drafted again. Three years later, however, Goodwin was disowned for wearing a ring, among other offenses of like nature. The war had already ended; otherwise, Goodwin would most likely have found himself in the same kind of difficulties as Newby had been in.

the potential Quaker objector, even when a special document for this purpose was not required by law. Sometimes, as we have seen, the authorities would in fact demand from the conscientious objector a certificate of membership drawn up in due form by his meeting before exemption from service in the militia was granted. Friends seem to have generally complied. But, at the outset of the Revolutionary struggle, New York Quakers had refused to supply the names of their male members between the ages of 16 and 60 on the grounds that it was not "consistent with our religious principles" to do so.[29] Their "truly conscientious scruple" in the matter, however, may have arisen at least in part from the fact that the request came from the local committee of safety, whose authority Quakers regarded as usurped. In Virginia, too, we find at least one of the meetings, Fairfax Monthly Meeting, refusing to supply its members when drafted with the certificates required by law on the grounds that this was an impermissible act of collaboration in war.[30] On the other hand, Friends in Rhode Island were prepared to issue certificates so long as militia service was required of them by law; yet they used the occasion to exclude from the benefit of the legal exemption not only those whom they did not consider genuine adherents of the peace testimony but also any who were felt to be wanting in regard to other facets of the discipline. This policy emerges clearly in the following words of advice circulated among local meetings by the (New England) Meeting for Sufferings:

> Let it be remembered, Friends, that if we give certificates to any whose life and conversation does not well answer to our profession, we must bear the reproach, and shall mar our reputation as a Society; and very likely lose the indulgence we now have, through much labour, obtained. Therefore, dear Friends, let there be great care to inspect the conduct of such as require certificates, and also their principle respecting war; and we desire that none may be granted to any others but such who are of sober lives and conversations, and who are clear in our ancient testimony against wars and fightings; and that such certificates be inspected and directed by, and signed in open meeting.[31]

The Quaker objector, even when in good standing with the meeting, as the vast majority were, was still faced (except where the state

[29] John Cox, Jr., *Quakerism in the City of New York*, pp. 75, 76.
[30] Mekeel, "The Quakers," p. 225.
[31] Mekeel, "New England Quakers and Military Service in the American Revolution" in *Children of Light* (ed. Howard H. Brinton), p. 252.

granted complete exemption) with the familiar requirement either to pay a fine, varying in amount from province to province and often from year to year, or to hire a substitute to replace him in his statutory military duties, at a cost that might be greater even than repeated fining. When the assembly in Pennsylvania in November 1775 imposed a draft on all able-bodied men between the ages of 16 and 50, it provided that religious conscientious objectors should be excused service on payment of a fine of £2.10s.[32] This sum was later raised several times largely on account of the inflation of prices as the war proceeded, until at the end of 1778 it reached the figure of £40, with a penalty for nonpayment of distraint of goods or imprisonment for four months for those who had no property on which to distrain. In the following years fines went even higher, first up to £100 and then over that figure, reaching as much as £1,000 in some cases. In the other provinces the pattern is much the same: a rising scale of fines as the years went by and currency depreciated in value, with distraint or imprisonment following for any who refused to pay. In both New Jersey and New York additional sums of money were demanded in the event of an emergency when the militia went out on active service against an invasion. Effective conscription in Maryland did not come until 1777 and in Delaware until 1778. Certified religious objectors were exempt in Virginia, except when the province was threatened by actual invasion. North Carolina, where, as in Virginia, conscientious objectors had been virtually exempt from militia service at the time war broke out, from 1776 on followed the pattern of the middle provinces. The two New England states where Quakers were thickly settled, Rhode Island and Massachusetts, both imposed selective service laws after the proclamation of independence. In Massachusetts, by a law of September 1776, persons refusing the draft or the hiring of a substitute were to be fined £10 or imprisoned for up to two months; but at the end of November, as the result of an amendment, Quakers who had been

---

[32] A month earlier Philadelphia Y. M. had presented an address to the assembly protesting against its intention of introducing military conscription without giving complete exemption to religious objectors. This, the address claimed, conflicted with the guarantees of "liberty of conscience" set out in the fundamental laws of the commonwealth, to enjoy which the first Quaker settlers had left their native land. See *Votes of Assembly, Pa. Archives*, 8th ser., VIII, 7326-30. In the previous June the assembly had indeed generously recognized that "many of the good people of this province are conscientiously scrupulous of bearing arms." Associators, therefore, were asked to "bear a tender and brotherly regard towards this class of their fellow-subjects and country-men." The pacifists of the province, in their turn, were required to "cheerfully assist, in proportion to their abilities, such Associators as cannot spend their time and substance in the public service without great injury to themselves and families." (Quoted from VIII, 7249.)

in membership before 19 April 1775 were allowed complete exemption, although this was withdrawn for a brief time in 1780 during a period of acute manpower shortage. In Rhode Island, at first, Quakers were subject merely to the requirement included in prewar legislation of performing in an emergency certain auxiliary noncombatant but paramilitary duties, such as acting as scouts or messengers, watching, fire-fighting, etc. However, after a brief period during which they were completely exempted from all military obligations, the assembly in April 1777 imposed the draft on all citizens, including Quakers, without the benefit of a conscience clause. Those who would not find substitutes were to have a distress levied upon their property.

If Friends, then, had been willing to pay the statutory fine for refusing service, their conscientious objectors would in most cases—except for certain emergency situations or brief periods when the law was temporarily made more stringent in one or another province—have suffered little beyond a certain financial inconvenience for their opposition to soldiering. But, as in the preceding years, the Society turned its face sternly against any compromise on this issue. The advice issued by Philadelphia Yearly Meeting in September 1776 was, indeed, but a restatement of an old position; its contents were echoed in the declarations of Friends throughout the continent.

It is our judgment [it laid down] that such who make religious profession with us, and do either openly or by connivance, pay any fine, penalty, or tax, in lieu of their personal services for carrying on war; or who do consent to, and allow their children, apprentices, or servants [presumably also Quakers] to act therein do thereby violate our Christian testimony, and by so doing manifest that they are not in religious fellowship with us.[33]

Mekeel[34] has calculated that a total of 469 members of the Society were dealt with during the war for either paying militia fines themselves or conniving at others paying on their behalf:[35] 3 in New York, 125 in

[33] *Rules of Discipline and Christian Advices of the Yearly Meeting of Friends for Pennsylvania and New Jersey* (1797), p. 132. A curious case is cited in Frank H. Stewart, "The Quakers of the Revolution," *Year Book. The New Jersey Society of Pennsylvania, 1907-1921*, pp. 48, 49, of a member of Haddonfield M. M. who was disowned for allowing his apprentices, some aged less than 16, to serve in the militia in his stead.

[34] Mekeel, "The Quakers," p. 301.

[35] Thorne, "North Carolina Friends and the Revolution," pp. 325, 326, cites several examples of this practice. William Townsend of Perquimans M. M., for instance, was accused of "being a partner in hiring a man to serve in a military capacity to save himself from the penalty of the law in that case." John Charles of the same meeting was dealt with for "agreeing to repay a person for paying a draughted fine."

New Jersey, 321 in Pennsylvania, 4 in Delaware, 11 in Maryland, 2 in Virginia, and 3 in the Carolinas. No cases are reported from New England, where fining did not constitute a penalty imposed on Friends. It is not possible, either here or in regard to the other statistics given by Mekeel of "dealings" for offenses against the discipline connected with the war, to say how many of those dealt with were actually disowned and what percentage showed due contrition for their infringement of the rules and were reinstated in good standing with the Society. But probably well over half the cases ended in disownment. In addition, any Quaker found hiring a substitute— a more serious offense and a practice that, in fact, was also condemned by the more conformist German peace sects that did not object to paying fines in lieu of personal service—would be peremptorily disowned, unless he agreed to cancel the arrangement.

Under 500 members (most of whom were probably adherents—if somewhat faint-hearted ones—of Quaker peace principles rather than unconscientious draft dodgers hiding under the Quaker name) defaulted by paying fines. In contrast, 1,000 names are recorded of Friends who were dealt with by their meetings for accepting military service—for acting "in the quality of a soldier," as the quaint Quaker phrase ran. Mekeel gives a total figure of 1,149 dealings on this count: 109 for New England, 59 for New York, 226 for New Jersey, 542 for Pennsylvania, 32 for Delaware, 28 for Maryland, 54 for Virginia, 67 for the Carolinas. Very few of these cases represented enlistment in the British forces: the vast majority joined the Continental army or its auxiliary provincial militias. The number of able-bodied male Quakers of military age who abandoned the peace testimony at this juncture was indeed small, and the majority of such cases date from the first year or two of war when enthusiasm for the Revolutionary cause ran high, especially among the younger men,[36] and before the Society had had time to consolidate its ranks and clarify its position on the various issues connected with the war. In Philadelphia, where the falling away was greatest, Sharpless estimates that "about one-fifth of the [eligible]

---

[36] Among the older men who joined up at this time, some had already earlier shown a proclivity to martial affairs. A good example is John Blackburn, sometime judge of York Co. (Pa.), a Quaker of Irish extraction, who was dealt with on this account during the Indian troubles of 1755, when "at a report of Indians doing mischief at a great distance [he] went out in a warlike manner to meet them contrary to our peaceable principles." Since he finally, though reluctantly, was prevailed upon to express his regret at his action, he was not disowned on this occasion. But early in 1776 his meeting received a report that Judge Blackburn had "enlisted as a soldier," and this act finally brought an end to his career as a Quaker. See Albert Cook Myers, *Immigration of the Irish Quakers into Pennsylvania, 1682-1750*, pp. 231, 232.

adult male Friends . . . joined the American army, or [took] places under the revolutionary government."[37] In the country meetings of Pennsylvania and in the other more rural yearly meetings, the percentage was certainly less. Some of those who joined up were purely nominal Quakers, whose right to the name was limited to their birthright in the Society; some were young people who were in the process of emancipation from the rather narrow social mores of eighteenth-century Quakerism—and thus it is that a disownment for a military offense is often coupled in the records with other forms of deviation such as cardplaying, dancing, frequenting places of worldly amusement, non-Quakerly apparel, or marrying out. On the other hand, many who incurred the penalty of disownment for their soldierly activities were men who had a genuine attachment to the practices and worship of the Society of Friends, except for their disagreement with the peace testimony, and for them the break with Friends was a serious and often painful process.

That in the early months of the war Philadelphia Quakers were those most easily infected with a war spirit is not surprising, since in the provincial capital, with its close political and trading connections with Britain and the other colonies, a worldly spirit had already begun several generations back to seep into the Society. Early in May 1775, James Pemberton reported to his English friend, Dr. Fothergill: "It is too sorrowful and arduous a task to describe our present situation; a military spirit prevails, the people are taken off employment, intent on instructing themselves in the art of war, and many younger members of our Society are daily joining with them, so that the distresses of this province are hastening fast." And John Adams, writing in 1775 from Philadelphia, expressed his surprise at seeing "whole companies of armed Quakers in uniform going through the manual." Even the country meetings began to feel the effects of the mounting tension in the country, and some of their people were carried away. The clerk of Philadelphia Yearly Meeting, summarizing the reports sent in by constituent meetings at the annual assembly in 1775, stated sadly:

All the accounts except that from Shrewsbury [New Jersey] lament the sorrowful deviation which has lately appeared in many members from our peaceable profession and principles in joining with the multitude in warlike exercise, and instructing themselves in the art of war which has occasioned painful labor to the faithful among us

[37] Sharpless, *A Quaker Experiment*, II, 151.

whose care has been extended to advise and admonish those who are concerned therein.[38]

In its epistle the yearly meeting, "in deep affliction and sorrow" at the failure of Friends "in this time of commotion and perils," admonished parents as well as Friends of experience and years to be more diligent in guarding the youth of the Society against the spirit of the world that had crept into it.[39]

However, within a comparatively short time the work of the local meetings in purging their ranks of "all backsliders and transgressors, who after being treated with in the spirit of meekness, cannot be reclaimed," had been completed. No one was spared because of previous distinction within the counsels of the Society or outside it. Among the earliest cases of disownment was that of the prominent Philadelphia merchant (and later general in the Continental army), Thomas Mifflin (1744-1800), whose home meeting, Philadelphia Monthly Meeting, first called him to account in March 1775. Owen Biddle was another prominent and respected Philadelphia Friend whose support of the war led to speedy disownment. He later returned to the Society ("the instance of O. Biddle shows that miracles are not ceased," commented James Pemberton with a touch of irony),[40] as did a few others similarly disowned, including the brothers Peter and Mordecai Yarnall, young men who were afterward to be active as Friends' ministers. But the greater number were lost to the Society for good.

The Society on the whole, however, emerged strengthened from the rather painful process of eliminating its nonpacifists. Philadelphia Yearly Meeting in 1776 noted the presence among its members of still "a large number of hopeful youth, [who] appear united with us in a living concern for the cause and testimony of truth, and the keeping to the good order of that excellent discipline which our ancestors were enabled to establish, and which as it is rightly administered, we have found to be as a hedge about us."[41] The only trouble was that the hedge

[38] Ibid., pp. 120, 121, 128, 129; Margaret E. Hirst, The Quakers in Peace and War, p. 400.
[39] Philadelphia Y. M. MS Minutes for 1749-1779, p. 335. For all the shortcomings of the Philadelphia Quaker merchant class, there seems little justification in the assertion by A. T. Gary [Pannell] ("The Political and Economic Relations of English and American Quakers [1750-1785]," D.Phil. thesis, Oxford [1935], pp. 371ff.) that, in addition to the Society's traditional pacifism, the economic interests of wealthy Philadelphia Quakerdom gave an added stringency to the dealings with those participating in the war against Britain.
[40] Sharpless, A Quaker Experiment, II, 209.
[41] Ibid., II, 139, 140.

might eventually become transformed into a prison wall. But most of those who had not been ejected from the Quaker plantation in the early period of the war were probably content to accept the Society's restrictive discipline as not merely a necessary cohesive force but as an essential part of Christian living.

Throughout the war, however, members continued to be cut off as a consequence of minor deviations from the peace testimony, although in many cases either unwillingness to suffer the penalties of disobedience to the new authorities or a lukewarm faith, rather than outright disagreement with Quaker pacifism, was responsible; and, as new members of the Quaker community grew to maturity each year, there were always some who saw their duty in service to their country in arms rather than in following the faith of their forefathers. For instance, to a young relative who was reported to have been attending militia musters, the distinguished Virginia Quaker, Robert Pleasants, wrote a letter of admonition in which he expressed the hope that the young man could be got to view his conduct as mistaken. Otherwise, he went on,

> Thou can't reasonably expect any other than to be excluded from a right of membership in a Society to whose discipline thou don't choose to conform. I wish, however, thou wouldst solidly consider the matter, and if thou canst not justify war from the doctrines and example of our Saviour, His apostles and the primitive Christians, would it not be a dangerous innovation, to set up thy own judgment in opposition to the highest authorities? Wherein, should thou be mistaken after having been favored with a different education, the greater will be thy condemnation.[42]

It is instructive to observe the author of this rather smug epistle appealing to "authorities" rather than inner personal conviction in his effort to recover the young brother for the Society.

As dangerous an innovation in the eyes of loyal Friends as compliance with the militia laws was submission to another demand of the Revolutionary authorities. By 1777 the legislatures of Pennsylvania, New Jersey, North Carolina, and most other states had imposed effective legislation requiring the taking of a test oath or affirmation, which included the renunciation of allegiance to the king and a statement of loyalty to the Continental cause. Severe penalties were attached for refusal, including fines (with distraint or imprisonment for nonpayment) and the loss of many civil rights. In Pennsylvania, where

[42] Adair P. Archer, "The Quaker's Attitude towards the Revolution," *William and Mary College Quarterly*, 2nd ser., I, no. 3 (July 1921), 181.

all schoolmasters were required to take the "test," many Quaker teachers preferred to sacrifice their means of livelihood rather than compromise on this issue. Refusal also entailed serious difficulty in traveling, which was so important an element in maintaining the close intercolonial relations of the Society of Friends, since the failure of a Friend to produce a certificate affirming that he had taken the test might lead the authorities to turn him back at the state or even the county boundary. Friends remained adamant in their refusal to take the test and systematically disowned all those who, for whatever reason, broke the discipline on this point. In 1783, for instance, a minute of Evesham Monthly Meeting in New Jersey recording the disownment of one of its members for this offense mentions that the man did so for "slavish fear of suffering imprisonment."[43] Mekeel gives a total figure of 353 dealings with members for having taken the test: 222 were from Pennsylvania and 49 from New Jersey, the two areas of greatest Quaker concentration. Both these states enforced the test with considerable strictness.

Two factors led Friends to refuse to cooperate with the authorities on this issue. In the first place, they were unwilling to give open recognition in this manner to the change in regime, for, as a minute of Philadelphia Yearly Meeting of 1778 expressed it, "we cannot be instrumental in setting up or pulling down any government."[44] This attitude was in line with all their political declarations since the outbreak of hostilities, and the authorities in Pennsylvania completely failed while the war was in progress to get their Quakers to come out with a clear-cut statement acknowledging president, executive council, and general assembly as the legal government of the state.[45] But there was a second source of Quaker objection to the test that was intimately linked with their whole peace testimony. If Friends were to take the test, it seemed to them that, quite apart from any question of disputed allegiance, they would thereby be giving tacit assent to the arbitrament of war. "We conceive," to quote this time from a statement by North Carolina Yearly Meeting, "that the proposed affirmation approves of the present measures, which are carried on and supported by military force." Later in the same document they optimistically expressed the hope that the administration would "consider our principles a much stronger security to any state than any test that can be required of us; as we . . . for conscience sake are submissive to the laws,

---

[43] Lois V. Given, "Burlington County Friends in the American Revolution," *Proceedings of the New Jersey Historical Society*, vol. 69, no. 3 (July 1951), p. 203.

[44] Ezra Michener (ed.), *A Retrospect of Early Quakerism*, p. 287.

[45] Sharpless, *A Quaker Experiment*, II, 197-200.

in whatsoever they may justly require." But, after the conclusion of peace when the issue was clearly settled in favor of independence and the taint of military means likewise disappeared, the Quaker objections were removed. And so we find North Carolina Friends, for instance, being advised: "Friends are at liberty either to take or refuse the said test according to the clear freedom of their minds."[46]

While there was unanimity among Friends concerning the test, there was more hesitation in issuing a categorical injunction in regard to two important aspects of war finance: the Continental paper currency and the payment of taxes of various kinds in a period of hostilities. Indeed, particularly in relation to the latter issue, members of the Society engaged in a long and sometimes heated controversy. Again, as in the case of the test, two basic reasons, one quasi-political and the other pacifist, lay at the source of Quaker opposition to the Continental authorities in this matter. The paper currency which Congress and state governments, acting on a timeworn principle of colonial administrations, began to issue from the outset of the struggle led inevitably to inflation and a very considerable depreciation in the value of the notes circulated. In the eyes of many Quakers, handling such currency—which, in addition, was the product of an authority whose legitimacy the Society did not acknowledge—was not financially honest, since transactions carried on with it, whether by the authorities or by private individuals, did not approximate the true values involved. Furthermore, Continental paper money was considered—not altogether unjustifiably—to be a covert means of taxation to finance the prosecution of the war.

At Philadelphia Yearly Meeting in the fall of 1775 the question was broached but no definitive conclusion reached. The scruples of those Friends who had "a religious objection" to handling paper money were to be respected. At the same time, Friends holding this position were to be tolerant of those who took a less radical view and were to refrain from censuring them.[47] Whereas Virginia Yearly Meeting, largely under the influence of the exacting Robert Pleasants, forbade its members to handle paper money, North Carolina after discussing the matter in early 1776 left it up to the conscience of every individual whether to accept the money or not. Currency objectors often met with opprobrium, and sometimes ill-treatment as well, from the populace and with the imposition of severe penalties by the

[46] Francis Charles Anscombe, *I have called you Friends*, p. 155; Thorne, "North Carolina Friends and the Revolution," pp. 330-33; Julia S. White, "The Peace Testimony of North Carolina Friends prior to 1860," *BFHA*, vol. 16, no. 2 (1927), p. 64.
[47] *A Retrospect of Early Quakerism*, p. 300.

authorities. Even the Quaker-born General Nathanael Greene (1742-1786), who had some understanding of Quaker views on war, considered such noncooperation an "effrontery" that quite naturally excited hostile sentiments among the people at large against those who practised it.[48]

One of those who objected to the use of Continental paper money was that earnest-minded Southern Quaker, Warner Mifflin (1745-1798). His decision not to handle it stemmed from an incident involving a fellow Quaker, John Cowgill, a farmer from Kent County (Del.), which he had read about in a newspaper. Cowgill had been proclaimed for his currency objection "an enemy of his country" by the county authorities. As a result, not only were his horses, cattle, sheep, and grain requisitioned, but an economic boycott was enforced against him, and his children were barred from attending school. On one occasion Cowgill himself was seized by some American troops and carried off to Dover, the state capital, where he was paraded up and down the town on a cart with a placard affixed to his back. Later, his daughter wrote of the family's experiences at this time: "When we went to bed at night, we did not know what would be the issue before day and in that way we lived for several years." Cowgill's protest started Mifflin thinking about the right Quakerly attitude in this matter. At first, he was torn first one way and then another by conflicting arguments in his own mind. He doubted, too, his strength to stand firm against the kind of persecution Cowgill was enduring. Finally one evening, greatly perturbed, as he relates, "under this exercise and concern I walked about my plantation after night, and seemed as if I never more should be able to make the stand, I thought if they took all my substance I could give that up, but the fear for the poor body prevailed." Returning to the house, he picked up his Bible and began to read in it. Slowly there took shape within him the resolution that it was his duty to refuse to have anything to do with this money.[49]

Another sensitive spirit who finally, after considerable travail of mind, adopted a similar line of conduct was the prominent Rhode Island minister, Job Scott (1751-1793). For a long time he worried over the various arguments pro and con. If he refused the currency, he knew that he would—not unnaturally—be suspected of pro-British sympathies and would have to face misunderstanding and considerable material hardship as well. Besides, many Friends evidently did

[48] Given, "Burlington County Friends," p. 206. See also Theodore Thayer, *Pennsylvania Politics and the Growth of Democracy*, p. 173.

[49] Warner Mifflin, "Statement concerning his Refusal to use and circulate Continental Currency" (1779), Misc. MSS, F.H.L.S.C.; John A. Munroe, *Federalist Delaware 1775-1815*, pp. 48, 49.

not entertain any scruples in the matter. Who was he to run counter to the opinion of those whom he respected? "Fears and reasonings of one kind or other prevailed on me to take it [i.e., Continental currency] for a season; and then it became harder than it would probably have been at first" to decide against acceptance. However, an increasing conviction that the use of such money was equivalent to aiding and abetting the war effort and to abandoning strict Quaker neutrality led him at last to decide to refuse the use of this money altogether. This decision brought financial difficulties, since scarcely any other currency was available, but, he tells us, he enjoyed an easy conscience thereafter.[50]

Mifflin and especially Scott were strict neutralists in their political views. As an example of a Quaker currency objector whose stand was motivated perhaps more by his hostility to the change in regime than by the money's association with the waging of war, we may take the case of the weighty Philadelphia burgher, Samuel Rowland Fisher (1745-1834), who, along with his father and brother, eschewed the use of the tainted paper currency. To accept it, in their view, would be to become a party "to . . . setting up and pulling down governments and the promotion of war in the land." Fisher's feelings emerge clearly in a remark he once made to a government official: "Your government," he told him, "if it can be so called, is exactly of a piece with the paper bills issued to carry on the war, which are the greatest lies, deception and hypocrisy and for these reasons I could not acknowledge their authority." Fisher would have liked all Friends to take the same course he did and boycott the Continental money. (In 1779, indeed, Philadelphia Yearly Meeting condemned its use as a dereliction of the peace testimony, while at the same time not making it actually a disciplinary matter and still leaving it up to the individual conscience to decide whether or not to discontinue handling it.)[51] In February 1776, as a result of their outspoken stand against the money, the two Fisher brothers were "advertised as enemies" of the American cause, and their stores were temporarily closed down by the authorities.[52]

[50] *Journal of Job Scott*, pp. 47-51.

[51] At Western Q. M. for Conference in August 1779, there arose a concern among some present "that Friends might exert themselves in laboring to have their brethren convinced of the pernicious consequences of continuing to circulate the Continental currency so called, it being calculated to promote measures repugnant to the peaceable principles we profess to be led by" (*A Retrospect of Early Quakerism*, p. 382).

[52] "Journal of Samuel Rowland Fisher, of Philadelphia, 1779-1781," *PMHB*, XLI (1917), no. 2, 149, 163, 193; no. 3, 291; no. 4, 401, 402, 431. Fisher was later one of the Virginia exiles of 1777-1778 and, in July 1779, was again arrested on charges—undoubtedly false, for Fisher for all his conservative loyalism was a

Among those Friends who disagreed with the view that Quaker pacifism required abstention from the use of Continental currency was Moses Brown, perhaps the most outstanding New England Friend of that day. "His position" on this issue, writes his most recent biographer, "was determined by sympathy for the American cause and by common sense." Brown believed that, in fact, no moral distinction could be made between handling paper money and using specie, which all Friends admitted to be necessary for carrying on everyday life. As a result largely of Brown's influence, New England Friends never made an issue of the Continental currency question; their unwillingness to do so, in turn, became a factor in creating better relations between the Society and the American authorities in this area than existed in most other parts of the continent.[53]

More intricate in its various ramifications than the paper money problem, and more apt to generate heat on both sides, was the controversy evoked within wartime Quakerdom by the tax question. As we know, this was by no means a new problem: indeed, it reached back to the early days of the Society. But the war had given it renewed urgency. Now, as earlier, there were really three questions at issue, although not all Friends seem to have been quite clear as to the distinction between them. In the first place came the question of "war taxes" for some quite specific military purpose: most Friends at this time agreed that such taxes should not be paid, but, as we shall see below, a small group in New England actively and publicly advocated compliance, a stand that led to their eventual separation from the main body of the Society. The next category was that of general taxes "in the mixture," where only a part—and usually a portion that was difficult to estimate exactly—went toward financing the war: about this issue there was less unanimity, indeed considerable confusion, in the minds of many Friends. Lastly came certain taxes and rates, for the upkeep of the highway, for example, or for the maintenance of the poor, where—except for the circumstance of their being levied by an administration that was waging a war—there was obviously no association with military objectives.

Most Friends at this date, then, had a clear sense that the payment of special taxes imposed for some military purpose was not compatible with the peace testimony and that both payment and collaboration with the machinery of levying such a tax[54] constituted a contravention

---

staunch Quaker pacifist—of having sent military intelligence to the British and was kept in prison for two years.

[53] Mack Thompson, *Moses Brown*, pp. 136, 137.

[54] As an example of a Friend who refused appointment as a collector of taxes,

of the discipline. Thus we find Friends being disowned for such offenses as "assisting in laying a tax for military purposes," "paying a fine for refusing to collect taxes for military purposes," or "paying taxes for hiring men to go to war."[55] As early as August 1775 we find a minute like the following appearing in the records of a New Jersey country meeting:

> John Gill, from Haddonfield Preparative Meeting, requested the sense of Friends respecting the present demand of money by the Provincial Committee for military purposes. The judgment of Friends was fully and clearly given. That paying it was a manifest deviation from our peaceable principles, and all under our name are desired deeply to attend to this principle which so distinguishes us as a people from other professions and seek for strength to live up thereto and not balk our testimony.[56]

The conviction expressed here of the incompatibility between assent to a demand of this kind on the part of Caesar and the Quaker profession of peace was typical of Friends' meetings up and down the country during the war years.

In the case of ordinary taxes which, especially in wartime, were obviously in part intended to finance military objectives, there prevailed in many parts of the Society a strong feeling that these, too, should be refused, despite the penalties that would follow for the tax objectors. As the war proceeded, Philadelphia Yearly Meeting and Virginia Yearly Meeting in particular, where perhaps—at least in influential Quaker circles—strong pro-British sentiment helped to exacerbate the reluctance to pay money to a rebellious administration, showed a widespread incidence of refusal to pay these mixed taxes, as well as specifically war ones. In 1778 Philadelphia Yearly Meeting passed a very sympathetic resolution concerning the increasing number of Friends who had scruples about paying general taxes in wartime. Although it did not state categorically that payment was con-

---

we may take the case of 26-year-old Eli Yarnall of Chester Co. (Pa.). In a letter explaining his rejection of the office, he stated: "I dare not do it, let my sufferings in consequence thereof be never so great," for many of the taxes he would be obliged to collect would be allocated for war purposes. As he expected, fine and distraint followed his action. See *Biographical Sketches and Anecdotes of Members of the Religious Society of Friends*, pp. 326-28.

[55] Cited in Sharpless, *A Quaker Experiment*, II, 134, 135, from the records of two monthly meetings within the city of Philadelphia.

[56] Stewart, "The Quakers of the Revolution," p. 42. On p. 44 Stewart cites the similar case of Woodbury Preparative Meeting, whose members in mid-1776 refused to pay a powder-tax imposed by the provincial convention and had their goods distrained as a result.

trary to Quaker principles, it did say that those Friends who felt "uneasiness to themselves" in paying should have the united support of the Society in their stand.[57] We hear of Pennsylvania Quakers spending periods of up to two years in prison for nonpayment of taxes.[58]

Philadelphia Monthly Meeting was later to claim, in reply to the assertions of the pro-war group of Free Quakers (see below), that "we know not of any of our members being disowned, for the payment of taxes, for the support of government, nor is there any rule of our discipline that requires it."[59] The latter part of the statement is undoubtedly correct, but it would seem that, if not in Philadelphia itself, at least in some of the rural meetings of Pennsylvania disciplinary action was taken against Friends who paid "mixed" taxes. The exact character of the various taxes referred to in meeting records is not always clear. But—to cite one case—the offense of the "ancient Friend" of London Grove Preparatory Meeting, Nathaniel Scarlet, who in 1779 was "dealt with" by New Garden Monthly Meeting for having "through weakness . . . paid a tax tending to the encouragement of war and commotion,"[60] surely concerned a "mixed" tax rather than a purely military one. The old man escaped disownment in this instance by expressing regret for his action, an acknowledgment of error that was accepted by the meeting. Or take the case of Kennett Monthly Meeting where we find this entry recorded for 15 January 1780:

The Friends appointed to extend labour in order to strengthen their brethren against the payment of taxes report, that they have visited some members, to some degree of satisfaction, in some places; but as the service is not fully gone through, they are continued, and desired to attend thereto, and report to next meeting.[61]

In North Carolina legislation passed in 1778 requiring Friends on account of their refusal to take the oath of allegiance to pay three times the ordinary tax, combined with the knowledge that the money thus raised would be largely allocated to the prosecution of the war, led to a lively discussion of the issue within the Quaker community. Some Friends urged a united refusal to pay a mixed tax of this kind,

[57] *Rules of Discipline* (1797), pp. 132, 133.
[58] Mekeel, "The Quakers," p. 151.
[59] Quoted in Charles Wetherill, *History of the Religious Society of Friends called by some the Free Quakers*, p. 67, from "An Address and Memorial on Behalf of the People called Quakers" presented in February 1782 to the general assembly of Pennsylvania.
[60] Gilbert Cope, "Chester County Quakers during the Revolution," *Bulletins of the Chester County Historical Society 1902-3*, p. 24.
[61] Kennett Monthly Meeting Sufferings 1757-1791 (MS in F.H.L.S.C.), p. 29.

arguing that a divided witness now would "tend to weaken and discourage those who [conceived] it to be their duty to suffer the loss of life, liberty and property, rather than violate the testimony of a good conscience." In October 1778 in its epistle the yearly meeting advised members to have "a close and solid consideration whether the payment of taxes under the present commotions" was in fact consistent "with our peaceable principles." But it did not impose any clear ban on payment. The upshot was that Quakers in the western regions usually paid their taxes, while those in the eastern part of the state more often refused compliance and in most cases suffered distraint of property by the authorities.[62]

In other areas the story is much the same. In Delaware many Quakers refused to pay the ordinary taxes to the state because of the association of these taxes with the prosecution of the war. Among members of Baltimore Yearly Meeting, which covered Maryland and some adjacent districts, feeling also ran strong against compliance. The annual gathering in 1781 reported: "Most Friends appear to be careful in maintaining our testimony against war by refusing the payment of taxes."[63]

Another part of the country where the problem of tax payment in wartime was keenly debated was New England. There the small group that advocated the payment of all taxes, including specifically military ones, was, as we shall see, ejected from the Society without causing too much dissension. In regard to mixed taxes there was a genuine division of opinion, and the matter cropped up repeatedly at successive yearly meetings. The powerful influence of Moses Brown was exerted in the direction of granting tolerance to differing viewpoints: in Brown's view, an explicit ruling on the part of the highest authority among New England Friends against paying the ordinary taxes—taxes "in the mixture," to use the Quaker term for them—would only have excited additional hostility against the Society on the part of the Continental authorities and might as well engender a still more serious split in the Quaker ranks.[64] Some weighty New England Friends like Job Scott opposed him, hoping that Friends would issue a clear condemnation where any considerable amount of money was destined for use in war. But New England Yearly Meeting continued to urge tolerance of both these points of view, while explicitly requiring noncompliance in the case of "all taxes, expressly or specially for the support of war, whether called for in money, provisions or otherwise."

[62] Mekeel, "The Quakers," pp. 233-35.
[63] Kenneth S.P. Morse, *Baltimore Yearly Meeting 1672-1830*, p. 22.
[64] Thompson, *Moses Brown*, pp. 139, 141, 143-45.

"Such Friends as do actively pay such taxes," it laid down, should "be dealt with as disorderly walkers." And the scruples of the more radical members must be given all respect. "We also desire," the yearly gathering of 1781 told members, "that all Friends carefully avoid discouraging a tender scruple which may arise in the minds of our brethren respecting the payment of such taxes, a part whereof is evidently for the support of war." The hardships they might encounter for taking such a stand were to be reckoned as sufferings on account of Friends' principles. And so the same yearly meeting goes on to record:

> The testimony of many Friends in the nonpayment of taxes, part whereof goes for the support of war, coming under consideration of this meeting,—It is our sense and judgment that the several monthly meetings collect accounts of the sufferings of our brethren on account of said testimony, and send them up to the Meeting for Sufferings, there to be recorded after due inspection in Friends' Book of Sufferings as our brethren's testimony for the truth against the appropriation of any part thereof to the purposes of war and it is recommended to Friends, that labouring to be preserved unbiased herein, as to the powers which are or may be, they keep an eye single to the testimony of truth against war and fighting.[65]

At the same time, however, the validity of the position of the moderates within the Society, who felt no compunction in rendering government what they believed to be its normal due in the way of tribute, was safeguarded.

Moses Brown himself felt that, in the existing circumstances, he could not pay mixed taxes since such a large proportion was allocated to war. But at the same time he disagreed with the chief reason on which many of the tax objectors based their refusal. In a letter dated 2 October 1780 to his Pennsylvania friend, Anthony Benezet, he explained his point of view. "We fear," he wrote, "some take up the testimony [i.e., of nonpayment], more on account of the authority that demands the taxes than because they are used for war. Such we fear instead of forwarding will eventually retard the testimony." He stressed that of equal importance to their peace testimony was Friends' "testimony of supporting civil government by readily contrib-

[65] New England Y. M. MS Discipline, H.C.Q.C. (*BX 7617 N5C5 1781), p. 432; *The Book of Discipline, Agreed on by the Yearly-Meeting of Friends for New-England* (1785), pp. 148, 149. These debates and resolutions of 1781 seem to be the ones referred to in Job Scott's *Journal*, p. 63, but there they are mentioned as having taken place in 1779.

uting thereto," a fact the Quakers opposed to the Revolutionary regime had lost sight of. "I understand," he told Benezet, "that some Friends have fallen in with or been overpowered by the common argument that civil government is upheld by the sword, and therefore they decline paying to its support, which appears to me a great weakness, for I see a material distinction between civil government and military or a state of war and on this distinction our ancient testimonies were and remain to be supportable of paying tribute and custom for the support of the civil and yet to refuse paying trophy money and other expenses solely for war. Civil government is the restoring and supporting power." Brown did look forward, however, to a time when, peace having returned and the proportion of tax money devoted to military purposes being thus substantially reduced, Friends would be able to work out in cooperation with the government "a separation" between the amount that they were prepared in good conscience to contribute and the sum destined for war that, for all their approval of the civil power, they felt obliged to withhold. If such a separation were not permitted, then Friends should consider refusal to pay the whole tax, even where only a small part went toward war.[66]

A third tax problem, alongside direct war taxes which Friends were required to refuse to pay and taxes in the mixture toward which a considerable number of Friends adopted an attitude of noncooperation, concerned unquestionably nonmilitary taxes. Here no definite ruling was ever adopted by any of the yearly meetings. Most Friends saw nothing wrong in paying these taxes in wartime, even to a *de facto* authority in rebellion against the established government. But a small minority objected. We hear, for instance, of New England Friends taking this stand[67] and of some Quakers in Pennsylvania refusing to pay even the poor rate and the rate for the upkeep of the roads on the grounds that payment would constitute acknowledgment of an authority set up by violent revolution.[68] But, though generally recognized as a possible alternative for a concerned Friend to take, this form of protest was clearly a minority position.

"The consistency of paying tax for war," Benezet wrote to Virginia's most outstanding Quaker of the period, Robert Pleasants, in March 1781, "is becoming so interesting a subject to the Society" that he was sure his correspondent would be glad to hear the results of the most

[66] Brookes, *Friend Anthony Benezet*, pp. 431, 432.
[67] *Ibid.*, p. 432. Brown informed Benezet: "Some Friends [i.e., in New England] refuse all taxes even those for civil uses as well as those clear for war and others that are mixed."
[68] Mekeel, "The Quakers," p. 141.

recent consideration of the matter among Philadelphia Friends.[69] Pleasants himself had long been deeply concerned with the taxation issue and in 1779 had been largely instrumental in getting Virginia Yearly Meeting to take an antitax position. In December of that year he had stated his position in a letter to a friend. "It appears clear to my judgment that Friends can no more pay than take the test, for they are both calculated to promote the same ends and make us parties to the destruction, the violence and confusion consequent to such intestine commotion; and would it not be repugnant to reason to contribute by taxes to the support of either party who may happen to prevail, whom we could not, under the present unsettled state of affairs, be free to acknowledge."[70]

The tax issue had indeed occupied the thoughts and prayers of many of the most concerned members of the Society right from the early days of the war, and it became an increasing preoccupation with many as the war proceeded and the demands for money grew larger and more insistent. All the yearly meetings grappled with the problem at one time or another. We find the antitax party in New England Yearly Meeting in 1780 drawing up a lengthy "Apology," "running to over 60 quarto pages," elaborating their point of view, which they hoped to persuade their Meeting for Sufferings to publish. In the summer of the same year a prominent New Jersey Friend, Samuel Allinson, a lawyer by training and sometime surveyor general of his province, sat down and put his "Reasons against War, and paying Taxes for its Support" onto paper. The 24 pages of his manuscript exercise book, which contain his essay,[71] give perhaps the most trenchant statement of Quaker objections to paying mixed taxes in wartime. "The thoughts on paying taxes of Samuel Allinson," wrote Moses Brown after a copy had been sent for the perusal of New England Friends, "is well thought of even by those who yet pay them."[72] The essay is indeed well argued and shows a logical and well-trained mind at work, which, despite a certain legalistic cast, was free of excessive reliance on either scripture or the Quaker discipline. For this reason, and because of the important role tax objection played in the thought and practice of Friends during the Revolutionary War, the little work deserves some attention at this point.

Allinson's main argument was that the payment of all taxes which in any way contributed to the prosecution of war must be rejected by

[69] Brookes, *Benezet*, p. 353.
[70] Archer, "The Quaker's Attitude towards the Revolution," p. 170.
[71] Now in the H.C.Q.C.
[72] Brookes, *Benezet*, p. 435. Letters to Benezet, 24 Dec. 1780.

Friends on two counts, one general and one particular. In the first place, if Quakers felt that conscience forbade them to fight, then the same conscience should not lead them to contribute money willingly to assist others to do what they scrupled themselves to do. Secondly, in the present conflict taxes imposed by the Continental authorities differed in kind from those imposed by the government in past wars, for in levying them the regime was pursuing an objective that Friends must disapprove, namely, the overthrow of the king's authority and its replacement by one that was new. Moreover, Allinson pleaded, the destructiveness of war in their own land should now serve to bring home effectively to Friends its thoroughly evil nature. "Can we look at the dismal consequences of war," he asked, "and immediately reflect that we give our voluntary aid to it any way and be easy under it? or think we are consistent throughout?"

After stating his premises, Allinson went on to discuss in turn a number of objections that might be lodged against his position. Did not St. Paul, for instance, enjoin his fellow Christians to pay tribute to the authorities without mentioning any possible use that Caesar might make of the money? The Roman Empire was then at peace and the question of specifically war taxes was not involved, Allinson answered—not altogether convincingly. But anyhow, he went on, implicitly challenging—so it would seem—the right of St. Paul to speak authoritatively on all questions for later generations: "If tribute is demanded for a use that is antichristian it seems right for every Christian to deny it, for Caesar can have no title to that which opposes the Lord's command." Again, it was often argued, both within the Society and outside it, that Friends in the past had normally paid their taxes as a religious obligation without enquiring too closely about their later use. Although this assertion was true, Allinson admitted, yet might not the same be argued of the buying and owning of slaves, now generally admitted to be inconsistent with Quaker principles? Knowledge of good and evil is in some ways a progressive revelation. "This therefore seems to be the criterion; whenever an act strikes the mind with a religious fear that the voluntary performance of it will not be holding up the light of the Gospel of Peace, or be a *stumbling block* to others, it ought carefully to be avoided." A third argument frequently urged against the tax objectors was that payment represents the fulfillment of a debt that we owe our government in exchange for the services that it has rendered us, that, in fact, it is as obligatory on our conscience as the completion of a contract once entered into. In his answer Allinson, showing here his lawyer's deftness in making subtle distinctions, differentiated between a debt where the service for which payment

174

was being made was in the past and the creditor was in no way obliged to render account of how he might spend the money repaid and a tax to be expended on future service to the state, where "he who gives has a right to *call to such an account* and therefore seems himself liable for and privy to the application." The citizen in a free polity, Allinson was arguing, has a responsibility for the actions of his government. If he does not approve morally of the purposes to which he knows his money will be put, he is under an obligation to withhold voluntary payment.

Considerations of this kind led Allinson on to a discussion of the vital and closely related problem of civil government. How did Quaker pacifism fit in with Friends' nice sense of obligation toward the powers that be (a dutifulness, we may add, that had led many to observe the strictest neutrality, if not to show considerable hostility toward the new American regime)? Since the first loyalty of man is to God, Allinson pointed out, a general approval of the institution of civil government "can never mean a compliance with every requisition." He went on:

We pay our proportion to the support of the poor, the maintenance of roads and the support of civil order in government (if the demand is unmixed with war or tithes), these include every benefit we ask or receive. We desire not war or any of its consequences, nor do we apprehend any benefit arising from it.

He agreed that "the sword of municipal justice" can rightly, indeed on some occasions must, be used "against an internal malefactor." But this action is not the same as war, for "municipal justice is conducted by known rules agreed upon in stillness and quiet, and may be done without injury to any one." On the other hand, war represents the victory of lawless force, destroys innocent and guilty alike, and can usually be avoided by the application in good time of appropriate measures to remove its causes. "Civil justice is an innocent dispassionate remedy; this cannot be said of war."

In one passage Allinson made a sly allusion to the possible connection between the wealth and respectability that many Friends had acquired, "which sometimes seems to need the arm of power to secure," and their reluctance to take a firm stand on this question of war taxes. Yet at the same time, like Moses Brown and many of the wiser spirits of the Society, he refrained from calling for uniformity, for making the tax question a disciplinary matter, and instead urged tolerance of differing but sincerely held views among Friends. In both his rejection of precedent as obligatory on later generations of Friends and in his concept of a slow growth in awareness of truth, Allinson succeeded in instilling a certain freshness in what was in danger of becoming a rather sterile argument.

It was not in Allinson's yearly meeting, however, but among New England Friends that the tax issue had become a direct cause of schism within the Society. Late in 1775, at the very outset of the war, a prominent member of Sandwich (Mass.) Monthly Meeting, Timothy Davis, had composed a short tract strongly urging Friends to comply with all tax demands made on them by the new provincial authorities. Failing to secure the sanction of New England Meeting for Sufferings, which was then required for all publications bearing on any of the Quaker testimonies, he had gone ahead and brought the essay out on his own early the following year under the title *A Letter from a a Friend to Some of His Intimate Friends, on the Subject of paying Taxes &c.* Although the work was published anonymously, all Friends of course knew who the author was. The Meeting for Sufferings attempted to prevent the circulation of the pamphlet, fearing that it would "have a tendency to suppress tender and religious scruples, in the minds of those who are or may be exercised respecting the payment of taxes, for the purpose of war"; and it therefore started disciplinary action against both Davis and his printer, who was also a Quaker, the ostensible offense committed by the two being, of course, the publication of the tract without official permission and not the nature of its contents.[73] Meeting for Sufferings' fears were by no means groundless, for in fact New England Quakers were deeply divided on this question of paying taxes. Although it contained a number of tax radicals like Job Scott, the yearly meeting also included, to use Moses Brown's words, "a number of concerned Friends and leading members"[74] who took the opposite view. Public discussion of the issue would only lead, it was feared, to internal dissension before any general consensus among Friends had been reached.

Davis in his tract had not abandoned his Society's pacifism. This fact he was careful to point out early in his argument. "The peaceable profession," he writes, "which we have long made to the world (which constitutes a very amiable part of our religious character) will not ad-

[73] Mekeel, "Free Quaker Movement in New England during the American Revolution," *BFHA*, vol. 27, no. 2 (1938), p. 76.

[74] Quoted in Brookes, *Benezet*, p. 431. After Davis's disownment, Brown, who was making great efforts to reclaim him for the Society, reported that Davis had admitted that recently he had received a tax demand that he felt unable to pay. Brown contrasted this with the position of some Friends still within the Society, "even some who had been on appointment to treat with Timothy," "who had paid all." (They escaped disciplinary action, of course, because they had not made a public issue of it as Davis had done.)

mit of our taking up arms." On this point he differed from the dissident group in Philadelphia (discussed later in this chapter) which was
to crystallize into the Free Quaker movement. But both were at one
in their positive attitude toward the new Revolutionary regime, and
it was largely this stance that brought down on the heads of both
groups the wrath of many weighty members of the Society.

Davis could see no reason why Quakers should not be taxed along
with their fellow citizens. While expressing his desire for a reconciliation between Great Britain and the colonies, he felt that Friends had
no cause to withhold payment either because the government in
control of their country had been set up as a result of revolution or
because the money paid would be used for war purposes. Had not
Friends in Cromwell's time paid taxes to the Commonwealth, which
was the outcome of a successful rebellion against a lawful monarch?
Or had a later generation of Quakers demurred from paying them to
the governments which succeeded the Glorious Revolution of 1688?
Indeed, almost any government was preferable to a condition of
anarchy. Christ urged his fellow countrymen to pay to Caesar, even
though they were in a state of subjection to Rome. Tax payment did
not signify an overall approval of every aspect of government: it did
not mean in the case of Friends that they were giving their blessing to
either violent revolution or military defense. It simply showed that
they appreciated that magistracy was an institution sanctioned by God.
Besides, had not Friends regularly paid taxes in wartime as in periods of
peace? "By all that I have been able to discover," he concluded,
"our Society in England have ever made a point of being careful and
exact in paying all taxes that are legally assessed, except the priest's
rate." He quoted from that old Quaker stalwart of two continents,
Thomas Story, to show that his own position had the sanction of the
apostolic age of their Society. Although Davis, like many contemporary Quakers, did not clearly distinguish between direct war taxes
and those "in the mixture" (his argument is directed toward showing
that the necessity of government makes the question of the use to
which taxes, once paid, are put irrelevant), he at least implicitly sanctioned the direct war tax along with the mixed ones. However, whatever had been the position of early Friends (and the surreptitious practice of some more recent ones), this was a viewpoint that was generally
rejected by American Quakers in Davis's day.

The machinery for dealing with Davis's case moved slowly, partly
because of the fact that he enjoyed a considerable following among
the members of his own monthly meeting, with which prime responsibility rested in handling the matter. The case was shuttled back and

forth from monthly meeting to yearly meeting until, finally, sentence of disownment was passed on Davis at the end of 1778. The delay may probably be attributed also to the hopes of reclaiming the erring minister that Moses Brown and other leading New England Friends who were not unsympathetic to Davis's point of view entertained, as well as to fears that, if Davis were ejected too precipitately, he might carry with him a considerable number of sympathizers. Delay was urged, too, by the tactful Anthony Benezet in Philadelphia.

In fact, the split when it came was on a small scale. Twenty-nine members of Sandwich Monthly Meeting followed Davis out in 1779, along with a dozen or so members from the neighboring monthly meeting at Dartmouth, where in 1781 the dissidents proceeded to set up their own separatist meeting. The usual disputes over meeting property ensued. The group enjoyed fairly close contacts with the more radically nonpacifist Free Quakers of Philadelphia. Even more quickly than the latter, however, the New England "Free Quakers" began to disintegrate.[75] In the mid-nineties Davis himself applied to be readmitted to the Society and was duly reinstated in membership after making acknowledgment of error.[76] After their leader had abandoned them, the tiny group disappeared altogether early in the next century.

As a pendant to the controversy that had at one time seemed to threaten to cause a severe breach in the Quaker ranks and in fact had made scarcely any impact on the Society, there was published in 1784, after the war had ended, a longish pamphlet by one Joseph Taber (1731-ca.1796) with the title *An Address to the People called Quakers*, in which the author set out to give a detailed defense of the views and conduct of his leader, Davis. Whereas Davis's original treatise had numbered a mere 8 pages, Taber's tract ran to 67. Taber had been angered by the Society's treatment of Davis, by what he considered their "impatience of dissent," behavior so inconsistent with the spirit of the "Christian liberty" that they professed.

Two points are worth bringing out in connection with Taber's pamphlet, which otherwise contains little that is of any special significance.[77] In the first place, in spite of their relations with the militant Philadelphia Free Quakers, Taber and, presumably, the group in whose name the pamphlet was issued (although the authorship is almost certainly Taber's) still adhered, as Davis had at the beginning, to the Quaker position on peace. The Society of Friends, stated Taber, has rightly been "called from the use of the sword . . . to hold the olive

[75] Mekeel, "Free Quaker Movement in New England," pp. 77-82.
[76] *Memoir of Henry Hull*, pp. 68, 69.
[77] See esp. pp. 22, 23, 30, 38-42, 44.

branch to the nations until it shall please infinite wisdom to call the rest of mankind in like manner from the use of the sword." Their role, however, he conceived as a strictly vocational pacifism; the sword-bearing magistracy was absolutely essential for the well-being of society in its present state, and it was imperative that Friends willingly support the magistracy by their taxes. Mankind in general, even Christians, would only be ready to adopt Quakerly peaceableness slowly, would have to grow gradually up to it; most men were not yet far enough advanced for this way of life. Secondly, while stating that his group opposed the antitax position, not because it was new, but because it appeared to them incorrect, Taber obviously felt that his strongest weapon against his opponents lay in his ability to marshal a whole array of proof texts in favor of tax payment, whatever the warlike implications. And indeed, with such authorities as George Fox, Isaac Penington, and London Yearly Meeting as late as 1756, it must be admitted that at this level at least Taber had the best of the argument, and it is clear that his claim that Davis's tract contained nothing "inconsistent with the ancient and approved practice of the Society, from their first appearance as such until very lately" was fully justified. The contention that Allinson had urged a few years earlier, that revelation even among Friends is progressive, was not a proposition that would have found assent among a number of Taber's and Davis's orthodox Quaker opponents. Equally, Taber's assertion that Timothy Davis was no more pro-American than a number of his opponents had been pro-British was also hard to deny. But, as we have seen, the root cause of disownment lay as much in the publicity which Davis chose to give his views and the decisiveness with which he endowed his pro-Continental sympathies as in his alleged failure in interpreting early Quaker practice in regard to tax payment.

The war had, in fact, ended by the time Taber wrote his apology for his group's defection, but the problem of war taxes continued to occupy the Quaker conscience for the rest of the decade (see Chapter 5). The peace treaty had legitimized the regime of independence in the eyes of even the strictest Friend, and tax money was no longer destined for the prosecution of war. But were Friends to begin to pay up with an easy conscience when some taxes were designed specifically to help sink the considerable debt accumulated during the war? Some Quakers who had previously withheld payment of the more obviously military taxes now complied, arguing that payment was permissible now that peace had come. But the yearly meetings came out strongly against payment: Baltimore, Philadelphia, and New England meetings equated this kind of demand with a direct war tax and required their subordinate meetings to disown members who persisted in paying. New York Yearly Meeting, however, while also recommending noncompliance, did not call for disownment.[78]

The tax issue was one of the hardest problems that faced the Quakers during the war, for, unlike direct military service and its alternatives or the "Test," it was extremely difficult for them to know where to draw the line between the legitimate demands of the civil power and the rights of religious conscience. Here the sensitive Quaker conscience, which has so often been a cause of irritation to the Society's less sympathetic critics, had plenty of scope to expand. The aim of the tax objectors was to avoid the taint of hypocrisy that would seem to be implied by their contributing money to the war effort. Yet the actual result of their objection, where the objecting Friend owned any property, was in most cases a larger contribution by way of excessive distraint of goods, although, of course, this was extracted without the Friend's willing participation.

This same delicacy of conscience was exercised in a wide variety of other ways in connection with the wartime activities of Friends, usually without the agonizing dilemmas presented in the case of war taxes. A whole array of actions came up before the Society at one time or another and were duly disapproved, often on the basis of past decisions or administrative practice, with disownment following if the delinquent member refused to express contrition for his un-Quakerly conduct (except a few instances where a recommendation of disapproval of a milder sort replaced the more frequent categorical prohibition of some action). These quasi-military activities, which will now be discussed, may be divided into three broad (and overlapping) classes: actions which, although technically noncombatant, involved direct assistance to the military; business and trade activities that implied indirect support of war; and nonmilitary conduct that seemed to imply giving approval to war.

Direct assistance to the military, whether American or British, was always a disownable offense, although, owing to the congregational nature of the Society of Friends and the responsibility delegated with-

---

[78] Mekeel, "The Quakers," pp. 278-80. Baltimore Y. M. (Meeting for Sufferings) in 1784 resolved as follows: "We are unanimously of the judgment that notwithstanding the offering of human blood appears to be stayed Friends cannot be clear in paying taxes for sinking the debt incurred by the late war, and that Friends ought to be very careful how they act in all such cases as may have a tendency to lay waste our peaceable testimony, and especially those who have heretofore suffered the spoil of their goods rather than contribute towards the support of war, and that they give no occasion for the truth to be evilly spoken of" (quoted in Kenneth L. Carroll, "Talbot County Quakerism in the Colonial Period," *Maryland Historical Magazine*, vol. 53, no. 4 [Dec. 1958], pp. 347, 348).

in it to the local meetings to enforce the discipline, some offenders may have escaped the penalty. Mekeel has given the figure of 91 dealings with members who had assisted the armed forces. But certainly the number must have been considerably higher, the exact figure depending, of course, on the researcher's definition of assistance. Many of the cases concerned Quakers who had agreed to work for the army or to make munitions ("making weapons of war formed for the destruction of his fellowmen" was how a Philadelphia city meeting termed the latter offense).[79] We hear, for instance, of a member of Kennett Monthly Meeting (Pa.) confessing to having made "wheels for gun carriages";[80] in Maryland another Friend admitted that "two years since he did make four or five shot bags and cover [for] one cartridge box, for a neighbor, a military man." Meeting records contain many instances of action against members who had hired themselves out as workmen in camps or army. The temptation in country districts to accept temporary service as teamsters with one or other of the armies was considerable, since refusal was likely to have led to the requisitioning of horses and equipment. Friends were solemnly warned that, if the military authorities did seize these supplies, no payment that the army might afterward attempt to press on them should be accepted. We find Jeremiah Brown of Brick Meeting (Calvert, Md.) confessing in 1778:

That when my wagon and team came back, which were forcibly taken to carry military stores, [I] did receive wages for the same and was paid for one of my horses which was lost in the journey, which compliance has not been easy to my mind, being convinced that the testimony of truth is against such, I do hereby acknowledge my weakness therein, hoping and desiring for the future to give closer attention to the inward principles which preserve out of error.[81]

And where a member of the family went along with the impounded horses to see that they were properly cared for, this action, too, was a matter of concern for the meeting.[82]

[79] Sharpless, A Quaker Experiment, II, 133.
[80] A Retrospect of Early Quakerism, p. 301.
[81] Bi-Centennial of Brick Meeting-House, Calvert, Cecil County, Maryland, 1701-1901, p. 55.
[82] Cope, "Chester County Quakers during the Revolution," p. 18. See also "Bucks County Quakers and the Revolution," Pennsylvania Genealogical Magazine, XXIV, no. 4 (1966), 297: "William Richardson offered a paper condemning his misconduct in sending a person to take care of his team that was pressed, expressing his sorrow for the same." This article prints extracts from the minutes of Middletown M. M., Bucks Co. (Pa.).

In the late seventies the American army frequently requisitioned foodstuffs and blankets for their ill-fed and ill-clad troops from among the well-stocked farms around Philadelphia. Although Quakers, as we have seen, were among the first to voluntarily assist the civilian victims of war, a demand of this nature came to them not as a humanitarian request but as a military imposition. Members, therefore, were forbidden to comply, and where they yielded, led either by a genuine wish to help or by a desire for gain, the discipline was rigorously enforced. Here is what the Committee on Sufferings of New Garden Monthly Meeting had to report for January 1777 of the reactions of their members in this situation:

> When military officers were going about collecting blankets for the use of soldiers, a number of Friends not being free to contribute to the support of war, had blankets taken from them for which they could not be free to receive any pay; others for want of due consideration received money themselves, or suffered some of their children or family to receive it; and some who received pay, and others who in their absence money was left at their houses, afterwards returned or sent the money to them that sent it.[83]

In similar fashion, Friends in New York City, then under British control, politely refused Governor Tryon's request made in 1777 to furnish money for the purchase of stockings for the army, explaining "that the proposed contribution is manifestly contrary to our religious testimony against war and fightings."[84] Later they were to refuse the rent, which the British authorities repeatedly attempted to make them accept, for the use of Quaker meetinghouses in the area that had been requisitioned for army use. In one instance, where the city meeting

---

[83] New Garden M. M. Committee on Sufferings, Minutes, p. 2. In the neighboring Kennett meeting we find the following rather complicated acknowledgment of error being accepted from a member in mid-1779: "To Kennet Monthly Meeting. Friends, I am free to acknowledge that when two armed men came to my house and demanded a blanket of me, that I ordered one to be handed to them, which they left pay for and I made use of it, but have had just cause to reflect on my misconduct therein; and some time afterwards complied to go with my team to draw fifty bushels of wheat to the mill, which they demanded of me; also consented for another person to take an order that was given for a horse that was pressed from me to answer a demand of substitute fine they had against him; altho' I forbad that any part of said order should go towards paying the demand they had against me, which he informed them, nevertheless when they received the order took it for satisfaction for both demands: which misconduct I have often to reflect on and acknowledge under others to my shame; with desires that I may be preserved from giving way when trials come. James Bennett" (quoted by Cope, p. 21).

[84] Rufus M. Jones, The Quakers in the American Colonies, p. 260.

had accepted some money on this account, the Meeting for Sufferings insisted on its refund; the army refused to take it, but eventually it was handed into the British Exchequer in London by the mediacy of an English Friend. The receipt he received ran as follows: "Paid by the Society of the People called Quakers of New York in America, by the hands of Daniel Mildred, being the money they had received for rent of their meeting house, which had been appropriated for the use of the army, as such they could not retain it consistently with their religious testimony against war."[85]

The same scrupulous care in avoiding the least contamination with military affairs as was shown in the case of those Friends who returned the money for their requisitioned blankets emerges, too, in the conduct of a young Quaker, Joseph Townsend, whose home was situated near the site of the battle of Brandywine. It was the British troops in this instance who tried to compel his collaboration as they marched past his house. His own account of the affair has been printed by Isaac Sharpless:

> I arrived at the bars on the road [Townsend later related] where I was met by several companies of soldiers who were ordered into the field to form and prepare for the approaching engagement. The openings of the bars not being of sufficient width to admit them to pass with that expedition which the emergency of the case required, a German officer on horseback ordered the fence to be taken down, and as I was near to the spot had to be subject to his requiring as he flourished a drawn sword over my head with others who stood by. On a removal of the second rail I was forcibly struck with the impropriety of being active in assisting to take the lives of my fel-

[85] Mekeel, "The Quakers," pp. 204-7. When at the end of 1776 American forces took over Middletown meetinghouse for use as "an hospital for their sick," Friends protested vigorously that "it was not consistent with their minds nor their principles that their meetinghouse should be put to the use of the soldiery" (*Pennsylvania Genealogical Magazine*, XXIV, no. 4, 299). For a contemporary account of the efforts of New York Quakers—whose meetings were divided between the areas under American and British control, with contacts between Friends thus seriously impeded—to preserve a strict neutrality, see Mekeel (ed.), "New York Quakers in the American Revolution," *BFHA*, vol. 29, no. 1 (1940). According to one Long Island Friend, Elias Hicks (1748-1830), who later became famous as the leading figure in the Quaker separation of 1827, neutrality was possible because, Quakers being "friends to . . . all mankind, and principled against wars and fighting, the contending powers had such confidence in [them] that they let [them] pass freely on religious accounts" (quoted in Bliss Forbush, *Elias Hicks*, p. 46). For the distraints levied on Hicks by the British authorities in lieu of fines for his refusal to muster at an alarm or to contribute to the upkeep of the fortifications, see pp. 38, 44.

low beings and therefore desisted in proceeding any further in obedience to his commands.[86]

A more serious question than the removal of a fence to let the military pass (although the Roman pinch of incense had been a small matter, too, in its time) was the problem of the town watch in a period of war, which bothered several Quaker communities at one time or another during the conflict. In 1775 Friends in Lynn and Salem in Massachusetts had been troubled with the implications of their continued participation in watching in the troublous times that were then beginning. They referred the matter to the Meeting for Sufferings which New England Quakers had recently established. This body recommended complete abstention from the duty, which they held to be "inconsistent with our religious principles, being mixed with, if not wholly for military purposes, and we conceive will have a tendency to leaven you into the prevailing spirit thereof." Those who continued to serve should be dealt with and, if they did not show themselves amenable to tender persuasion, must finally be disowned, so "that the cause of truth and its followers do not suffer." It seems that the authorities (whose attitude in New England during the Revolutionary War was singularly mild if compared to that of their predecessors a hundred years earlier) accepted the Quakers' explanations and henceforward did not call upon them to do duty.[87]

The problem does not appear to have arisen again for Friends until near the end of the war. Then, in the spring of 1782, the British administration in New York demanded that Quakers—who had been exempted from military duties by a proclamation of the British commandant of the city of January 1780 on the proviso, however, that they would be expected nevertheless "to exert themselves in any cases of emergency"—should now take over complete responsibility for the city watch. In a letter to the British commandant, Friends, who in this case, too, were evidently willing to take their turn in the watch along with their fellow citizens, endeavored to explain the grounds of their present refusal of what they believed was a sincere effort on the part of the military to give recognition to their scruples against fighting. In the first place, they told the general, their compliance in the present circumstances, "when military works and labour are carried on by the rest of our fellow citizens who at other times share with us in common the business of the watch," would be equivalent to "a composition in lieu of military service," which was contrary to their

[86] Sharpless, *A Quaker Experiment*, II, 189.
[87] Mekeel, "New England Quakers and Military Service," p. 245.

principles: for at this time Quakers, as we know, rejected the acceptance of any alternative to a service they believed was essentially unchristian. The letter went on, secondly, to urge the incongruity of entrusting a public service of this kind to a group of men who not only were too few in numbers for the purpose but were by virtue of their whole attitude unsuited for the task. As they said:

> Our peaceable principles . . . render the business of a watch kept altogether by ourselves, attended with inconveniences, and perhaps so many that its end might be frustrated. Riotous and ill-disposed people would be under small restraint from persons who cannot submit even to bodily defense, and who would therefore more likely meet with injustice and abuse themselves than be able to control boisterous and unruly men.[88]

It is clear from this letter that these New York Friends had not thought through clearly the relationship of their pacifism to civil government, the kind of problem that Pennsylvania Friends had had to face during the period of their power.

Alongside activities that Friends prohibited as, in their view, giving direct assistance to the war effort must be placed the business and trade practices that, being a community very largely of merchants and farmers, they felt would compromise the purity of their testimony for peace. "We affectionately desire that Friends may be careful to avoid in engaging in any trade or business tending to promote war," Philadelphia Yearly Meeting testified in 1776, "and particularly against sharing or partaking of the spoils of war, by buying or vending prize goods of any kind."[89] This, like many of the Society's official declarations on war, was old advice; but the war situation gave it renewed relevance. Of course, all connection with privateering or its profits, all arming of Quaker-owned ships, and all participation of Quaker crews in manning armed vessels came under the ban. John Harris, a member of a North Carolina meeting near the coast, for instance, was disowned since, as the record goes, he "contrary to advice and counsel of his Friends made a cruise on board a privateer vessel of war, a practice so inconsistent with our principle and holy peaceable Christian profession that we can do no less than publicly testify against such antichristian practices." A Friend from Pasquotank Monthly Meeting journeying to the West Indies was refused a certificate by his meeting because "the vessel he intended to enter on board of is to carry guns in order to make some defense." At Perquimans one Solomon Elliott "who

---

[88] Cox, *Quakerism in the City of New York*, pp. 77, 79, 80.
[89] *Rules of Discipline* (1797), p. 132.

justified himself in consenting to his sons entering on board a privateer was disowned."[90] In the Narragansett district, another coastal area where the sea held snares for the unwary Quaker, we hear of a Friend being disowned because he bought books at an auction that had been taken from a captured ship as war booty.[91] The ultra-scrupulous Warner Mifflin finally came to a resolve to abandon for the duration the use of all imported products (except for salt in food he ate away from home, since it would scarcely have been possible to extract it), as he was later to give up using the products of slave labor. "In a time of national hostility," he wrote, "those sweets I am so fond of come . . . at a manifest risk of the lives of fellow men."[92]

On land as on sea the Quaker community watched over its members to see that, if possible, they did not either by their buying or their selling help contribute one iota to the prosecution of war—a concern that was increased by the element of personal profit frequently implicit in such transactions that served to compound the offense. In Maryland, for instance, we find Hezekiah and Elizabeth Rowles expressing their sorrow before their meeting that "they had not stood clear as they ought in selling some small matters to soldiers, and suffering some of their family to make and wash some of their clothes."[93] Or take this instruction, which Philadelphia Yearly Meeting in 1779 handed down to its subordinate meetings to carry out: "We are desirous and earnestly recommend, that Friends in every quarter be encouraged to attend to their tender scruples against contributing to the promotion of war, by grinding of grain, feeding of cattle, or selling their property for the use of the army, or other such warlike purposes."[94]

[90] Thorne, "North Carolina Friends and the Revolution," pp. 325, 326. In October 1780, Robert Pleasants wrote to a Quaker friend: "Thy son . . . tells me that he is going to sea in an armed vessel, and that he has the full consent of his father and mother for so doing. From a tender regard for his good and the reputation of his worthy parents, I was induced to query with him whether he thought, in case of an attack at sea, he would have resolution to withstand the scoffs and threats of the people on board so as not to give up the privilege of peace in which he had been favored with an education. And also whether he had been plainly explicit with the Captain. For it appears absolutely necessary, if he has an intention of preserving the unity of his friends that the Captain should not be deceived in time of action." (Quoted in Archer, "The Quaker's Attitude towards the Revolution," p. 180.)

[91] Caroline Hazard, *The Narragansett Friends' Meeting in the XVIII Century,* p. 169.

[92] *The Defence of Warner Mifflin,* pp. 19, 20. Mifflin once told his wife: "If every farthing we were possessed of, was seized for the purpose of supporting war, and I was informed it should all go, except I gave voluntarily one shilling . . . I was satisfied I should not so redeem it."

[93] *Bi-Centennial of Brick Meeting-House,* p. 56.

[94] *Rules of Discipline* (1797), pp. 133, 134.

Lastly, although the preceding account has by no means exhausted the list of activities forbidden to Friends as assisting more or less directly in the war, we must now turn briefly to certain other forms of conduct only remotely military, yet also disapproved on account of their implied sanction of the war. More than once American Quakers, like their English brethren, refused to illuminate their windows in celebration of an American victory, often having them smashed by angry crowds as a result;[95] many objected, also, to shutting up their shops on the public fast days or days of public penance proclaimed by the American authorities in connection with the war. In 1775 Philadelphia Yearly Meeting warned its members against seeming to give approval to war by attending military spectacles or watching the marching of troops. In the same year we find Providence (R.I.) Friends refusing the deputy-governor's order to produce their hunting guns for registration in connection with the impending war. All the men in the meeting signed a paper stating that to comply was against their conscience. (In reply the deputy-governor, instead of getting angry, told them that religious conscience was man's natural right—an answer that was in line with Rhode Island's tradition of toleration.)[96] Or again, to give still another instance of this type of Quaker peace witness, in the following year we find New York Friends refusing to give a bond of security to the local authorities that they would prevent their cattle from straying across into the British lines:[97] to do so, in their view, would have implied a certain degree of approval, however distant, to the prosecution of the war.

III

As a basic prerequisite to the whole Quaker wartime strategy that we have outlined, which constituted a withdrawal of collaboration in all aspects of public and private life connected in any way with either the British or American war effort,[98] the Society soon came to

[95] In extenuation of their brethren's behavior in the victory celebrations after Cornwallis's surrender at Yorktown in 1781, Philadelphia Meeting for Sufferings protested to the Pennsylvania assembly that, "as they could not fight with the fighters, neither could they triumph with the conquerors." (Their "Representation" is printed in *Pa. Archives*, 1st ser., IX, 450-54). In Virginia, on the other hand, Friends' refusal to participate in the official celebration on this occasion does not appear to have aroused serious ill-feeling among the populace (perhaps because Friends there did not live in towns, where nonconformity of this kind was more conspicuous). See Mekeel, "The Quakers," pp. 150, 151, 228.

[96] *Journal of Job Scott*, p. 47.

[97] Jones, *The Quakers*, pp. 259, 260.

[98] As a prominent Nantucket Quaker, William Rotch, expressed it during a hearing before the authorities in Boston: "Our principles are active obedience, or

posit a withdrawal starting at the top from all association with government. This was mainly a problem in Pennsylvania where, as we have seen, the Quaker retreat from politics begun in 1756 had only been partial, leaving a number of at least nominal Friends in the assembly (members of the so-called Quaker party) and a still larger proportion of members in good standing holding various lesser offices, especially at the local level. Thus the retreat was by no means a rout, and it is doubtful whether such orthodox Quakers as James Pemberton, who had accepted reelection in 1765 after the conclusion of the Seven Years War, had completely given up hopes of reasserting Quaker ascendancy in the province. Quakers were still to be found in the lesser ranks of officialdom in several other provinces; they also accepted election to the Second Continental Congress in 1774 and to some provincial conventions of that time. Indeed, the mild Benezet was driven to deplore "the violent spirit which some under our profession are apt to show, more particularly in the [Continental] congress."[99] Most of these fiery Quaker patriots, like the radical Assemblyman John Jacobs of Uwchlan Monthly Meeting (Chester County, Pa.) who "endeavoured to justify defensive war" to the committee appointed to labor with him and was finally disowned "for . . . having joined with things in the House of Assembly inconsistent with our testimony against wars and fightings,"[100] were of course weeded out as the disciplinary machinery of the Society went into action. Others, like Evan Thomas (1738-1826) of Baltimore who had participated in the first Maryland convention without feeling that his presence there conflicted with his obligations as a good Quaker, soon withdrew alto-

---

passive suffering" (*Memorandum*, p. 5)—i.e., active obedience to legitimate authority where religious conscience was not infringed and passive endurance of suffering for refusing the orders of illegitimate rulers or commands contrary to conscience.

[99] Brookes, *Benezet*, p. 322. Benezet, however, was an admirer of Quaker rule in Pennsylvania, when, as he wrote, government was "chiefly in the hands of a people principled against war." "They experienced the protecting hand of Providence, and enjoyed an uninterrupted tranquillity for more than sixty years." "The force used in the support of civil order, to regulate the weak and ill disposed" was not equivalent to war, in his view. Government was God-ordained and would always be necessary for the maintenance of order and man's happiness. Where good order was endangered, "restraint becomes necessary as mentioned in scripture." See Benezet, *The Plainness and Innocent Simplicity of the Christian Religion*, 1782 edn., pp. 14ff., 22, 23.

[100] Cope, "Chester County Quakers during the Revolution," p. 25. See Charles Francis Jenkins, "Joseph Hewes, the Quaker Signer" in *Children of Light* (ed. H. H. Brinton), pp. 211-39, for the story of a birthright Friend who was one of the signatories of the Declaration of Independence on behalf of North Carolina. However, Hewes (1730-1779), though never disowned, was by that date a purely nominal member of the Society.

gether from public life—a course of action that was not without sacrifice in the case of men like Thomas who nourished political ambitions.[101]

In the lower magistracy, where Friends had often served without clashes between their civil duty and their Quakerly conscience having been of too frequent occurrence, even before the fighting broke out many Friends had begun to doubt if they could in good conscience continue in service. In 1774, for instance, Warner Mifflin resigned as a justice of the peace, feeling that a post of this kind was too intimately bound up with both armed coercion and the slave system for a good Quaker to hold. "I revere magistracy," he wrote some years later, "confiding in the sacred text, that it is an *Ordinance of God,* and believing it a great benefit to mankind when executed under his holy and preserving fear. But in the present state of governments, I apprehend my brethren cannot be active therein consistent with our high profession . . . in the support of our principle against war, with which the various governments among men have so much affinity." Acting as exemplary citizens in every other respect, Quakers, he believed, would be permitted the enjoyment of their scruples on this point by government and community alike.[102]

The decisive moment came at the yearly meeting in Philadelphia in September 1776 when the assembled Friends declared categorically against continued participation in any kind of public office—legislative, executive, or administrative—which was even remotely connected with the prosecution of the present war. The minute ran as follows:

> As we have for some years past been frequently concerned to exhort and advise Friends to withdraw from being active in civil government, it now appearing to us that the power and authority exercised at this time over the several provinces within the compass of our Yearly Meeting are founded and supported in the spirit of wars and fightings: We find it necessary to give our sense and judgment that if any making profession with us, do accept of or continue in public offices of any kind either of profit or trust under the present commotions, and unsettled state of public affairs, such are acting therein contrary to the profession and principles we have ever maintained since we were a religious Society: And we therefore think it necessary to advise, exhort, and caution our brethren in profession against being concerned in electing any person, or being them-

---

[101] *Friends' Miscellany,* II, no. 8 (July 1832), 360-62.
[102] *The Defence of Warner Mifflin,* pp. 7, 8.

selves elected to such places and stations . . . which is . . . recommended to the several quarterly and monthly meetings, and the members of our religious Society in general, in order for the promotion of our Christian peaceable testimony, by a life and conduct conformable thereto.[103]

This statement did not, indeed, mark a reversal of the positive attitude toward government taken up by Friends on both continents since the Society's beginnings more than a century before—the belief that somehow the state could be purged of its excessively coercive features, that pacifism and magistracy were not *ipso facto* incompatible. It did not mean that American Friends (for the other yearly meetings on the continent followed Philadelphia's initiative in this question) had gone over to the Anabaptist-Mennonite position, although in the decades to come the views of some influential Friends and of a wide cross section of the rank and file of the Society became almost identical with it. It did signify, however, that—so long, at any rate, as the war was being fought—the Quakerly withdrawal from politics must be complete, and it gave notice that all who refused to accept this situation would be cut off from the Society. Mekeel has calculated that 47 members of the Society were dealt with during the war period for accepting public office, 34 of whom came from Pennsylvania and 9 from New Jersey, the two provinces where Quaker participation in public life was most widespread; the complete figures may have been considerably higher than this.

Undoubtedly, the ban on politics put a strain on the loyalty of many members who still sympathized in general with their Society's pacifism. The ban seems to have had this effect particularly on Friends in rural areas where officeholding, even in wartime, was not so obviously connected with warmaking as it was in the centers of government like Philadelphia and where, too, a more positive attitude toward the American authorities seems to have existed. In rural New York, for instance, toward the end of the war when active fighting in the area had ceased, some Quakers began to take part in town meetings, considering such participation no longer in conflict with the peace testimony. But they met with stern disapproval from the Quaker leadership: "in the present commotions of public affairs," they were told, "Friends being in any ways active in government is inconsistent with our principles." Abstention from politics had to be absolute if the testimony "against wars and fightings" was to be "maintained and supported inviolate." In Pennsylvania we hear of Quakers during the war

[103] Philadelphia Y. M. MS Minutes for 1749-1779, pp. 356, 357.

refusing to serve even in the capacity of overseers of the poor and suffering fines and distraint of goods as a result. With the conclusion of war it once again became theoretically possible for a consistent Friend to hold public office. But feeling within the Society still ran strongly against such activity; the yearly and quarterly meetings issued advices underlining the dangers lurking in this region for the unwary and seldom endowed officeholding Friends with positions of trust within the Society.[104]

Friends in the city of Philadelphia had been the mainspring of the great movement of withdrawal from political life that took place in 1775-1776. The city was the scene, too, of the establishment of a small independent group of dissident Quakers, known as the Free Quakers, who supported the armed effort of the American revolutionaries. "The differences" between them and their orthodox brethren, their historian has claimed, "were not of faith, but of practice."[105] This assertion is true—if one does not count Quaker pacifism as an element of the Society's faith. The Free Quakers claimed complete toleration for all sincerely held religious opinion as their central tenet and the main body's abandonment of what they considered a basic component of primitive Quakerism as their chief reason for separation. But, in fact, the ranks of the new Society were filled exclusively by those who had abandoned the old Society's traditional pacifism: none who held to the latter felt sufficient attraction in the new body's liberty to take the step of joining it. In addition, only a small percentage of those who were disowned within the confines of Philadelphia Yearly Meeting for support of the war adhered thereafter to the Free Quakers.[106]

The *spiritus movens* behind the creation of the new group was Samuel Wetherill, Jr. (1736-1816), a minister of the Society and a prosperous cloth manufacturer by trade. From the outset of the struggle Wetherill, like the rest who eventually became Free Quakers, was heart and soul behind the struggle against Britain and was strongly set against the neutrality, if not mild loyalism, that marked most of his fellow Philadelphia Quakers. In particular, he opposed the policy of disowning Friends who gave active support to the colonial cause by entering military service or accepting public office or giving assistance of one kind or another to it. "Disowning is wrong in any case," he wrote, "but to disown a man for defending his life, or the life of his

---

[104] Mekeel, "The Quakers," pp. 204, 286-88; James, *A People among Peoples*, p. 244.

[105] C. Wetherill, *History of the Free Quakers*, p. 22. The author was a descendant of one of the founders of the group, Samuel Wetherill, Jr.

[106] Mekeel, "The Quakers," p. 271.

friend, or the government under which he lives, are extraordinary cases . . . the criterion of fellowship is made to consist, . . . in so acting, as not one man in an hundred thousand could act, were he brought to the test." And he made plain his belief that pacifism was a perfectionism such that only very, very few, even within the Quaker ranks, could meet its requirements. He pointed out the inconsistency between Quaker support of government, albeit now only passive, and their pacifist scruples. "The government cannot exist without defence, the sword being its sinews. Government in its essence is a defensive war; a defensive war of that kind is not sinful."[107] And for Wetherill and his associates, government meant the regimes set up by the Continental authorities in the various provinces.

Wetherill's disownment did not actually take place until August 1779 when he was dealt with for, among other charges of a similar nature, having taken the test in the previous year. Among those who labored—unsuccessfully—to keep such a valued member within the Society was Anthony Benezet, whose earnest devotion to the peace testimony did not preclude a recognition of the inadvisability of coercing those members who could not genuinely accept it for themselves. But Wetherill would evidently have been satisfied with nothing less than a complete abandonment of any official stand in the matter on the part of the Society. "I have repeatedly begged he would consider," wrote Benezet with a hint of exasperation, "that however he might think hardly of England's design with respect to us, in which he however might in part be mistaken; yet we, as a people, ought not to have taken any other part but mildly and tenderly to have exhorted people to follow after peace."[108]

In the fall of 1780 the first meetings of the emergent group began to be held in the homes of Wetherill himself and of Timothy Matlack (ca. 1735-1829), political radical, Revolutionary army colonel, and a member of the Pennsylvania Committee of Public Safety. The Religious Society of Friends "by some styled" the Free Quakers was formally set up in February 1781. Membership was confined almost entirely to the Philadelphia area, although tiny groups also emerged in Chester County (Pa.) and at West River (Maryland), and contact was of course maintained with the dissident Quakers of New England. After an unsuccessful attempt had been made to persuade the Pennsylvania legislature to give them the use of an existing Quaker

---

[107] Samuel Wetherill, *An Apology for the Religious Society, called Free Quakers, in the City of Philadelphia*, pp. 32-34. Although this pamphlet was published toward the end of the eighteenth century, Wetherill's views here substantially coincided with those he had expressed earlier.

[108] Brookes, *Benezet*, pp. 334, 335.

meetinghouse for their worship (the orthodox Society having replied to accusations of disloyalty made by the dissidents by pointing out that they had every right to remove the latter for violating the traditional rules of their body), the Free Quakers proceeded to build their own meetinghouse by public subscription, a brick building that still stands in Philadelphia today at the corner of Fifth Street and Arch Street, "erected," says a plaque on one of its walls, "in the year of our Lord, 1783, of the Empire 8."[109]

Among leading members of the Free Quakers, alongside Wetherill and Matlack, we may mention the names of Colonel Clement Biddle, quartermaster-general in Washington's army, William Crispin who acted as one of its commissaries, Christopher Marshall, a prominent member of the Pennsylvania Committee of Public Safety, Peter Thomson who helped to print the Continental paper money, and "Betsy" Ross who allegedly made the first American flag with its familiar stars and stripes. Some of the Free Quakers had not been expelled from the Society recently for their disagreement with its wartime stand but, like Christopher Marshall or Timothy Matlack who had been disowned as far back as 1751 and 1765, respectively, for what their meetings regarded as un-Quakerly business practices, had been forced to leave it in the prewar period. The group also attracted a few adherents, who had been hitherto unconnected with the Quakers. However, it remained a small group, never reaching more than about a hundred members, and in the early years of the next century it began to dwindle rapidly as the old members died off and new accessions became infrequent, until meetings for worship were finally discontinued in the mid-1830's. Descendants of the original members (many of them ultra-patriots) continued to maintain a formal organization, mainly for the purposes of property ownership, until this century. Thus ended the only schism within Quakerism that centered directly on the issue of its peace testimony.

The Free Quakers had modeled their discipline on that of the orthodox body in matters of worship and business, with the single difference that all mention of disownment for deviations in doctrine and practice was omitted. "No public censures shall be passed by us on any," they stated in the seventh article of their discipline. "Neither shall a member be deprived of his right among us, on account of his differing in sentiment from any or all of his brethren." However, al-

---

[109] Asked to explain the meaning of the somewhat cryptic phrase "Of the Empire," one of the Free Quakers answered: "I tell thee, Friend, it is because our country is destined to be the great empire over all the world" (quoted in Wetherill, *History of the Free Quakers*, p. 39).

though they claimed, not altogether without foundation, to be waging defensive war against "ecclesiastical tyranny" in the Quaker hierarchy because the Quaker nabobs would not "permit . . . that Christian liberty of sentiment and conduct which all are entitled to enjoy,"[110] rather than attempting to introduce innovations that were rejected by the vast majority in the Society, yet their separation was primarily a protest against the failure of Quakers as a body to come out squarely on the side of "the present great revolution."[111] In essence, not the virtues of religious tolerance and broadmindedness, but what they considered the sins of neutrality and passivity were the root causes of the schism.

The Free Quakers at the beginning had issued a goodly number of short pieces—addresses, testimonies, and declarations—setting forth their differences with orthodox Friends and pressing their legal rights against them. But although they included several members, like Wetherill himself, who were able at wielding the pen, they produced at this time no lengthy apology for their separation. In fact, the most considered statement of what may be called the Free Quaker position came from one who was never formally to become a member of the group. Its author, who tried to mask his unorthodoxy by anonymity, was Isaac Grey of New Garden Monthly Meeting; the publication without the official sanction of the Society of this defense of the Revolution and Quaker participation in it earned him speedy disownment. The pamphlet, a production which his meeting branded as likely "to spread discord and disunity in the Society"[112] and whose very title appeared as a challenge to official Quakerdom—*A Serious Address to Such of the People called Quakers, on the Continent of North-America, as profess Scruples relative to the Present Government: exhibiting the Ancient Real Testimony of that People, concerning Obedience to Civil Authority*—came out in 1778. The first edition was bought up by the yearly meeting in an effort to suppress its contents, but Grey and several friends (among whom, apparently, was Samuel Wetherill) succeeded in bringing out a second printing within a short time.[113]

Grey did not attempt directly to attack the Quaker peace testimony

[110] The spirit of Free Quakerism at its boldest and best was exemplified by young Thomas Ross, Jr., of Wrightstown M. M. in Pennsylvania. After the clerk had stood up in meeting and read a testimony of disownment against him for his part in military affairs, Ross got up and delivered his own statement claiming that Friends themselves had deviated from their traditional sense of liberty. "They are become," he told the meeting, "extremely partial, inconsistent, and hypocritical," and he had no desire to continue in membership.

[111] Wetherill, *History*, pp. 13, 27, 32, 47, 48.

[112] Cope, "Chester County Quakers during the Revolution," p. 23. Grey's disownment was also attributable to his having taken the test.

[113] Joseph Smith, *A Descriptive Catalogue of Friends' Books*, I, 71.

(although he leaves a distinct impression that he himself did not share it); he confines himself mainly to the task of persuading his fellow Friends that the Revolutionary government was the lawful one, to whom taxes of all kinds ("except those in lieu of personal service") and allegiance must be rendered willingly and in the fear of God, and that defensive war on the part of the magistracy was a duty, the refusal of which would be defiance of God's will. "If any man be appointed by God to defend my life," he asks, "is it possible that God can authorize me to call him a sinner for doing his duty; or is it possible that I can consistent with my duty, refuse him that tribute which is absolutely necessary to enable him thus to defend me?" Grey, like Timothy Davis of New England whom he quotes copiously, makes great play with the writings of early Friends like George Fox, Edward Burrough, Isaac Penington, Francis Howgill, William Penn, etc., which give a prominent place within God's order to the sword-wielding magistrate and stress the need for strict subordination to the latter. And, above all, Grey emphasizes that early Friends did not attach special importance "to any particular form of government merely as such": they had declared their loyalty first to the antimonarchical regime of Oliver Cromwell and then to the shifting changes in monarchical government which followed the Restoration. "It appears to me," he argues cogently, "that it is for those who choose not to have any hand in the formation of governments, to take governments as they find them, and comply with their laws, so far as they are clear of infringing rights and matters of faith toward God." Like the Free Quakers, Grey calls for tolerance of various standpoints within the Society on a level of equality, pro-war sentiments alongside pacifist scruples, and brotherly regard for the freedom of conscience of all.[114] Such views, however, could scarcely find acceptance within the carefully guarded seclusion of contemporary American Quakerism.

If by some chance the policy urged on the Society by the Free Quakers had been accepted by Friends, adherence to the peace testimony would have been reduced to a merely vocational pacifism, a transformation that has, indeed, almost been accomplished in our own day. As it was, the conscientious objector, nonconformist in regard to the community at large, was still the conformist in relation to his own Society.

IV

In the Revolutionary War the tax and the test objector were as prominent a feature of the Society of Friends as the straight conscien-

[114] Isaac Grey, A Serious Address, pp. 1-9, 12-15, 18, 21, 22.

tious objector to military service. But the wartime draft embraced a fair proportion of the younger men. Although, as we have seen, most consistent Friends of military age suffered fines and distraint for their refusal of service, as they had done before the war, a few among them nevertheless found themselves in jail or under arrest for a period of time.

Neither in the former Quaker commonwealth of Pennsylvania nor in any other place where we find a number of young Friends being put in prison for refusing service in the militia are any reliable statistics available, so that it is impossible to say even approximately how many persons suffered this penalty. Nor is it always possible in reported instances of imprisonment to tell whether the prisoner was a tax objector, test objector, or military service objector. Sometimes the offense was compounded of more than one form of protest. Since fine and distraint for nonpayment was the usual method of penalizing militia objectors, many of those who were put in prison were presumably propertyless men, whose goods did not suffice for repeated distraints. But undoubtedly in some cases the propertied also suffered, sometimes through local officers' ignorance of the law or through their animosity against a group that they considered unpatriotic or even sympathetic toward the enemy. In times of emergency, when the need to mobilize all available manpower overpowered all other considerations, Quakers' claims to exemption were liable to be overlooked along with the rights of their nonpacifist fellow citizens. Occasionally the imprisoned man may have only attended Quaker meetings but not been a full member of the Society and was therefore not literally entitled to the degree of exemption granted by the law.

The journal of John Pemberton, the unpolitical brother of Israel and James Pemberton, makes mention not infrequently of young Friends in prison as conscientious objectors from 1776 on. In December of that year, for instance, when a British attack on the city was expected and the Continental authorities were desperate for men to stem the enemy advance, two men from a Philadelphia meeting were jailed "for refusing to bear arms or work at the entrenchments near the city." They were released after Friends had intervened with General Israel Putnam. Again, to cite another instance in April 1778, when Pennsylvania was still the scene of battle, Pemberton noted in his journal: "At York, Henry Drinker and myself visited a young man [presumably a Friend] who was confined in jail for his religious testimony against war; we found him in a tender disposition."[115] In most cases the

---

[115] *Friends' Miscellany*, VIII, no. 2 (Jan. 1836), 61, 82. See *Exiles in Virginia*, pp. 296-99, for other examples of imprisonment of Pennsylvania and New Jersey

Quaker was released after several months in jail, if not before. In late 1779, however, two Friends were imprisoned in Lancaster jail, and, despite the efforts of the Meeting for Sufferings to gain their release, they were kept there for a period of over two years.[116]

One of the most detailed and graphic accounts from this period of the experiences of a Quaker conscientious objector in prison may be found in the manuscript minutes of New Garden Monthly Meeting. The report runs as follows:

> Some account of the suffering of Stephen Howel, a young man belonging to New Garden Monthly Meeting. He was taken on the 17th of the 4th month 1778 by several armed men who were by order of Andrew Boyd called Sublieutenant collecting fines said to be to hire substitutes to serve two months in the militia in the room of such as refused to go themselves or send others. On which account they demanded fifty two pounds ten shillings of Stephen (tho' he had not been called upon to go nor had any account of such demand before) which he refusing to pay they had him before said Boyd and he ordered him under guard to a magistrate and being taken to Lancaster he was had before several under that character one after another who used many persuasions for him to pay the demand and not go to prison which he steadily refusing (as being inconsistent with his religious principles) was at last took [sic] to the house of the under-burgess and kept at the door by one of the guards while the other went in and procured the following order Viz "To the Gaoler for the County of Lancaster. This is to command you in the name of the Commonwealth of Pennsylvania to receive the body of Stephen Howel into your custody and him safely keep until you receive further orders. Given under my hand and seal this 19th day of April 1778. Henry Dehuff." (Seal) And being conducted there when he entered the prison he felt such sweetness of mind as encouraged him to persevere on in suffering for the testimony of a good conscience. He was kept close prisoner upwards

---

Friends taken from the year 1777. See also *Friends' Miscellany*, vol. I, no. 3 (June 1831), where an account (by John Hunt of Moorestown) is given of the trials of New Jersey Quakers during the last quarter of 1776. Not only did they have to face heavy requisitioning by the Continental troops, but, "about the middle of 12th month, there was great talk of pressing men to go to war, and very great fear fell on our young men in general; many strove to keep themselves hid for fear of being forced to go to war, for the [American] army now began to approach so near as Burlington and there away. It was said that many of our young men fled to barrens and cedar swamps at this time." In such circumstances those who refused to hide were sometimes caught up by the military.

[116] Mekeel, "The Quakers," p. 149.

of three months and favoured to bear his confinement with a good degree of patience and resignation. Several Friends being then on a visit to men in office found the said Dehuff under some exercise of mind for his conduct in this case and being treated with he readily ordered Stephen's release without any demand for fees or otherwise.[117]

Here we see on one hand the almost radiant joy of young Howel himself at being called to suffer "for the testimony of a good conscience," an attitude not too frequently found in sober eighteenth-century Quakerism and more reminiscent, indeed, of the ecstatic utterances of a seventeenth-century Friend like William Dewsbury, and on the other hand the sympathetic stance of the Lancaster County magistrate Dehuff, reluctant to hold a man in prison on account of religious scruples with which almost every educated Pennsylvanian was well acquainted from childhood.

The only cases recorded of severe ill-treatment of Quaker conscientious objectors come from the Southern states. We hear of a North Carolina Friend living in an isolated area "being drafted" in 1779 "to stand guard over part of Burgoyne's army, prisoners in Virginia" and, for his refusal to comply, being sentenced by a court-martial "composed of young officers" to forty lashes, "which [were] executed in the presence of some hundred spectators. Forty stripes were very heavily laid on, by three different persons, with a whip having nine cords; but the Friend, though much torn, was supported; and persuasions and threats were afterwards offered in vain, to prevail on him to yield to service." He refused to accept any kind of noncombatant duty, such as working as a medical orderly with the troops. After a little while, however, some of the officers became more sympathetic: "one captain, it was said, laid down his commission, declaring that if innocent conscientious men were thus treated, he would not serve any longer." The objector, however, was only released on the expiry of his draft period.[118]

In the summer of the previous year a milder instance of ill-treatment had occurred in regard to fourteen young men belonging to Hopewell Monthly Meeting in Frederick County (Va.). The cause of their summary drafting for active service in the Continental army lay in the

[117] New Garden M. M. Committee on Sufferings, Minutes, pp. 6-8.
[118] *The Life and Travels of John Pemberton*, pp. 97, 98; *A Journal of the Life of William Savery*, p. 6. There are small discrepancies in the two accounts, but both Pemberton and Savery visited the South in the ministry soon afterward, and it was then that they learned the story from local Friends. The conscripted Quaker may possibly have been from Virginia instead of North Carolina.

American reverses farther north, where the British army had recently occupied Philadelphia and a considerable part of Pennsylvania. The men were therefore marched northward, while unsuccessful efforts were made by the officers to force them to carry muskets. On one occasion "with drawn swords" they "pushed the Friends into rank threatening they would have their blood if they did not comply." Several had the muskets tied on their backs and were forced to march along in this way. The men also refused to draw army rations, considering that acceptance would compromise their resistance to military orders. Finally, after about half of them had been allowed to go back home on account of their poor physical condition, the remainder were brought, along with other draftees from Virginia, to Washington's encampment outside Philadelphia. Here Colonel Clement Biddle, the quartermaster-general, who was well acquainted with Quaker peace principles since he had himself been disowned by the Society in the previous year for his warlike activities, intervened with Washington to have the men released. The commander-in-chief, who, as we know, had already during a previous war come into contact with the Quaker conscientious objectors of his homeland, readily complied. As a result, "they were, by his order, discharged, and liberty given them to return home."[119]

In New York, Friends, although they suffered hardship in other ways, were not subjected to duress on account of their refusal of military service to the same extent as their brethren in other areas. We do hear of some young Quakers from Purchase Monthly Meeting on the left bank of the Hudson being put in prison in 1779 for this reason, but they were soon released. Many New York Friends lived in areas under British control, and the British military authorities did not impose conscription on Friends. (Indeed, some loyalist journals readily seized on instances of Quakers being imprisoned by the Continental regime for their refusal to fight as examples of military tyranny exercised on innocent victims.[120])

It was New England, and Massachusetts in particular, that seems to have provided the greatest number of cases of imprisonment of military service objectors, at least in proportion to the total number of Friends in the area. On the other hand, treatment under duress was not harsh on the whole, and imprisonment resulted from certain special circumstances and not from the settled policy of either central or local

[119] Mekeel, "The Quakers," p. 224; *Exiles in Virginia*, p. 181; Paul F. Boller, Jr., "George Washington and the Quakers," *BFHA*, vol. 49, no. 2 (1960), p. 73. More instances of Friends being drafted into the armed forces during this crisis period were reported from other Virginia monthly meetings.
[120] Mekeel, "The Quakers," pp. 161, 162.

officials. Mekeel, indeed, speaks rightly of "the sincere attempt made [by the Rhode Island and Massachusetts governments] to spare the Quakers and others with conscientious objections from suffering for their testimony against war." "The Quakers might have fared much worse," he adds. The two governments were careful to avoid impinging on religious conscience in this question wherever possible, only departing from this policy for a more rigorous one either where the demand for manpower became extremely acute or in communities with a large proportion of Quakers where the draft quota could not easily be filled. Referring to Massachusetts' wartime policy toward Friends, Mekeel comments: "In its consideration for the conscientious scruples of the Quakers against bearing arms the Puritan Commonwealth went far toward redeeming itself for the treatment accorded them a century before."

In Rhode Island a few Quakers suffered brief periods of imprisonment (as well as the more frequent distraints) during the early months of the Revolution for refusing the alternative service which was allowed objectors by law but which was unacceptable to the Quaker conscience. The stringent militia law of April 1777, which withdrew the recent very generous exemption, led to the jailing of at least one young Quaker, David Anthony of Greenwich Monthly Meeting. This caused New England Meeting for Sufferings to take the matter up with the general assembly, and Anthony was released after spending only nine weeks in prison. Although the law was not then repealed, as Friends had hoped, the situation became easier for them, especially after the British evacuation of Newport in 1779 removed the immediate threat to the province's security.

The Quaker community in Massachusetts, despite the generally well-disposed attitude of the government toward Friends, encountered greater difficulty in regard to military service requirements than did their Rhode Island brethren. When a selective service draft was established in September 1776 with a penalty of up to two months imprisonment for not paying the fine imposed for failure to muster or hire a substitute, three young Quakers from Worcester County soon found themselves behind bars. With the help of their elders they drew up a petition to the general court suitably larded with scriptural passages, in which they stated "that they profess themselves Friends and cannot in conscience take up arms on either side in the unnatural war subsisting between Great Britain and the American colonies or in any other wars whatever because they think it is contrary to the precepts of Christ as set forth in many places in the New Testament and in no ways lawful to such as will be the disciples of Christ." Their release and a blanket exemption for all who had been members of the Society prior to the war followed soon afterward. For several years the situation eased for Friends. But they were not altogether immune from the attentions of overofficious local authorities, for in January of the following year we hear that three more Worcester County Quakers were in jail for refusing the draft. They complained to the general court of their incarceration in "a crowded loathsome gaol in Worcester among prisoners of war and our health endangered by filth and vermin."

There were two classes of Quaker conscripts, however, who did not qualify for exemption under the recent law: those who joined the Society after 19 April 1775, the date set in the act, and those men who attended Quaker meetings but had not become full-fledged members. Cases of arrest and imprisonment of new Quakers and near-Quakers continued to occur, especially when, as in the summer of 1777, a general shortage of available troops made the need for fresh draftees urgent. Thus, in August 1777, four young men from East Hoosack in the northwest corner of Massachusetts (the meeting there was actually attached to Saratoga Monthly Meeting and thus formed part of New York Yearly Meeting) found themselves in prison for not answering the draft. With the support of their meeting they petitioned the general court, asking that the court "not for the bare want of certificates to leave us to suffer, although we do really believe the principles of truth as professed by our Friends." They were lucky in also being able to enlist the support of their local committee of safety, which backed their request for release on the grounds that it was a waste of time to try to force such men to serve and that in prison, too, they would be useless to the community. The committee confirmed the existence of "divers . . . persons within our township under the denomination of Friends (but not members of their Society) who profess with them, that it is against their consciences to take up arms either offensive or defensive." In all such cases the general court, upon receiving an appeal, ordered the release of the imprisoned men.

But in mid-1780, with the rising demand for new recruits, the existing Quaker exemption was withdrawn altogether. Now not only the fringe members of the Quaker community were threatened, in the words of the new act, with "all the penalties of the laws for desertion," but all who professed their peace principles. Almost at once arrests began: seventeen members of Dartmouth Monthly Meeting were taken, as well as some from the Quaker communities on Cape Cod. The New England Meeting for Sufferings was obliged to take the matter up with the Massachusetts executive council then in session, handing them a "Remonstrance" which asked "for redress in this interesting matter from the lenient disposition of the Council." Quakers expressed their trust that the authorities in fact did not intend to treat Quaker objectors on a par with deserters or to oppress religious conscience. Once again we find local officials intervening on behalf of the Quaker conscripts. In this case the officer commanding the militia in Sandwich, obviously a local man who knew his neighbors well, sent a supporting letter along with the appeal of his Quaker draftees. In his letter he stated his conviction that these men could not be

... marched unless by force, and if forced to camp I do not suppose they would be active in a single particular; nor do I think it would be practicable here to get any body to have any hand in dragging them off against their consciences. It was with reluctance the officers drafted them, but the resolve makes them as liable as others, and the towns here are called upon for men ... in proportion to their polls, Quakers included, which makes such uneasiness among said poor distressed inhabitants this way that to draft of the non-Quakers much more than their proportion would be drawing the cords so as to break ... the Quakers drafted are less than their proportion according to numbers.

The arrested men were all soon released, but the position of Friends remained anomalous. The root of the trouble lay in the dilemma touched on in the Sandwich militia commander's letter quoted above: while Quakers stubbornly refused to serve and their neighbors were loath to attempt the distasteful and probably fruitless task of coercing them to become soldiers, the statutory quota of militiamen remained and the gaps caused by Quakers' martial delinquency had to be filled by the township, if the law was not to be flouted. So we find the officer in charge of the Bristol County militia, where Friends were fairly numerous, grumbling to the authorities in Boston of his difficulties in getting together enough men in places where "more than half the number of the male inhabitants ... had rather submit to be trampled on like the meanest reptile than by a vigorous exertion to defend himself." "Therefore," he concluded, "I desire the General Court will condescend to separate this burdensome class of men from the militia, in such a manner as their wisdom shall direct." And on Cape Cod the officer in charge of the militia of Barnstable County (another Quaker stronghold) bewailed: "The hardships of getting men among Quakers is inconceivable and what makes great uneasiness I cannot say unjustly." Several counties sent in requests to the executive council to excuse them from not filling the draft quota assigned them on account of the high proportion of Quakers among their inhabitants. As a result, to quote Mekeel's apt comment, "the very size of a large Quaker

community was a strong reason for the difficulties of its members."
However, the adoption of a new constitution for the commonwealth
of Massachusetts in the same year, 1780, with a clause exempting
Quakers from the duty of serving in the militia, resolved the difficulties and dilemmas of both Quakers and their military neighbors.[121]

For the first time almost during the wars of the seventeenth and
eighteenth centuries, very few Quakers during the Revolution were
subjected to the possibility of Indian attack. The only area settled by
Friends in any numbers where this danger existed was Saratoga
County in upper New York, which had only recently been opened to
colonization. Here in 1777 the approach of the British army under
Burgoyne, says a contemporary Quaker account,

. . . was preceded by very alarming reports of the scalping
and devastation committed indiscriminately by the Indians, yet
Friends were generally preserved quietly to await on their own habi-
tations the trials that approached them, and not to neglect the as-
sembling themselves for public worship, altho' to outward appearance the hazard was great from scouting parties from both sides, and
at one of these times near the conclusion of the meeting, came a
party of Indians with two Frenchmen [i.e., French Canadians], and
surrounded the house. One of the Indians after looking in, withdrew
and beckoned his hand, upon which a Friend went out, and was
asked by signs whether there were soldiers there, the Indians upon
being answered in the negative, shook hands with him, and the rest
came into the house, they were marked, painted and equipt for war.
And it being about the conclusion of the meeting, they shook hands
with Friends and one Friend having [a knowledge of] the French
tongue could confer with them, by the assistance of the two Frenchmen. When they understood Friends were at a religious meeting, they
went to one of their houses, got some victuals, of which a prisoner
with them partook, and they quietly departed.[122]

[121] Mekeel, "New England Quakers and Military Service," pp. 246, 248, 256,
257, 274, 275. The small community of Quakers in New Hampshire does not
appear to have had any serious troubles connected with military service during
the Revolution. The experiences of a Quaker attender in Maine, Moses Sleeper,
who was arrested for refusing to join the militia, imprisoned in a fort, court-
martialed and sentenced "to receive forty-five lashes on the naked back," are
printed in the Philadelphia *Friend*, LII, no. 37 (1879), 272, 273. The sentence,
however, was never carried out, and Sleeper soon afterward gained his release.
Given the chance to escape, Sleeper had refused, explaining that, if he had
accepted this offer, he would have acted contrary to Quaker principles; "though
I am not a member of the Society of Friends," he stated, "yet I am one with
them in profession, and by my acquaintance am considered as one of their
number."
[122] Mekeel, "New York Quakers in the American Revolution," pp. 54, 55.

Another contemporary account of what is certainly the same incident[123] is given in the journal of a Quaker minister, who was then farming in the district, where there were about a dozen Quaker families living. He reports that, as the rival armies approached, "the skulking Indians seemed to strike the greatest dread, the more so because we could not converse with them: but they did not do so much damage by far, as to plundering, as our own people did." He tells of how a party of Indians arrived at their meeting "just as it was breaking up." "Their warlike appearance was very shocking, being equipped with their guns, tomahawks and scalping knives: they had a prisoner and one green scalp taken from a person they had killed but a few hours before: but they went away without doing any violence." General Burgoyne's defeat shortly afterward brought quiet back to the neighborhood again.[124]

Friends, like their non-Quaker neighbors, of course suffered from the plundering, requisitioning, and depredations the two conflicting armies inflicted on the settled population with whom they came into contact. On occasion Quaker pacifism seems to have served to aggravate the situation. We are told, for instance, of Thomas Lamborn, a farming Friend of Chester County (Pa.), that "his plainspoken advocacy of the principles of peace as held by Friends" did not appeal to the British troops when they were in the area. "They took everything available; almost everything that could be carried or driven away, beating the wheat battens against the posts in the barn to get the grain out, then throwing back the balance into the mow, saying 'there, Lamborn may have that.' At another time he was plowing in the field, when some officers of the [British] army detached the horses from the plow and unceremoniously appropriated them to the use of the army."[125]

This was, indeed, the first occasion when a major war was being fought on territory thickly populated by Friends; farmers in particular —and most Quakers during this period were country people—endured the most hardship on this account, exposed as they were to the

[123] Mekeel (p. 55) considers that this episode was probably also the foundation of the story related by Violet Hodgkin in her popular *Book of Quaker Saints* (London-Edinburgh, 1917) under the title "Fierce Feathers," pp. 347-55.

[124] *A Journal of Rufus Hall*, pp. 17, 18.

[125] *Two Hundredth Anniversary of the Establishment of the Friends Meeting at New Garden, Chester County, Pennsylvania, 1715-1915*, pp. 24, 25. In addition, Lamborn suffered fines from the American authorities to the value of almost £760. As a result of his losses (the property taken in distraint having been, as in most cases, probably greatly in excess of the money demanded), Lamborn's farm had to be sold by the sheriff at a low price, only to be bought by a non-Quaker who returned it to him after paying off the debts.

marchings and counter-marchings of the often hungry, ill-disciplined, and ill-clad troops by their farms. New York Friends suffered a special trial in having to cross a kind of "no man's land," which separated the two occupying armies and, also, the several Quaker communities from each other. This zone had to be crossed frequently by groups of Friends wishing to attend monthly, quarterly, or yearly meetings, who thus not only risked interception by the authorities of either army but had to pass "over ground rendered still more perilous by desperate men" who lived by plundering unprotected travelers. In addition, about a hundred families lived in this border zone, refusing to flee as most of their neighbors had done and suffering considerably from the depredations of the gangs and desperadoes who infested the area. "Yet," as a Quaker report on their wartime experiences in New York, written shortly afterward, observed, "watchful providence preserved in these trying seasons, that we don't find the lives of any were suffered to be taken and the Friends thus tried were supported firm in this testimony committed them to bear."[126] The only recorded case of a Quaker meeting death at the hands of either of the armies is apparently the one reported from Rhode Island in the journal of a traveling Quaker minister from Maryland, George Churchman. He tells of a Friend there who was set upon by some looting German mercenaries in British pay who, accusing him—ironically—of being a rebel, "stabbed and killed [him] in his own house, his wife and small children present."[127]

The main hardship endured by Quakers during the Revolutionary War was neither loss of life nor harsh physical treatment nor imprisonment on the scale of the early "heroic" period of Quakerism of the third quarter of the seventeenth century. It consisted rather in the very considerable financial burden laid upon members of the Society

---

[126] Mekeel, "New York Quakers in the American Revolution," pp. 49, 50, 54, 55.

[127] H. J. Cadbury, "A Quaker Travelling in the Wake of War, 1781," *NEQ*, XXIII, no. 3 (Sept. 1950), 400. The case of the two Pennsylvania Quakers, John Roberts, a miller from Lower Merion, and Abraham Carlisle, a Philadelphia carpenter, who were executed in November 1778 on a charge of high treason for assisting the British military forces, is a special one. Their Meeting for Sufferings, while (quite correctly) considering their sentences unduly harsh and the result of "a party spirit" in the court trying them and while refraining, therefore, from passing the private Quaker sentence of disownment on them (particularly since the two Friends eventually expressed sorrow at their conduct), was at the same time unwilling to intervene officially on behalf of the two men, regarding their behavior (again correctly) to have been inconsistent with Friends' peace principles. See Sharpless, *A Quaker Experiment*, II, 192-97; Mekeel, "The Quakers," pp. 142, 143. It is interesting to note that John Roberts had suffered very severely from the requisitioning and confiscations of American troops: his losses, according to the Radnor M. M. Minutes of Sufferings, amounted on one occasion to as much as £500 worth of property.

by the confiscation of their property resulting primarily from distraints. Although some property losses stemmed from the general requisitioning of the armies mentioned above, a hardship that was shared by a large section of the non-Quaker population of varying political sympathies, the greater part was the outcome of Friends' loyalty to the demands of their peace testimony as they conceived them. As Mekeel has rightly remarked: "The record of disownments and dealings is a story of failure to abide by the religious ideals of the Society and is an indication of weakness. This record, however, is more than counterbalanced by the account of sufferings borne by the Friends in maintaining their principles. This latter story is a convincing testimony to the basic strength of the Society of Friends at that time."[128]

Undoubtedly, the witness was upheld by some Friends more imperfectly than by others. Apart from those members cut off for their obvious unwillingness to accept the peace testimony in part or in its entirety, there were occasionally serious backslidings because of a desire to escape the hardships of the war resister, as in the case of a wartime Quaker of Core Sound Monthly Meeting in North Carolina who, according to the meeting records, "for a small season sheltered himself under our holy profession, but could not stand in it and bear his testimony of the truth when suffering appeared at hand." Although he had, through joining Friends, been "screened from mustering . . . a few years past," he had now, in order to avoid having his goods distrained, consented to act "as commissary in supplying troops with provision."[129]

But we can see the impact that the collective witness for peace, borne consistently and often at considerable sacrifice on the part of the overwhelming majority of members, could make on a young and impressionable mind from the pages of the journal of Henry Hull. The son of a devout Quaker minister, Hull had revolted against the ancestral religion, and at the outbreak of war, although as yet much too young, he had wanted to go off to join the American forces. Later, in his teens, seeing the readiness with which his parents' people suffered the loss of their material possessions in their endeavor to uphold their pacifist witness, he underwent a change of heart.[130] Moreover, something of this respect for the Quaker willingness to suffer for their beliefs seems to have been felt by at least some of the officers entrusted with the task of enforcing the law against Friends; it was shown, too, in the course of the periodic visits Quaker representatives made to

[128] Mekeel, "The Quakers," p. 155.
[129] Thorne, "North Carolina Friends and the Revolution," p. 329.
[130] Memoir of Henry Hull, p. 27.

Continental officials in the government for the purpose of explaining the Society's point of view and of pointing out, in particular, that their own refractory conduct flowed not from partiality toward the British but from deep religious principle.[131]

The list of items seized from Quaker households—in the words of a contemporary Quaker account—"for not complying with the unjust requisition of men to become instrumental in shedding human blood"[132] would cover many pages of print. It would include livestock and farm equipment, furniture and household equipment, clothing, stocks of food and animal fodder; in very many cases the value of the goods taken far exceeded the amount of the fine on account of which the distraint was being made. Complaints were voiced by Friends about "the insolent conduct of collectors and others under them," of their arbitrary assessments and ruthless exactions, which had reduced many Quaker farmers to penury.[133] Friends were warned to "be careful not to balk our testimony against war, in giving way to collectors, either in letting them know what we can best spare, or by manifesting

[131] See, e.g., the following comment on the attitude of local magistrates and officials taken from the records of Western Q. M. (Philadelphia Y. M.) and printed in A Retrospect of Early Quakerism, p. 380: "They generally appeared friendly, and to receive our visit kindly, some of them particularly so; and most of them acknowledged that the prophecies concerning the disuse of carnal weapons, pointed to the gospel dispensation, and was much to be desired."

[132] James W. Moore, Records of the Kingwood Monthly Meeting of Friends, Hunterdon County, New Jersey, p. 25.

[133] A Retrospect of Early Quakerism, pp. 390-92. See also pp. 386-92. A "Memorial" of grievances presented by the Quakers of Chester Co., where the losses of Friends were among the highest, to the president and executive council of Pennsylvania has this to say about the behavior of the distraining officers: "Power has been put into the hands of rapacious and unreasonable men, who have sported with property; often selling and exposing goods to sale without having them present, representing them unfairly and purchasing them, themselves, at so low a rate as sometimes to double their money and more the same day; often seizing to the worth of double or treble their demand, and afterwards utterly refuse to give receipts, in some instances they have seized goods for the same fines over again, and when considerable overplus has been in their hands, fresh seizures have been made for others—to the whole amount, and often charging exorbitant fees. Fines have likewise been levied and collected for not marching where notice had not been given. And where goods have been taken for fines which had previously been obtained and the same made [to] appear they have seized and detained property to pay their costs. And when endeavours have been used to put a stop to those and like extravagances by laying it before superior officers we have been put off with 'Such conduct was not by their allowance,' also that the captain's return must be their rule of discrimination, and unless we have receipts we must suffer for requisitions which have been fully satisfied. Thus instead of being redressed or those covetous men restrained, who are endeavouring to enrich themselves by the ruin and spoil of their neighbours' goods, they have been encouraged by extending their jurisdiction over several townships and continuing them in office from year to year." (From an undated manuscript [possibly 1781] in the H.C.Q.C.)

a disposition contrary to the peaceable principle we profess."[134] Cases of Friends being disciplined both for conniving with the distraining officers at a lighter imposition as well as for un-Quakerly behavior toward them are met with in the records. New England Meeting for Sufferings in July 1776 adjured Friends in that area to remember "that they have enlisted themselves as soldiers under the Prince of Peace; for if any be so unwary as when distraint is made, and their goods taken from them, to be caught in that spirit, in which wars are fomented, and carried on, such instead of maintaining our peaceable testimony, will thereby wound the cause of truth, . . . and bring reproach on our holy profession."[135]

In the South we even find an occasional slave seized for his master's military delinquency, thereby giving an admirable opportunity for the latter's yearly meeting to deliver a timely warning on the bad effects of Friends' delaying manumission. In December 1779, for instance, the sheriff seized a 6-year-old Negro child from Robert Hunnicutt of Blackwater Monthly Meeting in Virginia "because of [his] testimony against war," and for not paying his war taxes in particular. This monthly meeting, despite the promptings of Virginia Yearly Meeting to make more rapid progress, was apparently extremely tardy in ridding itself of slaveownership, which had almost disappeared in most sections of the Society by this date. In official captivity the child, it was reported, had "suffered sorrowful neglect"; in addition, of course, it was now impossible to free him since he was no longer in Quaker hands.[136]

In coastal areas Quaker sailors and fishermen suffered loss of employment. Moreover, Quaker-owned vessels were frequently impounded by one or other belligerent on the pretext that their owners were trading with the enemy.[137]

The "crimes" for which Friends were thus penalized ranged from vague suspicions of Toryism (or, in some instances, of pro-colonial sympathies) to specific offenses such as refusal of military service and

[134] Kennett M. M. Sufferings, p. 54.
[135] Mekeel, "New England Quakers and Military Service," p. 250.
[136] *Encyclopedia of Quaker Genealogy*, VI: *Virginia*, ed. W. W. Hinshaw *et al.*, 95, 96.
[137] For the hardships inflicted on Nantucket Quakers on this account, see Rotch, *Memorandum*, pp. 5ff., 16-24, 36, 39, 82-89. Under the leadership of Rotch (1734-1828), a wealthy whaler and shipper, the island Quakers, who formed the majority of its inhabitants, attempted to steer a strictly neutral course between the two contestants. The non-Quaker minority backed this policy on grounds of expediency, except for a handful of pro-American enthusiasts. Despite their neutral stance, however, the islanders still had to endure plundering by British troops on land and by British privateers by sea and sporadic hostility and suspicion from the American side.

its alternatives in the way of fines or hiring of substitutes, failure to pay taxes of various kinds connected with the war, refusal to take a test oath or affirmation, "nonassociating," and, more rarely, refusal to handle the Continental paper currency.[138]

Just as Philadelphia and New York Yearly Meetings had established Meetings for Sufferings after the London model during the French and Indian War of mid-century, so similar meetings were set up during the Revolutionary War by the yearly meetings in New England, Baltimore, and Virginia, with an equivalent body, too, in North Carolina. Their prime function, as in the case of London Meeting for Sufferings in its early days, was to provide institutional support for members of the Society in a period of heavy trial. Abundant evidence of Friends' "sufferings" during the Revolutionary War exist in the Society's meeting records, since each meeting was required to keep a full and accurate account; excerpts have been published in such documentary compilations as Ezra Michener's *Retrospect of Early Quakerism*[139] and in histories of central and local meetings. However, no completely reliable statistics on the total losses in property incurred by American Quakers at this time are readily available. The figure given by Mekeel—£103,195. 8s. 11 3/4d.[140]—may be taken as reasonably close to the actual amount, even if hardly accurate to the last pound, shilling, and pence. For Pennsylvania, where the largest number of Friends were located and where army requisitioning and distraints for the various military and paramilitary delinquencies had been among the heaviest of all Quaker communities on the continent, Mekeel gives a figure of £38,550. 9s. 5 1/2d., with the greater part of the sum carried by Friends in Chester and Bucks Counties and with 1778 as the most burdensome year.[141] Indeed, everywhere it was naturally the pe-

---

[138] This last became a capital offense; no Friends, however, actually suffered the death penalty on this account. See *A Retrospect of Early Quakerism*, pp. 303-6, where details are given concerning the case of Thomas Watson, a prosperous Quaker farmer in Bucks Co., who during the winter of 1779-1780 became convinced that he must bear "a testimony against such money," as a hidden instrument of war, by refusing to handle it. After his refusal had been reported to the American military authorities, Watson was court-martialed and sentenced to be hanged; however, his wife's intercession with the commanding general, who had probably not realized the motives of Watson's conduct and mistook it for intent to help the enemy, brought about his pardon and release.

[139] See esp. chap. XXXII, which prints copious extracts concerning Friends' sufferings from the records of Western Q. M. of Philadelphia Y. M. and of its seven constituent monthly meetings covering Lancaster Co. and the western part of Chester Co., esp. for the period starting in 1777 when the systematic recording of "sufferings" was begun.

[140] Mekeel, "The Quakers," p. 299.

[141] *Ibid.*, pp. 155, 156. The losses of Philadelphia Friends amounted only to £1,283. 13s. 2d., thus illustrating once again the fact that it was the rural com-

riods when fighting was taking place in or near Quaker settlements that brought the severest strain between Quakers and the authorities, military and civilian.

It was in a period of serious military crisis, when Philadelphia was threatened by British troops (which soon afterward were to capture the city), that the *cause célèbre* occurred—the arrest by the Revolutionary authorities and subsequent detention of seventeen leading Philadelphia Quakers who, along with three well-known Anglicans (including that exacting critic of Quaker pacifism in the previous war, Provost William Smith), were accused of treasonable relations with the enemy.[142] Among those caught up in the net were the three Pemberton brothers, Israel II, James, and John—all of them among the foremost in the counsels of the Society—leading city merchants like Thomas Wharton, Henry Drinker, and Samuel Rowland Fisher, and prominent Quaker ministers like Thomas Gilpin and the English-born John Hunt. The arrests took place between 2 and 5 September 1777; on 9 September the men were removed for safekeeping to Winchester, Virginia, where they were held in honorable and not very onerous custody until April 1778. Two members of the group, Thomas Gilpin and John Hunt, died during their detention. The rest returned home.

The charge of Quaker complicity with the British was undoubtedly false; it was based in part on hearsay, in part on forged documents (the spurious Spanktown papers), and in part on the known neutralist and quasi-loyalist sentiments of these leading members of the Pennsylvania Society. The evidence against them was spiced by the rancor of Quaker renegades like the "Free Quaker" and Revolutionary radical, Timothy Matlack, who in his capacity as secretary of the supreme executive council of Pennsylvania was responsible for preparing the case against the men and for the decision to incarcerate them.

---

munities that suffered the heaviest losses in worldly possessions. In his *Quaker Experiment in Government*, II, 176, Sharpless estimates the aggregate losses of Pennsylvania Friends to have been at least £35,000; in his chapter in Jones, *The Quakers in the American Colonies*, p. 568, he gives an estimate of nearly £50,000, but this sum may include the losses incurred by New Jersey members of Philadelphia Y. M. For estimated losses among Friends of North Carolina Y. M., see Thorne, "North Carolina Friends and the Revolution," p. 335. The total for the period from 1778-1783 is given there as £9,888 in "good money." La Verne Hill Forbush provides some rather fragmentary information about the material losses suffered by Quakers belonging to Baltimore Y. M. during the Revolution ("The Suffering of Friends in Maryland," *The Maryland and Delaware Genealogist*, vol. 3, no. 2 [Winter 1961-1962], pp. 36, 37; vol. 3, no. 3 [Spring 1962], pp. 59, 60).

[142] The main source for this episode is the compilation of documents edited by a later namesake of one of the exiles, Thomas Gilpin, under the title, *Exiles in Virginia*. See also Thayer, *Israel Pemberton*, pp. 215-31.

Whether one should class the hardships of the exiles as part "Tory" sufferings, which form such a deplorable chapter in the of the Revolution, or as part of Quaker pacifist opposition to u.. is a difficult question to resolve. The Revolutionary authorities obviously considered these Friends as "the Tories of the Quaker Society"[143] and would not have taken such action against them if they had believed them to be pure Quaker pacifists. In a resolution of late August 1777 issued by the Continental Congress, which had initiated the action against the Philadelphia Friends, the wartime "testimonies" of Philadelphia Yearly Meeting (discussed earlier in this chapter), especially the most recent of 20 December 1776, were quoted to show that "a number of persons of considerable wealth," who were in control of Yearly Meeting policy, had become "with much rancour and bitterness, disaffected to the American cause." Treasonable communication with the enemy was presumed to be an inevitable consequence of such an attitude.[144] On the other hand, the exiles themselves and Pennsylvania Yearly Meeting as a whole, which stood united behind its leaders both in its public utterances and by personal intervention with the Revolutionary authorities, maintained with at least equal sincerity that their behavior had not deviated from a strict adherence to Friends' peace testimony.

Protesting their innocence, the exiles in a number of remonstrances to Congress and the Pennsylvania authorities, which were permeated —it is worth noting—with the traditional Quaker insistence on their rights as citizens, branded their imprisonment as "arbitrary" and "illegal" and demanded a fair trial. "The testimony of the Quakers is against all wars and fightings, and against entering into military engagements of any kind," they expostulated; "surely then, it was the right of the representatives of the Society, to caution their members from engaging in any thing contrary to their religious principles." Their refusal to fight applied to both sides.[145] In denying that they harbored any hostility to the American cause, however, the exiles were undoubtedly a little disingenuous; although all convinced Quaker pacifists, the men formed an assortment of political views ranging from the religious apoliticism of John Pemberton to the cryptoloyalism of Samuel Rowland Fisher.

Among the efforts undertaken by Philadelphia Yearly Meeting in connection with the imprisonment of their brethren was the dispatch at the beginning of October 1777, just after the battle of Germantown,

---

143 *Exiles in Virginia*, p. 187.
144 *Ibid.*, p. 261. See also Sharpless, *A Quaker Experiment*, II, 151-53.
145 *Exiles in Virginia*, p. 101. See also pp. 58, 59, 75, 83, 240-45, 247, 248.

of a committee of six weighty Friends, including Warner Mifflin and Nicholas Waln (1742-1813), to interview the commanding generals on both sides, Howe and Washington.[146] Although at this time Washington shared the view, common among supporters of the Revolution, that identified Quakerism and Toryism,[147] he was convinced by the arguments of the delegation, at least of the inauthenticity of the Spanktown papers. As the delegation passed through the lines while moving from one camp to another without the support of either passports or armed backing to protect them from the overwhelming might of the two forces, which both in their different ways stood for principles in direct contrast to the quiet testimony of Friends, the six Quakers suddenly felt the powerlessness of their position, symbolic perhaps of the situation of the whole Society caught up in the turmoil of war and unable to identify itself with either of the contestants. One of their number, the ever sensitive Warner Mifflin, was thereby led to compare their present situation, at the mercy of arbitrary power, to the plight of the Negro slaves in their own land. "Herein," he writes, "I was brought into renewed sympathy with our oppressed African brethren, who are many of them exposed to the uncontrolled power of man, without any tribunal on all the earth whereunto they can appeal for redress of grievances."[148]

Suspicion of Friends' intentions continued on the part of the Pennsylvania Revolutionary authorities. On 14 November, for instance, we find the executive council telling its representative in Chester County "to watch the meetings and especially the Quarterly meetings of the Quakers. At these assemblies, agents of this nature [i.e., of a subversive

[146] *Ibid.*, pp. 52, 59-61. See also Sharpless, *A Quaker Experiment*, II, 160-71.

[147] See Boller, "George Washington and the Quakers," pp. 72-77. Washington spoke on one occasion of the "unfriendly Quakers and others notoriously disaffected to the cause of American liberty." On 20 March 1778 we find him writing to General Lacey from Valley Forge: "Sunday next being the time on which the Quakers hold one of their general meetings, a number of that Society will probably be attempting to go into Philadelphia. This is an intercourse that we should by all means endeavour to interrupt, as the plans settled at their meetings are of the most pernicious tendency" (quoted in Devere Allen, *The Fight for Peace*, pp. 559, 560). On the other hand, both the French general, de Choisy, who was in command of the troops of America's ally stationed in Rhode Island, and his officers spoke warmly of the Quaker peace testimony. "They knew our principle in that respect," they told some visiting Friends, "and allowed it to be good, that we were a people who were known and revered throughout the world on account of our peaceable sentiments and conduct, and that the French people had a very favorable opinion of us" (Cadbury, "A Quaker Travelling in the Wake of War, 1781," p. 399). The first comment perhaps only goes to show that the legend of the "good Quaker" was not one of the ideas of the French Enlightenment that easily found acceptance among the cultured class of Washington's Virginia.

[148] *The Defence of Warner Mifflin*, p. 17.

kind] will without doubt, be busy, and mischievous."[149] Fears that British spies lay concealed beneath the Quaker drab died hard; so, from the Quaker side, did Friends' hostility to the new political order.

Once the war was over, however, and American independence had been recognized by Britain in the Peace of Paris of September 1783, the Society of Friends, along with its brethren among the Mennonites, Dunkers, and Moravians who had likewise caviled at being privy to the overthrow of monarchies, soon accommodated itself to the new regime.[150] Some Friends, nevertheless, were unable to accept the transition from monarchy to republic. And so it happened that the earliest large-scale migration of Friends to Canada (if we except a small Quaker group that moved from Nantucket for economic reasons in 1762 and settled at Barrington, Nova Scotia) came about as a result of the American Revolution.

These immigrants were all loyalists. Some of them had abandoned their pacifism to fight or otherwise support the British cause and thereby earned disownment from the Society, along with their brethren who had espoused the Continental cause. Some were the wives and

[149] *Pa. Archives*, 1st ser., VI, 4.

[150] For the loyal address presented by Philadelphia Y. M. to Washington in October 1789 soon after his election as the country's first President, see *Exiles in Virginia*, pp. 235-37. It was signed by Nicholas Waln as clerk of the meeting and presented in person to the President by a delegation of Friends. "We can take no part in warlike measures on any occasion or under any power," the address stated, "but we are bound in conscience to lead quiet and peaceable lives." "As we are a people," it went on, "whose principles and conduct have been misrepresented and traduced, we take the liberty to assure thee, that we feel our hearts affectionately drawn towards thee, and those in authority over us, with prayers that thy presidency may, under the blessing of Heaven, be happy to thyself and to the people." Washington's reply to this address is printed on pp. 237, 238. Thanking Friends for their "affectionate address," he told them that their "principles and conduct" were well-known to him and "that (except their declining to share with others in the burthens of common defence) there is no denomination among us, who are more exemplary and useful citizens." Nonetheless, despite his disagreement with their pacifism, he stated it as his opinion that "the conscientious scruples of all men should be treated with great delicacy and tenderness" and as his earnest hope "that the laws may always be as extensively accommodated to them, as a due regard to the protection and essential interest of the nation may justify and permit." The well-known remark he made to Warner Mifflin (quoted in Boller, "George Washington and the Quakers," p. 68) when the latter was expounding Quaker pacifism in the course of his interview with the President—"Mr. Mifflin, I honor your sentiments; there is more in that than mankind have generally considered"—is just one more illustration of the fact that, if the Quakers subsequently moderated their wartime attitude toward the Revolutionary regime, the passing of the years also considerably mellowed the sentiments of the Revolution's great leader toward Friends. In the postwar years prosperous Quakers in Philadelphia and elsewhere gave their support to the Federalists; Quakers who sympathized with the Democrats were rare.

families of these men, who, though not held responsible for the delinquencies of their near relatives and therefore able to escape the penalty of expulsion from the Society, wished to accompany the latter in their exile from their native land. Still others were good Quaker pacifists whose sympathies, however, had been very decidedly with the old regime and had earned them a reputation for "Toryism" that made it inadvisable for them to remain in their old homes. Among such people those who still retained their Quaker membership were probably a minority.

Beginning their trek in 1783, more than 500 of these Quaker—or former Quaker—loyalists settled at Pennfield in New Brunswick. The settlers in this wilderness area experienced many difficulties and hardships at first. Quakerism among them was a tender plant that soon died off: it had disappeared altogether by the end of the century. Another group made for Upper Canada, where Quaker settlements sprang up in the Niagara district and at Adolphustown near the Bay of Quinte. There from the beginning the genuine Quaker element was stronger than in the New Brunswick settlement; and it soon began to be reinforced by newcomers from the United States, who were attracted to Canada by cheap land and generous terms of settlement. The earliest regular monthly meetings in Upper Canada date from 1797-1798. Probably some memory of the benefits Friends had enjoyed under British rule acted at first as a further incentive to move northward. However, this whole movement of Quaker settlers into Upper Canada (which later became the province of Ontario) that was to last into the 1820's should be regarded as one wing of the great "westward" movement of Friends—and many more thousands of others—into the free spaces of the continent that were now being gradually opened up for settlement.[151]

Friends in Upper Canada were first exempted from militia service by a law of 1793 (33 Geo.III c. 1), an exemption which was retained in subsequent legislation; this law, however, did not free them from payment of a fine in lieu of actual mustering. Thus the same pattern prevailed again here as in the land that they had left of distraint of goods and occasional imprisonment as a result of Friends' absolutist stand, with disownment for any members who consented to pay the fine or attended a militia muster. In 1809 and 1810 we hear of Friends being censured by their meetings for taking out government land set aside for United Empire loyalists. Since land of this kind was awarded ostensibly for services to the British Crown's military effort, its

[151] Arthur Garratt Dorland, *A History of the Society of Friends (Quakers) in Canada*, pp. 47-55.

acquisition was considered a contravention of the Quaker peace testimony. In the War of 1812, which saw fighting on Canadian territory, Friends who agreed to drive their teams of horses after they had been requisitioned for army use or who behaved, on the other hand, in an aggressive fashion when their animals were impressed for service were disciplined and required to make acknowledgment of faulty behavior. In the rebellion of 1837 a few young Quakers took up arms on the side of the insurgents; as usual, only by expressing regret for their conduct before their meeting could they escape disownment. In the second half of the nineteenth and on into the present century a steep decline in numbers became apparent in Canadian Quakerism. This, combined with the isolated rural character of the Canadian membership and the removal of any serious demands for military duties on the part of the government, made the peace witness of Canadian Friends during the half century and more before the First World War appear rather ineffective.[152]

In addition to the first Quaker migration to Canada, a second and, in the long run, more important legacy of the war period that was to influence the Society for many decades to come was a widespread aloofness from politics, a withdrawal from society which—apart from the Holy Experiment—had to a limited degree always been a feature of American Quakerism but which their wartime experiences had served greatly to intensify. A more compact body, more closely disciplined and more uniform in outlook, a body, too, that had become more sensitized to the needs of suffering humanity, emerged from the testing period of the Revolution. But, at the same time, the American Society of Friends as a whole, and the great concentration of Quakers comprising Philadelphia Yearly Meeting in particular, was in the post-Revolutionary period to be spiritually more narrow and culturally less variegated than it had been in the rather more relaxed years that had preceded the upheaval.

If the effects of the war years on the Society, with their subtle intermixing of positive and negative factors, are not always easy to assess, the verdict on Friends' role during the Revolutionary struggle is even more debatable. The interplay of forces within their ranks had been extremely diverse, and the gamut of opinions gathered under the overshadowing umbrella of the Society's peace testimony extraordinarily wide: it had ranged from the passivism of some of the Philadelphia Quaker grandees, scarcely distinguishable from authentic Toryism, through every neutral shade of pacifism to the pacific procolonialism of many country Friends and of such Quaker bourgeois as Moses

152 *Ibid.*, pp. 308-23.

Brown in New England and old Elizabeth Shippen of Wilmington (Del.), who prophesied on her deathbed the ultimate expulsion under the Lord's power of "the invader of our land."[153] Genuine abhorrence of war and of all its fruits, traditional loyalty to the ancestral taboo on every activity connected with physical fighting, or a compound of the two might have provided the impulse toward the varied manifestations of Quaker war resistance. Their premises may have been incorrect; yet it was not partiality toward the enemy, as so many colonial enthusiasts thought, but a scrupulous regard to keep their conscience clear of what they believed was wrong that formed the basis of most Quaker conduct. The understanding verdict of a French observer, the future Girondin J. P. Brissot de Warville, who traveled widely in the United States half a decade after the end of the American Revolution, may be quoted as a suitable conclusion to this account of Friends' witness during the War of American Independence:

I believe that it was wrong to persecute them so ruthlessly for their pacifist neutrality. Had this been the first time they had refused to fight, had this refusal been dictated by devotion to the British cause, and had it been only a cloak to cover their true feelings, then they would have certainly been guilty and the persecution would have perhaps been justified. But their neutrality was dictated by religious beliefs which they had always professed and have continuously practiced. Whatever prejudiced or misinformed writers may say, the truth . . . is that the majority of Quakers did not favor more one side than the other, and that they helped anyone who needed help, no matter who he was. If a few Quakers did serve in the English army, a few . . . also served in the American army, and the Society expelled indiscriminately all who bore arms.[154]

[153] *Friends in Wilmington 1738-1938*, p. 36; Elizabeth Waterston, *Churches in Delaware during the Revolution*, pp. 47-49.

[154] J.P. Brissot de Warville, *New Travels in the United States of America 1788*, 1964 edn., pp. 328, 329. Among the Federalists during the postwar years there was increased understanding of the Quaker position on war. In June 1789 James Madison, speaking in Congress on behalf of his party, proposed that exemption from personal military service be guaranteed for religious objectors in the Bill of Rights, then under discussion. The bill became law in December 1791; however, by that date the provision for conscientious objection had been dropped. See Lillian D. Schlissel (ed.), *Conscience in America*, p. 47.

Chapter 5

The Quaker Peace Testimony,
1783-1861

Seventy-eight years passed between the end of the Revolutionary War and the outbreak of the war between the states. These years saw immense changes in every aspect of the new nation's affairs. Economic life was revolutionized; political institutions and parties were molded and remolded; social customs were transformed; new and vital intellectual trends sprang up among the educated; the religion of all classes was swept by the fires of revival and the cold winds of skepticism. Inside the three major American peace sects important developments were taking place, too. Some were beneficial to the health and well-being of these groups; others were harmful and represented a retrogression.

Whatever gains and losses the records of these sects (or "historic peace churches," as they are collectively known today) may show for this period of over three quarters of a century, their peace witness was marked on the whole by a decline in vitality. These years were for the most part years of peace. True, war was being waged in Europe almost continuously from 1792 to 1815, but only during its last few years—the War of 1812—was the United States involved directly. Thereafter, if we exclude trouble with the Indians and occasional abortive war crises, peace was punctuated only by the limited Mexican War of 1846-1848 until, nearly a decade and a half later, the rising tide of sectional conflict flooded over into open war. During these years separations stemming from disputed theology, or even from personality conflicts, occupied far more of the peace sects' attention than the maintenance of their historic testimonies against war.

I

The story of their continuing, if somewhat pallid, peace witness is to some extent fragmentary. The most coherent picture comes from the Society of Friends—as might be expected, both on account of the careful keeping and preservation of Quaker records and because of the higher educational level maintained within the Society. Quakers of both town and country were more articulate, more given to self-expression, more introspective than the German dialect speakers of the

Mennonite and Dunker faiths, whether back in their Pennsylvania home state or pushing out westward into the ever retreating wilderness. Quakers, not unlike the German sects, had grown increasingly isolated as a community from the surrounding world. They had come to pursue their advocacy of peace like their other activities as in "a garden enclos'd" (to use the words of the eighteenth-century English Friend, Samuel Fothergill). But the Quaker enclosure, for all its stifling narrowness in many respects, was still broader than the sectarian world of the pious Mennonite and Dunker farmer and backwoodsman.

Early in the second half of the eighteenth century, as we have seen, a movement originating in Philadelphia Yearly Meeting had begun in the American branch of the Society, aimed at the regeneration of the peace testimony as well as of the other aspects of the Quaker witness. To restore the purity of their faith and practice, the movement's leaders had insisted on the Society's separation from the world. Purged of its worldliness, the Society could then act—so it was hoped—as an agent of regeneration within the wider society of America. A reinvigorated Quaker pacifism, along with other humanitarian concerns, was thus part and parcel of this renewal of the Society of Friends as a whole. Yet, "in spite of being pacifists," Friends strove to be "essentially good Americans"[1] by holding up the Quaker enclosure as an example for the whole American nation.

In this period the Quaker as pacifist was concerned with a number of issues both in their direct impact on his personal life and in their theoretical implications for the religious life of the Society. What response should he make if called upon to muster with the state militia? Should taxes be paid if, wholly or in part, they were destined for military purposes? Might Revolutionary veterans who had become convinced Friends go on drawing their pensions? Where should the conscience of the Quaker merchant draw the line between peaceful trade and the profits of war? And, as Friends followed the frontier and thereby came into contact with the lawlessness of such regions, how would they meet the challenges this brought to their philosophy of nonviolence? These questions, and others like them, were practical matters which required individual decision. They were mostly questions which had had to be met in earlier periods—indeed, ever since Friends had come together in England around the middle of the seventeenth century. Friends also continued to concern themselves with the theoretical problems of war and peace. They composed treatises

[1] Sydney V. James, "The Impact of the American Revolution on Quakers' Ideas about Their Sect," *William and Mary Quarterly*, 3rd ser., XIX, no. 3 (July 1962), 375.

or drew up shorter statements expounding Christian pacifism in general or as it related to some particular situation. They did not neglect altogether the thorny old question of the relationship between pacifism and civil government. Finally, we may mention their reaction to the new focus of pacifism which developed outside the historic peace churches from 1815 on in the nondenominational peace societies, and to the radical philosophy of nonresistance in particular.

The conclusion of peace in 1783, though it greatly diminished the sufferings of Friends for their faithful maintenance of the peace testimony, did not end conscription for the state militias. In almost all states the law continued to require all able-bodied men to muster under arms for several days of training each year, with fines for nonattendance and distraints on property or short periods of imprisonment for failure to pay such fines. The law was not enforced with equal regularity or efficiency in all areas and, as time passed, the training period tended, except during national emergencies, to become more and more an occasion merely for junketing rather than for a serious military operation. Exemption might always be purchased by paying enough money to hire a substitute to train in one's stead. Quakers and the other peace sects were sometimes specifically granted exemption in a state's militia law—provided they were ready to pay a small sum in exchange. This, of course, the Quakers as a body refused to do, regarding it still—as they had done hitherto—as an infringement of the rights of conscience and freedom of religion. And, as before, distraints on property and occasional imprisonments ensued whenever and wherever the militia officers took their jobs seriously. More often, of course, neighborly friendliness, mixed with the unmilitary disposition of the majority of the American people, inhibited a harsh enforcement of the law on otherwise law-abiding citizens whose consciences had in this instance converted them into temporary law violators.

When in 1790 and again in 1795 proposals were put forward in Congress, then deliberating in Philadelphia, to exempt Quakers from the obligation of mustering with the militia provided they paid a sum of £2 to be used for nonmilitary purposes, protest came from Friends both individually and collectively. In 1790 a committee of twelve, including such weighty members of Philadelphia Yearly Meeting as James Pemberton, William Savery, and Warner Mifflin, drew up on behalf of the meeting an "Address and Memorial," which was duly presented to President and Congress.[2] In it they judiciously mixed in appreciation of the concern shown by the legislators for tender con-

---

[2] Quoted in full in Hilda Justice, *Life and Ancestry of Warner Mifflin*, pp. 178-82. See also Ezra Michener, *A Retrospect of Early Quakerism*, p. 306.

sciences with a warning that the conditional exemption proposed would not, in fact, be sufficient to allay Friends' scruples. In addition to refusing direct military service, they stated, Friends "have also considered themselves conscientiously bound to refuse the payment of any sum required in lieu of such personal service or in consideration of an exemption from any military employment, however laudable the purposes are to which the money is intended to be applied, as it manifestly infringes on the right of conscience."

Five years later, when the question was still being discussed in the legislature, an anonymous Friend attempted to argue the case for unconditional exemption in more detail. His views were originally expressed in private correspondence and published, apparently without permission, by the non-Friend sympathizer to whom they were addressed. The writer, naturally, recognized the religious foundation of the Society's pacifism and the importance of early training in inculcating its precepts. "The ardor of youth, ambition, and other powerful springs, which exist in the human breast," he explained, "are common to the members of our, as well as to those of every other society; but it is the early and assiduous care, which is bestowed upon the formation of our minds, and the direction of our ideas, which first initiates us into the habit of restraining our ambition, and other passions; and finally deters us from engaging in the field of battle." However, he based his case primarily on the liberties of the freeborn American, on "the ground of unrestrained freedom of opinions, which is the birthright—the constitutional right—of every citizen of these states, whether in religious or other concerns." If a man's conscience, his religion, forbids him to do military service, then it is an infringement of his freedom to require him to pay a "tax" for permission to follow his conscience, which is in itself an inalienable right. The objection that granting complete exemption to members of the Society would open the doors to a flood of slackers unwilling either to drill themselves or to pay a monetary equivalent was groundless. The exactitude with which the Society kept its membership records would prevent its being used as a cover for militia dodgers.[3]

After the bill became law in 1795, it remained, as before, the official policy of the Society that members should, if necessary, suffer the penalties of the law rather than buy their exemption at the cost of principle, however seemingly innocuous were the ends to which their exemption money might be put by the authorities. "Where deviations in this respect occur," states a minute of Philadelphia Yearly Meeting

[3] *A Letter from One of the Society of Friends, Relative to the Conscientious Scrupulousness of its Members to Bear Arms,* pp. 2-5, 10-12, 17.

of 1805 which expresses the practice then current among Friends, "tender dealing and advice should be extended to the party, in order to their convincement and restoration; and where they continue so regardless of the sense and judgment of the body, that the labor of their Friends proves ineffectual, Monthly Meetings should proceed to testify against them."[4] Thus Quaker absolutism, the refusal of all conditional exemption to military service, continued to be officially endorsed by the Society and enforced with the threat of disownment.

Lobbying state legislatures on behalf of their conscientious objectors became a frequent practice with the various yearly meetings, particularly when new militia legislation, or an amendment to the old, was being discussed. We find Philadelphia Yearly Meeting, for instance, doing this—not for the first or last time—in 1808. A delegation complete with a memorial drawn up by the Meeting for Sufferings was dispatched to the state capital, then situated at Lancaster. Its four members, so it is told, entered the legislative chamber just at the moment a representative, Michael Leib, was denouncing Friends as instigators of the attempt to insert into the militia bill then under consideration a clause giving religious objectors complete exemption. Looking up and recognizing among the delegates his old friend and neighbor, the prominent Quaker minister Thomas Scattergood, Leib immediately changed his tack and now began to praise the Society as warmly as he had only a few minutes before condemned it—much to the amusement of his fellow assemblymen.[5]

Perhaps the most cogent example of memorializing in favor of complete exemption was provided by the documents drawn up toward the end of 1810 by the talented clerk of Virginia Yearly Meeting, Benjamin Bates, and presented to the state legislature in the meeting's name. Both the "Memorial and Petition" and Bates's accompanying letter were subsequently reprinted several times and used by other yearly meetings even as late as the Civil War to support their claims to exemption. These documents do, indeed, argue the Quaker case with skill and clarity and show the author to be a man of education and culture, well versed in the political philosophy of his day.

The rights of religious conscience, the "Memorial" states, do not need to be proved. They should be "self-evident . . . in this enlightened age and country," and, besides, they had been guaranteed in federal and state constitutions. To confine freedom of conscience to the realm of mere thought and not to extend it also to action flowing from thought

---

[4] *Yearly Extracts for 1805* (folder issued by Philadelphia Y. M. in F.H.L.S.C.), pp. 2, 3. See also Michener, *A Retrospect of Early Quakerism*, p. 307.
[5] W. W. Cadbury in *Friend*, vol. 119, no. 10 (8 Nov. 1945), pp. 150, 151.

would be an injustice. Friends, following what they believed to be the example of the early church and many other good Christians, and also of their own society since its beginning, had always held it to be wrong for Christians to bear arms. "To require it under legal penalties, is to reduce them to the alternative of refusing a compliance with the laws of their country, or of violating what they most solemnly believe is, to *them*, a law of God, clothed with the most awful sanctions." Their conscientious scruples in this respect had been recognized as genuine by the Virginia Legislature immediately after the Revolution, but recent changes in the law had withdrawn this liberal exemption. Friends were now required to pay commutation money for their unwillingness to train, and the amount of these fines was fixed arbitrarily "at the discretion of the courts martial, and become in numerous instances, extremely oppressive." "The voluntary payment of a fine imposed for adhering to religious duty, or the receiving of surplus money arising from the sale of their property seized for the satisfying of these demands, would be to acknowledge a delinquency, which they cannot admit, and to become parties in a traffic or commutation of their principles."[6]

In his supplementary remarks, Bates stressed that Friends had no wish to escape from their civil obligations under the cloak of religion or to contest the right of the state to conscript, if such were the people's will, those of its citizens whose consciences were not opposed to militia training. At the same time, he explained in further detail why Friends felt unable to pay commutation money ("a muster-fine in disguise," he called it), even when, as in the present instance, it was to be put to some good use like the upkeep of schools.

I am paying [he told the legislators] what is considered by the government as a debt—and for what consideration? Plainly for being allowed to enjoy the liberty of conscience. But I do not derive the liberty of conscience from the government; I hold it from a tenure antecedent to the institutions of civil society. It was secured to me in the social compact, and it was never submitted to the legislature at all. They have therefore no such privilege to grant or withhold, at their pleasure; and certainly no pretence or authority to sell it for a price.

Absolute exemption for religious objectors, then, was a natural, inborn right which their nonpacifist fellow citizens were powerless to barter away. "If the powers they surrender for themselves," Bates wrote of the

---

[6] *Memorial and Petition of the Society of Friends, to the Legislature of Virginia: with a Letter of Benjamin Bates, on the Subject of Militia Fines*, pp. 2-4.

latter, "involve the constitutional rights of others, they are binding only on those who have consented to them." The Quaker absolutist, in following his conscience and his God in refusing to obey a man-made law and in patiently suffering the consequences, was in fact defending at the same time the civil rights and the constitutional liberties of all free Americans.[7]

Benjamin Bates and his fellow memorialists were acting during a period of peace when the continental war had not as yet involved the United States in direct military conflict. The year 1812, however, saw the outbreak of hostilities between the United States and Great Britain. Although North America was only briefly and intermittently the scene of actual battle, so that the devastation and loss of life nowhere equalled that suffered back in Europe and the day-to-day existence of the majority of the country's citizens went on unchanged, the war years brought new and more acute problems to the Society of Friends. The edge of their peace witness, always liable to become blunted in periods of protracted peace, was sharpened, too.

The yearly meetings exhorted their members to maintain a consistent testimony against war in the face of increased pressures to conform. In 1813 Baltimore Yearly Meeting—to give just one instance—urged Friends to avoid any conduct that might "violate in any way this most precious testimony." History had shown the disastrous character of war and the fair fruits of peace, and it was incumbent on them to be prepared to face trials and sacrifices on its behalf.[8] Early in 1815 its Meeting for Sufferings warned members against even an "indirect payment of fines or other military demands."[9] As the Quakers had found in the past, it was not always easy to know just where to draw the line in defining action inconsistent with their peace witness. For example, a minute dated 14 August 1813, from a Pennsylvania rural community, the monthly meeting at Center, runs as follows: "This meeting requests the judgment of the quarterly meeting on that part of the discipline relating to military service whether the voluntary or involuntary furnishing of waggons, where compensation may be received for the owners, for the use thereof will bear a testimony."[10]

The main trials faced by Friends during the war years were naturally those connected with service in the militia. The rigor with which the military enforced its requirements was increased as the demand for men became greater. Again the practice differed even from county to

[7] *Ibid.*, pp. 10-12.
[8] Kenneth S.P. Morse, *Baltimore Yearly Meeting*, p. 34.
[9] Minute dated 4 Feb. 1815, copy in the Janney MSS, F.H.L.S.C.
[10] From Thomas Jenkins Papers, F.H.L.S.C., R G 5.

county within the same state. In Virginia before the outbreak of war, we are told, the "sheriffs of the counties to the southwest of Richmond were unrelenting in their collection of fines for failure to muster, whereas in other counties at the same period the county officials were either indifferent or purposely lenient with the Quakers." The harassment in the former area reached a climax in 1813. Eleven young men from Upper Monthly Meeting were arrested and taken off to prison in Norfolk or Petersburg.[11] Elsewhere in the same state Friends fared no better. The records of Western Branch Monthly Meeting show that funds were raised early in 1813 among members of the meeting to assist the families of those who "are carried off in the militia," as well as Friends who were suffering severely from distraints for nonpayment of militia fines. "On the 17th of the 3rd," it was reported, "three young men were taken and carried off into the army in or near Portsmouth and for refusing to bear arms they were by orders of Colonel Francis B. Boykin confined in the dungeon about 48 hours and are still detained in the army."[12] These were not isolated cases. But Friends in Virginia, a small minority group whose popularity was not increased by their outspoken opposition to slavery in this slaveholding state, often seem to have fared worse vis-à-vis the military than was usually the case with their brethren farther north and west.

True, poorer Friends anywhere who did not own enough property on which distraint could be levied might find themselves cast into the local jail until such time as the military or public opinion relented. This contrast in treatment comes out clearly in the narrative of an Indiana Quaker (later converted to Methodism), Henry Hoover, whose family was among the first to settle in the upper Whitewater Valley. Friends' views were not as well known there as in the older settled areas, and frontier mores were in any case intolerant of pacifist inclinations; thus, even before the outbreak of war, public opinion had forced the territorial legislature to withdraw the exemption they had granted Quaker objectors in 1810.[13] When war came, young Hoover was or-

---

[11] Hinshaw, *Encyclopedia of American Quaker Genealogy*, VI, 127. In the editor's opinion, the severity with which the militia regulations were enforced over the years—along with the unpopularity and embarrassments connected with Friends' testimony against slavery—were the chief reasons for the westward migration of most Quaker families from this and neighboring meetings in the course of a couple of decades after the war.

[12] *Ibid.*, pp. 48, 292.

[13] In August 1811 Indiana Friends had written to the governor, General William H. Harrison, and to the general assembly to thank them for the generous exemption given them in the previous year. "If," they say, "we may be useful in harmonizing our fellow citizens, or civilizing our Indian neighbors, we will with unreserved alacrity contribute thereto; as we hope ever to participate in the peaceful

dered out for eight days' service with the military. "A compliance would have ejected me from the Church," he writes, "and moreover brought trouble on the minds of my parents, who had taught me that all wars were antichristian." And so, upon refusing to serve, he was fined $16 by the court, and soldiers were sent to seize his sheep to cover the fine which, as a loyal Friend, he could not pay himself. "Others were used more severe," he adds, "not having property on which to levy, their bodies were seized and cast into the jail in Salisbury, in the dead of winter. . . . The jail had neither chimney, stove or bed. . . . They were for weeks confined in jail, but were ultimately discharged, but not until public opinion had begun to do its work of mercy."[14]

In the North, however, Quakers in many areas enjoyed considerable social prestige. In New England, New York, and Pennsylvania the Society included many prosperous merchants and traders in its membership. There, especially in Pennsylvania, arrest and imprisonment for refusing military service occurred only rarely, though fines were often heavy and, as usual, the value of the property distrained was frequently in excess of the amount of the fine.[15] This latter fact would seem to invalidate the stories told at that time (and later) of conversions to Quakerism in order to evade military service,[16] especially in view of the strict requirements laid down for membership. Sometimes, however, Friends were treated with remarkable sympathy and understanding—presumably because the Quaker peace testimony and the individual's membership in the Society were well known in the community. The experience of William Evans (1787-1867), then a young

---

improvement of our country's welfare." This letter and Friends' memorial of 1810 asking for complete exemption from militia service are printed in Rufus M. Jones, *The Later Periods of Quakerism*, II, 720, 721.

[14] Bernhard Knollenberg, *Pioneer Sketches of the Upper Whitewater Valley*, pp. 29, 41.

[15] See *Pennsylvania Colonial Records: Minutes of the Supreme Executive Council of Pennsylvania*, XV, 418, for an early example in a protest, dated March 1788, from Friends in Chester Co., whose goods were being made by the collectors liable to repeated distraint for the same fine.

[16] Samuel H. Cox, *Quakerism not Christianity*, p. 235: "In the last war [1812] some became sudden converts to Quakerism; growing quite conscientious in the time of danger against such profane exposures of life—and either joined the Society, or pleaded a kindred exemption from responsibilities." Dr. Cox was a convert from Quakerism to Presbyterianism. Pp. 234-56 of his bulky refutation of Quakerism are devoted to a discussion of the peace testimony. A more plausible, though equally partisan, criticism is that contained in a short political pamphlet published in 1808, *A Serious Expostulation with the Society of Friends in Pennsylvania, and Parts Adjacent*, where "Pacificus" comments (pp. 5, 6) on the lack of a genuinely pacific spirit among even many weighty Quakers where "their mercantile interest" is involved. See also *To Pacificus, in Reply to his Essay*.

man of 27 and a birthright Friend, is a case in point. He relates in his journal how in 1814 he was summoned "before a court-martial" in Philadelphia to answer for his failure to muster with the militia. The court gave him a respectful hearing, listening patiently to his explanation that, as a Friend, he would suffer the penalty of the law rather than comply with an order that went against his conscience. Evans heard nothing more from the military authorities, who evidently decided to leave the young Quaker in peace and not to proceed against him further.[17]

Thus, as earlier, in the Revolutionary War, the sufferings of Friends on account of their pacifist witness during the War of 1812 stemmed mainly from the heavy distraints on their property which refusal to pay the fines imposed by the military entailed. As usual, careful record was kept by most meetings of the losses endured. An example of the scrupulousness with which this accounting was carried on is shown in the case of Baltimore Yearly Meeting. In February 1815, Meeting for Sufferings admonished monthly meetings, when gathering information concerning "military" sufferings,

> . . . not to admit of any case as a suffering which may not appear to have been faithfully borne. We believe also that when goods are distrained, an advantage would arise from obtaining as far as practicable consistently with our peaceable profession from the officer making the distraint a certificate containing the articles taken, and the amount and nature of the claim they were taken to satisfy.[18]

In 1815 an era of external peace and of domestic "good feelings" came to the United States. In the internal affairs of the Society of Friends, however, the spirit of schism was growing, until finally it spilled over into the great separation of 1827, dividing the Society into Orthodox and Hicksite branches, each of which excommunicated the other. The deplorable discord within a religious denomination collectively dedicated to the gospel of peace did not, it is true, directly affect the maintenance of its historic testimony against war. This testimony continued as part of the heritage claimed by both branches. Nevertheless, energy and thought were channeled off into the problems generated by the factional conflict. One of the Friends' activities that suffered—but, of course, by no means the only one—was their peace witness.

For many decades the problem of militia service continued to occupy the main place in Friends' concern for the peace testimony. The

---

[17] *Journal of William Evans*, p. 32.
[18] Minute dated 4 Feb. 1815, copy in the Janney MSS, F.H.L.S.C.

pattern did not change very much. The heaviest burden still arose from the imposition of fines on the younger men for failure to appear for training at the annual musters and the subsequent distraints levied for their conscientious refusal to pay. It was calculated that during the single decade of the 1820's property amounting to the total value of $16,021.85 was taken from members of Philadelphia Yearly Meeting (which of course included, in addition to the Pennsylvania meetings, Friends living in western New Jersey as well as some in Delaware and Maryland).[19] The accuracy with which monthly meetings kept records of militia "sufferings" vouches for the reliability of these figures. There was frequent complaint about the rapacity of the collectors, usually shady characters who seized from their victims goods much in excess of the value of the original fine. "The office is so disagreeable," complained an Ohio Quaker, "it is seldom undertaken by a man of generous feeling." Self-respecting citizens were usually unwilling to undertake the task of confiscating the clothing, bedclothes, furniture, and household utensils of neighbors whose religious scruples they respected, even if they did not share them. Consequently, either the law was ignored or its execution was placed in the hands of the unscrupulous.[20] A writer in the Orthodox *Friend* provides several examples of these extortions. "For a fine of four dollars," we are told, "one of these deputies came into a store, took up the shears, and cut himself off two yards of the finest broadcloth, then selling at nine dollars per yard." "Another of these abandoned fellows actually seized a man's account books, and took them to a neighbour's to sell."[21]

We have a detailed description of how the system worked where the law enforcement officers were reasonably honest in the account left by Benjamin Hallowell (1799-1877), the Quaker schoolmaster (one of whose pupils was to be Robert E. Lee!). In 1824 he was teaching in Alexandria (then within the limits of the District of Columbia), and at the end of his first year there he was presented with a bill for $15 for failing to attend the statutory militia trainings. The militia captain, who in this case had the task of levying distraint on Hallowell's property when the latter persisted in his refusal to pay the fine, was obviously somewhat embarrassed at his assignment and asked the young man to point out to him what objects he could spare most easily. His Quaker conscience, however, restrained Hallowell from collaborating with the military even to this extent. So, in the end, the captain

---

[19] *Friend; or, Advocate of Truth*, N.S., I, no. 2 (Feb. 1832), 35.
[20] "Extract from an Address to the People of Belmont, Ohio, by Charles Hammond" in *Extracts from Several Writers on Militia Fines and War*, pp. 3, 4.
[21] *Friend* (Phila.), 29 Dec. 1832, p. 96.

took away a number of pieces of "our parlor furniture" to be sold by special auction where, however, because no respectable people attended "from a reluctance to make a profit from their neighbours' religious scruples," the goods went for a ridiculously low figure. The following year Congress exempted all teachers within the District from the obligation of militia service, and thus Hallowell's trials came to an end.[22]

The militia laws, in peacetime as in wartime, touched not only the purses of the Friends but upon occasion their persons as well, and, hence, we find that young Quaker conscientious objectors were sometimes dragged off to spend short periods in prison for nonpayment of their fines. Usually, as we have seen, it was the poorer brethren who suffered in this way, but not always. In the early 1820's, for instance, young James Mott (1788-1868), a fairly well-to-do Philadelphia merchant newly wed to the famous Lucretia, found himself in the city jail on Arch Street until, without his knowledge or consent, an unknown sympathizer paid his fine for him.[23] As late as 1845 the Hicksite New York Yearly Meeting could record: "Beside the loss of property taken from our members by distraint, three of our young men have suffered imprisonment for different periods rather than submit to military requisitions."[24] Constant distraints on property and occasional imprisonment continued—though with decreasing intensity—to be the lot of many Friends of militia age into the 1850's.

That most young Friends followed the Society's official line and refused to pay the fines imposed on them seems clear from the surviving evidence. That many did so more or less reluctantly appears equally certain, and, it seems, too, that, at least by the thirties, a few did pay and escaped the disciplining by their meetings that would almost inevitably have been their lot earlier. The issue, after all, was not as clearcut as the original refusal of service from which it had resulted. The penalties—whether in the form of distraints on property or brief imprisonments—were more inconvenient than harsh or cruel, and the whole position had a slightly ridiculous aspect. The sympathies of the community were often with the lawbreaker rather than with the law. The very mildness of this law, indeed, offered a temptation to relax opposition to its enforcement. So we find that even a man like Hallowell, who "cheerfully" suffered his furniture to be removed and auctioned for a song, had his inner doubts about the wisdom of his Society's uncompromising stand and its right to impose it on members

[22] *Autobiography of Benjamin Hallowell*, pp. 210-12.
[23] A. D. Hallowell, *James and Lucretia Mott*, p. 8.
[24] From Thomas Jenkins Papers, F.H.L.S.C., R G 5.

who had different views, feeling that the payment of a fine was a legitimate submission to the penalty for noncompliance with the law. "But," he went on, "estimating very highly the privileges my birthright membership in the Society of Friends has given me . . . I will not pay such fines while the Discipline of the Society requires its members not to do so."[25]

Not all members who failed to go along with the discipline, which regarded the payment of fines as compromising their conscientious objection to war, were so loyal or so scrupulous as Hallowell. Thus, in an article which an anonymous writer contributed to the *Friend* in 1835 under the pseudonym of "Pacificus,"[26] we discover that not only the special efforts of "the present collector of militia fines in the city of Philadelphia" to enforce payment, but the evidence of "the very small number of cases sent up to our late quarterly meeting" of persons refusing payment, indicated (in the writer's opinion) that this testimony was growing lukewarm among the present generation. There were undoubtedly some who did not hesitate to pay outright; more often, there was resort to subterfuge through connivance at payment, usually by some non-Quaker friend. " 'Have you no friend to pay it for you?' is the enquiry of the collector; 'Friend so-and-so always *has* his paid.' 'Mr. S—— is a Friend and he pays me his fine; so does Mr. T——; they never make a disturbance about it.' " "Pacificus" goes on to point out what he regards as the insidious effects of this disobedience on the Society's discipline and brands the willingness to pay on the part of non-Friends as "mistaken kindness." It helps, he says, to bolster up "the onerous militia system," and it makes it more difficult for consistent Friends to maintain a clear testimony for peace.

By the fifties the pressure had been largely relaxed. Distrainment became infrequent, and imprisonment for nonpayment of fines ceased almost entirely. But for Pennsylvania Friends a new danger arose: they might inadvertently pay their militia fine along with their general state tax bill. An extra 50¢ (which by this time was the total exacted for militia delinquency) might not easily be noticed, and the whole amount might be paid willingly by the unsuspecting Friend. The state was probably not aiming at conscious deception when it sanctioned tacking militia fines onto the general tax bill in this way but, rather, was out to save on the costs of collecting at a time when, for most citizens of the state, this small fine had taken the place of the obligation to attend musters. For the militia system had fallen into decay, and delinquency had become almost universal among those

[25] *Autobiography*, p. 212.　　　　[26] *Friend*, 14 Feb. 1835, p. 151.

who did not entertain any conscientious objections. The Quaker conscience, however, was distressed at the thought of giving even unwitting support to the war system, and throughout the decade the Quaker weeklies, all published in Philadelphia during that period, continued to sound the alarm from time to time lest Friends relax their vigilance.

I was on the point of paying my militia fine to the tax collector a day or two since [runs a letter in the *Friend* of 6 July 1850], and that without thinking at all on the subject. No open reference is made to it in the tax bill, but the item of State *Personal* tax is 50 cents higher than usual. Some little occurrence excited my suspicion, but it was not until I had repeatedly and pointedly questioned the collector, that I learned from him, that the additional 50 cents was for my militia fine. As the time when our taxes are to be paid is now at hand, would it not be well to put Friends on their guard, lest they be led in this manner to support the militia system, without being aware of it?[27]

In the 1850's the war clouds were already mounting, and the testing period of the early sixties would make a storm over the 50¢ look small indeed. Nevertheless, a question of principle, the pinch of incense, was at stake here for Friends, and ultimately this, not the size of the stake, is what is important.

We have briefly surveyed the history of Quaker conscientious objection during the decades following the conclusion of the Napoleonic Wars. Friends collectively or individually, were active in upholding their conscientious objectors in various ways, too. As we have seen, they addressed state legislatures in favor of exemption, placed the case for such exemption before the public, and attempted, more generally, to prove not only the moral harm but also the practical uselessness of the militia system.

Among the most active in encouraging conscientious objectors was Elisha Bates (ca. 1780-1861), who was one of the leaders of Ohio Quakerism until his fervent evangelicalism led him in 1835 to leave Friends for the Methodist Episcopal Church. In the *Moral Advocate*, which he edited in Mt. Pleasant from 1821-1824, he included, along with material on "duelling, capital punishments and prison discipline," a number of articles—mostly from his own pen—protesting against the imposition of fines and other penalties on Friends for refusing militia service and explaining the grounds of the Quaker objec-

---

[27] *Ibid.*, 6 July 1850. See also *Friends' Review*, 30 April 1853, p. 521; *Friends' Intelligencer*, 12 March 1859, p. 822; *Journal of William Evans*, p. 661.

tion to war. Not much of this writing was original, but, in a time when no regular Quaker periodical press had yet appeared, it served a valuable function in freshening the traditional teaching on peace learned at home, school, and meeting. The paper closed at the end of 1824, and in the last number Bates gave the place of honor to his "Address to Young Men who believe in the Unlawfulness of War."[28] In it he explained to them the importance of Friends' peace testimony, "this noble testimony," to the Society to which they belonged. They must be prepared in their turn to make sacrifices for it, to face unpopularity as their forefathers had done, and the opportunity to do so they should welcome as a privilege rather than as a burden. They must see that gentle behavior and blameless conduct match their words of peace: this is the best means of disarming hostility. They should try to direct their thoughts to the source of Friends' peace testimony and not accept pacifism passively as merely an inherited belief. On this point he gave some sound advice to those who might have to take their stand as conscientious objectors:

In declining to render to the laws, that active obedience they require, you should recur to principle, rather than rest on the example of your elder friends. In giving to those who inquire, the reasons for your conduct, still recur to the principle in your minds, rather than to any train of reasoning which you may have learned from others, or formed to yourselves by mere speculative reflection.

Bates had grasped one of the main weaknesses of an inherited religious testimony, whether it be against all wars or in any other sphere: that it would come to be accepted merely as a part of this inheritance and cease to have vital meaning, or any meaning at all perhaps, apart from the desire to maintain the traditions of the group as they had been handed down from the forefathers.

Friends' collective statements on militia service during our period tended to concentrate on the practical disabilities faced by members of military age. Often, however, they dwelt, too, on the general principles which lay behind the peace testimony. In protesting against a new act passed by the Delaware legislature requiring commutation money from religious objectors, we find Wilmington Monthly Meeting in 1827 explaining that their peace testimony was based not only on religious conviction but also on "right reason and the dictates of experience." Christian love coupled with a readiness to suffer without retaliation "would if collectively practised, be found equally effectual

[28] *Moral Advocate*, III, no. 12 (Dec. 1824), 192-94. For Bates's pacifism, see the M.A. thesis on Bates by Robert J. Leach, pp. 76-86.

in the preservation of *nations*" as it was for individuals.[29] Three years later, in 1830, when New York Friends faced similar revisions in the militia laws of their state, they appealed to the good feelings of the law-makers. They were sure, they said, that imprisonment for following conscience, to which members of their Society had recently been subjected, was repugnant to the legislators.[30] Again, in 1833, Philadelphia Yearly Meeting (Orthodox) issued on behalf of its members living in New Jersey a memorial discussing proposals in that state to relieve conscientious objectors by allowing them to pay a special tax, that would go to the school funds, in place of the straight militia fine. Although the memorial recognized that the idea was well meant, "yet it is due to ourselves," it went on, "to state that so far as *we* are concerned, the proposed change in the law will not afford us the intended relief." Commutation money in any form was a tax on conscience, an infringement of religious freedom. The attempt to exact it at the cost of distrainment and imprisonment would prove as useless as it was costly.[31]

The convention, which met at Harrisburg in 1837 to frame a revised constitution for the state of Pennsylvania, aroused deep interest among Friends. The Orthodox Yearly Meeting drew up a "Memorial and Petition" to the convention, pleading for unconditional exemption for all religious objectors. It also reprinted a non-Quaker pamphlet published in Boston nineteen years earlier—*A Dialogue between Telemachus and Mentor on the Rights of Conscience and Military Requisitions*—which stated the case for all types of militia conscientious objectors. (The *Dialogue* is discussed in the full version of this book.) The "Memorial" was presented to the convention by a Quaker member, Thomas P. Cope (1768-1864). After telling his fellow members that, "in this land of Penn, the Quaker has been deprived of his conscientious privileges," Cope went on to compare the provisions now made for Quaker conscientious objectors in the commonwealth of Massachusetts, Friends' fiercest persecutor in the seventeenth century, with those at present existing in the Quaker state—to the disadvantage of the latter.[32] The "Memorial" itself emphasized the civil liberties aspect of the Quaker case. Friends hoped "that the Society of Friends will not, in the nineteenth century, be deprived of those rights, which their predecessors, on the same soil, in the beginning of the eighteenth,

---

[29] *Address of the Wilmington Monthly Meeting . . . on the Subject of the Militia Law*, pp. 3, 4.
[30] *Memorial . . . on the Subject of Imprisonment, for Non-Compliance with Military Requisitions*, p. 4.
[31] *Friend*, 27 July 1833. [32] *Ibid.*, 5 Aug. 1837, pp. 347, 348.

extended to every class of natives and emigrants." The right to the free exercise of religious conscience was the birthright of every American citizen; therefore, those who had genuine scruples concerning the bearing of arms, whether Quaker or non-Quaker, should be relieved of all obligation under the militia laws.[33] "It is the payment of an equivalent, as the purchase of a religious right; not the purpose to which it may be applied, to which we conscientiously object." Friends, by their sufferings for conscience in the past and their readiness to pay taxes and contribute to the public welfare, had shown that they were not actuated by a desire to contract out of their social obligations or to escape persecution or the hardships of battle. Moreover, by the very fact of firmly maintaining their pacifist ideals, they were making a contribution to the welfare of the whole, since "the diffusion of opinions, such as Friends have always held, must operate in favour of peace."[34]

One of those delegated to present the "Memorial" was Enoch Lewis (1776-1856), who was also responsible for drawing it up.[35] Lewis was by profession a lawyer, by inclination a scholar, in his religious views close to the evangelical party within the Society of Friends, and in the next decade was to become editor of its organ—the *Friends' Review*. In 1831 he had compiled a 35-page pamphlet entitled *Some Observations on the Militia System*, some of whose arguments were repeated in the "Memorial" six years later. Lewis's *Observations* were addressed to a broader audience than the Society of Friends, and it seems to have been quite widely read, since by 1846 it had gone through three editions. The author states his intention at the outset not to discuss the question of absolute pacifism (though he makes his own sentiments clear throughout and at times strays off into arguing about the merits of a peaceful over a warlike policy for a nation); his avowed object was to plead for the scrapping of a compulsory peacetime militia such as existed in all states at that date.

The first objection raised—and it was perhaps the most important one for Lewis—concerned the compulsory character of militia service.

[33] Friends always contended for the inclusion of all genuine objectors within the scope of any legal exemption, although state legislators were rarely as liberal, limiting the right to Quakers alone or to members of other specified peace churches. For instance, when the Maine constitution was being framed, the small group of Friends there attempted to get the rights of all C.O.'s written into it. Only "when we found that to urge so general an exemption was of no avail, we then confined ourselves to the narrow limits of our society." See Rufus M. Jones, *The Society of Friends in Kennebec County, Maine*, pp. 11, 12.

[34] *Memorial and Address of Friends on Military Exactions*, pp. 2, 3, 5, 6, 8.

[35] See Joseph L. Lewis, *A Memoir of Enoch Lewis*. Pp. 25-28 relate Enoch Lewis's personal witness as a young man against seeking security in armed defense when in the 1790's he was employed in surveying the frontier wilderness of western Pennsylvania.

How ironic it was that in the province founded by the peaceful William Penn, where religious freedom had been guaranteed from the beginning, men should be required to pay money to exercise a right which belonged to all, whether Quaker or not. "To presume that a plea of conscientious scruple is insincere, and upon that assumption to found a right to impose a penalty, is to reverse an established principle of law, which always presumes innocence where guilt is not proved." Therefore, all who desire exemption by reason of conscience should have this guaranteed them by law.[36] Lewis went on to present, in the second place, a series of utilitarian arguments against the militia system. Many Friends had attacked the institution on these grounds. A decade before, Elisha Bates had described it as "futile and contemptible in the estimation of military men: demoralizing to those who conform to it, and oppressive to those who conscientiously cannot."[37] In many states during this period, also, a widespread feeling existed, outside the peace movement, that the militia system had become outmoded and that it was merely burdensome to the citizen, fulfilling no useful function to offset the time and money expended on it. And so Lewis could write: "Scarcely any person acquainted with the subject pretends to believe that militia trainings, as practised in this state, are anything better than a ridiculous farce." He quotes from a number of statements by high-ranking military officers, showing that even they shared this opinion. Militia musters had become scenes of drunkenness and vice rather than exhibitions of the martial virtues. Lewis cites extensively from recent reports of the auditor-general of Pennsylvania, in order to show the large sums the state was lavishing on its militia. And it was for their refusal to participate in all this display that the conscientious continued to be fined and imprisoned. Let us disband the militia, Lewis pleads, and spend the money on some more useful purpose such as the education of deprived children.[38] Lewis's tone here is distinctly secular, his argument antimilitarist rather than pacifist, his appeal to persons outside the Quaker enclosure.

What of those Friends who overstepped the Quaker discipline and participated in military service in one or another capacity? Our period saw no change in the rigid enforcement of the discipline in regard to delinquents on this score. The procedure remained unaltered: the member was first "labored with" in an effort to bring him to acknowl-

[36] Enoch Lewis, *Some Observations on the Militia System, Addressed to the Serious Consideration of the Citizens of Pennsylvania*, pp. 4, 8-23.
[37] *Moral Advocate*, II, no. 2 (Aug. 1822), 22.
[38] Lewis, *Some Observations*, pp. 24-34.

edge his fault, but, where he remained adamant, the final step of disownment followed sooner or later. The records of local monthly meetings are filled with minutes to this effect.[39] The scions of aristocratic
Quaker families were dealt with impartially along with the sons of
humble rural farmers. When Dr. George Logan (1753-1821), son of a
Quaker councillor, nephew by marriage of a Quaker speaker of the
Pennsylvania assembly, and grandson of Penn's secretary and confi-
dant, joined the militia, he too did not escape. "Friends were hesitant
to take action against a Logan of Stenton, whose family history was
so closely entwined with William Penn's 'holy experiment.'" He was
visited by a series of weighty Philadelphia Friends who tried in vain
to persuade him to withdraw. Although Logan was no militarist and
believed "all war unlawful to a Christian except that which was strictly of a defensive kind" (a view that was held, in fact, by some who
remained all their lives within the Society), he refused to change his
course. In January 1791 came the final breach, and Logan was
disowned.[40]

Usually, a decision by some young Friend to attend militia musters
(the form infringing the peace testimony most often took) was, as
has been shown earlier, part and parcel of a more general drifting on
his part away from his Quaker moorings, one more step toward loosen-
ing the ties with his home environment. In these circumstances the
elders were unlikely to reclaim the prodigal. We can see this clearly
in a case like the following one, which is taken from the minutes of
Cedar Creek Monthly Meeting (Va.) for 1807:

> Whereas, Micajah Crew, Jr., son of Nicholas Crew, of Hanover
> County, has so far deviated from our known rules as to use spirituous
> liquors to excess, also has engaged in military services, for which
> conduct he had been dealt without the desired effect, and has sub-
> sequently entered into marriage contrary to the rules of our Disci-
> pline, we do, therefore, disown him from being any longer a mem-
> ber, until he shall make satisfaction for his conduct.[41]

Sometimes, however, a young man might be led by local pressure, by
desire not to seem different, or might be influenced perhaps by the
glamor of the military to assume only temporarily a role in conflict
with his family, to which he still remained closely bound by ties not
only of sentiment but of genuine devotion. On other occasions, it might

---

[39] Several examples from this period are cited in Jones, *The Later Periods of
Quakerism*, II, 721; Edward Needles Wright, *Conscientious Objectors in the Civil
War*, p. 12.
[40] Frederick B. Tolles, *George Logan of Philadelphia*, pp. 106-8.
[41] *Our Quaker Friends of Ye Olden Time*, p. 146.

be a wish to escape the material inconvenience involved in a persistent refusal to train which led to action frowned upon by the Society. "Dear Friends," wrote one William Betts, a Virginia Friend, on 15 January 1798, "I hereby condemn my conduct in having been active in procuring a substitute to serve in the Militia, although by indirect means. . . . Hoping my future conduct may be more consistent, I desire Friends may accept this my acknowledgment and continue me under their care."[42] In cases of these kinds, meetings would have some chance of reclaiming the erring member and then, as with William Betts, proceedings would be closed by an acknowledgment of error.

Friends, as we have seen from the previous period, regarded all forms of noncombatant service in the armed forces as incompatible with the Society's peace testimony. And this held even for work which might be regarded by many as humanitarian, whose object was to save life (but, of course, within the framework of an institution, Friends maintained, whose aims were the exact opposite). In 1806 we find Birmingham Monthly Meeting disowning their member Dr. William Darlington, one of the leading Friends in Chester County, for accepting the post of surgeon to the militia.[43] However, the question of noncombatant service for the conscientious objector as an alternative to military service really does not arise before the Civil War.

In North Carolina, where Friends were for most of our period completely exempt from service in the militia, a requirement came into force in the early 1830's that conscientious objectors make an affirmation before the military authorities that they were unwilling to bear arms. Yearly Meeting thereupon advised members against compliance with the regulation: "it would be best for Friends to remain quietly at home."[44] In this advice, as we know, they were merely echoing decisions of the previous century.

The problem of war taxes had been one of the most trying ones for Friends during the Revolutionary War, and no satisfactory solution was reached at that time. It did not cease to be a problem with the coming of peace, for the previous conflict had still to be paid for and, after that, the long period of the European war which involved the United States itself in 1812 meant continued armaments and the need for money to finance them. Although the Society was united in its opposition to the payment of commutation money, a tax in lieu of personal military service, unanimity still did not exist—especially now

---

[42] *Ibid.*, p. 164.
[43] *Two Hundred Fifty Years of Quakerism at Birmingham 1690-1940*, pp. 25, 26.
[44] M. P. Littrell, M. E. Outland, J. O. Sams, *A History of Rich Square Monthly Meeting of Friends*, p. 23.

that hostilities had ceased—on the matter of general war taxes, and even less on those "in the mixture." Some members paid both, but many —especially among the more concerned—continued to regard doing so as a serious compromise of the peace testimony. They were prepared to go to prison rather than pay, even if their attitude was not shared by the whole Society. The following entry in the journal of a New Jersey farmer and craftsman, John Hunt (ca. 1740-1824), though taken from the beginning of the period covered by this chapter, reveals the spirit in which many Friends continued to act:

> 10th mo. 24th [1787]. This evening the constable took our son, Samuel, off to jail for refusing, to pay his tax. He went in a composed, commendable disposition, having, I believe, well considered the matter. I went to see him in prison, and he appeared to bear the trial in a proper manner, in thus suffering for his refusal to pay a tax for defraying the expenses of war. On the 29th, he returned home, being discharged by the sheriff; and we suppose somebody paid the constable his demand, while we had no desire should be done. It was a favoured time with us while he was in prison, which made it easy to us and to him; and I never was more fully and clearly confirmed that the Truth owned this testimony against war.[45]

Sometimes a war tax might be concealed under the guise of an import duty whose purpose it was less easy to distinguish. But here, too, the consciences of some Friends were aroused. An example of such scrupulousness is to be found in the pages of another Quaker journal, that of the New Jersey Friend and minister, Joshua Evans (1731-1798), who throughout his life bore a steadfast witness against slavery, war, and social injustice. Evans had regularly refused to pay taxes which, he considered, went mainly to the support of war and military preparations: "my refusal was from a tender conscientious care to keep clear in my testimony against all warlike proceedings." Early in the 1790's a duty was laid on imported goods, which he had good reason to believe was being substituted for a tax to raise money for military expenditure. "When the matter was brought under my weighty consideration," he writes, "I could see no material difference between paying the expenses relating to war, in taxes, or in duties." It is true that for some time now he had refrained from buying imported articles "because of the corruption attending the trade in these things." As a traveling minister, however, he had partaken of imported salt when it was used in cooking by his hosts—"people generally used it in almost every kind of food," he explains. But now not merely corrupt trading practices but support of war were involved; new scruples were aroused in Evans, and he prayed for guidance. As a result, he writes,

> I was made sensible, that it would be better for me to live on bread and water than to balk my testimony. . . . I therefore thought it right for me to make a full stand against the use of all things upon which duties of that kind were laid. Since which, I have to acknowledge, my way has been made easier than I looked for.[46]

During the War of 1812 we find the apothecary Isaac Martin (1758-1828) taking the same stand that Joshua Evans had earlier taken and reaching the same peace of mind after arriving at the decision that Evans had found. If it had involved the traveling minister in occasional embarrassments with the lady of the house where he was staying, it brought considerable financial loss to Martin the shopkeeper. "Scarcely a day passed," he relates, "that I had not to turn customers away who applied for articles which I had on hand, but could not sell" on account of the duty imposed for war purposes.[47]

The most trying problem, perhaps, arose in connection with taxes "in the mixture." Friends had been grappling with this problem for a century and more. Although, as we have seen, the general opinion among Friends was that such taxes might be paid without compromising the peace testimony, the issue still recurred from time to time as some more sensitive conscience was troubled about the implications of conformity.

Once again, it is to a Quaker journal that we are indebted for insight into how the issue developed in a typical country meeting. Rufus Hall (1744-1818) relates how in June 1800, while his meeting (Northampton, Montgomery County, Pa.) was drawing up answers to the queries, discussion arose on the question of how far members might contribute money to the government by way of taxation which they knew was largely to be expended for military purposes—to construct fortifications and build ships of war, etc. "But this tax," says Hall, "being so blended with other taxes and duties, made it difficult; some Friends not being free to pay it, as believing it inconsistent with their religious principles and testimony against war; while others had paid it." Friends now hoped some decision could be reached so that they would be able to present on this issue a consistent witness for peace. Two views were represented among members of the meeting. The more

[46] A Journal of . . . Joshua Evans, pp. 40, 41. Cf. the rather less uncompromising stand on this question taken by another Quaker tax radical, Warner Mifflin, at the time of the Revolutionary War. See p. 186.
[47] A Journal of . . . Isaac Martin, pp. 113, 114.

traditionally minded claimed that before the Revolution Friends had always paid such mixed taxes to the king, that New York Friends, among others, paid them to Congress today, and that this example should be followed. Others, however, felt that it should be individual conscience and not precedent or the conduct of other Friends, however respected, that should be decisive. "Friends would not do well," they said, "to look to New York or London, nor even to former customs, for direction; seeing we had to go forward and not backward, nor yet to stand still with the work of reformation." The discussions, Hall notes, were conducted in a spirit of unity and friendliness; there was no ill feeling nor heated tempers—"which is too often the case in such matters"—and in the end Friends agreed to differ. Most members, it was found, were against paying this kind of mixed tax, "but as the subject was new to some, and others were not altogether clear, by reason of long custom, so as to see the inconsistency of paying it,—it was thought best to let every Friend act according to their freedom therein."[48]

Calls for personal military service or for the payment of taxes and duties connected with war did not exhaust the areas in which Friends, especially the more concerned members, felt obliged to keep a vigilant witness for peace. The numerous disownments for infringing the peace testimony in one or another way, by means of which the Society had enforced the discipline during the Revolutionary War, had probably removed most of those who did not share, or were lukewarm toward, Friends' views on war, and the widespread unpopularity and sporadic persecution of the war years served to reinforce this process. Nevertheless, the coming of peace brought new temptations: in 1791, for instance, Philadelphia Yearly Meeting was compelled to threaten with disownment all found dealing "in public certificates issued as a compensation for expenses accrued and services performed in the late war."[49] Sometimes a veteran of the Revolution would join Friends, and the problem then arose (as it was to do again after the Civil War) whether he might be permitted to go on drawing his war pension. It was decided that this should be forbidden on pain of disownment, and the ban soon became incorporated in the disciplines of the yearly meetings.[50] The disciplines took a firm line, too, against Friends mak-

---

[48] *A Journal of . . . Rufus Hall*, pp. 112, 113.

[49] *Rules of Discipline and Christian Advices* (1797), p. 135.

[50] In areas where Quakerism had only spread among the inhabitants after the Revolution was over, the problem of pensions could become quite important. This was the case in Maine, for instance, where many who became Friends had fought in the recent war. Several were subsequently disowned for unwillingness to forego their pensions. See Jones, *The Society of Friends in Kennebec County*, pp. 22, 29.

ing profits out of war—a special temptation to a group of which many members, and among them some of the most influential, belonged to the merchant class. "Let all be careful not to seek or accept profit by any concern in preparation for war," Philadelphia Yearly Meeting warned its members, "for how reproachfully inconsistent would it be, to refuse an active compliance with warlike measures, and at the same time, not hesitate to enrich ourselves by the commerce and other circumstances dependent on war."[51] And we do, indeed, find a man like the Quaker millionaire, Nathan Trotter (1787-1853), who dealt in a large range of businesses from metals to real estate and stocks and securities, carefully refraining in the years after 1815 from the purchase of government bonds ("except when he purchased to make payments abroad," his biographer qualified) because of their association with the financing of the War of 1812 and, later, of the Mexican War.[52]

This sensitivity to the wider implications of one's actions—mingled, of course, with a strong sense of loyalty to the Society's collective decisions—was felt not only by the big merchant, whose wide business interests could absorb some losses without too much difficulty, but also by the small man for whom losses were less easy to take. Consider the case of a simple New Jersey smallholder, a Negro who had become a Quaker by convincement. He had made a living chiefly by selling the produce of his holding for the use of workers in a nearby iron foundry. In the War of 1812 the foundry began to make cannon for the army; so he now became "very uneasy at the thought that he was supplying that establishment with articles of produce, whilst they were principally employed in the manufacture of arms." The decision he reached to stop supplying the foundry and to try to find some other outlet for his produce unconnected with war meant temporarily endangering his livelihood.[53] The Society of Friends, despite its conservatism during this period and its failure to reach out with its message of peace to circles beyond the influence of the meeting, remained unique among the peace groups in its quest to relate its peace testimony to the widest ramifications of the war spirit.

We have dealt so far with the negative aspect of Friends' personal

[51] *Christian Advices* (1808), p. 108.

[52] Elva Tooker, *Nathan Trotter*, p. 176. Another example among the well-to-do merchant class of the conscientious Quaker pacifist is Elias Hicks's cousin, Isaac, of New York City. Isaac Hicks consistently refused to handle goods if he was aware that the transaction was in any way connected with military activities. "With regard to the Quaker testimony on war," writes his biographer, Robert A. Davison (*Isaac Hicks, New York Merchant and Quaker 1767-1820*, pp. 161, 162), "Hicks is a better Quaker than he is a businessman." See also pp. 114, 205.

[53] *Proceedings of the First General Peace Convention . . . in London . . . 1843*, p. 30.

witness for peace. This witness was, indeed, expressed mainly in the form of protest: refusal to serve in the militia, to purchase an exemption by one of the several means then open, to pay war taxes, to buy goods on which duty was levied to finance war preparations, to draw a war pension, or to accept financial profit tainted by its connection with war. In this way Friends attempted to preserve the integrity of their own individual consciences and the collective testimony of their Society to the Christian spirit of love in a warlike world.

After the Revolution, Friends in the old settled areas in the Eastern states seldom had the opportunity to test their pacifism in any direct encounter with the spirit of violence. One reason was that, except for occasional outbreaks of mob violence which occurred throughout most of the nineteenth century, law and order were firmly established in these areas. The frontier had retreated beyond the mountains, and the Indian peril had long since disappeared. Again, even in places where we might expect Quakers to have been the victims of rough treatment, they rarely encountered it during this period. They were a peculiar people—and a peculiarly respectable people, who could be permitted the indulgence of some peculiar ideas. Although, as we have seen, they were subjected to various minor hardships for their objections to fighting and in the Southern states endured considerable unpopularity for their abolitionist stand, these views were not usually regarded as too serious a threat to the institutions of either war or slavery; for the message was directed primarily to those inside the Society, and few outside it were ready to enter into the closely guarded Quaker enclosure. The chances that any wide area would be tainted by their obnoxious views were thus much reduced. This did not at all mean, of course, that Quakers tended to play down their views on war or on any other unpopular subject in their dealings with the outside world. Many were fearlessly outspoken, and the itinerant ministers, in particular, bore testimony not only within the confines of the Quaker meeting but, on occasion, outside among the general populace as well.

The case of Joseph Hoag during the War of 1812 is not an isolated example. In the autumn of that year he set out to visit Quaker communities in the South, and there at public meetings, although "it was thought dangerous," he spoke out against both war and slavery. In Washington, D.C., where by 1813 pro-war feeling ran high, he encountered strong opposition in his exposition of Quaker peace views.[54]

[54] Another Quaker visitor to Washington during the war was the rural Friend, Jesse Kersey of Chester Co. (Pa.), who succeeded in gaining access to both President Madison (whose wife was of Quaker stock) and his secretary of state, James Monroe. At these interviews Kersey urged the statesmen to conclude peace as soon as possible. See *A Narrative of . . . Jesse Kersey*, p. 195.

"When I mentioned that," he relates, "a number of them straightened themselves up and stared me full in the face with all the defiance of confident-countenance that they were able." However, after some hesitation he persevered and in the end succeeded in winning the respect, if not the agreement, of his hearers.[55]

Although the Society of the first half of the nineteenth century may not have produced a Woolman, it did contain many devoted souls willing and able to present Friends' views on war to an unsympathetic public when occasion required. Yet the withdrawal from society which marked the development of Quakerism as a whole during the half-century and more after the Revolution affected its peace witness, too, preventing any widespread missionary outreach in this area. And this withdrawal, along with the long period of external peace and internal security (the War of 1812 and the Mexican War, as we have seen, did not seriously affect the rhythm of life in the country), shielded Quaker pacifism in the East, at least from any serious trials.

For the practice of nonviolence in Quaker experience during this period we must turn, therefore, to the Western territories which were only then being opened up for European settlement. There, on the frontiers of civilization, the organs of orderly government functioned only with difficulty, or not at all, and the arm of the strongest laid down the law in many communities. In some areas, too, trouble broke out from time to time with the Indians, who were now being gradually forced out of their remaining hunting grounds by the advance of land-hungry white men. The danger from this source, which had ceased altogether in the Eastern states, continued to present, along with the disordered conditions of life, a challenge to the Quaker settlers coming to these territories in the great tide of western migration, which from toward the end of the eighteenth century, progressively enveloped the areas that eventually became the states of Ohio, Indiana, Illinois, Iowa,[56] Kansas, etc.

[55] *Journal of . . . Joseph Hoag*, p. 190. See pp. 199-204 for an account of his conversations on the subject of the Quaker peace testimony with the general in command of troops at Knoxville (Tenn.) in the summer of 1813. It was a time of alarm, owing to the possibility of an Indian invasion, and the general expressed his disgust to Hoag at local Quakers for not obeying the order given for a general muster of the able-bodied, attributing their disobedience to shirking and cowardice. In the end, after listening to Hoag, the general, though still a little puzzled, was ready to admit their sincerity and expressed his willingness to help get them exempted. A bystander who had listened attentively to the whole exchange of views between the Quaker and the general turned to Hoag and said: "Well stranger, if all the world were of your mind, I would turn in and follow after"—to which Hoag at once replied: "Then thou hast a mind to be the last man in the world to be good. I have a mind to be one of the first, and set the rest an example."

[56] Iowa contained a small group of Norwegian Quaker immigrants who, begin-

These Quaker farmers, some of them escaping from the unfriendly atmosphere of the slave states and others from Pennsylvania, New York, or New England seeking a more promising future than their home environment seemed to offer, were mostly simple men whose struggle with the wilderness left little time or inclination for recording their experiences and impressions. Friends' meetings, which as conditions became more stabilized were established wherever Quakers settled, continued to keep careful records just as they had done back in the East, but, of course, these records do not usually provide evidence for the practice of nonviolence on the part of these frontier Friends.

The conditions of frontier lawlessness and disorder, as we have said before, presented a lively challenge to those trying faithfully to uphold the Quaker peace testimony. Back in the home states the enforcement of the discipline had served to buttress the influence of Quaker home and school and the promptings of individual conscience in keeping the Friends a defenseless people. The carrying of weapons in an emergency was, of course, forbidden, and those who infringed the discipline on this point were brought to account. A single example will suffice. A Virginian Friend, one Enoch Robarts, sent the following declaration, dated 20 June 1789, to his meeting: "Dear Friends: Having so far deviated from the peaceable principles professed by us as to suffer the spirit of anger and resentment so to prevail as to procure firearms for my safety, all which conduct I condemn, hoping at the same time that my future conduct will evince the sincerity of this my acknowledgment."[57] Suppose now that this same Enoch Robarts were to migrate to the West, as so many Virginian Friends soon did, in families or as individuals. There, with wife and children as an added responsibility, he would be alone, isolated perhaps by many miles of virgin wilderness from the nearest Quaker family and therefore thrown on his own inner resources to face the menace of hostile Indians or equally dangerous white-skinned marauders. In such circumstances the temptation to seize a hunting rifle or knife in self-defense—or to flee for safety to some larger settlement or to an area where other Friends, who shared Quaker principles of peace, were more thickly settled—must sometimes have been almost overwhelming.

ning in the 1840's, left their native land—in part to escape the severe penalties imposed there on conscientious objectors to military conscription. They retained the Norwegian language in their meetings until near the end of the century. See H. F. Swansen, "The Norwegian Quakers of Marshall County, Iowa," *Norwegian-American Studies and Records*, X (1938), 127-34.

[57] *Our Quaker Friends of Ye Olden Time*, p. 163.

We can see something of all this, and of how in this instance the dilemma was successfully resolved, in the story of William Hobbs (1780-1854), who, along with a few other Quaker families, had come from North Carolina early in 1812 to settle in what was then the Indiana Territory. After war broke out in June between the United States and Britain, the Indians in the territory began to grow restless. As near as sixteen miles away some white families were killed, and the scattered group of new Quaker settlers grew alarmed.

> To quiet our families [Hobbs relates], we built little huts and lived together, that is, Friends, and those that held that way. Altho' I made no preparation to defend myself and family, having no gun, I did not feel peace of mind in so living. . . . After living so a few weeks, my wife and I felt the most peace of mind to move home. After we returned to our habitation, I do not remember of ever feeling the least alarmed, though the Indians killed a man about seven miles from us.[58]

In the middle of the nineteenth century, when already conditions over large parts of the "old" West had become more settled and the framework of law and order was more firmly established, the territory of Kansas became the scene, with the passing of the Kansas-Nebraska Act of 1854, of endemic civil war between pro and antislavery forces that added ideological hatred to the other ingredients of frontier lawlessness. Settlement was only just beginning. Quakers began to arrive just after the passing of the notorious act. "Bleeding Kansas" of the second half of the 1850's did, indeed, prove to be a testing ground for Quaker peace principles. Friends' sympathies were naturally with the antislavery elements: the ancestors of many of those settling had originally left the South because of the difficulties of living in a slaveowning environment. Their relatives back East were frequently engaged in helping the Negroes—as participants in the "Underground Railway" or in numerous philanthropic activities on behalf of colored freemen or runaway slaves. In fact, one of the reasons that Friends settled in this territory, apart from the lure of cheap and abundant land, was the desire to preserve it from becoming open to slavery. Friends in Kansas, therefore, placed their votes as well as their moral influence behind the free-soil movement. At the same time, Quakers as a whole could not sanction the attempt to maintain Kansas as free territory by the use of armed force against the aggression of Southerners mainly from across the Missouri border; still less, of course, did they approve the moral and material aid given by northern Chris-

---

[58] *Autobiography of William Hobbs*, pp. 7, 8.

tians, including many ministers even (Theodore Parker, for example), to the antislavery guerrillas. "Who can tell what scenes of blood may be chargeable to their counsels?" asked the evangelical *Friends' Review*, and the paper went on to recommend "resistance by suffering" as the Christian way to confront evil. This had been the method used by seventeenth-century Friends in their struggle for religious and civil liberty; nothing, the editor believed, had occurred since to disprove "that the same peaceable resistance to aggression and outrage would have been equally availing in Kansas."[59]

This advice might have been all right for peaceful Philadelphia, but it could easily have seemed oversimplified to the small communities of Quakers out in Kansas caught in the midst of a fierce struggle for predominance between two equally determined groups, both convinced of the rightness of their objectives. Friends, in fact, lived in the very area that was swept by sporadic border fighting. Quaker farms were raided, horses or cattle were seized, and occasionally a Friend was roughly handled.[60] A mission school founded by the Society back in 1836 among the Shawnee Indians was forced to close down temporarily. No lives were lost—but perhaps more because of luck than anything else. However, it is true that Friends did have a champion in the person of a former Quaker, Joel Hiatt, who moved in proslavery circles and spoke up there on behalf of his former coreligionists. "Stock men, peaceable, wouldn't fight," was Hiatt's description of them, "obedient to the laws no matter how things were settled"—antislavery, certainly, and in favor of a free state, but unwilling to impose a solution by force or to stir up rebellion among the slaves. His Quaker nephew later commented as follows on renegade "Uncle" Joel's unrequested, but not unuseful, intercession with the slavers: "We did not take much interest in this kind of talk; but it was our best policy at this time to keep still, and act when we had the opportunity to effect anything, which I believe we all bravely did."

So Quakers voted for the antislavery candidates at the polls but steered clear of active politics as much as possible. One young Friend,

[59] *Friends Review*, 8 March 1856. I have found occasional references to Quaker abolitionists carrying arms in order to defend fugitive slaves from recapture. The stories are not well documented but may well be true. However, such cases were not typical and probably occurred infrequently. If conduct of this kind were known to his meeting, a member would almost certainly have been disciplined.

[60] See Cecil B. Currey, "Quaker Pacifism in Kansas 1833-1945" (M.Sc. thesis, Fort Hays State College), p. 27, for an instance of this kind. On p. 24 the author relates a story concerning this period of a Quaker farmer who had purchased two expensive horses. One was seized later by a proslavery marauder. The Quaker, to counterbalance the advantage given thereby to the slavery side, then presented the remaining horse to the captain of a free-soil band—and thereafter traveled himself by mule!

however, was almost beaten to death for his official activities in connection with the elections of mid-January 1856. And it is at the time of these elections, too, that we find one of the most interesting examples of the workings of the Quaker spirit of nonviolence. Shortly before polling day a gang of proslavery marauders from over the Missouri border, which went by the name of the "Kickapoo Rangers," swept through the area where the Quakers were settled in widely scattered homesteads. On one such lonely farm lived young William Coffin (who was, incidentally, Joel Hiatt's nephew and also cousin of Levi Coffin of "Underground Railway" fame). He was alone, except for his wife and children, when he received warning that the Kickapoo Rangers, along with other marauding gangs from Missouri, were moving his way and that they were spreading terror in the whole neighborhood in an attempt to intimidate the antislavery vote in the forthcoming elections. Let us hear the story in William Coffin's own words:

> We could expect no favor from such a body of men, composed, as they were, of the worst description of border men, of the Jesse James type. . . . I do not think that I was afraid at that time, being young and excitable; but my education was such that I could not, with conscience, kill a man; but when I got to reasoning with myself about my duty in the protection of my family, my faith gave way. I had an excellent double-barreled gun, and I took it outdoors and loaded it heavily with buckshot. It was near bed time; my wife and children soon went to sleep, and I barred the door and set my gun handy, and made up my mind I would shoot any man or set of men that undertook to break in. A cabin, built as they were, of logs at that time, made a pretty good fort; but I could get no sleep, having laid down with my clothes on. Finally, towards midnight I got up, wife and children peacefully sleeping, drew the loads from my gun and put it away; and then, on my knees, I told the Lord all about it and asked His protection; and so casting all my care upon Him, I felt easy, went to bed, was soon asleep, and slept until sun-up the next morning.[61]

The Kickapoo Rangers, as it turned out, had followed another route, and to Coffin it seemed that his simple faith was justified. For us, the story illustrates the firm foundation which Quaker training and educa-

[61] William H. Coffin, "Settlement of the Friends in Kansas," *Transactions of the Kansas State Historical Society, 1901-1902*, pp. 332, 334, 335, 341, 343. See also Cecil Currey, "Quakers in 'Bleeding Kansas,'" BFHA, vol. 50, no. 2 (Autumn 1961), pp. 96-101.

tion were able to build for the Society's peace testimony in many of its members.

From mid-century, however, "fear of war over slavery continually oppressed Friends' minds." Opposed to both war and slavery, Quakers were faced with a difficult choice. A few Friends, even before the fighting broke out, decided in favor of a violent solution if this could win freedom for the oppressed.[62] We see here the struggle, especially in the minds of the young, between two seemingly irreconcilable loyalties: antislavery and pacifism. It was this conflict, for instance, that led the two young Quakers from Iowa, the brothers Edwin and Barclay Coppoc,[63] in 1859 to join John Brown in his famous and ill-fated raid on Harpers Ferry. Brown, after taking part in the guerrilla warfare in Kansas, had spent the winter of 1857-1858 in the Coppocs' home community of Springdale where he made many friends among the largely Quaker population. Most disapproved, of course, of his resort to arms; the young Coppocs, however, were fired by the image of the old warrior to abandon the nonviolent way in which they had been reared.

II

If we turn now from the practical implementation of Friends' peace principles to the contribution of American Quakers to the theory of pacifism during our period, we are struck at once by the paucity of material and the lack of creative thinking in most of what was written. British Quakerism produced Dymond (1796-1828), and "the masterly and altogether irrefutable arguments of Jonathan Dymond,"[64] contained in his writings on war, were to provide a staple source for American pacifists of the nineteenth century, both Quaker and non-Quaker. Although the Society in the United States produced some half-dozen pacifist tracts, occasional discussions in wider expository works, sporadic pronouncements on the subject of the peace testimony by various yearly meetings, and—with the rise of a Quaker periodical press from the end of the 1820's on—a number of articles discussing the implications of pacifism from the Quaker point of view, it cannot be said that any of this writing was of major significance. During this pe-

---

[62] Thomas E. Drake, *Quakers and Slavery in America*, pp. 190, 194-97.

[63] Edwin, however, had been disowned in 1857 for dancing; Barclay was not disowned until January 1860. See *The Palimpsest*, XLI, no. 1 (Jan. 1960), 22-30. This number is entitled "John Brown among the Quakers" and is edited by William J. Petersen.

[64] From the lecture by William J. Allinson (1810-1874), quoted in *Friends' Review*, 20 Sept. 1862.

riod the main contribution of the Society to religious and social thought was being made elsewhere. However, this Quaker writing on peace is worth reviewing briefly insofar as it may throw light on the condition of the peace testimony against war existing at the time.

The Society, as we know, exercised a considerable degree of censorship over the writings of its members, as much in regard to the subject of peace as in regard to other topics. The discipline printed by New York Yearly Meeting in 1810, for instance, threatened with ultimate disownment those who persisted "in promoting the publication of writings which tend to excite the spirit of war."[65] The Society thus found it easier to guard against the public expression of heterodox opinion than to promote vital thinking on peace. However, most of the peace tracts which Friends wrote, if hardly original, are competent pieces of work which succeed in giving a fairly adequate presentation of the traditional Quaker view.

The first tract on peace to appear from a Quaker pen after the end of the Revolution was the 52-page *Essay on War*, which John I. Wells (ca. 1769-1832) published in 1808. Wells himself had recently refused, when called on, to serve in the militia of his native Connecticut. As he wrote in the preface to his pamphlet: "Not long since, I was called upon as a delinquent on the military account." The author's object in publishing his booklet was to provide a reasoned case for refusal of such service on religious grounds, a necessary task in view of the overwhelming weight of opinion hitherto in favor of the legitimacy of war in certain circumstances. There is little that is especially striking in most of the arguments put forward; they are derived—as might be expected—mainly from the appropriate texts of the New Testament. In Wells's words, the Christian alternative to war is to trust in God for protection in all adversity. Calamities like war are usually the result of transgression of God's commandments, though Christians may have to suffer persecution for righteousness' sake. More interesting is his treatment of Old Testament wars, always a ticklish problem for pacifist writers before the development of Biblical criticism. Where success was granted, he claims these wars were waged "for the glory of God, and the punishment of sinners." "Under the Mosaic dispensation it was consistent that this most favoured nation should war and fight; the plan of the divine government at that time admitted of it. But . . . in the Jewish wars, it was only when they were commissioned, or authorized by express orders from the Lord, that they were prosperous." Christ's new dispensation, however, "forecloses all liberty to

---

[65] *Discipline*, p. 46.

engage in war."[66] Wells's tract was used as peace propaganda at that time by the American Quakers.[67]

The War of 1812 naturally turned the minds of Quakers, as it did the minds of such non-Friends as Dodge or Worcester who would later become leading advocates of peace, toward a reconsideration of the whole problem of war and peace and toward the need to put the Christian case against all war once again before the general public. There was a risk of misunderstanding here, of course, a danger that the pacifism of the Society would be misinterpreted as a purely political objection to the war at hand. This difficulty was not new; Friends had encountered it during the Revolution and were to meet with it again in subsequent wars. Answering charges of this nature which had been laid against its pacifist stand, Philadelphia Yearly Meeting felt bound to issue a statement in October 1814 that "subjects of a political nature make no part of the deliberations of our religious assemblies."[68] The yearly meetings in their pronouncements confined themselves chiefly to defending the sincerity of their conscientious objectors.

Some Friends, though, were thinking more deeply on their own— and not necessarily with publication in mind. We find William Evans, a future Quaker minister, for instance, wrestling at this time with the problem of what would happen if a nation accepted Friends' views on war and abandoned its arms. They were likely to be unmolested, he reasoned, not only because God would protect them against the aggression of their neighbors, but because other nations would no longer fear attack or interference and would be ashamed to start unprovoked aggression of their own against a defenseless people. His reasoning is superficial, his approach unduly optimistic, the problem oversimplified; yet it does show at least one Friend's mind reaching out beyond the traditional concern with scriptural interpretation and moral objection and with the problem of individual self-defense to the implications of Quaker pacifism if adopted on a nationwide scale. Evans's thoughts, however, were not intended for publication and were confided to the intimacy of his journal.[69]

The only substantial Quaker tract on the subject of pacifism that was directly inspired by the war came from the pen of James Mott, Sr. (1742-1823), Lucretia Mott's father-in-law. In 1814 he published a 33-page pamphlet entitled *The Lawfulness of War for Christians, ex-*

66 J. I. Wells, *An Essay on War*, pp. 11, 25. See also Robert H. Morgan's article on Wells in the *Friend*, vol. 114 (1940), no. 6, pp. 89-91.
67 Merle E. Curti, *Peace or War*, p. 35.
68 *To our Fellow Citizens of the United States*, broadsheet dated 21 Oct. 1814.
69 *Journal of . . . William Evans*, p. 35.

amined. His object in writing it, he tells us, was "to remove the prejudices of those who, through the influence of education, custom, or public opinion, have been induced to conclude that war is allowable for
christians." Mott frankly acknowledged his debt to his predecessors
in the peace movement, in particular to Erasmus, and to Mott's own
contemporary, the Anglican Clarkson, whose studies of the attitude
of the early Christian church to war were often used by nineteenth-
century pacifists, and he did not himself bring anything new to the
discussion. But it is interesting (though Mott here, like Wells, was
only voicing the general view of the Society at this time) to note his
qualified acceptance of Old Testament warfare. "The Jews," he writes,
"went to war at the command of God, and against nations, whom
for their wickedness he, in his inscrutable wisdom, had determined to
extirpate from the earth. But it was only at his immediate command
that they were to do it." We shall see a little later how his daughter-
in-law Lucretia was to be regarded by conservative elements in the
Society as something of a heretic (a reputation she had already acquired on many other counts) for contesting, in the name of Christ's
teachings, the belief that God could ever have approved war at any
time. It was, of course, on the gospels that the elder Mott rested his
case for Quaker pacifism, and he calls the contemporary argument for
war on the basis of the Old Testament "but a fig-leaf covering."[70]

In the years that followed the war, one of the most prolific exponents
of the Quaker peace testimony was the Ohio publisher and publicist,
Elisha Bates, whose fervid evangelicalism, as we have seen, eventually
led him to abandon even Quaker Orthodoxy and to break completely
with the Society of Friends. However, his exposition of the *Doctrines
of Friends*, which first came out in 1825, long remained a standard
work on the subject. In it he devotes a chapter of 30 pages (chapter
XVI) to the subject of war, where he briefly reviews the evidence
for the "non-resistance" of the gospels and the early church and urges
the need for Christians to follow the example of their church's
apostolic age. Though a useful summary of Friends' views, his argument yet brought nothing fresh to the development of the Quaker
peace testimony.[71]

A regular Quaker weekly press did not come into existence until the
founding in October 1827 of the Philadelphia *Friend*, which became

[70] Mott, *The Lawfulness of War . . . examined*, pp. 3, 14.
[71] Elisha Bates was also largely responsible for the drawing up in 1829 of a
Testimony of the Society of Friends on the Continent of America, which was published in the following year in the name of eight Orthodox yearly meetings. It
contains a brief section on war (pp. 27, 28), which is mostly taken up by cita-
tions from the Bible or from past Quakers' statements on the subject.

the organ of the Orthodox branch of the Society. The Hicksites did not establish a permanent paper of their own until the appearance of the *Friends' Weekly Intelligencer* in 1844, and it was not until three years later, in 1847, that the evangelical wing within the Orthodox branch began to produce the *Friends' Review*. Yet now that these journals (all of which were published in Philadelphia) had emerged, in the second quarter of the century, opportunity opened for a wider, more public discussion of the peace question among Friends, in which rank-and-file members could participate without the necessity of going to the expense of publishing a pamphlet of their own. They could get to know the views of other members more easily than before, and also, since the new papers reprinted from time to time articles from the press of the non-Quaker peace movement, they could become familiar with the thinking on peace being carried on outside the Society. Most of the material presenting the utilitarian case against war and attacking its economic waste, the failure of the war method to produce a lasting settlement, the horrors of battle, and the moral depravity of army life was reprinted from the publications of the American or British Peace Societies. Excerpts from the peace classics were also presented to readers from time to time. The contributions of Friends were confined mainly to discussion of the religious aspects of pacifism. In general, we may say that, although in the period before mid-century the Quaker periodicals devoted quite a lot of attention to the problems of peace (the two Orthodox papers rather more, perhaps, than the Hicksite *Intelligencer*), the amount of space given to this issue was indeed small compared to the total amount available. This fact seems to indicate that the peace testimony was not then one of the primary interests either of the leaders of the Society or of the rank-and-file members, whether Hicksite or Orthodox.

The original articles in these papers did not on the whole make any very original contribution to the debate on pacifism. But, occasionally, a Friend came out with some interesting suggestion or thought. A case in point can be found in the two articles contributed in 1837 to the Orthodox *Friend* by "L.S." under the title "Observations on War." In them the anonymous author, almost certainly influenced by the ideas of the peace societies, advocated the establishment of international courts of arbitration acting under an agreed international law to settle disputes between the nations. The power of world opinion, as well as some form of economic sanctions (the writer does not go into the details), would usually, in his view, be enough to bring about compliance with the court's decision. In rare cases, however, these factors might not be sufficient. "L.S." writes:

It may be imagined that wars would arise out of this system; as nations might refuse to comply with the award of referees, and thus nullify the whole procedure unless they were compelled by military force. Even supposing this effect to follow, the plan would still be an improvement upon the present barbarous mode of settling national disputes. For a government which should refuse to submit to the award of the national arbiters, would be placed in hostility, not merely to its original opponent, but to the civilized world. The object on the side of the national confederacy would be, not to redress a particular grievance, but to support the supremacy of the law of nations. Such a contest would probably be soon decided.[72]

This argument strikes a note that was only infrequently heard in the Society in those years. Yet it represents one strand, and an important one, in the tradition of Quaker pacifism running from William Penn's scheme for European federation to the Quaker supporters of the League of Nations and the United Nations. "L.S." believed as firmly as any of his brethren in the incompatibility of war with the Christian dispensation and supported the Quaker refusal to participate in it; at the same time, however, he sanctioned on the sub-Christian level measures which fall short of this Quaker ideal, provided they are directed toward the same goal of establishing peace on earth.

The outbreak of the Mexican War presented a twofold challenge to Friends. On the one hand, their pacifism made them reject resort to arms; while, on the other, a consideration that had not been present, at least to the same degree, in the War of 1812—the aggressive foreign policy and the threatened extension of the Southern slave system which lay behind the opening of hostilities—offended their antislavery feelings and their sense of political justice. These factors account for the outspokenness of their condemnation of the war. The evangelical *Friends' Review*, in particular, took a strong line against the government's policy and branded the war as one of aggression by the United States; even the more conservative *Friend* took a decided antiwar stand, reprinting the speeches of members of Congress against the war and increasing the space it devoted to antiwar material. Not untypical, probably, are the reactions of an anonymous woman Quaker, who, after reading accounts of military action in the press, wrote as follows to the *Friend*: "Is not this a time to proclaim more earnestly than ever to the world our Christian testimony against all war, and the spirit of war, now that our country is actually engaged in a

[72] *Friend*, 27 May and 15 July 1837.

barbarous contest with a neighbouring nation?" She was especially disgusted by the prayers being offered up in the churches for the success of the United States' arms. In her eyes, the war was "iniquitous," a reversion to savagery on the part of a civilized nation and not a subject for national pride. "We earnestly desire," she concluded, "that our young Friends may beware of catching the infection of the war-spirit, even so far as to feel any degree of exultation on account of this *gallantry* and *valour* of the American soldiers which is so loudly extolled."[73] This kind of antiwar protest, of course, was shared not only by Quaker and other pacifists but, in the North, by wide circles within the churches and outside them. Quaker pacifism had temporarily overlapped with a political movement against an imperialist war.

During the years of war the various Quaker yearly meetings of both branches issued a series of statements on the peace testimony, urging members to testify faithfully to principle in thought and deed and including at the same time undertones of political protest.[74] For Ohio Yearly Meeting (Orthodox) in its "Address on War" of September 1846, the conflict was "not surpassed, perhaps, in atrocity by any previous contest to which this nation has been a party . . . [a] horrid affair." What practical steps could Friends take, the "Address" asked, to express their aversion to it? Let them refrain from supporting military men or those in favor of the war at the polls. Let them boycott where possible imported products when they knew duty had been levied on them to provide income for the war. "Friends are also advised against performing any labor on the public roads in lieu of paying a military fine, or in any way give a sanction to military laws."[75] Baltimore Yearly Meeting in a small pamphlet issued on 19 December 1846, while urging Friends "to be separated from the spirit and the policy of this world," recommended arbitration to settle disputes between the two combatants.[76] The Hicksite Yearly Meeting of Philadelphia in its statement of 15 January 1847 concentrated on the need for young Friends not to compromise their pacifism by conniving at the payment of their militia fines.[77] We find their Orthodox brethren on the same day memorializing Congress on the subject of the war and taking a more political stand (while at the same time stressing, of course, that Friends' opposition was religious in principle and not motivated by any party considerations). The United States was especially favored

[73] *Ibid.*, 21 Nov. 1846, p. 71.
[74] Clayton Sumner Ellsworth, "The American Churches and the Mexican War," *AHR*, XLV, no. 2 (Jan. 1940), 317.
[75] *Friends' Weekly Intelligencer*, 19 Dec. 1846.
[76] *The Unlawfulness of All Wars and Fightings under the Gospel*, p. 7.
[77] Extracts from Minutes 1847 (printed folder in F.H.L.S.C., S G 2).

by Providence, they pleaded, and it was the country's duty to provide an example to the world of peace and international morality.[78] New York Friends, too, issued declarations in support of the peace testimony on 4 January 1848; the statement of the Orthodox branch, like that of its Philadelphia Yearly Meeting, was in the form of a memorial to Congress, while the Hicksites published a pamphlet addressed to the Christian churches throughout the country which summarized Quaker doctrine on the subject of war.[79] The Orthodox memorial, perhaps because it was destined for a political body, dwelt more on the unjustifiability of the present conflict, deploring the fact "that our citizens now compose an invading army within the acknowledged territory of a neighbouring nation, towards whom this country has heretofore been on terms of amity and peace" and calling for a speedy conclusion of peace. The Society's testimony was, indeed, against all wars, but some conflicts (including the present war, it was implied) might be more calamitous than others. The Philadelphia *Friends' Review* called the document a "strong memorial."[80]

The Mexican crisis inspired one Friend to compose a more detailed defense of Quaker pacifism than could be done within the limits of the kind of statement that we have been reviewing. In 1846 John Jackson (d. 1855), a respected minister of the Hicksite Yearly Meeting in Philadelphia, set down his *Reflections on Peace and War* in a booklet which he evidently hoped would find readers outside as well as inside the Society. There was nothing startling in most of what he had to say; once again, we find the familiar arguments for pacifism drawn from the New Testament, and expatiation on the horrors and waste of modern war in particular. But when (in chapter IV) Jackson came to discuss the question of the wars waged by the Jews in the Old Testament, he introduced an unfamiliar note in the literature of American Quaker pacifism by denying categorically that God had ever sanctioned such conflicts, even within the framework of the old dispensation. "Once take the ground that men have been divinely commissioned to fight," he said, "and there is no war for which this authority will not be claimed." The Jewish chroniclers of that time had been mistaken in believing that their warfare was divinely inspired. "These authors, whoever they were, were fallible men like ourselves, liable to mistaken views of the divine character and will." His reasons for doubting their claims Jackson drew from his understanding of God's love

---

[78] *Friend*, 6 Feb. 1847.

[79] *Considerations respecting the Lawfulness of War under the Gospel Dispensation.*

[80] *Friends' Review*, 19 Feb. 1848.

THE QUAKER TESTIMONY

as revealed by Christ in the New Testament. How, he asked, could the barbarous policy of extermination pursued by the ancient Jews against the Canaanites and other tribes be reconciled with the spirit of Christian forgiveness? The Old Testament was an excellent historical source, but it must be judged primarily as history.[81]

Jackson's little book caused quite a flutter in the Quaker dovecote. In a short while it had gone through two editions. But the author's liberalism was regarded by most Friends, even in the more liberal Hicksite branch to which he belonged, as sheer heresy. To doubt the literal veracity of everything in the Old Testament was, in the view of many Friends, to undermine religious belief. This Biblical literalism entailed, as we have seen, the acceptance of the view that for his inscrutable purposes God had on occasion commanded his Jewish people to wage wars of atrocity against their neighbors, while later through his son Jesus Christ he enjoined an undeviating pacifism.[82] One of those who shared Jackson's rejection of this view was the redoubtable Lucretia Mott (1793-1880). Early in 1847, Mrs. Mott reported to an Irish Quaker concerning the reaction of Friends to Jackson's arguments: "This has brought up a new issue among our Friends, and many of us are now charged with unsound doctrine."[83] In the following summer, while out in Indiana attending Western Yearly Meeting, she took occasion to recommend Jackson's tract as suitable reading for young people. "This," her companion reported in her diary, "immediately brought out a spirited reply from a minister of this meeting . . . in which she expressed her 'astonishment' that such a thing should be recommended, as to read a book 'that despises the Bible.'" The same writer goes on to describe the strong feelings aroused in many members against Jackson's tract: "many would be afraid to suffer it in their houses, much less read it."[84]

Lucretia Mott was, in fact, mistaken in thinking that the literal inspiration of the Old Testament and the divine sanction for the Jewish wars chronicled there constituted a new issue for American Friends. The problem had been keenly debated at the beginning of the century in the case of a young woman Quaker from New York Yearly Meeting, Hannah Barnard (née Jenkins). It is, therefore, worthwhile at this point to review briefly the facts in the Hannah Barnard affair.

[81] John Jackson, *Reflections on Peace and War*, chap. IV.
[82] In the very same year that Jackson was writing, we find Baltimore Y. M. in the pamphlet cited above (n. 76) conditionally justifying wars "under a former dispensation." These, it stated, the Jews had waged with God's approval.
[83] Letter to Richard D. Webb dated 21 Feb. 1847, quoted in Hallowell, *Motts*, p. 283.
[84] *Ibid.*, pp. 290, 291.

Hannah had been born in a family of Baptists in 1754 but, at the age of 18, had become a convinced Friend. After marrying a fellow Quaker and becoming the mother of a family, Hannah was chosen a minister by her local meeting, which apparently regarded her highly on account of her character, intelligence, and gifts as a speaker. Her departure in July 1798 for a pastoral visit to the British Isles, in the company of another woman minister from Rhode Island, had the full approval of New York Friends. No suspicion of unorthodox views appears to have been felt at this time. Yet already, it seems, her espousal of the peace testimony had led her to have strong doubts whether a beneficent deity could really ever have sanctioned war under the old dispensation. If he had, so she reasoned, did not this constitute "an impeachment of the divine attributes" of love and goodwill toward the creation? Surely, Old Testament wars, like modern ones, stemmed wholly from men's passions and lust. Opinions of this kind had, indeed, been held by American Friends like Anthony Benezet or Job Scott in that century: Hannah did not think she was uttering any very novel views.

Now, while visiting Ireland, she came into contact with a group of liberal Friends, led by Abraham Shackleton of Ballitore and John Hancock of Lisburn, who at that very moment were pressing similar views on the British Society. Suspected of deism and influenced undoubtedly by the ideas of the Enlightenment in trying to bring their Quaker Christianity into line with the findings of reason, these Friends were soon either to be disowned by their fellow members or to resign themselves in protest at their Friends' illiberality.

Of course, the same suspicions fell on their young American disciple who, during her travels, could not contain herself from expressing her opinions on the subject. Like the Irish dissidents, Hannah not only denied that there had been any divine sanction of the Old Testament wars against the Canaanites but quite logically contested the infallibility of the scriptures as a whole and cast doubt on some of the miraculous stories contained within their pages. British Friends, among whom the evangelical trend was increasing in weight and importance, were shocked at their American visitor's impiety and were fearful of the effect it might exercise over weaker minds—feelings that were supported vigorously by another American visitor, the strongly evangelical Friends' minister, David Sands, who was in Britain at this time.

In May 1800, in the course of the annual gathering of London Yearly Meeting, an Irish Friend accused Hannah of "holding erroneous opinions concerning war." To this charge she replied that she believed

war was always and in all circumstances wrong, "a moral evil" resulting from man's abuse of the free will granted him by God. That she
also asserted disbelief in (among other miraculous incidents in the Old
Testament) any heavenly command to Abraham to sacrifice his son
served only to further incriminate the intrepid young woman in the
minds of a majority of her hearers. At the end of June, London Yearly
Meeting forbade her to travel any longer in the capacity of a Quaker
minister and requested that she return forthwith to the United States.
Hannah lingered on for another year hoping, perhaps, to vindicate
her orthodoxy in the eyes of her British Friends. "As to war," she
once again told them her view "that in no age of the world [had] the
great and merciful Creator ever commissioned any nation or person
to destroy another; but that they were formerly, as at present, only
permitted so to do."

On returning home her case was dealt with by her monthly meeting (Hudson), which, after lengthy deliberation, in June 1802 gave
sentence of disownment. Her appeals to quarterly meeting and then to
New York Yearly Meeting were rejected. Hannah Barnard certainly enjoyed some support in her views from her fellow members. However,
the rising tide of evangelicalism, which was already apparent in the
American branch of the Society as it was on the other side of the
ocean, swept aside her protest against the avenging God of the old
dispensation. A Quaker disowned for refusing to give support to
war is a curious—and somewhat disturbing—incident in the history
of Friends' peace testimony.[85]

The Hannah Barnard affair created quite a stir at the time among
both British and American Friends. It was many years before another
remonstrance of this kind was heard on this side of the Atlantic—even
among the Hicksite opponents of Quaker evangelicalism in the
Orthodox camp. Jackson's little effort, therefore, appears to be the first
work to contest once again the compatibility of the concept of an all-
loving God with his alleged approval of the bloodthirsty contests in
which the ancient Hebrews had engaged. Again, the matter caused
somewhat of a flutter in Quaker circles. But Jackson's Hicksites, although his ideas were as yet too radical for most of them, were not
inclined to proceed against him as their fathers had been willing to

<hr>

[85] [Thomas Foster], *A Narrative of the Proceedings in America of the Society
called Quakers, in the Case of Hannah Barnard. With a Brief Review of the Previous Transactions in Great Britain and Ireland*, pp. x-xiv, 5, 6, 9, 50, 53, 120-24;
*An Appeal to the Society of Friends, on the Primitive Simplicity of their Christian
Principles and Church Discipline*, pp. 43-79, 115-17, 120, 158-63, 168, 169, 177,
184, 185, 193, 195, 207-10. See also Jones, *The Later Periods of Quakerism*, I,
292-307.

do in regard to poor Hannah Barnard. And so, after none too long a time, the excitement over Jackson's booklet died away, and, with the Mexican War ended, the issue of peace again retreated from the forefront of Friends' interests.

The period of the 1850's in America was one of mounting war clouds, but the tension between the sections as yet impinged only indirectly on the Quaker peace testimony. None of the Quaker periodicals at the time devoted much space to the testimony, and this neglect was reinforced by the fact that, in comparison with previous decades, Friends in the fifties came only infrequently into conflict with the law over the matter of militia service. Yearly meetings occasionally issued statements on peace,[86] but they lacked the urgent note of those of the Mexican War period.

We have noted already the absence of a missionary spirit in the Quaker pacifism of our period. The peace testimony was still cultivated assiduously, but on the whole only within the confines of the Quaker enclosure.

Aggressive championship of the peace position—taking its message outside the circle of Friends' meetings in an effort to bring it to non-Quakers instead of merely striving to strengthen the adherence of members of the Society to its principles—was unusual. A rare example of this militant spirit is to be found in the action of a mid-Pennsylvania woman minister of the 1830's, Ellen McCarty. A contemporary journal relates of her: "Hearing of a militia muster about three miles from her residence, she felt drawn to go there, and by her faithful dealing with some of the young men there assembled, she convinced two of them of the unlawfulness of war; and they afterwards joined the Society of Friends."[87]

More often than not, it was the very peculiarities of Friends, the distinguishing characteristics that marked Quakers off from the rest of society, that were also regarded as the surest means of preserving their peace testimony intact. Pacifism without the plain dress seemed almost a contradiction in terms to many nineteenth-century Quakers, young and old; so we find Maine Friends, for instance, heartily agreeing with the view voiced by outside critics that Quaker applicants for

---

[86] An example is the 8-page *Address on Peace*, which New England Y. M. issued in 1854 in connection with the outbreak of the Crimean War. In it Friends exhorted parents to bring up their children in the spirit of the peace testimony. "The exhibitions of military show and preparation should be set before them in their true light, and they early taught that they are parts of the antichristian system of war, and should be considered in that light, and not as attractive displays for recreation and amusement" (p. 7).

[87] *Journal of . . . William Evans*, p. 202.

exemption from military service "ought to certify by their appearance to whom they belong."[88] We can see the same attitude, the feeling that there was a vital connection between the Society's objection to bearing arms and to the whole method of war, on the one hand, and the peculiarities of garb and speech which it had retained from an earlier century, on the other, expressed even more clearly in an article by "Pacificus" published a decade and a half later in the columns of the Orthodox *Friend*:

> One weakness begets another. The laying waste of one part of the enclosure of the Society, enfeebles and makes way for the prostration of another portion of the hedge. When called upon to pay militia fines, some of our members who have already departed from plainness of dress and address, are *ashamed*—yea, *ashamed*—to acknowledge the motive which should induce them to refuse compliance with these demands, from a consciousness *that they do not look like Quakers*, that if they are sheep, they are not in their clothing, and, through weakness begotten of this very cause, they fancy themselves compelled to act in accordance with their appearance.[89]

III

Although a sectarian attitude toward peace may have had considerable psychological justification in earlier periods, it became less understandable in the decade after 1815, when an organized peace movement began to develop outside and independent of any of the peace denominations. This movement, and its absolute pacifist wing in particular, is discussed in the full version of this book. Something should be said now, however, concerning the relationship between the Society of Friends and the burgeoning non-Quaker pacifism, which was finding expression in such organizations as the American Peace Society, its affiliates and forerunners representing the right wing of the movement, and the later and more radical New England Non-Resistance Society on the left.[90]

By temperament and outlook Friends might be expected to have felt close sympathy with the more conservative wing of the peace movement. The gradualism of these peace societies had something in common with the long-term range of the Quaker objectives. The societies frankly acknowledged their debt to the peace witness which the Quak-

---

[88] R. M. Jones, *The Society of Friends in Kennebec County*, p. 12.
[89] *Friend*, 14 Feb. 1835, p. 151.
[90] See Peter Brock, "The Peace Testimony in 'a Garden Enclosed,'" *Quaker History*, 54, no. 2 (Autumn 1965), 67-80.

ers had upheld for almost two centuries. They quoted in their publications from Fox and Penn and from many of the Quaker journals. The Quaker experiment in the government of Pennsylvania (pictured in rather an idealized fashion, it is true) provided them with one of their most frequently used examples of the safety of peaceable principles; and they also drew for illustrative material upon the experiences of Irish Quakers during the rebellion of 1798, as described in the book by Dr. Thomas Hancock. The essay on war of the contemporary English Quaker Jonathan Dymond was, as we have said, immensely influential on the thinking of American pacifists throughout the whole nineteenth century. As a Delaware Friend wrote: "Many of the important testimonies which were maintained by Friends and were almost peculiar to them as a people are now picked up and become matter of deep interest to those very people, who reviled and persecuted Friends on account thereof—Peace Societies, Temperance Societies, Abolition Societies."[91]

True, the membership of the moderate peace societies was never confined to absolute pacifists. This was considered by many Friends a stumbling block in the way of collaboration. Others, however, joined with non-Friends on a common platform, agreeing, despite their different approaches, to labor together in the interests of international peace. Such a man was the venerable Moses Brown, a leading figure among New England Quakers. Around the time of the War of 1812, Brown became a friend of the two founding fathers of the American peace movement, David Low Dodge and the Rev. Noah Worcester, and in 1818 was himself instrumental, along with several other local Quakers, in getting a peace society started in his native Rhode Island, which he continued to support with his time and money.[92] Members of the Rhode Island Peace Society, in which Quakers were influential, were no more obliged to pledge themselves to complete pacifism than those of the other groups which eventually merged into the American Peace Society. On the whole, however, we do not find many Quakers among the leading figures of the early American peace movement. The initiative came from outside the Society, from Unitarians and Presbyterians, Congregationalists and Baptists, rather than from any of the peace sects. In some places, for instance in the small Pennsylvania Peace Society, Friends predominated, but its influence was confined to Philadelphia and its environs; in the movement as a whole Friends played a subordinate role.

This fact surprised—and disappointed—many non-Quaker peace

[91] Quoted in James A. Munroe, *Federalist Delaware*, p. 49.
[92] Mack Thompson, *Moses Brown*, p. 282.

workers. "Why it is thus, we of course do not know," remarked William Ladd, and he pointed out that, in England, Friends' participation in the London Peace Society was both larger and more effective.[93] Indeed, even though its support was to come mainly from non-Quaker sympathizers, a large part of the initiative in founding the British body had come from Quaker sources. It is not too difficult, perhaps, to resolve the enigma which puzzled William Ladd. Friends in America were slower in emerging from the social isolation into which the Society on both continents had retreated during the previous century. The reaction against the active participation of Pennsylvania Friends in political and social life, which had set in at the middle of the eighteenth century, had been felt more strongly, of course, on this side of the ocean, and other factors, such as the separations and the westward expansion, served to delay the return of the Society to a more active role in national life. For the bulk of American Quakers, then, the activities of the peace societies were worldly, creaturely. Friends were not, of course, actually hostile: they did give the societies a certain slightly condescending approval. Moreover, Friends' periodicals drew extensively on the literature of these societies, American and British, for their peace material, reprinting in their columns extracts from the British *Herald of Peace* and the American *Advocate of Peace* and other papers and drawing, too, on the declarations issued by the respective societies. But a narrowly conceived separatism prevented most Friends from throwing their energies into organized peace work, and as a result the whole cause of peace suffered. A representative example of the thinking of the Society in this respect is found in an article published in the Philadelphia *Friend* in the mid-thirties. Its author declared:

> These societies, in their collective capacity, do not fully come up to the Christian standard according to our estimate of . . . the New Testament doctrine bearing upon this subject; and it therefore may not be expedient that our members should be found in their ranks. The Society of Friends as a body, . . . has emphatically been a Peace Society from its foundation, declaring to the world . . . that war in all its forms, offensive and defensive, is utterly at variance with the glorious gospel dispensation of "peace on earth, goodwill to men." And it is safer, at least in the present state of the world, that we keep much to ourselves, and not act as a body in reference to this important testimony, lest by joining with others we should unawares be led into a compromise or evasion of any of its requisitions.[94]

[93] *Calumet*, I, no. 15 (Sept.-Oct. 1833), 450.
[94] *Friend*, 30 Aug. 1834.

If Friends tended to assume a cautious attitude toward such bodies as the American Peace Society for, among other reasons, falling short of an uncompromising testimony against all wars, their reaction to the New England Non-Resistance Society, which came into being in September 1838 as a result of the efforts of William Lloyd Garrison and his abolutionist disciples, was more often than not one of downright hostility. To understand the reasons for this reaction, we must recall once more the principles governing the Quaker attitude toward civil government, since one of the key points in the platform of the New England nonresistants was their belief in the incompatibility between Christian pacifism and participation in any of the activities of government as then constituted.

The experience of the final years of Quaker rule in Pennsylvania, reinforced by the quietist trend which was a powerful influence at that time on Friends on both continents, had left American Quakers profoundly disillusioned with the world of politics and determined to keep themselves as far as possible separate from its corrupting influence. The strife engendered by party struggles and the lust for office were contrary, Friends now argued, to the spirit of Christian love that had led them to abandon reliance on armed force.[95] Yet the withdrawal was never complete. A few Friends continued to sit in the Pennsylvania legislature right up through the nineteenth century and to act as magistrates and hold various other offices, provided they did not conflict directly with the peace testimony. Above all, Friends went on voting in large numbers at elections, on both state and federal levels. "The peaceable exercise of the right of suffrage, Friends have always left to the private judgment of the members," states an epistle issued by the Meeting for Sufferings of the Philadelphia Yearly Meeting (Orthodox) in 1834.[96] Belief in the possibility of so organizing the protection of society that armed force would be eliminated altogether or reduced to an absolute minimum was still widely held. As an Ohio Friend wrote at the time of the Mexican War: "The civil power has, perhaps in ninety-nine cases out of a hundred been sufficient to bring criminals to punishment."[97] The same thought was developed further by the Hicksite leader Benjamin Ferris (1780-1867), who wrote: "The Society

[95] See, e.g., the *Christian Advices* issued by Philadelphia Y. M. (1808), pp. 9, 109.

[96] *Friend*, 13 Sept. 1834.

[97] *Remarks by a Member of the Society of Friends on the Subject of War*, p. 2. Its author "E.C." (probably Elijah Coffin) wrote the pamphlet in answer to a Roman Catholic who had published a pro-war "Address to the Society of Friends on the Subject of War" in the *Eaton Register* on 3 June 1847.

never set up the doctrines of *nonresistance*."[98] Approval of the positive aspects of government was expressed frequently in the official statements of yearly meetings, and participation rarely led to disownment where a connection with the military was not clearly apparent.[99]

Thus we see that opinion regarding the practical application of Quaker pacifism in the realm of government was by no means uniform within the Society. The majority, though as yet remaining somewhat on the fringe of political life, maintained basically the positive view of the state that had held sway throughout most of the period of the "Holy Experiment."[100] Nevertheless, a minority, whose exact strength it is very difficult to estimate, had veered over to a position that was not far removed from the Anabaptist-Mennonite view, rejecting participation in civil government even where questions of military force or war taxation were not involved. This antistate attitude, a kind of Christian anarchism, had been strongest perhaps in the last

[98] Ferris Collection (R G 5), ser. 4, box 12, MSS in F.H.L.S.C. Ferris had been a militia C.O. in the War of 1812.

[99] A more unbending attitude, however, was exhibited by some yearly meetings during the Revolution and the years immediately succeeding it toward members who held any kind of office. See, e.g., F. C. Anscombe, *I have called you Friends: The Story of Quakerism in North Carolina*, p. 156. But the question of the use of armed compulsion was only one contributory factor here along with such matters as the enforcement of a test and the question of slavery.

[100] It is interesting to note that the viewpoint of the "political" Quakers of the period of the "Holy Experiment," that compulsion backed by armed force might be dispensed with in individual relations but must be retained by Friends who acted in a public capacity, still had adherents a half century later. (Very similar considerations had led some Friends to advocate a complete withdrawal from political life.) We see opinions of this sort expressed in a letter Israel Foulke wrote to his brother on 22 Sept. 1793 (misc. MSS F.H.L.S.C.): "I . . . must confess I see no way to avoid giving my assent to thy conclusion, that civil government, and defensive war, is [sic] indivisibly connected for (under the present situation of mankind) it seems morally impossible that the former should be at all times supported, without the aid of the latter." He goes on, however, to say: "I think the doctrine of nonresistance may be of considerable use to mankind notwithstanding the above conclusion; especially in private citizens and religious societies for two reasons, 1st as being conducive to the internal peace and tranquillity of the state and secondly, as I look upon it to be a very delicate point to keep to the exact bounds between defensive and offensive war, which has [sic] perhaps never been clearly ascertained . . . so I conceive that the doctrine of nonresistance may be of use in the present state of things as a counterpoise even to defensive war. Thus as a private citizen or subject I think it my duty to encourage the doctrine of peace on earth and goodwill to men universally. But were I a legislator I should look upon myself entrusted as a guardian of the state, and should I apprehend an invasion intended, I should think it my duty to use every means in my power to prevent it, first by putting the state in a posture of defence, and at the same time preparing just and reasonable terms of peace, and if that proved ineffectual, to exert every power to repel force by force."

quarter of the eighteenth century, when the crisis of 1756 and the hard years of the Revolutionary War had still been fresh in the minds of Friends. But we find many individuals sharing it in the period up to and beyond the Civil War.

Perhaps the best known exemplar of this way of thinking among Friends during the first half of the nineteenth century is the Pennsylvania Hicksite minister, Jesse Kersey (1767-1845), whose zeal for nonresistance led him to condemn all existing governments and to advocate total Quaker abstention from politics. "My fears have been," we find him writing in 1815 in his often reprinted *Treatise* on the fundamentals of Quaker belief, a volume that was published with the *imprimatur* of Philadelphia Yearly Meeting, "that many are in danger of departing from the true ground of this testimony." He goes on to propose a boycott of political activity that in many ways foreshadows—although in more moderate language—the later theories of the Garrisonian nonresistants:

I know of no constitution or government in the world that, at this day, agrees with Christianity: they all make provision for war, they all complete their ends by force. And therefore, it becomes a people who cannot act upon opposite principles, to be on their guard how they connect themselves with the measures of government. The Christian may live in the world, he may comply with all the commands of government, either actively or passively, and there is nothing to fear from him, if he be a Christian. And if all men were Christians, the principles of civil government would be changed from compulsion to consent, the subjects from force to submission without it.[101]

In 1847 we find the Hicksite *Friends' Weekly Intelligencer* complaining that the antipolitical current within the Society was on the increase: "The number of those who adopt this view is, we think, large and increasing; and we are informed, that in the neighboring Yearly Meeting

[101] Jesse Kersey, *A Treatise on Fundamental Doctrines of the Christian Religion*, pp. 93-101. Later Kersey had contacts with Garrison's New England Non-Resistance Society. We find him writing to the *Non-Resistant* (vol. II, no. 2, 22 Jan. 1840): "There is no doctrine, in my view, which can be embraced, more important to mankind than this." He went even further than most nonresistants in advocating that they refrain from petitioning Congress on behalf of oppressed minorities like the slaves—on the grounds that, however great our sympathies with the latter, such action was inconsistent with "no-government" principles. This statement brought a rejoinder from the paper's editor, Edmund Quincy, who explained to his readers: "We cannot pray Congress to make slaveholding a penal offence, but we think that we may ask for the abrogation of all the slave laws, so as to leave the slave system, unsustained by legislation, to the force of public sentiment."

of New York, so general is the feeling against voting, in many places, that a prominent Friend is rarely seen at the polls."[102] This was probably an exaggeration. But the activities of the non-Quaker nonresistants from around 1838 on seems to have made a certain impact on the Society of Friends, even though few of its members were to be found actually enrolled in the New England Non-Resistance Society.

John Jackson, the Hicksite minister whom we have met as the author of a tract expressing doubts about the justifiability of Old Testament wars, had come out six years earlier with a small pamphlet, which well illustrates this influence. Jackson did not swallow the whole nonresistant doctrine, but his approach is very similar to theirs. Although Friends might legitimately take part in government where it was carried on without the use of armed force, "it is our duty," he went on, "to abstain from a participation in the administration of such governments as are conducted upon anti-christian principles." Friends should exercise the suffrage only when a pacifist was standing for office. Since in Jackson's view (and in that of the nonresistants) the positions of President or Congressman under the existing constitution were inextricably involved in military affairs and the upholding of slavery, and a consistent pacifist who believed this could scarcely stand for office, Jackson was in fact advocating a total withdrawal from the political arena, to the point of complete abstention from voting.[103]

Jackson was an educated man and a representative of the upper ranks of Quaker society. But the same kind of view was expressed by many rural Friends. Take, for example, Edward Hicks (1780-1849), painter of the "Peaceable Kingdom" and a village coachmaker. In the mid-forties he had felt a concern to address the youth of the Society, and he therefore composed "A Word of Exhortation to Young Friends: presented to them without money and without price. By a poor illiterate Minister." In it he instructed the younger generation in regard to the peace testimony as follows:

> His kingdom being a blessed state, arrived at by the redeemed soul, where there is no qualification for either war or politics, our young Friends could neither elect others, nor receive any office of honor or profit in the governments of this world, that are set up by the sword, and defended by the sword; but would feel conscientiously

[102] *Friends' Weekly Intelligencer*, 21 Aug. 1847.
[103] John Jackson, *Considerations on the Impropriety of Friends participating in the Administration of Political Governments*, esp. pp. 3-6, 11, 12. Cf. the similar views of Ezra Michener, who wrote around 1860 in regard to the upper governmental echelons: "We cannot consistently give our suffrage to others to fill any office, the duties of which we could not conscientiously discharge" (*A Retrospect of Early Quakerism*, p. 276).

265

bound, in justice, to leave these offices to such as are better qualified to fill them.[104]

A small number of Friends did join the New England Non-Resistance Society and collaborated wholeheartedly in its work, thereby sometimes risking disciplinary action if their meetings (as was quite likely) were unsympathetic. The nonresistants' first president was a highly respected New England Quaker, Effingham L. Capron; but he does not appear to have come into collision with his meeting. However, some of the lesser lights among Massachusetts' Friends who were active among the nonresistant abolitionists, men like William Bassett of Lynn, Joseph S. Wall of Worcester, and Clothier Gifford of Fairhaven, found themselves in trouble.[105]

Since the Non-Resistance Society's activities did not reach out much beyond the Northeast, a direct clash of this kind mainly affected New England Friends. However, mention should be made of Lucretia Mott's interest in the work of the Non-Resistance Society. Mrs. Mott, at least during the early years, attended its annual meetings in Boston as regularly as her domestic and philanthropic duties in Philadelphia permitted and took an active part in its proceedings. The militancy of the movement, the lack of compromise on vital issues like war or slavery, attracted a rebel spirit like Lucretia Mott. When a memorial meeting was held in Philadelphia after John Brown's execution, Mrs. Mott was one of the speakers. She expressed her admiration for him as a martyr for liberty, though at the same time making clear her disapproval of the methods he employed for its attainment. Afterward, a friend told her that she was "the most belligerent Non-Resistant he ever saw." Mrs. Mott was immensely pleased. "I have no idea, because I am a Non-Resistant, of submitting tamely to injustice inflicted either on me or the slave. I will oppose it with all the moral powers with which I am endowed." And she went on to expound her interpretation of Quaker pacifism. "Quakerism, as I understand it, does not mean quietism. The early Friends were agitators; disturbers of the peace; and were more obnoxious in their day to charges which are now so freely made than we are."[106]

Views of this kind had long before aroused strong resentment against Mrs. Mott inside her own Hicksite society; many of the more respectable felt that she was setting a dangerous example and that something

---

[104] *Memoirs of . . . Edward Hicks*, p. 346.

[105] *Non-Resistant*, vol. II, no. 21, 11 Nov. 1840.

[106] Otelia Cromwell, *Lucretia Mott*, pp. 61-63, 170. Mrs. Mott was also a warm (though not altogether uncritical) admirer of Kossuth and the cause of Hungarian independence.

should be done to prevent further harm. So in September 1842 when she was passing through New York on her way back home from the Non-Resistance Society's annual meeting in Boston, attempts were made to bring her to book. "The elders and others there," she wrote, "have been quite desirous to make me an offender for joining with those not in membership with us and accepting offices in these Societies. But our Friends here [i.e., in Philadelphia where Mrs. Mott held her membership] know full well that such a position is neither contrary to our Discipline, to Scripture, to reason, nor sense."[107]

Behind the action attempted against Lucretia Mott undoubtedly stood the figure of George F. White (1789-1847), minister and elder in the Hicksite meeting of New York. White may be taken as typical of the extreme conservative and sectarian element which dominated many meetings at this time—as much in the Orthodox branch as among the Hicksites, it should be added.[108] Only the previous year White's meeting had disowned the saintly Quaker bookseller, Isaac T. Hopper (1771-1852), for his abolitionist activities. For White and his fellow conservatives, those Friends who had thrown their energies behind the various reform movements of the day, whether peace or abolition or even temperance, and were prepared to work there alongside non-Friends were betraying the peculiar mission of the Society and by their creaturely activities helping to lay waste the fences so arduously erected around the Quaker enclosure. "Hireling lecturers," "hireling book-agents," "emissaries of Satan," White called the abolitionists. "I had a thousand times rather be a slave, and spend my days with slave-holders, than to dwell in companionship with abolitionists."[109] Despite a genuine devotion to the Quaker peace testimony, which was part and parcel of the heritage of the Society, White and his kind took

[107] *Ibid.*, p. 111. Despite her "no-government" views, Mrs. Mott supported women's right to the franchise, even though she felt they should refrain from exercising it until the existing political system was reformed. In a *Discourse on Woman* which she delivered in December 1849 (quoted *ibid.*, p. 150), she had the following to say on this subject: "Would that man, too, would have no participation in a government recognizing the life-taking principle—retaliation and the sword. It is unworthy of a Christian nation. But when . . . a convention shall be called to make regulations for self-government on Christian principles, I can see no good reasons why women should not participate in such an assemblage, taking part equally with man."

[108] See, e.g., the Orthodox *Friend* for 15 Oct. 1842: "The editor is aware that a class of people,—a sort of hair-brained sciolists,—has of late risen up in several of the eastern states, who, under the specious guise of reformers, and of superior degrees of enlightenment, propagate opinions, the tendency of which, if permitted to be carried out, would be to break up the foundations of all order in society, civil and religious." These were "abominable doctrines" of which no Friend could possibly approve.

[109] John Cox, *Quakerism in the City of New York*, p. 100.

up from the outset a position of implacable hostility toward the radical nonresistant movement, tainted as it was with the stigma of abolitionism, and did everything they could to counter its influence, particularly on the younger generation of Friends.

On one occasion, after White had blasted the nonresistants while on a pastoral visit to Philadelphia, a young Friend from Philadelphia Yearly Meeting's western quarter wrote to Lucretia Mott: "The attack upon non-resistants was most unexpected. I almost shuddered as he heaped his denunciations upon them . . . and my spirit sank with despondency, and yet with something of indignation, when I recollected that he was an accredited Minister of the Society of Friends."[110] Another young man, Oliver Johnson (1809-1889), who was one of Garrison's close collaborators in his work for abolition and nonresistance, had been led by his pacifist and abolitionist sympathies not merely to change his intention of becoming a clergyman in one of the orthodox churches but to withdraw from it altogether and seriously contemplate joining Friends. "My own experience," he says, "was similar to that of many others" (in much the same way, we may note, as many conscientious objectors in both the World Wars were later to become Quakers in no small part as a result of their common antiwar sympathies). The violent attacks of White and the social conservatives on the Non-Resistance Society came as an unpleasant shock to a man like Johnson (if we may trust his account, which he obviously wrote in a state of considerable emotion). "How surprising . . . that a minister of the Society of Friends can utter the language of scorn and reproach toward an institution based upon the identical principles" of his own church.[111] Johnson finally threw in his lot with the antislavery rebel spirits who formed the Progressive Society of Friends.

White told Johnson in a lengthy correspondence they had around 1840 that the Non-Resistance Society was a body framed "in the will of man."[112] The unorthodox religious opinions of many of its members, combined with their militant opposition against "human governments," was enough, indeed, to arouse conservative Friends against it. The obstructionist tactics and strong language adopted by the Non-Resistance Society's members in their campaigning, especially in their role as abolitionists, offended many Friends who had long favored quiet and unassuming methods of forwarding their aims. This emotional incompatibility made it extremely difficult for Quakers of this kind to find common ground with radical nonresistants, despite the similarity

---

[110] Hallowell, *Motts*, pp. 207, 208.
[111] *Correspondence between Oliver Johnson and George F. White*, pp. 21, 38.
[112] *Ibid.*, p. 5. White's side of the correspondence is characterized by a rancorous and sarcastic tone.

of their ultimate objectives. Thus in 1840, for instance, the Orthodox yearly meetings in New England and New York in official pronouncements castigated the nonresistants roundly and dissociated themselves from "the views of those who deny the necessity of human government." The Hicksite *Friends' Weekly Intelligencer* was still fulminating some years later against the nonresistants, "whose souls were not baptized into the Spirit of the Lamb. . . . While they are preaching up forgiveness of injuries, and love towards enemies, they indulge in denunciations towards those who differ from them."[113]

Conservatively minded Friends in both branches clearly underestimated the earnestness and sincerity of the men and women who threw in their lot with the Non-Resistance Society. Differences regarding means and the debate on civil government were genuine sources of disagreement. But, as we have seen, they were issues which at this date divided Friends themselves. When Sarah Pugh (1800-1884), a Philadelphia school teacher who was a close friend of Lucretia Mott and her collaborator in many reform causes, first attended an annual meeting of the Non-Resistance Society, she was agreeably surprised by what she saw there. As she wrote with a tinge of surprise: "Here was a large body of people zealous and earnest for the right, dressed as the worldly dress."[114] Sarah Pugh, of course, was something of a rebel, and in fact only a handful of Friends ever came directly in contact with the nonresistant movement.

How did the latter react to Quaker attacks? At first, many nonresistants seem to have expected considerable support from Friends, and they stressed the similarities between their two viewpoints. However, as it became apparent that such support was not forthcoming, that, instead, downright hostility was all that they could expect from the Society as a whole, a note of anger appeared; the differences in approach were now emphasized, and Friends' official stand was sub-

---

[113] *Friends' Weekly Intelligencer*, 21 Aug. 1847. Cf. the "Admonitory Address" of the Hicksite Y. M. in Indiana (quoted in the *Practical Christian*, vol. IX, no. 19, 20 Jan. 1849): "But who are these that are running to and fro in the earth, in their own time, and will, and strength, babbling of temperance and nonresistance, and slavery and benevolence, and communities and the Scriptures, and the sabbath and woman's rights. These are the thieves that cannot abide the way of humility and the cross, but climb up some other way, and steal the testimony of Jesus, and are lifted up in their self-sufficiency."

[114] *Memorial of Sarah Pugh*, pp. 30, 31. The Rev. W. H. Furness, minister of the First Unitarian Church in Philadelphia, suggested that possibly his fellow nonresistant abolitionists "should wear Quaker hats as a method of telling the world that they abhor all *forcible* measures" (*Non-Resistant*, vol. I, no. 21, 2 Nov. 1839). Perhaps the sight of Garrison in a Quaker broadbrim burning his copy of the Constitution of the United States might have led to a speedier abandonment of Quaker peculiarities in dress on the part of the traditionalists!

269

mitted to critical analysis.[115] Nonresistant criticism of the Quaker position of giving a large degree of support to government measures for internal security, and to a police force in particular, as inconsistent with their pacifism comes at times extremely close both to that of Mennonite writers and of many nonpacifists.[116] That ardent nonresistant, Henry C. Wright, concluded that it was a realization that police duties under the present system were incompatible with their peace testimony that really kept Friends from entering this branch of government service.[117]

Responsibility for the use of armed force by a government rested in part on those who had voted that government into power, the nonresistants told their Quaker critics. One could not contract out of the unpleasant aspects of government, they argued, and say that one cast his vote for the President only in a civil capacity and not as commander-in-chief as well, or that one would act as magistrate or legislator only where armed force was not involved. In all law enforcement as practised at present "the bayonets are none the less present because unseen," wrote Edmund Quincy, editor of the *Non-Resistant*, in answer to a Quaker correspondent. Granted that a country might be run on Christian, pacifist lines—"*we* know that such a government is possible, and our object is to establish it in the land by first changing the hearts of the people"—these were still not the guiding principles "in *existing* government, which Friends support." Since, then, all present-day governments were based on the "life-taking principle," Quincy went on, "we pronounce the Society of Friends, as a body, false to their own principles, in taking part in such governments."[118]

How far the influence of liberal-minded Friends was able to counteract that of the conservatives it is hard to say. After a decade of inter-

[115] See, e.g., *Selections from the Writings and Speeches of William Lloyd Garrison*, p. 94.

[116] See the remarks of a nonpacifist critic of Quaker views on war, William Logan Fisher, *A Review of the Doctrines and Discipline of the Society of Friends*, 1854 edn., p. 61: "The Society of Friends have never been a non-resistant society. All their property is held by the power of the sword; their deeds and title papers are acknowledged before a magistrate, in order to place them under the protection of the law, sustained by the military force of the country, and yet they disown a man for paying a militia fine. They use the magistrate's sword to preserve order; others use their own; there may be a material difference in results, but they rest on the same foundation." Fisher was of Quaker ancestry and later associated with the Progressive Friends.

[117] Wright, *Six Months at Graeffenberg*, pp. 164-66. See also pp. 155-57, 161, 162.

[118] *Non-Resistant*, vol. III, no. 3, 10 Feb. 1841.

mittent scrapping between nonresistants and radical abolitionists, on the one hand, and their conservative opponents who dominated most Quaker meetings, on the other, H. C. Wright wrote of the latter: "Their sole business now seems to be to administer their Discipline to keep their members 'out of the mixture.' "[119] And, undoubtedly, many Friends who might have given the radical pacifists a more sympathetic hearing were led by the denunciations of White and his sort to close their minds to an impartial consideration of nonresistant doctrines. But it is very uncertain if at that date the majority of Friends in either branch were ready to throw down the walls which separated them from society and, while maintaining intact their own specific peace witness, to place their energies at the disposal of the common pacifist effort. For this situation, of course, the extremism and fanaticism displayed by many of the nonresistants were not altogether without responsibility. In any case, there was perhaps something inherently incompatible between the militant "immediatism" and perfectionism of the non-Quaker nonresistants and the "harmless" pacifism of nineteenth-century Friends, which, in the words of one of its advocates, "carries no enmity in its bosom; and leaves the rest of the world in the quiet possession of their own principles."[120]

The story of the Society of Friends' relations with the radical nonresistants illustrates both the strength and the weakness of the Quaker peace testimony during our period. The sober, traditional character of its witness against war prevented it from swallowing the extravagancies and eccentricities which were associated with the New England Non-Resistance Society. Friends continued on their way (we cannot quite say unruffled, since some of the utterances and actions of meetings and their leading members were marked by considerable heat and acrimony), bearing a personal testimony against military service when called upon, considering carefully and prayerfully the implications of their pacifism in such matters as paying taxes and carrying on business, and occasionally demonstrating the depth of their pacifist principles in a situation of violence. Yet this witness, so carefully nurtured and so rigorously guarded, only too often lacked the vital spark. There was little creativity in Friends' thinking on peace, especially if we compare it with the contribution of the radical nonresistants. As pacifists, Friends now made little impact on society. The organized peace movement, both its left and its right wings, though drawing immense in-

---

[119] *Non-Resistant and Practical Christian*, vol. IX, no. 12, 14 Oct. 1848.
[120] From Elisha Bates's "Letter to a Military Officer of Distinguished Rank," in the *Moral Advocate*, I, no. 6 (Dec. 1821), 84.

spiration from Friends' witness in the past, gained little assistance or backing from the Society in the present. This was, indeed, a misfortune for the cause of peace, which needed to rally all the support it could get in its uphill struggle with widespread indifference on the part of many and actual hostility from a militarist minority in the nation.

Chapter 6

The Quakers in the Civil War

The story of the Quakers during the Civil War period has been told on more than one occasion. Edward Needles Wright, for instance, devoted the greater part of his study on *Conscientious Objectors in the Civil War* (1931)[1] to the stand of the Society of Friends, while back at the end of the last century the Quaker minister, Fernando G. Cartland, compiled an artless yet moving account of the trials and tribulations of Friends under the Confederacy with the title *Southern Heroes* (1895). That there were many Friends who took the traditional conscientious objector position of their Society and that there were also others who in the North broke with tradition and joined actively in the struggle against slavery and secession are facts known to all who are at all acquainted with Quaker history. In truth, the pattern of conduct among Friends in the war period was more complex than this simple dichotomy implies, and it caused some confusion at times in the minds of the authorities. Even among those who upheld the Society's peace testimony, there was by no means always unanimity as to what reaction to the various demands of a war situation this testimony required of members.

The peace testimony of the Society of Friends, as we know, was not in its essence a literalist belief, a dogma based on any one, or any number, of Biblical texts. It sprang from the spirit that underlay the scriptures and that might be revealed to the perceptive soul directly in the present, as it had been revealed nearly two thousand years before. The spirit of peace might speak to the Indian untutored in the Christian scriptures. The evangelical trend that had come to predominate in many meetings of the Orthodox branch did not succeed in altogether obliterating this spiritualism in the pacifism of the Friends. The peace testimony at bottom resulted from an outpouring of the Inner Light, a discipleship of the spirit, and not merely from the keeping of the letter of the gospel. We find an excellent illustration of this attitude in one of the wartime epistles of the Orthodox Yearly Meeting of Philadelphia. "Our testimony against all war and fighting," it states, "is founded on the precious precepts contained in the New Testament,

---

[1] As the author points out (p. 1), the term "conscientious objector" was not yet in use at the time of the Civil War. The men were described as "non-resistants," "non-combatants," "those scrupulous against bearing arms," etc.

and the immediate openings made on the mind by the same Spirit which dictated it."[2] It was a loving spirit that was needed to conquer the forces driving toward war; it was this that must provide the impulse toward asserting the primacy of peace. As an address of the Meeting for Sufferings of Baltimore Yearly Meeting (Hicksite this time), which was published early in the war, put it: "Let us keep ever in mind, that the practical ground-work of our profession . . . is love, universal love—love to God, and love to all men."[3]

It was, nevertheless, this very principle of universal love, when Friends tried to apply it in practice, that from the outset of the war created one of the most trying dilemmas that beset them. In spite of the fact that the first Emancipation Proclamation was not promulgated by the Lincoln administration until September 1862, for most Quakers, as for many millions of their fellow citizens then and since, the war seemed from the first to be fought with the slavery issue in the foreground. The *Friend*, organ of the Philadelphia Orthodox Yearly Meeting, for instance, describing the war as "a wanton and unjustifiable attack on the Union" by the South seldom paralleled in the whole course of history, went on to affirm "the real causes of their treasonable and murderous proceedings, to be the maintenance and extension of the abominable system of human slavery."[4] How in these circumstances was universal love to be reconciled with universal peace? How was a desire to see our fellow men freed as soon as possible to be squared with an abhorrence of shedding the blood of human beings, even in order to free the oppressed? It is true that this was not a new dilemma for Friends, but the war presented it to them with a new urgency and in new ways that demanded in many cases some immediate and decisive action.

Their long held testimony against slavery had been so conceived as not to conflict with their viewpoint on peace. They advocated gradualism in getting rid of the peculiar institution, the use of persuasion

---

[2] *Friend* (Phila.), 16 May 1863.

[3] *Friends' Intelligencer*, 19 Oct. 1861.

[4] *Friend*, 23 Aug. 1862. A postwar pacifist, the Rev. John M. Washburn, in his book *Reason vs. the Sword* (1873), pp. 374, 375, criticizes this kind of attitude even on the part of those Friends who upheld their Society's pacifism throughout the war. He writes: "Their testimony had become traditional and shadowy, and existed rather as a dogma than as an active principle; but the question of slavery, constantly agitated, was vivid in their minds, and so led them very generally to sympathize with the work of the sword . . . so, too, the Quakers were seduced into the common but erroneous belief that *the act of the South in seceding was in itself a wrong and sin*, apart from violence and war." Washburn, though anti-slavery and pro-Union, maintained that the Confederacy had possessed the same right to a separate existence as Ireland or Italy. His remarks on the Quakers, penetrating in some ways, lack understanding of the issues involved.

and example. Yet Friends were not slow to recognize that difficulties must persist among members in reconciling these two separate expressions of what was fundamentally one organic faith. The position was aptly described by a contributor to the Hicksite *Friends' Intelligencer,* writing after Lincoln's final Emancipation Proclamation of 1 January 1863 had made the question more acute:

> There is danger, under present circumstances, of allowing our testimony against war to be modified or lessened, from the fact that this war will certainly be the means of putting down slavery. This war having been begun by slaveholders more firmly to secure themselves in their authority over slaves, we cannot be sorry to see that authority overthrown; yet it is done by a means that we, as Christians, cannot recommend or uphold.[5]

This general sympathy with the Unionist cause on the part of most Friends may be illustrated by an incident told of old Thomas Garrett (1783-1871), a Wilmington (Del.) Friend, who had devoted many years to the cause of the slave, helping the "Underground Railway" in smuggling runaways up north. Garrett remained loyal to Quaker pacifism during the war. He did not hesitate, however, to encourage a former slave, whom he was assisting, to join up with the Union army. "Am I naughty, being a professed non-resistant, to advise this poor fellow to serve Father Abraham?" he inquired of a friend.[6]

I

Friends of all branches of the Society in the Union states, to whose wartime experiences we turn first, continually stressed their loyalty to the administration, their lack of all sympathy with the Confederate cause, and their willingness to undergo all the burdens of citizenship except where these infringed on their conscientious scruples. As opposition grew within the Northern states to a continuation of hostilities—an antiwar trend not based on any abstract pacifism but on indifference or hostility to the war aims of the Union administration, combined usually with some degree of sympathy for the South—and as the party of "peace democrats" or "copperheads" (as they were derisively dubbed by their opponents) gradually consolidated in the country, the Quakers carefully pointed out the clear-cut distinction between their own stand and that of the political antiwar party. In a document drawn up in September 1863 (the year of the antidraft

---

[5] *Friends' Intelligencer,* XX, no. 30 (3 Oct. 1863), 474.
[6] Thomas E. Drake, "Thomas Garrett, Quaker Abolitionist," in *Friends in Wilmington, 1738-1938,* pp. 85, 86.

rioting in New York City) by their Meeting for Sufferings for trans-
mission to its counterpart in London, the Orthodox Yearly Meeting
of New York stated:

> Although our religious Society is known as the unfeigned advocate
> of peace, it is cause of embarrassment to us at this time, that un-
> scrupulous men, assuming the name of peace makers, are doing all
> they can to further the objects of those who seek to destroy our
> general Government, and to rivet the chains of slavery in this land.
> And while we find it our duty to refrain from all connection with
> war, both in spirit and in practice, we cannot do or say anything
> calculated, even remotely, to identify our members with these men.[7]

We shall find in the course of the story that the authorities in the
North, particularly Lincoln and some members of his administration
in Washington, showed on many occasions both consideration and a
large measure of understanding for the Quaker position on the war.
Wright has commented on the astonishing freedom in which Friends
were allowed to spread peace propaganda. Tracts expounding Quaker
pacifism were sometimes distributed even among the military. A
major-general, on being presented with one such document by an
Indiana Friend, is reported to have remarked: "That tract is true,
and the doctrine right, but we must wait to put it in practice, until
after the war closes."[8] We read again, to give a second illustration, of
the woman minister, Ann Branson (1808-1891), an Orthodox Friend
from Ohio, who felt a concern to visit two recruiting officers and
inform them of Friends' testimony against war and of the wrongness
of oppressing those whose consciences led them to refuse to bear arms.
Despite a recent law threatening imprisonment for any who tried to
discourage men from enlisting, she determined to regard "the law of
the Lord more than the law of man, and paramount to the laws of the
land." "I used great plainness of speech," she tells us, "in regard to
the inconsistency of war with the gospel dispensation." Nevertheless,
the officers listened courteously to what she had to say, and no bad
consequences resulted from her outspokenness.[9] A fairly widespread
recognition of the fact that Quaker opposition to war stemmed from
opposition to it as a method, rather than from any hidden sympathy
with the enemy, and that, therefore, it did not constitute a subversive
influence in the land, seems to have existed in the American community at that date.

[7] Quoted in E. N. Wright, *Conscientious Objectors in the Civil War*, p. 2.
[8] *Ibid.*, pp. 166, 167.
[9] Martha H. Bishop, "Ann Branson" in *Quaker Biographies*, 2nd ser., II, 84, 85.

The militant antimilitarist propaganda of Ann Branson was perhaps less usual than the quieter form of nonpolitical lobbying in favor of peace that is exemplified in the activities of Eliza P. Gurney (1800-1881), the American-born widow of the famous English evangelical Friend, Joseph John Gurney. In October 1862 Mrs. Gurney, accompanied by three other Quakers, felt called upon to make "a religious visit" to the President. Her message to Lincoln was one of peace. She told him of her own and the whole Society's sympathy for him in his responsible position, of her people's oneness with him in his aim to free the oppressed, and of their need to trust in God. Lincoln was deeply moved and wept; they all knelt in prayer together. She did not dwell particularly on the Quaker peace testimony, either during this interview or in the subsequent correspondence with Lincoln in which she engaged at the President's request, though this was obviously in the thoughts of both. On 4 September 1864 Lincoln wrote to her: "Your people, the Friends, have had and are having a great trial. On principle and faith opposed to both war and oppression, they can only practically oppose oppression by war. In this hard dilemma some have chosen one horn and some the other." He assured Mrs. Gurney that he would do all in his power, consistent with the law and the obligations of his office, to help any Quaker conscientious objectors in difficulties, whose cases became known to him.[10]

Ann Branson exhorting the recruiting officers and Eliza Gurney praying beside Lincoln were both seeking to give expression to the Quaker peace testimony, each in the manner which most suited their individual temperaments. Collectively Friends were active, too, in spreading the same message during the years of war. The various yearly meetings of the Orthodox and Hicksite branches, as well as the smaller Wilburite Conservative one, all contributed a steady flow of petitions, addresses, and memorials. These were usually drawn up for presentation to the state or federal legislatures; sometimes they were addressed to some other body or to the general public. Very often they were occasioned by one or another piece of draft legislation and had as their object to expound the reasons for Friends' refusal to comply. They appeared quite frequently as pamphlets or leaflets, and many of them were printed in a Quaker periodical—either the Orthodox *Friend*, the *Friends' Review* (belonging to the same branch but more evangelical in tone), or the Hicksite *Friends' Intelligencer*. The con-

---

[10] *Memoir and Correspondence of Eliza P. Gurney*, pp. 307-22. In her last letter to Lincoln written on 8 Sept. 1864, one that he is known to have valued highly, Mrs. Gurney, agreeing with the President that "Friends have been placed . . . in a peculiar and somewhat anomalous position," went on to give him a straightforward exposition of the grounds of Friends' objection to war.

tents of these documents followed traditional lines: innovation on such an issue was, indeed, alien to the thinking of most sections of the Society at that time, even if conservatism was not so deeply ingrained as among the German peace sects. Friends brought out their love of country and loyalty to its authorities, their recognition of the need for civil government, and their abhorrence of "the wicked rebellion"; they pointed out, too, that obedience must be limited by conscience and that Friends had shown by their former sufferings the sincerity of their devotion to pacifist views, which they believed were the only ones compatible with the message of the gospels. They often mentioned the peaceable nature of Quaker government in Pennsylvania as an indication of the practicability of their principles. And, finally, they frequently stressed the view that liberty of religious conscience, which was their constitutional right as American citizens, included the right to unconditional exemption from military service, that the government was not entitled to demand any alternative service or payment in exchange for the free exercise of conscience.[11]

The Quaker press also printed a large amount of material on the pacifist issue in the form of editorials and articles contributed by individual Friends. The discussion centered on the implications of Christianity in regard to war; the political and economic aspects of war were only occasionally touched on. The Philadelphia *Friend* devoted most space to the subject, but its style tended to be duller than the contributions of the other two Quaker papers.

The presentation of war news presented a special problem to Quaker editors. Some Friends considered that such news might have an inflammatory effect on those who read it. A typical illustration of this viewpoint is to be found in an epistle issued by the men's meeting of New York (Hicksite) Yearly Meeting: "Might not the inquiry be made of us individually," they ask, "whether the perusal of the war news of the day, unless guarded against, is not calculated to excite and foster those passions in our breasts, which are in direct opposition to the blessed precepts of our Saviour, as expressed in his most excellent Sermon on the Mount?"[12] And so we find some Friends in all branches

---

[11] A typical example of this kind of memorializing is to be found in the address of the Ohio (Wilburite) Y. M. sent to the governor of Ohio on 30 August 1862. "The Governor," it stated, "may rest assured that as a religious body we are loyal to the government and deeply regret the difficulty which has beset it. But acting on the ground of our religious principles we can neither engage in military service nor hire substitutes. Nevertheless it has always been the practice of the consistent members of our religious society, in cases where they cannot comply actively with the requisitions of the law, passively to submit to the penalty if not released therefrom." (Quoted in Charles P. Morlan, *A Brief History of Ohio Yearly Meeting of the Religious Society of Friends [Conservative]*, p. 82.)

[12] *Friend*, 22 June 1861.

of the Society uniting in their disapproval of either reading or print-
·ing news on the progress of the war. But there existed a second, and
less narrow, attitude which held it to be desirable for Friends to keep
informed on the momentous events of the day. They regarded it as an
advantage that this news should be presented "in the least objectionable manner" by journals which were edited in the spirit of Quaker
pacifism. "Many take no newspaper," it was reported, "being unwilling to admit within their family circle, the contaminating literature
they so frequently contain." For such Quakers, for instance, the "Summary of Events," which the *Friend* printed weekly (until pressure
from those who disapproved led the editor to suspend this item for a
time), was welcome. On the whole, the bulk of Friends, including the
editorial staffs of their papers, saw no inconsistency between an interest in the news of the day, even if this were mainly concerned with
battles, and a strict adherence to the peace testimony.[13]

Quaker papers were read by few outside the ranks of the Society,
while the statements on their peace witness, which we have seen them
issuing from time to time as the need arose, were *ad hoc* affairs not
intended as full-length expositions of their peace testimony. We have
seen that a not inconsiderable literature on peace had been produced
by Friends on both sides of the Atlantic, and some of these works
continued to be used effectively during the Civil War period. But
the war years were singularly lacking in any original contributions to
the pacifist debate. An example of the conservative, traditional nature
of Quaker peace propaganda is the continued use made of even such
a minor piece as Benjamin Bates's letter and memorial to the Virginia
legislature of 1810 (discussed earlier), which was not only given a
prominent place in several Quaker papers but was also presented by
Ohio (Orthodox) Yearly Meeting to their state legislature on the
occasion of its discussion of the exemption of conscientious objectors
to the wartime militia. That new literature on the peace testimony was
so meager can be explained in large part by the absorption of Friends
in the immediate exigencies of the war situation and, in particular, in
the defense of Quaker conscientious objectors.

The first summer of the war saw the composition of two small
pamphlets on war from the Quaker point of view. In September 1861
a Rhode Island Friend, John W. Foster, disappointed at the failure of
the New York *Tribune* to print a letter he had written defending
Christian nonresistance against attacks made on it in that paper, sat
down to compile a pamphlet, which he entitled *War and Christianity
Irreconcilable: An Address to Christians*. It was printed privately at

[13] *Ibid.*, 28 Dec. 1861. See also Wright, pp. 45, 46.

the author's expense. The work consists largely of extracts from other pacifist writers, including Dymond on war and a couple of pieces from local Providence nonresistants outside the Quaker fold, and contains little that need detain us here.

At about the same time, in Philadelphia, a young man by the name of Alfred H. Love (1830-1913), who was to make his mark on the postwar peace movement, had also taken up his pen to defend pacifism, this time against attack from a former nonresistant and onetime treasurer of the Pennsylvania Peace Society, a Baptist minister who had left the peace ranks on the outbreak of war to become a regimental chaplain. As mentioned in the full version of this book, Love, although not an actual member, was very close to the Society of Friends and had been reared in a Quaker home. He therefore felt keenly disappointed when this man, the Rev. William J. Mullen, had urged his fellow Christians to support the struggle as "a defensive war," "an honorable resistance in the cause of justice." It was the effect that Mullen's utterances would have among the little band of Philadelphia peace workers that chiefly prompted Love to compose his *Appeal in Vindication of Peace Principles*. Love did not attempt to prove that pacifism presented a practicable political alternative in the existing situation. He appealed instead to the central teaching of the Christian gospel and contrasted this with the essential nature of war, even for the best of causes. "Think of it," he went on, "each section appealing to the same Father for directly opposite ends! There is but one God, he is not a 'God of Battles.' He cannot answer both prayers—is it likely he will hear or answer either?" Christians must work quietly for peace between the two sides, acting in the faith that would move mountains and not being carried away by the folly of believing that one side was perfect and the other wholly evil. Slaveholders, though thoroughly misguided, were still people.[14] Love's pamphlet, it is true, went through two editions, yet the circulation was very small and this quiet voice of reason was barely audible above the battle.

In 1862 three further pamphlets on war of a general nature appeared from Quaker authors. Ezra Michener (1794-1887), self-educated scholar, scientist, and medical practitioner, and throughout his long life a keen pacifist, published under the imprint of the Book Association of Friends a 34-page piece entitled *A Brief Exposition of the Testimony to Peace, as exemplified by the Life and Precepts of Jesus Christ, and the Early Christians, and held by the Religious Society of*

---

[14] Love, *An Appeal in Vindication of Peace Principles*, pp. 2-6, 7, 9-11, 13, 14, 16, 17.

Friends. His object was to answer compendiously the questions being asked by many both within and outside the Society concerning Friends' peace testimony; he had found out himself, he tells us in the preface, how difficult it was to refer questioners to suitable literature, "which would afford them a ready answer, without cost, or laborious research." The treatment is rather disorderly, but the author covers the ground fairly adequately, ranging from the pacifism of the New Testament and the early church through a number of later Christian advocates of peace, including the Quakers and their Pennsylvania experiment (in which Michener was particularly interested). For further reading he recommended Barclay's *Apology,* Clarkson's *Portraiture of Quakerism,* Dymond's *Essays on Morality,* and Adin Ballou's works on Christian nonresistance.

In the same year that Michener produced his little book, two thin pamphlets were published by Friends in New York state, both named Cornell. W. T. Cornell's effort was entitled *On the Incompatibility of War with the Spirit of Christianity* and was aimed, in the words of the preface, to give "proof that should forever shame and put to silence the professor of Christianity who is an advocate of war." Follow Christ and do not look to the consequences was its simple message. John J. Cornell (1826-1909) was clerk of Genesee Yearly Meeting in upstate New York at the time war broke out. The *Address* on the peace testimony, which he published in 1862 with the approval of his fellow members, was meant primarily for internal consumption, to strengthen Friends in his yearly meeting in upholding the Society's opposition to all war by bringing them back to the sources of Quaker pacifism in the Sermon on the Mount and the other teachings of the gospels. He had been led to write it, he stated, by observing that

> There are some amongst us who, either from inattention to the unfoldings of Divine Light, or by intermingling with the strivings and contentions of political life, or from inexperience in the school of Christ, are yet either hesitating to carry out this noble testimony, or have suffered their feelings to become so enlisted in favor of what they deem to be the right in the present contest, that they have given their allegiance to the doctrine that a war conducted for self-defense, or to put down rebellion, is admissible and even right.[15]

After 1862, members of the Society of Friends published little or nothing new relating to the peace testimony for the rest of the war (apart from the official pronouncements of the various meetings and contributions to the Quaker periodicals). Yet the Society included in

---

[15] J. J. Cornell, *An Address,* pp. 1, 2.

its membership at least one concerned Friend with outstanding literary gifts, a figure of note in the world of letters who, moreover, felt a deep obligation to place his pen at the service of humanitarian causes. Was John Greenleaf Whittier, then, ardent abolitionist as he had shown himself in the prewar years and with his passionate temperament, one of those Quakers who had been carried away by their hatred of slavery to put their allegiance to the peace testimony into cold storage for the duration of the war? We find that his patriotic verse written in the early years of the conflict and published in book form under the title *In War Time and Other Poems* (Boston, 1863) did, indeed, act as a great boost to Northern morale. They gained the poet an invitation in 1864 to visit the Army of the Potomac and the eulogy there of a brigadier-general: "Your loyal verse has made us all your friends, lightening the wearisomeness of our march, brightening our lonely campfires, and cheering our hearts in battle."[16] Yet Whittier never relinquished his personal adherence to the peace testimony and rejected the appellation of war poet. "I have never written a poem in favor or in praise of war," he remarked many years later.[17] He always admitted to feeling profound sympathy with the better aspects of the Unionist cause and deep admiration for those who had selflessly given their service, and sometimes their lives, to the struggle. But, as he wrote to the Newburyport *Herald* at the beginning of the war when that paper published a report that he had contributed toward raising volunteers, "as a settled believer in the principles of the Society of Friends, I can do nothing at a time like this beyond mitigating, to the extent of my power, the calamities and suffering attendant upon war, and accepting cheerfully my allotted share of the privation and trials growing out of it."[18] And, after he had watched the youthful Colonel Shaw marching off at the head of his Negro regiment, the 55th, to the battlefront from which he was not to return, Whittier, deeply moved, wrote to Mrs. Lydia Maria Child, an old friend who shared his brand of nonresistant abolitionism: "I have longed to speak the emotions of that hour, but I dared not, lest I should indirectly give a new impulse to war."[19] With the two impulses

---

[16] Samuel T. Pickard, *Life and Letters of John Greenleaf Whittier*, II, 476.

[17] Letter to John J. Pratt, 7 Dec. 1878, quoted in *Bulletin of Friends' Historical Society of Philadelphia*, vol. 9, no. 1 (1919), p. 43.

[18] Letter dated 15 May 1861, quoted in *Friends' Review*, 1 June 1861. A month later, on 18 June, Whittier addressed an open letter to members of the Society of Friends, urging them to give their utmost to relieving the suffering of war, whether on the battle front or back at home, as an essential part of their peace testimony. "Let the Quaker bonnet," he wrote, "be seen by the side of the black hood of the Catholic Sisters of Charity in the hospital ward." See Pickard, *Whittier*, II, 441.

[19] Quoted in A. T. Murray, "Whittier's Attitude toward War," *Present Day Papers*, II, no. 7 (July 1915), 216.

of peace and antislavery warring in his heart, it is not surprising, therefore, that we do not find Whittier an active protagonist of the Quaker peace testimony. He felt it his task rather to urge his fellow Quakers to acts of mercy for suffering humanity than to expound nonresistance to a people fighting oppression.[20]

The same deep commitment to the purposes of the war (or what were thought ought to be its purposes), combined with a purely personal pacifism, is to be found in a small group of intellectuals and radicals on the fringe of the Quaker world. The Progressive or Congregational Friends of Pennsylvania, because of the high moral and intellectual caliber of many of the members and the fact that both leadership and rank and file were leavened with a goodly number of militant nonresistants, might perhaps have been expected (at least by one not acquainted with the wartime attitudes of other survivors of the nonresistant movement of previous decades) to make some contribution to the ideology of Quaker pacifism. The reverse rather was the case.

The group, which dated from 1853, belonged to an offshoot of the Hicksite branch of the Society, which had arisen in the late forties and early fifties. Its activities were centered in the Philadelphia area, with smaller groups in New York state and in the Midwest. The movement represented a protest against Quaker sectarianism and theological intolerance, as well as against the predominance of conservative authority in the Society in general. Its main interest lay in the promotion of humanitarian reforms, and in antislavery work in particular. There was no formal membership and no set discipline—and, therefore, no disownments. Its theology was liberal: all were welcome who believed in God and in the brotherhood of man. There was, indeed,

[20] Merle E. Curti ("Poets of Peace and the Civil War," *World Unity*, X, no. 3 [June 1932], 151) has suggested that, if Whittier had not felt bound by his loyalty to his Society's peace testimony, he would probably have given unqualified support to the war. As it is, "one looks in vain in Whittier's war poetry for anything like a condemnation of the War; he does not see fit to observe that even so holy a cause as freedom might be ill-served by bloodshed." (It may be noted, too, that the militant revolutionary nationalist, Garibaldi, had always been one of the poet's heroes.) A certain ambiguity remained in Whittier's attitude toward peace in the postwar years. Witness his admiration and praise for what he considered the heroic Christian spirit of General Gordon ("a providential man") at the time of his death in the Sudan in 1885, an attitude which brought down on him the censure of John Bright. (See Murray, *Present Day Papers*, II, no. 7, 217, 218.) As an old man he reaffirmed his basic agreement with the peace testimony of the Society to which he belonged in a letter to Hannah J. Bailey on 1 January 1890. "The cause of Peace," he wrote there, "lies very near to my heart. War seems to me now to be the great evil to be abolished. While it exists there are no *Christian* nations. I am glad to see thee so earnestly devoted to the cause of Peace. It is the great mission of our Society." From MS letter in the Whittier Collection, F.H.L.S.C.

within this framework a wide diversity of opinion. It included within its ranks those who retained membership in the old established Hicksite meetings, like Lucretia Mott and her husband or Thomas Garrett, former members of the Society who had been drummed out of one or another of its branches for transgressing the discipline, and also a number of sympathizers from other churches or of no defined religious affiliation, ranging from the near-Quaker Alfred H. Love to religious liberals like Samuel J. May, William Lloyd Garrison, Cyrus M. Burleigh, and a number of others.

Although nonpacifist associates participated in its activities, its prewar stand had been strongly pacifist, and the influence of radical nonresistance of the Garrisonian variety on its pronouncements on war was marked. However, after war had broken out, enthusiasm for overthrowing slavery led the Progressive Friends into denunciations of the opposite side that were rarely outdone in the most warlike sections of the popular press. Take, for instance, this extract, dealing with the Confederate authorities, from the published proceedings of their yearly meeting held at Longwood (Pa.) in June 1862:

> Of the crimes and barbarities these conspirators have committed since they madly commenced the war—outraging all the claims of humanity and civilization—it is needless to speak at length. They will make such a volume of horrors as can scarcely be paralleled by the most savage warfare in the darkest ages of the world. Scalping, poisoning, and assassinating the living—mangling the bodies of the dead—making the skulls of Northern soldiers into drinking cups, and their bones into ornaments for barbarous display—repeatedly and persistently hoisting the white flag of truce, only to betray and slaughter those to whom they thus professed to surrender—carrying desolation and war everywhere in their train—these are but specimens of the almost numberless deeds of treachery and ferocity that have marked their bloody career.

Curiously enough, the passage is taken from the meeting's "testimony" for peace! In the same document the government is denounced—for not carrying on the war with enough vigor and for "dealing with the rebels as misguided brethren rather than as enemies of mankind." Yet the "testimony" also goes on to state its opinion that "in thus expressing our [general] sympathy with the government, we do not conceive that we repudiate or invalidate even the most radical peace principles that may be cherished by any of our Society."[21]

[21] *Proceedings of the Pennsylvania Yearly Meeting of Progressive Friends . . . 1862*, pp. 11, 12. This "testimony" and several other documents issued by the

In 1864 its yearly meeting proceedings contain alongside a "testimony" on "the evils of war," which "was adopted without discussion," exhortations to the administration not to weaken its efforts to crush the "slave oligarchy" completely. They saw no reason why "scrupulous non-resistants" should hesitate in collaborating (so far as conscience permitted) in their government's efforts "in suppressing the rebellion." Although it should respect the scruples of religious objectors, the administration had both "the right and the duty" to impose federal conscription on the country.[22]

If avowed nonresistants of long standing felt this way, what wonder that many young men who had been reared in Quaker homes and in the teachings of the peace testimony, ignoring the subtle distinction between conscious support of the war and a purely personal pacifism such as Garrison and the Progressive Friends nursed throughout the war years, decided—some only after long hesitation—to go against the discipline and traditional behavior of their church and participate actively in the struggle. Comments from both the major branches of the Society[23] indicate that many young Friends had been insufficiently grounded in the meaning of the peace testimony by the education they received at home and in school and that they were easily swept off their feet by patriotic fervor and enthusiasm for the cause of the oppressed slave—Friends' other great testimony which seemed to conflict in the moment of crisis with their pacifism.

A few days after the shelling of Fort Sumter, the poet, Bayard Taylor, himself of Quaker stock, wrote of his home town of Kennett Place (Pa.): "All the young Quakers have enlisted. The excitement and anxiety is really terrible. We are so near the frontier." Two days later he reported in another letter: "The women are heroes. Old Quaker women see their sons go, without a tear."[24] Early the following month we find Sarah M. Palmer, daughter of the Quaker abolitionist, Isaac

---

assembly were drawn up by Garrison, who was present at its sessions. See Garrisons, W.L.G., IV, 52. In his *Liberator*, Garrison retailed equally gruesome and gory stories of Southern barbarities in battle. (See John L. Thomas, *The Liberator*, p. 413.) Garrison's associate, Oliver Johnson, was clerk of their yearly meeting for many years. The yearly meeting for 1861, scheduled for June, had not in fact been called, ostensibly on account of the tense war situation but perhaps principally because of the inflamed feelings of many associates of the group, and not only the nonpacifist minority. The movement declined after the war and eventually disappeared altogether.

[22] *Proceedings . . . 1864*, pp. 11, 14-16.
[23] See, e.g., *Friends' Review*, 11 May 1861; *Friends' Intelligencer*, 30 Nov. 1861, 20 Dec. 1862.
[24] *Life and Letters of Bayard Taylor* (5th edn.), I, 375-77: letters of 21 and 23 April 1861.

T. Hopper, whose antislavery activities had eventually earned him disownment from the Society, describing the situation in Philadelphia in the following words: "Quakers are drilling, contrary to all the peace principles of the sect; indeed from all appearances we may suppose their hopes are based on war. I'm opposed to war—to cutting down men like grass—but if ever war was holy, this one, in favor of the most oppressed, most forbearing, most afflicted, downtrodden, insulted part of humanity, is a holy war."[25] In July 1862 the English-born Friend, Mrs. Elizabeth L. Comstock (1815-1891), who was active in the ministry and in various Quaker philanthropies, wrote to a friend: "We hear of many young Friends taking up arms for the North." She went on to relate the story of three young Union soldiers previously unacquainted with each other who fell into a casual conversation. Soon it transpired that all three were birthright Quakers: one the son of Dr. Samuel Boyd Tobey, clerk of New England Yearly Meeting, another the son of Sybil and Eli Jones, well known as Quaker ministers in Maine, and the third the son of a leading Friend, William Henry Chase.[26] On the whole, however, the rural meetings contributed "very few volunteers"; more came from Quaker communities in urban areas.[27]

Garrison's words, spoken to his Quaker friends to comfort them in their distress at seeing so many of their young men abandon the traditional position on war, probably to a large extent coincided with the feelings of Friends themselves at this time:

> I told them [he wrote in the autumn of 1861] that however much they might regret that their sons could not meet the test when it was applied they should at least rejoice that the boys were true to their real convictions when the shot at Sumter revealed to them that they were simply birthright Quakers, and had not fully comprehended and absorbed the principles of their fathers. They had imagined they were on the plane of the Sermon on the Mount, and they found they were only up to the level of Lexington and Bunker Hill; but they should be honored none the less for their loyalty to truth and freedom.[28]

Owing to the regular record keeping of the Society of Friends and the preservation in good condition of almost all of the materials dat-

---

[25] *Life of Abby Hopper Gibbons told chiefly through her Correspondence,* I, 292: letter from Sarah H. Palmer, dated 5 May 1861.

[26] *Life and Letters of Elizabeth L. Comstock,* p. 109.

[27] Rufus M. Jones, *The Later Periods of Quakerism,* II, 729. Jones reached this conclusion after examining a number of monthly meeting records.

[28] Garrisons, *W.L.G.,* IV, 37.

ing from the Civil War at least, a systematic examination of these records would probably yield a reasonably accurate figure of the number of Friends who entered the Union army and the proportion this figure bears to the total number of Friends drafted. But in the absence of a study of this nature generalizations have to be based to some extent on probabilities and surmise rather than on statistical fact. Assertions have been made that the number of Friends serving with the forces was higher in proportion to total numbers than was the case with any other religious group.[29] But, as Rufus Jones correctly remarks, there appears to be "no historical evidence whatever to justify such a statement." The "deviations" from pacifism, he goes on, "were more numerous than one would have expected in a conservative body which made the testimony an absolutely essential feature of its faith." However, in view of the strong pressures exerted on the young in the direction of active participation in the war, "the total number appears small."[30]

According to the minutes of the Meeting for Sufferings of Philadelphia (Orthodox) Yearly Meeting, to take one example, 150 men were drafted. Although some were rejected on grounds of health or for some other disability, only 4 actually accepted military service.[31] On the other hand, if we take a small Orthodox preparative meeting, that of Jericho (Randolph County, Ind.), out in the Midwest near the frontier where the weight of traditional authority would have been less than in metropolitan Philadelphia and its environs, we find a rather different pattern. There 16 young men connected with the meeting served in the Northern army, and only 9 appear to have become conscientious objectors.[32] And on another frontier, the borderland area between North and South, it is possible that in the Baltimore (Hicksite) Yearly Meeting fewer men of military age abided by the traditional peace testimony than were drawn by loyalty to the union and devotion to the antislavery cause to join the ranks of the army. In September 1861 the address issued by the yearly meeting lamented concerning members' attitude toward war: "There are few among us who have fully realized the evils connected with this anti-christian practice."[33] Two years later one of its monthly meetings had this to say on the way its members were upholding the peace testimony:

[29] This was stated, for instance, in regard to the Hicksite branch by Albert G. Thatcher, "The Quakers' Attitude to War," *Advocate of Peace*, LXXIX, no. 8 (Aug. 1917), 238.

[30] Jones, *The Later Periods of Quakerism*, II, 736-40. See also Wright, pp. 184-86, 188, 189.

[31] Wright, p. 183.   [32] *Jericho Friends' Meeting and Its Community*, pp. 53, 54.

[33] *Friends' Intelligencer*, 19 Oct. 1861.

Our testimony against a hireling ministry, oaths, clandestine trade, prize goods, and lotteries appears to have been generally maintained, but we have mournfully to acknowledge a wide departure on the part of most of our members from our Christian testimony against war. Many of our young men have taken up arms, and are actively engaged in the unhappy contest now desolating the country. Whilst many also of more mature years and even among the elder class have openly advocated war, and countenanced, encouraged and assisted those performing military [service]; nevertheless we believe there remains a remnant who are concerned for the preservation of our members and humbly desire to adhere faithfully to this ancient testimony against war.[34]

This situation, where only "a remnant" of the meeting continued to uphold Quaker pacifism, was surely exceptional if we consider the Society in the Northern states as a whole. But it is true that the considerable number of deviations from the peace testimony, especially among the younger members, indicated that in large sections of the Society this part of Quaker belief lacked the vitality and living reality it had possessed at times in the past among American and British Friends.

What happened to those Friends who contravened the Society's discipline and took up arms? How did meetings react to what in a few cases amounted to almost a mass desertion of Quaker pacifism and in almost every instance presented a problem for the Society? Again, no overall statistical data have been collected, and we are dependent here, too, on only partial evidence.

The act of becoming a soldier constituted an infringement of the Quaker discipline similar to marrying outside the Society, taking an oath,[35] or committing some offense against the Society's moral code. Disownment was the usual penalty for such infringement, unless due contrition was expressed.

Sometimes, disownment may have been carried out while the war was still in progress and the delinquent members on active service. We read of this happening soon after Gettysburg, for instance, to several young Quakers belonging to an Ohio country meeting, who had taken part in the battle. One of them was Benjamin Butterworth, (1837-1898), later to become a prominent figure in the Republican

[34] Report of an unnamed monthly meeting, dated 15 Aug. 1863, from Thomas Jenkins Papers, F.H.L.S.C.

[35] Curiously enough, Friends who had contravened their Society's testimony against war by entering the army were usually reluctant to break a minor commandment by taking the oath of allegiance and, in most cases, were permitted on request to substitute an affirmation. See the article by Thaddeus S. Kinderdine in the *Friends' Intelligencer*, LXVII, no. 25 (24 June 1911), 395.

Party in Ohio, whose own father on this occasion was responsible for proposing that proceedings should be commenced against the young men. "His father had not heard from him since the great battle and did not then know whether he was asking for the disownment of a dead son, or a live soldier."[36] But such almost Roman severity was rare. In most cases where a Friend had joined up, final action was postponed until the conclusion of hostilities.[37] Generally, postponement of a decision stemmed from a desire not to deal too harshly with their young people, who had been carried away by the enthusiasm of the hour to uphold, by un-Quakerly methods it was true, a cause with which most Friends sympathized. A minute of Genesee (Hicksite) Yearly Meeting passed at the end of the war summed up feelings that were widespread throughout the Society when it expressed the hope concerning "delinquent" members that

> . . . now, as the conflict has ceased, and as they return to their peaceful homes, they may become so convinced of the superiority of the principle of love to that of force, and that it is better to suffer wrong for a season than to do wrong, that they may so live in the future as not only to give satisfaction to their friends, and thus be continued in the bosom of Society, but by being convinced by experience . . . of this divine principle become its devoted advocates.

The returning soldiers were to be dealt with in a spirit of "sympathy and affectionate solicitude" (to use the words of Philadelphia [Hicksite] Yearly Meeting), brought to a renewed trust in the principles which underlie the Quaker peace testimony, and then received back lovingly into the religious community of their friends.[38]

There were some, of course, whose wartime experiences caused them to drift away from Quakerism altogether; some among these, even before the war, may have been only nominally attached to the faith of their ancestors. Others, although unwilling to break their association with the religion in which they had been reared, were yet not ready to condemn their conduct in taking up arms. "Those friends who entered the military forces and later justified their actions on patriotic or other grounds," as Wright says, "were generally 'disowned'

<hr/>

[36] H. E. Smith, *The Quakers, Their Migration to the Upper Ohio, Their Customs and Discipline*, p. 53. Yet Butterworth was listed later as a member of the Society, a fact which seems to cast some doubt on the accuracy of Smith's account.

[37] Wright is mistaken in asserting (p. 153) that General Henry W. Halleck retained membership in the Society throughout the war. In fact, General Halleck was never associated with Friends, and hence there could be no question of disciplinary action by the Quakers against him.

[38] *Friends' Intelligencer*, 8 July 1865. For a similar attitude on the part of Philadelphia (Hicksite) Y. M., see *ibid.*, 10 June 1865.

by their local Meeting."[39] Proceedings were not taken, however, or were stopped if already begun, when the returned soldier presented "an acknowledgment of error." Many examples of these acknowledgments have been preserved in the records of monthly meetings. They differ considerably in their exact wording, but their purport and content are remarkably similar. Here is one, a collective acknowledgment taken from the records of Westbury Monthly Meeting, a country meeting in New Jersey:

> Dear Friends, Having so far departed from the discipline and testimonies of Society, as, under an impression of duty, in view of the peculiar circumstances by which we were surrounded, to take up arms in defence of the government, sensible of our deviation from the principles of our education, yet desirous of retaining our rights in membership we hope that this with our future conduct may reconcile us to our Friends again.[40]

How genuine such repentances actually were it is difficult to say. Many who joined up continued to regard the peace testimony as a lofty ideal. Although they themselves had felt unable to live up to it in the existing circumstances, they were glad that the Society still remained loyal to its principles. Others, while finding it hard to comprehend how they could have acted otherwise than they did when their country seemed in danger and while continuing to hold inner reservations on the subject of Quaker pacifism, were yet willing to make concessions to the weight of opinion within the religious Society to which they were attached by so many bonds of affection.

We find, on the one hand, a young Quaker like Cyrus W. Harvey (1843-1916), who later became a weighty Friend out in Kansas and a keen pacifist, not being satisfied with the formal acknowledgment of error that he had presented to his home meeting in Indiana, along with several other boys who had served like him with the Union forces. Therefore, several months later, in fear "that he had not done his full duty in the matter," he stood up in meeting to make "a clear confession of his wrong-doing, and of his sorrow on account of it, condemning all carnal warfare as being un-Christian."[41] The sensitive conscience of the veteran, now turned pacifist, is matched on the other side by those who, anxious to return as soon as possible to full communion with their fellow members and prepared to recognize the Society's pacifist position as a whole, still did not feel it in their

[39] Wright, pp. 209, 210, where several examples of testimonies of disownment in such cases are given in full.

[40] MS in F.H.L.S.C.   [41] *Memorial of Cyrus W. Harvey*, pp. 8, 9.

hearts to condemn their wartime conduct. An example of this attitude is to be found in the dignified statement presented by Wilmer Atkinson (1840-1920), who later founded the *Farm Journal*, and a number of other young men and accepted by Horsham Monthly Meeting (Hicksite). They wrote:

> We, the undersigned members of Horsham Monthly Meeting, having been engaged in the service of our country in her peril and need . . . individually acknowledge we have departed from the injunctions of the discipline of the Society of Friends. In extenuation of this deviation we plead the regard and love of our common country, her laws and civil institutions, endangered . . . by a wicked and causeless rebellion involving us all in one common desire to maintain and perpetuate them. Feeling desirous that the testimonies of our Society may be maintained as founded in truth we present this declaration as an acknowledgement which we request to be placed on the minutes of the Monthly Meeting with our names appended and renew our desires of continued membership and ask that any proceedings had on account of our deviation may from henceforth cease.[42]

Most meetings, in fact, took great pains in trying to reclaim the strayed member. We can see the extent of such efforts in an example taken from the records of Kansas Friends. One of their members, Samuel Worthington, enlisted early in 1863, and his preparative meeting appointed a committee to speak with him. It was reported that "he manifests love for Society, but is not yet willing to acknowledge his deviation, whereupon after full consideration, the meeting comes to the judgment to continue the case." The matter dragged on for nearly three years; only at the end of 1865, when, perhaps, Worthington's term of service was finished, did he express the necessary sorrow for his "error."[43]

The general feeling in the Society at that time seems to have been in favor of enforcing the discipline at least against those who had participated in warmaking so far as to bear arms. Opinion, however, was by no means unanimous, especially among Eastern meetings of the Hicksite branch and also in some communities of Orthodox Friends in the Midwest.[44] As might be expected, such reservations were strong-

[42] Dated 28 Dec. 1866, in Thomas Jenkins Papers, F.H.L.S.C., cf. Wright, pp. 212, 213.
[43] Cecil B. Currey, "Quaker Pacifism in Kansas, 1833-1945," M.Sc. thesis, Fort Hays Kansas State College, pp. 32, 33.
[44] Thaddeus S. Kinderdine, *op. cit.*; Jones, *The Later Periods of Quakerism*, II, 738.

est among those rebel spirits, many of whom, like Lucretia Mott, were associated with the Progressive Friends. The New York *Friend*, which was connected with this group of religious liberals, commenting in June 1866 on the disownment by the Hicksite monthly meeting in New York City of a young Quaker soldier who maintained the rightness of his action in enlisting, wrote: "We have serious objection to any clause of discipline which requires a Friend to be disowned for acting up to his highest conviction of duty. Warfare is horrible in the flesh—but it is heaven-born innocence by the side of a war upon conscience."[45]

In some meetings, however, it does not seem to have been primarily a theoretical stand in favor of liberty of religious conscience so much as a very deep-seated division of opinion among even weighty Friends in the meeting as to the validity of the peace testimony, at least in relation to the circumstances of the recent war, that led to opposition to the disownment of the unrepentant Quaker fighters. In the Hicksite Yearly Meeting in Indiana, feelings were so divided that in the autumn of 1867 the yearly meeting appointed a committee of twenty to investigate the question. In its report the committee recommended that, since those who had deviated from the peace testimony had done so "from motives of conceived duty and patriotism" and, therefore, were "unable truthfully to say they are convinced of the error of their course," "the spirit of our discipline" and "the best welfare of our Society" did not require the disownment of those former soldiers who wished to continue in membership, were in unity with Friends' other testimonies, and yet felt that they could not in good conscience denounce their military activities.[46]

It was the Baltimore (Hicksite) Yearly Meeting that included some of the most deeply divided Quaker communities. At its yearly meeting in 1865, "the Committee appointed to consider the question" of deviations from the peace testimony recommended that "a lenient course should be pursued." Where possible, "voluntary acknowledgements" of error should be obtained verbally; when such endeavors proved ineffectual, "the names of the delinquents shall be reported to the Monthly Meeting."[47] What further action, if any, should be taken

---

[45] *Friend* (N.Y.), I, no. 6 (June 1866), 85. See pp. 87, 99, 119, 147 of the same volume for letters from readers pro and con allowing freedom in the matter to the individual conscience.

[46] From Thomas Jenkins Papers, F.H.L.S.C. The author of a recent study of one of the meetings in Indiana, which produced a goodly number of Quaker soldiers, comments: "On the whole, however, the minutes of the White River Monthly Meeting are singularly free from condemnation of the boys who had borne arms" (*Jericho Friends' Meeting*, p. 54).

[47] Quoted in Wright, p. 211.

was not specified: this, presumably, was the individual responsibility of each monthly meeting. In country meetings, always strongholds of Quaker traditionalism, disownment seems to have followed fairly regularly on the failure of a returned soldier to express contrition. But among urban Friends within this yearly meeting, and especially in the case of Baltimore Monthly Meeting, no action seems to have been taken against deviants from the peace testimony. The minutes of the latter meeting record for 8 March 1866: "There has been a general deviation on the part of our membership." A half century later Joseph J. Janney, a highly respected member of the meeting in Baltimore (he had himself volunteered for the Union army but was never called to account for his conduct), wrote: "There were not enough members who were entirely innocent to pronounce judgment on the alleged violators." He relates how, when the question of taking disciplinary action against the returned veterans came up, an aged Friend, "a much beloved minister . . . who sat at the head of the Meeting," arose and said: "If the discipline is to be applied in these cases commence with me. Although I did not enlist in the army I am not innocent, in some ways I am as guilty as those who did."[48] In this meeting, at any rate, no attempt was made to exclude the delinquent members.

An interesting case where an unrepentant veteran was permitted to retain membership is that of William J. Palmer (1836-1909) of Race Street (Hicksite) Monthly Meeting in Philadelphia. After volunteering at the outset of the war, Palmer achieved the rank of brigadier-general before he was finally demobilized in 1867. The young man viewed his wartime service quite unapologetically. He wrote to another young Friend on 19 April 1867 after being approached by a committee of his home meeting:

I have every desire to retain my connection, and hope they will look upon my case with that liberal and charitable spirit which I think distinguishes them from most other sects and which is one of the strongest incentives in my mind towards remaining a member of the Society. I think my views on the subject of Peace can hardly differ in essential points, from those of our Meeting, or at least of a majority of the members as I have incidentally learned them through their conversation and actions during and since the war. Of course under the same circumstances as existed in the summer of '61 I would act precisely as I did then and I do not understand that Friends desire me to think or say otherwise—as they would be the last to believe that principle should be compromised for the sake

48 From Thomas Jenkins Papers, F.H.L.S.C.

of avoiding troubles ... one of the most essential principles of Friends is obedience to conscience—much more essential than a belief in non-resistance. I do not ask more than that my case should be treated in that light. I think that Peace is holy and should be encouraged constantly—and that an unjust war is only legalized murder. But the inner light made it very plain to me in the summer of '61 that I should enter the army.[49]

Palmer was correct in his assumption that his meeting would accept his statement without requiring any expression of regret for his past actions.[50] A pacifist church (as the Society of Friends might still be considered at that date) may be congratulated for its liberalism in retaining a brigadier-general on its roll of members, but it is clear that the war had wrought a profound change in the position the traditional peace testimony held within the framework of the Quaker ethos.

II

The fighting Quaker, a seeming contradiction in terms, might catch the public eye by the very incongruity of his action. The Quaker who, though of military age, remained in one way or another a noncombatant was a less unfamiliar figure. He was following the traditional pattern of the Society and, although a nonconformist in relation to the general behavior of a community at war, was, as we have seen, a conservative in relation to his own background and home environment. Nevertheless, the pattern of behavior of the Quaker pacifist in wartime was a complex one, whether it was a case of a young man facing the challenge of conscription or of an older Friend who had to decide how he would meet the various demands of the authorities connected with the prosecution of the war. We must now turn, therefore, to consider how this group, which undoubtedly constituted the majority of Friends taken as a whole, and especially those of more mature years, fared under wartime conditions.

In the early months of the war Friends, along with the other peace sects, had hoped that enough recruits would be raised for the armies of the North by the voluntary method. But this optimism slowly faded

[49] *Letters 1853-1868: Gen'l. Wm. J. Palmer*, pp. 87, 88. It appears that the Philadelphia Y. M. of the Hicksite branch was laxer than most other sections of the Society is disowning its ex-soldiers who failed to make acknowledgment of error. See T. S. Kinderdine in *Friends' Intelligencer*, LXX, no. 27 (5 July 1913), 420-22.

[50] See his obituary in *Friends' Intelligencer*, vol. LXVI, no. 5 (10 April 1909). General Palmer remained a Friend until his death.

during the first half of 1862. On 17 July of that year Congress passed the Federal Militia Act, which, although it left enrollment of men between the ages of 18 and 45 in the hands of the state authorities, provided for the intervention of the President in case the latter were unable to execute the law properly. And, in fact, in the following month, by his General Order of 9 August, the President summoned 300,000 men to the colors for a period of nine months. Since the position of those who had religious scruples against bearing arms was far from clear under the new legislation, Friends busied themselves with trying to obtain satisfactory assurances from the state authorities that such scruples would actually be respected. To some extent, as shown in the full version of this book, conscientious objection had been recognized in the prewar militia legislation of many of the states at least, and this fact was frequently alluded to in the discussions over wartime conscription which now ensued. "Before the end of the year 1862 Friends and other noncombatants realized the seriousness of the military situation, and braced themselves for the struggle ahead." It became obvious that the Act of the previous July was proving inadequate for providing the men necessary to carry on the struggle and that the introduction of full federal conscription was not far away. Friends, therefore, now turned their attention to the Federal administration, and a series of memorials setting out the Quaker position on war and asking for adequate provision to be made in forthcoming legislation for the rights of conscience were presented to President and Congress by a number of yearly meetings. The final draft of the Conscription Act as it passed Congress on 3 March 1863 proved extremely unsatisfactory to all sections of the Society of Friends. Those drafted and unwilling to serve were permitted to furnish a substitute to take their place in the ranks, or, if they preferred, they might pay the sum of $300 in commutation money to procure such a substitute. No mention was made of conscientious objection.

E. N. Wright comments as follows on the reaction of Friends to the contents of the Act:

> The provision for the payment of commutation money in lieu of personal service was satisfactory to many noncombatants, but not to those who were most conscientious in their attitude toward military requirements. Quakers, especially, rightly surmised that the commutation money would be used for the purchase of substitutes and that payment of the fee was therefore a direct aid to the military authorities and virtually an equivalent to personal service . . . throughout 1863 and the years which followed, the attitude of the

Society of Friends as a whole remained consistently opposed to the payment of commutation money or the procuration of substitutes.[51]

Yet, as Wright goes on to point out, although the official attitude of the various yearly meetings remained set—at least at first—against any compromise on this issue, considerable variations in opinion and practice existed among individual Friends.

Throughout the war Quaker meetings attempted to provide counsel and care for those younger members who faced the ordeal of the draft. There was at times something a little condescending, a certain patriarchal note, in the way advice was dispensed. We find the *Friend*, for instance, early in the war, while summoning older Friends to show "patience and forbearance" in guiding the Society's sometimes faltering, bewildered, and brash young people of draft age, making it plain that, in return, the latter should properly "appreciate the privilege of being under the care and partaking of the sympathy and Christian regard of those of riper experience, more mature judgment, and greater stability in the Truth than themselves."[52] Those young folk whose youthful exuberance had led them to deviate from the sober behavior that was thought to befit a Friend, either by abandoning the plain attire or by attending dances or participating in one or another of the world's amusements, were sternly rebuked in another issue of the same paper. "In the present trials consequent on drafting for the army," it was pointed out with obvious satisfaction, "many of our gay young members have found how much harder it has been for them to appear before the commissioners to claim exemption on the ground of conscientious scruples, than it would have been had their conduct, conversation and clothing, all borne witness for them that they were bearing the cross of Christ."[53]

But if on occasion there was a note of priggishness in the manner in which Friends expressed their sympathy for the young people on whose inexperienced shoulders rested the main burden of upholding the Society's testimony against war, the records do show a widespread and genuine concern at this time of crisis to help "our precious young Friends," who were struggling to reach a decision on the conscription issue, and to strengthen those of them whom conscientious conviction brought into conflict with the authorities. Many meetings at various levels appointed special committees entrusted with the task of overseeing their conscientious objectors, and from time to time these committees issued reports of their activities. They show older Friends not

[51] Wright, pp. 39, 40, 49-65.
[52] *Friend*, 23 Aug. 1862.
[53] *Ibid.*, 8 Nov. 1862.

only in the role of advisers but active in accompanying Quaker conscripts to the boards of enrollment and helping them state their case to the authorities, in keeping in regular contact with those who had been arrested for noncompliance and placed in military camps, and in negotiating on their behalf with, and lobbying, the whole gamut of civilian and military authorities concerned, from the lowest rung right up to the President in Washington.[54] Some of the more fiery spirits in the Society occasionally complained of the timidity of elders and of their lack of sympathy for those drafted Friends who refused all compromise with the making of war.[55] But on the whole, and despite considerable difference of opinion among Friends who upheld the peace testimony on a number of points of behavior in connection with the war, the Quaker conscientious objector was well supported by his Society.

We spoke a little earlier about the complexity of the pattern of behavior among Quaker pacifists during the Civil War. Let us take first the question of hiring substitutes. Opinion was fairly unanimous here that a Quaker who paid another man to fight in his place was offending against the spirit of the peace testimony as much as, perhaps even more than, if he had taken up arms himself. The editor of the Orthodox *Friend* of Philadelphia was speaking for all branches of the Society when he wrote: "If it is wrong for me to fight and kill my fellow-creatures, it must be wrong to pay my money to hire another to do it; just as it would be to pay my money to hire a man to steal or murder." How do we know, he added, that the substitute may not be a brutal fellow who will commit various atrocities, when given the occasion, in addition to the routine killing of a soldier's career.[56] In the past, as shown earlier in this history, the penalty of disownment was regularly meted out to Friends who resorted to this practice when called upon for military service. Yet in the Civil War some Friends when drafted did undoubtedly furnish substitutes, and their meetings in many instances failed to take action against them. The Thomas Jenkins Papers (F.H.L.S.C.) contain several examples of such cases. Henry Dillingham of Granville Monthly Meeting (N.Y.) was drafted for service "but found a man who was going any way, and so he paid him the amount required to buy a substitute. As he was a poor man he was glad to get the money." Another Dillingham, Reuben by name, escaped the draft because his aunt hired a substitute for him. The fact that in this meeting members who had volunteered for the army were

[54] Wright, pp. 70, 190-98.
[55] For an example of such criticism, see the letter from Gideon Frost in the *Friend*, 22 Oct. 1864.
[56] *Friend*, 1 Aug. 1863.

not dealt with perhaps explains why no action was taken, either, against the two Dillinghams. In Brooklyn Monthly Meeting, too, some members paid for substitutes when drafted. These examples are all drawn from Eastern Hicksite meetings where, as we have seen earlier in this chapter, enforcement of the discipline for infringements of the peace testimony was laxer than in other parts of the Society. Disownment for hiring substitutes was certainly practised during the war.

When we come to the question of paying commutation money, the right course to follow was not quite so clear even to concerned Friends. Under the act of March 1863 the problem was in a way simplified by the probability that the money paid in this manner would be used for the purchase of recruits and was thus very little, if at all, distinguishable from straight hiring of a substitute. This objection, however, was removed by the clause in the subsequent act of 24 February 1864 (see below), whereby religious objectors would pay their commutation fine into a fund for the benefit of sick and wounded soldiers (a provision, however, that still might not be acceptable in itself to strict pacifists). It still left unchanged, of course, the major reason why Friends as a body now, as before the war, considered it wrong to pay commutation money: that no government was entitled to exact any penalty, or demand any service, in exchange for permission to follow the dictates of conscience. This absolutist point of view, the claim that it implied for unconditional exemption from military service, was well summed up in a minute, dated 13 April 1865, of the Meeting for Sufferings of Philadelphia (Orthodox) Yearly Meeting. "Believing," it stated, "that liberty of conscience is the gift of the Creator to man, Friends have ever refused to purchase the free exercise of it, by the payment of any pecuniary or other commutation, to any human authority."[57] That the state's demand was for something otherwise quite innocuous, perhaps highly commendable, could make no difference to the principle involved, which was one that, in fact, concerned not so much pacifism as the inborn rights of man.

An interesting discussion of the problem was carried on during the second half of 1863 in the columns of the Hicksite *Friends' Intelligencer*. The exchange of views started at the end of June with the publication of the first of three articles on the subject of "Friends and Government Requisitions" by a Byberry (Pa.) Friend, who signed himself "N.R." In his articles "N.R.," using arguments reminiscent of Mennonite or Dunker writers, urged that there was nothing inconsistent with Quaker pacifism in paying a fine in exchange for exemp-

[57] Quoted in Wright, p. 217. See also pp. 48, 49, 65-70.

tion: it should be regarded as a form of tribute paid to Caesar in the spirit of Christ's injunction. True, government had no right to control conscience, but it might dispose of our property within certain limits; the use that government then made of it, the writer implied, was not our responsibility. Even if, as some correspondents pointed out, payment was forbidden by the Society's discipline, surely the books of discipline were not so sacrosanct that they might not be a subject of discussion and changed, if not found to be sound on some point. Advice on how to respond to the small militia fines of prewar days might not be the appropriate answer to demands of the magnitude of $300 and to the exigencies of a war situation.

On the whole, the other contributions published by the editor disagreed strongly with "N.R.'s" views. Some writers feared their effect in undermining trust in the discipline and doubted the editor's wisdom in giving them publicity and, in particular, in stating that the matter was "a disputed point" among Friends. A Long Island Quaker gave expression to the predominant opinion when he wrote: "If Friends cannot themselves fight, it is wholly inconsistent for them to pay a fine, or tax in lieu of it, as that would be an acknowledgment that the demand is just, and that liberty of conscience is not due." "He is already a conscript in the Lamb's peaceable warfare," wrote another correspondent rather quaintly, and, therefore, no further demand for service in connection with terrestial warfare could rightly be made of him.[58]

The consensus of opinion on the pages of the *Intelligencer* went against "N.R.," but undoubtedly many among both the Hicksites and the Orthodox resorted—whether willingly or perhaps with an uneasy conscience, it is not often easy to say—to the method of paying commutation in exchange for exemption from service. We know that in the Philadelphia (Orthodox) Yearly Meeting, which kept more strictly to the discipline in such matters than its Hicksite brethren, 24 members were listed as paying their $300, with 7 hiring substitutes, in comparison with only 19 who rejected all forms of alternative service. (And, it should be added, 34 men had been discharged as a result of others paying their fines, usually without their consent, and in a further 5 cases the county officers, and not the men themselves, had hired substitutes.)[59] The same story is repeated in other sections of the So-

[58] *Friends' Intelligencer,* 27 June, 11 July, 18 July, 1 Aug., 8 Aug., 15 Aug., 29 Aug., 5 Sept., 12 Sept., 3 Oct., 5 Dec., 26 Dec. 1863; 9 Jan. 1864.
[59] Wright, p. 183. See pp. 164, 165, for details concerning two young Friends whose relatives paid their fines without their knowledge and contrary to their wishes.

ciety.[60] Official expressions of regret were certainly expressed frequently in meeting minutes or reports of committees. "They have been pained to find," the members of a committee of Philadelphia (Orthodox) Yearly Meeting "to assist Friends who are drafted" wrote at the conclusion of the war, "that some of our members have compromised our peace principles by paying the penalty imposed: thus lowering our profession of religious scruple in the estimation of those in authority, and greatly adding to the embarrassment and difficulty of such members as could not for conscience sake comply with the demand." But these offenders against the discipline—for such, indeed, were those who paid fines—rarely appear to have been penalized. Therefore, no schism such as had taken place within the Society at the time of the American Revolution, when the group led by Timothy Davis was disfellowshipped for supporting the payment of fines, resulted from the even more considerable falling away from the letter of the discipline during the Civil War period.

When new and more stringent draft legislation was under preparation in Washington toward the end of 1863, Edwin M. Stanton, the secretary of war, wishing to make some concessions to the position of the Society of Friends although not feeling empowered to press for the unconditional exemption that the Quakers hoped for, proposed the creation of "a special fund for the benefit of the Freedmen" into which the Quaker conscripts would pay their $300. To two delegates from Baltimore (Orthodox) Yearly Meeting "he expressed deep interest in organized, and individual efforts of Friends to elevate the moral, and physical condition of the manumitted Slaves"—a field of philanthropic endeavor in which the Society had long enjoyed a deserved reputation. However, Friends as a body were unwilling to accept this form of alternative, regarding its compulsory nature as an infringement of religious liberty. Such scruples, when communicated to him, Secretary Stanton found hard to comprehend.

He said he could understand no such abstraction as that—that it was a work of mercy, and in accordance with the commands of Christ, and that if our members did not choose to accept so liberal

[60] See Louis Thomas Jones, *The Quakers of Iowa*, pp. 333, 334, for the case of a monthly meeting borrowing in order to pay the fines of members unable to raise the money themselves. Meetings of the evangelically minded Western Y. M. seem to have done the same thing (see Wright, p. 195; *Semi-Centennial Anniversary Western Yearly Meeting of Friends' Church 1858-1908*, p. 198). But these instances probably occurred after the February 1864 act, when the use to which commutation fines were being put was less objectionable to Friends than under the earlier act.

300

an offer, he could do no more for them, and the law would have to take its effect.[61]

Despite the rejection by Friends of all forms of alternative service and despite a steady stream of memorials and petitions to this effect from their various meetings and a number of delegations dispatched by them to Washington to explain Friends' absolutist views, the new act, which came into force on 24 February 1864, did (in Section 17) provide specific alternatives to army service for all genuine members of the pacifist denominations. They might choose either to "be assigned by the Secretary of War to duty in the hospitals, or to the care of freedmen" or to pay the same commutation fine of $300 as before, but with the guarantee that it would "be applied to the benefit of the sick and wounded soldiers" and not to hiring further recruits or some other military purpose. Although minor amendments were made subsequently in the federal conscription law, the provision for conscientious objectors remained unaltered.[62]

The reaction of Friends to the considerable concessions which the February act made toward satisfying the scruples of religious pacifists was mixed. These concessions did not, as we have seen, remove the fundamental objections held by many Quakers who were most active and concerned about peace: indeed, nothing short of unconditional exemption could satisfy the most scrupulous. The Quaker papers stressed the appreciation which Friends felt for the good motives of the administration in trying to meet their case. But, as an editorial in the Orthodox *Friend* once more made clear,

We do not see how it can relieve our members, or they consistently avail themselves of any of its provisions; inasmuch as to be sent into the hospitals or serve as nurses, &c., or to be assigned to the care of freedmen, is just as much a penalty imposed for obeying the requisition of our religion in not performing military service, as is the fine of three hundred dollars. It matters not whether the commutation for military service is money or personal service in some other department; in either case it is an assumption on the part of the government of a right to oblige the subject to violate his conscience, or to exact a penalty if he elects to obey God rather than man.[63]

A further argument urged by the same paper against accepting such work of national importance as was being offered conscientious objec-

[61] Quoted in Wright, p. 75. See also p. 218.
[62] *Ibid.*, pp. 71-86.
[63] Quoted *ibid.*, pp. 83, 84. See also p. 217.

tors was that such employment, whether in military hospitals or even in the camps for freedmen which were under army control, was in fact aiding the prosecution of the war. "None of us would hesitate to relieve the sufferings of a sick and wounded fellow-being because he was a soldier; but this is wholly different from connecting ourselves with a military establishment got up expressly as a part of the machinery for . . . maiming and destroying our fellow creatures." The aim of the army medical service was to get the men fit again to return to the battle front. Additional arguments against accepting such service were provided by another editorial in a later issue of the *Friend*. It brought up the undesirability of Friends' wearing military uniform, which they would probably be required to do in army medical work, and the fact that any relaxation of the Society's official support of unconditional exemption hitherto would only serve to make things more difficult with the authorities for those young Friends who continued to take an unconditionalist line.[64] In the opinion of the *Friend* and that of many other Quakers, not only was the principle of requiring from genuine conscientious objectors civilian service in place of military service untenable, but the actual alternatives offered were to a greater or lesser degree unacceptable in themselves.

This view was, however, contested by some influential circles within the Society of both the major branches. Samuel Rhoads in an editorial in the *Friends' Review*, a periodical evangelical in tone but belonging like the Philadelphia *Friend* to the Orthodox camp, spoke out in favor of accepting the work provided by the government. "We presume," he wrote, "few of our members can be found who are unwilling to aid in the care of the freed-people, or, to a certain extent, in the relief of the sick and wounded. . . . We cannot but regard it as a mistaken view, to look upon the service substituted for arms-bearing, as a *penalty* or as a *purchase* of religious liberty." Friends had never refused to make an affirmation in place of an oath because the former was required as an alternative. We should rejoice that the government, in the midst of a bitter and prolonged struggle, had devised this scheme for alleviating Friends' conscientious scruples. A similar positive position was taken up by the Hicksite yearly meetings of New York and Ohio.

In a later issue the *Friends' Review*, while conceding that differences of opinion as to the consistency of Quakers' working as nurses or doctors in military hospitals might exist, maintained that absolutely no objection could properly be raised against rehabilitation work with freedmen. Do not let us make crosses for ourselves, the paper ad-

[64] *Friend*, 27 Aug., 29 Oct. 1864.

vised.[65] For the most part, the various yearly meetings left it up to the consciences of individual Friends to determine whether they felt able, if drafted, to participate in one or other of the forms of alternative service offered by the government. In this spirit the Meeting for Sufferings of Indiana (Orthodox) Yearly Meeting urged members to display "a large measure of Christian charity" toward those who were faced with the difficult choice of accepting the government's terms or disobeying the law.[66]

But even if on the whole meetings were tolerant of differing responses to the call for military service on the part of their conscientious objectors, it was undoubtedly the absolutists—those rejecting the alternatives provided by the government in the name of a higher law of spiritual liberty—who at this point in the Society's history most nearly expressed its peculiar testimony as found in the requirements of the books of discipline and in the thinking of its most concerned members.

By no means all such objectors had to suffer for their radical stand, in spite of the fact that the law made no provision for unconditional exemption. In many areas, and among the civilian authorities at least, the Quakers' uncompromising objection to fighting was well known and often respected, if not fully understood. Refusal to pay the commutation fee was usually punished by distraint of the property of the delinquent Friend, as we have seen in previous chapters had been the practice since colonial times.[67] But now, as earlier, the rigor of the law was often tempered by neighborly kindness and administrative good feeling. In one such case, Allen Jay (1881-1910), a young Quaker minister in Indiana who later became prominent in the evangelical movement leading to the setting up of Five Years' Meeting, was drafted but refused either to serve or pay commutation, which at that time was still being used to purchase recruits. "I would prefer to go myself," he told the officer, quoting to him antiwar utterances from the early church fathers, "rather than to hire someone else to be shot in my place." Later, an inventory of the livestock on Jay's farm was made in preparation for distraint, but, apparently on orders from Governor Morton, the sale was indefinitely postponed. Jay heard later that his non-Quaker neighbors, reluctant to see a man penalized because of sincerely held religious principles, had determined, when the sale took

---

[65] *Friends' Review*, 30 July, 20 Aug. 1864; *Friends' Intelligencer*, 24 Sept. 1864. Cf., e.g., *Friend*, 29 Oct. 1864; *Friends' Intelligencer*, 22 Oct. 1864.

[66] Wright, p. 84.

[67] *Ibid.*, pp. 183-87. Wright (p. 185) quotes the figure of $2,217.76 for the value of property distrained from members of the two New York yearly meetings for nonpayment of commutation fines during the period of the war.

place, to buy up his goods and return them to him as a gift.[68] Or take the case of another future evangelical leader of the postwar period, Samuel A. Purdie (1843-1897). Although of military age and in good health, he was left by the authorities to work on the family farm; for his continued absence from local militia musters, he received nothing worse than a mere $5 fine on one occasion (which presumably had to be distrained).[69]

A number of Friends, however, were drafted into the army as a result of their refusal to accept the alternatives offered by the government and thereby came under the control of the military authorities and were subject to all the rigors of military law. That the fate of such men was not worse than it was resulted in large part from the sympathetic stand of the highest authorities in the land, to whom Friends made direct appeal from time to time on behalf of their conscripted brethren. "Religious objectors to military service," says E. N. Wright, "were particularly fortunate in having President Lincoln and Secretary Stanton show a friendly attitude at all times." Lincoln's understanding and appreciation of the Quaker peace testimony emerges clearly in Wright's book, as does his desire to prevent anything in the nature of a persecution of religious conscience.[70] After his assassination many tributes to his efforts to relieve Quaker objectors came in from Quaker meetings. "We hold in grateful remembrance," wrote Friends of Green Street (Hicksite) Monthly Meeting in Germantown (Pa.), for instance, "the consideration with which he regarded our conscientious scruples in relation to military enactments, and believe he did for us in this respect all that his position allowed."[71] The method that the administration devised to deal with the Quaker unconditionalists, whose scruples were not met by the existing law, was that of paroling or furloughing them for an indefinite period: in fact, in such cases the men were not called up again before federal conscription was ended. The practice, while used earlier as a way of gaining release for objectors who had been caught up in the army, was employed fairly regularly from the end of 1863, on the orders of Secretary Stanton, to prevent such men from being taken into the army at all.[72]

The entanglement of Quaker objectors in the army machine occurred in most cases, therefore, in the years 1862 and 1863, though a

[68] *Autobiography of Allen Jay*, chap. X.
[69] James Purdie Knowles, *Samuel A. Purdie*, pp. 35, 36.
[70] Wright, pp. 121-30.
[71] F. B. Tolles (ed.), "Two Quaker Memorials for Abraham Lincoln," *BFHA*, vol. 46, no. 1 (1957), p. 42. See also Wright, pp. 90, 125, 126; *Memoir and Correspondence of Eliza P. Gurney*, p. 321.
[72] Wright, pp. 86-88, 124-26, 192-95.

few instances are to be found in the last year and a half of the war. No overall figures of the number of men involved have been compiled; in a few meetings records are defective. The most complete account kept by Friends in the North appears to be that compiled by the Philadelphia (Orthodox) Yearly Meeting soon after the end of the war from reports sent in by its constituent quarterly and monthly meetings. Of its absolutists it records:

> Two of those who refused on conscientious grounds to serve in the army, or to pay a commutation, or to hire a substitute, were arrested as deserters, but prompt application to those in authority, procured a speedy release on parole. Five were arrested, forced into military clothing, and sent some to Barracks, and some to a Camp in Philadelphia. On application to the Secretary of War, they were all released after periods of confinement, varying from a few days to 5 weeks. Three were drafted and sent to Camp Curtin, near Harrisburg, but on application for them to those in authority by Friends of Philadelphia, they were in a few days released. One was sent to the army, but after two months of trial and suffering, his release was obtained by application to the Secretary of War. Four of those who appeared before different Provost Marshals and stated their conscientious scruples were heard with kindly consideration and were not afterwards molested.[73]

This bare factual statement shows among other things the interplay between, on the one hand, Quakerly intercession for the release of the impressed men and, on the other, willingness on the part of many authorities, both locally and at the top in Washington, to relieve genuine conscience, if they could, within the framework of the existing law.

Those young Friends whose refusal to pay what Caesar considered his due led to their arrest and incarceration in one or another of the military camps that dotted the country met on the whole with courteous treatment. Sometimes they had to face threats of punishment and even the firing squad from senior, or more often, junior officers, but here, too, a more tolerant attitude frequently resulted from the objector's steady purpose and a somewhat closer acquaintance with, if not always much greater comprehension of, sincerely held opinions on the rightness of fighting. E. N. Wright in his book on the conscientious objectors of the Civil War relates several experiences of this kind on the part of young Quakers forcibly inducted into the army, and they seem, on the basis of admittedly rather scanty evidence, to

[73] Quoted in *ibid.*, p. 183.

have been more typical than instances of severe brutality toward the unwilling soldier.

Take the case of A. M. Jenkins, a country lad from around Dayton (Ohio). After he had been brought to camp, the "Captain of the Day" refused to place him in the guardhouse, saying that "it was a shame to put a decent man" there, as it "was full of the worst characters in the camp." (A couple of years later two other Ohio Quaker conscripts, who found themselves in the guardhouse of Todd Barracks in Columbus for refusing to drill, found a sympathetic guard there who told them: "Men, I do pity you, as it is such a filthy place and such hard cases to be your company but I do like to see men live up to their principles.") Despite the expressed wish of the colonel of the camp to which Jenkins and another Quaker boy were eventually transferred "to see how Quakers would look drilling," they received good treatment there, too; when they were permitted to return home not long afterward, the colonel told them good-humoredly "that he could give us an 'honorable discharge,' as we had maintained our 'conscious [sic] principles.'"

The story of another Ohio Quaker, Barclay Stratton, who was drafted in the autumn of 1864, two years after Jenkins's release, provides us with a further example of respect shown in the army to "conscious [sic] principles." Ordered to put on military uniform, Stratton quietly explained his reasons for refusing to exchange his Quaker garb for army blue, and, instead of the harshness he had expected to follow, the major in charge patted him on the shoulders and said: "My friend, I admire your candor." They soon came to an understanding whereby the uniform was put on the unresisting Quaker by one of the army clerks, without Stratton having to give actual consent. The major told him that "he did not blame me in the least for not doing it myself." Although Stratton and another young Quaker from his home area, who had been drafted to the same camp, were eventually sent south to Richmond (Va.) and although the two men steadily refused to accept offers of hospital work which were made to them by the military authorities, they continued to receive mostly kindness and consideration from both officers and rank and file, until at last they were sent home on indefinite parole.

Wright points out that sometimes hostile treatment was replaced by a more friendly attitude on the part of the military when it was realized that the recalcitrant soldier was in fact a member of the Society of Friends, whose peculiar views on the subject of war were fairly well known in the community. He cites the case of Joseph G. Miller, a Hicksite Quaker from Brooklyn, who, after being taken to a camp on

Rikers Island, had been forced into uniform and harshly treated there by the officers.

But when it became known that he was a Friend [relates a minute, dated 6 April 1864, of New York Monthly Meeting, to which Miller belonged] and was actuated by conscientious scruples their manner towards him underwent an entire change. After a detention of about three weeks on this Island he was on the 23d of 10th month removed to Governors Island, where he was furnished with a comfortable bed in the hospital, was permitted to resume his own clothes, and was required to do nothing contrary to his feelings, on the 11th of Eleventh Month he was liberated under parole.

In the summer of 1863 some yearly meetings—the Orthodox of Philadelphia and New York are examples[74]—prepared special statements for presentation by drafted members to the provost marshal and other military officials concerned with the draft. The statements mentioned the draftee's membership in the Society of Friends and his objection, as a Friend, to all forms of conditional exemption as an infringement of "the free exercise of his natural right to liberty" of conscience, while at the same time stressing the Quaker's entire loyalty to the Union government and its laws, "so far as these things are not inconsistent with his religious obligations." In this way, it was hoped that, however the fate of the objector was decided, the authorities from the outset would be left in no doubt as to the position he took and the fact that it had the backing of his church.

In some cases, a statement of this kind must have contributed toward a decision by the authorities to send the drafted man home without further ado or release him after a few days. But it did not always prove effective, as was shown in the case of the Smedley cousins, William and Edward, from Delaware County (Pa.). Although they had provided themselves with such a paper, as their Friends had advised them to do, they soon found themselves en route for Philadelphia under military escort. The lieutenant in charge was an old schoolmate of Edward's who, disliking his enforced task, treated the cousins with as much consideration as he could. But, when on arrival in the Quaker city, Edward relates,

... the officers ... were informed of the circumstances of our declining from conscientious motives to participate in any warlike measures, they utterly repudiated such notions, commanded our immediate compliance with their orders, and when we quietly declined,

[74] See *ibid.*, pp. 69, 70.

manifested great resentment by wordy abuse and threatenings of punishment. After their passions were pretty well spent, we were sent to the third floor of the building, turned in with some hundreds of drafted men and substitutes, and left to make the best we could of the situation till morning.

During their subsequent sojourn in the Philadelphia barracks the Smedleys were well treated, although there was a danger that they might be sent south. Meanwhile, Friends outside were busy trying to obtain their release; after seventeen days they were so far successful that the boys were given their liberty on condition that they reported daily to the barracks until further notice. A month or so later, on Secretary Stanton's orders, the two Quakers were "honorably" discharged from the United States Army.[75]

Some uncompromising unconditionalists at times fared better than this, however, since they never found themselves under military control at all. Take the case of Benjamin P. Moore, a Hicksite Quaker who kept a general store in a small Maryland village. When war came, writes this staunch antisecessionist, "and the military spirit broke out among my associates (chiefly on the 'rebel' side) . . . I emptied the powder I had left into the street, refused to sell ammunition to anyone, or to pay a state tax in aid of the war, for which some of my goods were levied and sold." Upon receiving notice that he had been drafted, in the late fall of 1863, he hurried to Washington to put his case before the President. That this obscure country shopkeeper succeeded in gaining a personal interview with Lincoln, who listened patiently to him before sending him on to the Secretary of War, bears witness to the surprising accessibility of the President even during the crowded years of war. Stanton told Moore that he would be assigned to work in a military hospital. "Now I had no objection to nursing the sick and the wounded," the Quaker wrote later, citing the fact of his volunteering for such work in the emergency after the battle of Antietam in September 1862, but he was not willing to do so as an alternative to military service. In the end, he received an indefinite parole before he could actually be inducted into service.[76]

In contrast to the mild experiences of a man like Moore, already in his thirties and with his mind made up as to the course he should pursue in face of the draft, we may instance those of 22-year-old Jesse Macy (1842-1919), a birthright Quaker from Iowa who much later,

[75] The above paragraphs are based on the accounts given in Wright, pp. 153-63. Jones (*The Later Periods of Quakerism*, II, 731, 732) prints young Miller's story as told in the minutes of Westbury M. M.

[76] *Friend*, vol. 114, no. 17 (20 Feb. 1941), pp. 297-99.

after he had left the Friends for the Congregationalists, was to gain a considerable reputation as a political scientist and historian. At the outset of the war, the antislavery enthusiasm of this son of free-soil pioneers led him almost to the point of volunteering. Loyalty to the faith of his fathers held him back. (Macy already seemed marked by his exceptional intelligence and obvious moral earnestness for leadership in the Quaker community in Iowa, and he had already begun, young as he was, to play a significant role in it.) In addition, until after Lincoln had proclaimed emancipation, the war to a fervid emancipationist like young Macy was scarcely one for the liberation of the slave: this also was a factor in dissuading him from joining up in the early days. In September 1864 Macy, then a student at Grinnell College where he was later to spend much of his life as a teacher, was at last drafted. His parents would willingly have seen him pay his $300 commutation and come back to work on the farm. But their son was anxious to seize this opportunity to do something positive to help the oppressed, now that the administration had given them their freedom, and so he decided to report for service, with the determination to accept only hospital duty or work with freedmen that the law had granted his people.

In spite of being furnished with a certificate of Quaker membership, however, he was told on arrival in camp that his exemption would not be recognized and that he would be required to serve as an ordinary soldier. His regiment, the 10th Iowa, was soon sent south to join the army there. Macy refused to draw a gun, feeling quite correctly that, if he once did so, even with the intention of never using it to kill, it might be difficult for him to prove his noncombatancy when they arrived in the battle zone. Then, and in the days following, all his former doubts and hesitations about what it was right for him to do, the inner conflict between his pacifist heritage and the militant antislavery feelings that were both his inheritance and his own heartfelt convictions as well, came again to the fore. His was, indeed, a "perplexing and intolerable situation," as he described it later.

> I had endured and was still enduring a good deal of mental agony with reference to my own personal duties in respect to the war. My role as representative of a church was not in harmony with my convictions as a man. . . . I had believed that I could enter the army and fight for liberty while still remaining worthy of the Christian's name; but such action *now* I felt would be a betrayal of trust reposed in me, a sacrifice of loyalty and truth and so of true manly integrity.

Therefore, he decided that his policy should be only to obey orders relating to the care of the sick and wounded and to regard all others as essentially illegal, since they ignored the noncombatant status that the law had granted him. He does not appear to have been in contact with any others of similar views: spiritual loneliness and his isolation must have compounded his difficulties. Nevertheless, he stuck to his resolution throughout the period when, with his regiment, he participated in Sherman's march to the sea; his fellow soldiers showed him sympathy, and the officers on the whole left him alone. In March 1865, on orders from the Secretary of War, he was sent to Springfield (Ill.) to work as a camp medical orderly; several months later he received his discharge from the army.

Macy's reflections on his wartime stand, as written down some years later, may serve as an example of the inner conflict set up by divided allegiances in the minds of many young men reared in the Quaker community, even among some of those who, like Macy, preserved an outward adherence to the Society's peace testimony. He writes:

At the close of the war I felt a lasting regret that my peculiar position in the army had been a source of annoyance to military officers whose work I regarded with sympathy and approval. I would have been willing to sacrifice my life to further the great work of saving the Union and abolishing the iniquity of slavery; but I was not clear in my mind as to the proper attitude of the Society of Friends. Each individual Quaker in North and South prayed daily for the success of the Union Army. . . . I felt that I had done practically nothing. Many [i.e., young Friends] had accepted full military service, others, like myself, had passed through the momentous period in a troubled state of mind, uncertain what was the path of duty. One of my cousins, Elwood Macy, believing when it was too late, that his own failure of duty to his country was due in large measure to the attitude of the Friends' Church, in which he had been educated, abandoned the Society and joined the Methodist Church.[77]

[77] *Jesse Macy: An Autobiography*, pp. 36, 41-46, 48ff., 63, 69, 75-77. Cf. an interesting correspondence relating to this subject carried on between Garrison and Elizabeth B. Chace in the summer of 1862, which is printed in L.B.C. and A. C. Wyman, *Elizabeth Buffum Chace 1806-1899: Her Life and Environment*, I, 241, 242. Mrs. Chace, daughter of the Rhode Island Quaker hatter and abolitionist, Arnold Buffum, was an ardent Garrisonian nonresistant who had resigned her membership in the Society of Friends in 1843 because of its hostility to abolitionism and had then slowly drifted away from organized religion during the subsequent years. From her Quaker heritage, however, she retained her pacifism, and this, together with her strong maternal instincts, led her to use all her influence on her two sons, Samuel (b. 1843) and Arnold (b. 1845), to dissuade them from enlisting in the army—despite the strong desire of the elder one, at least, to do so. Their father, Samuel B. Chace, had remained a Quaker, joining the Wilburite

When we turn from the torn and divided hearts of birthright Quakers like Jesse and Elwood Macy to the single-minded devotion to Quaker pacifism of a convinced Friend like Cyrus Guernsey Pringle (1838-1911), we breathe another atmosphere. Sincerity and high-minded idealism and loyalty to a cause there was aplenty in men like the Macys, but they were directed toward a different object. For them, some of the traditional testimonies of their Society had grown cold and formal, lacking the vital spark of a personally felt faith. Pringle was a convert who had joined the Friends only in 1862. For him, the peace testimony formed a living cell of his new found belief. This devotion shines clearly from every page of the diary that he kept of his draft experience, the manuscript of which was only uncovered a short time after his death. Although it has since been published and twice reprinted, this minor classic of conscientious objection deserves more than a bare mention in these pages. Its most recent editor, Professor Henry J. Cadbury, rightly calls it "a vivid, intimate human document," a simple record of the "timeless problem of a sensitive conscience."[78] Pringle in later life made a reputation for himself as a botanist, but he was mainly self-educated and during the Civil War was working on the small family farm in northern Vermont. On 13 July 1863 he received notice that he had been drafted. His reaction to the news, as he recorded it in the opening page of his diary, was typical of the man. "With ardent zeal for our Faith and the cause of our peaceable principles, and almost disgusted at the lukewarmness and unfaithfulness of very many who profess these, and considering how heavily

Conservative group when it was formed. Parental pressure, therefore, weighed heavily on the boys. On one occasion the mother told Samuel, Jr.: "I think the time will come in which thee will be very glad thee did not go into the army"; to which her son replied: "No, I shall never be glad that I did not help to save the Union." In her distress Mrs. Chace wrote to Garrison for advice. "Conjure them to act as duty may seem to require" was the essence of Garrison's answer, and he warned her that, if the boys were drafted eventually, they could not plead their parents' veto in extenuation of their unwillingness to serve. Nevertheless, the Chace boys, as was undoubtedly the case in a number of other Quaker households, seem to have yielded to family influence in holding back from service rather than following the light of personal conviction into active participation in the war. See also *ibid.*, pp. 216, 219, 220.

[78] *The Civil War Diary of Cyrus Pringle* (1962 edn.), p. 4. In his foreword, Professor Cadbury remarks (p. 6): "The almost naive approach of a single individual a century ago has relevance today among nations that toy under various pretexts with the possible guilt of mass extermination. The ultimate preventive against the commitment of such evil is the human conscience. It is the moral deterrent. For that reason the simple modest testimony of Cyrus Pringle may have more lasting meaning than appears on the surface. Human moral progress has often depended on the spontaneous response of one or two sensitive persons to quite unexpected situations, when that response became convincing and contagious."

slight crosses bore upon their shoulders, I felt [able] to say, 'Here am I, Father, for thy service. As thou will.'"

Friends and acquaintances, during a short period of grace granted him by the enrollment board to think matters over, urged the young man to pay the commutation, which would have extricated him from the clutches of the military. This, however, Pringle would not do from "a higher duty than that to country." He asked, he said, for "no military protection of our government and [was] grateful for none, [denying] any obligation to support so unlawful a system, as we hold war to be even when waged in opposition to an evil and oppressive power." There followed a final appearance before the provost marshal and involuntary induction into the army. Sent first to Brattleboro (Vt.) and then on to Boston, Pringle, who was joined by two other Quaker boys, shared the discomforts of the first days of army life along with a miscellaneous selection of conscripts and substitutes from country and town. Their final destination was the military camp on Long Island in Boston Harbor. We find Pringle recording in his diary for 28 August: "All is war here. We are surrounded by the pomp and circumstance of war, and enveloped in the cloud thereof. The cloud settles down over the minds and souls of all; they cannot see beyond nor do they try; but with the clearer eye of Christian faith I try to look beyond all this error into Truth and Holiness immaculate: and thanks to the Father, I am favored with glimpses that are sweet consolation amid this darkness." A consolation, too, was the sympathy and kindliness displayed by the ordinary soldiers in the camp, who showed no signs of resentment at the fact that the Quakers did not partake in all the drills and fatigues that were their own portion. Some of the officers, however, were hostile, and refusal to obey orders soon brought confinement in the guardhouse and threats of worse treatment and even of shooting.

Pringle's diary brings out the continual alertness of himself and his companions in maintaining an undefiled witness to the truth as they believed it to be expressed in the Quaker peace testimony. Back at the beginning of their army days there had been the problem of uniforms: they agreed to wear them but were unwilling to sign for them since they felt that would imply an acceptance of military service. Finally, they certified merely that the clothes were "with us." Later, after arriving in camp, they were confronted with the choice of performing, when ordered, certain seemingly quite innocuous chores or facing the consequences of disobedience. On one occasion they were required to help in cleaning the camp and in fetching water. "We wished to be obliging," Pringle recorded, "to appear willing to bear a hand toward that which would promote our own and our fellows' health and convenience; but as we worked we did not feel easy." It seemed too great an acquiescence in the military service, and, when a command from the sergeant bidding them "Police the streets" followed their fears were confirmed. And this time disobedience brought punishment. But most distressing of all the decisions they had to make, not least because compromise was recommended by respected members of their own Quaker community (Friends in both New England and New York Yearly Meetings were active on behalf of their conscientious objectors who were facing the trials of the army camp),[79] was the resolve to turn down the offer the authorities now made. This offer, put forward with the best intentions, proposed that they be transferred to work in the camp hospitals, a privilege that as yet was not formally guaranteed to objectors by law. They wrote to Henry Dickinson, a leading member of the Representative Meeting in New York: "We cannot purchase life at cost of peace of soul." Their situation now looked serious indeed, for, if they maintained their unwillingness to serve in the hospital, the alternative would be shipment south with one or another of the contingents that left the island at frequent intervals bound eventually for the scene of battle.

And so at last, in the middle of September, we find Pringle embarked for the final and hardest part of his adventure. After its arrival in Virginia, the regiment was sent on to a camp near Culpeper. Pringle and two companions refused to handle the gun which was issued to each of them for the march, "even though we did not intend to use it"; "in the hurry and bustle of equipping a detachment of soldiers," it was not easy for them to explain satisfactorily the reasons for disobeying orders. As they marched through the war-devastated Virginia countryside, with their rifles and equipment strapped onto them by order of the officers, Pringle found confirmation in the scene of the rightness of their stand. "When one contrasts the face of this country with the smiling hillsides and vales of New England," wrote the Vermonter in his diary, "he sees stamped upon it in characters so marked, none but a blind man can fail to read, the great irrefutable arguments against slavery and against war." In the days following their arrival at Camp Culpeper, there ensued the most trying period for the three Quakers. Harsh treatment and threats of court-martial and shooting were followed by attempts on the part of the colonel in command of the 4th Vermont regiment, to which they were now assigned, to get them to accept work with the medical service. "He urged us to go

---

[79] For further details in regard to New England Friends who were drafted into the army and of the efforts made to gain their release, see Ethan Foster, *The Conscript Quakers*; Wright, pp. 124, 125, 192-95; Jones, *The Later Periods of Quakerism*, II, 735.

into the hospital, stating this course was advised by Friends about New York. We were too well aware of such a fact to make any denial, though it was a subject of surprise to us that he should be informed of it." Once more they were faced with the same dilemma. If they refused his offer contrary to the advice of older and more experienced Friends, they would seem fanatics, irresponsible and deaf to the needs of the unfortunate around them. Active service on behalf of those urgently needing help—"we saw around us a rich field for usefulness in which there were scarce any laborers"—appeared so much more satisfying than a passive and perhaps sterile witness for an abstract principle. "At last," writes Pringle, "we consented to a trial, . . . reserving the privilege of returning to our former position."

But inner peace of mind did not follow. "At first a great load seemed rolled away from us; we rejoiced in the prospect of life again. But soon there prevailed a feeling of condemnation, as though we had sold our Master. And that first day was one of the bitterest I ever experienced. It was a time of stern conflict of soul." So eventually they returned to the colonel and told him that they were unwilling any longer to set aside their previous position: a clear testimony against war could only be borne by refusing to accept any alternatives to combatant service. The colonel, angry at what he considered their unreasonableness, now lost patience with them. Pringle's diary records the story of the punishments which followed their declaration of defiance. "I dreaded torture," he writes, "and desired strength of flesh and spirit." The climax came as a result of refusing an order to clean his gun, which was already becoming yellow with rust. What followed must be told in his own words, written down shortly afterward:

> Two sergeants soon called for me, and taking me a little aside, bid me lie down on my back, and stretching my limbs apart tied cords to my wrists and ankles, and these to four stakes driven in the ground somewhat in the form of an x. I was very quiet in my mind as I lay there on the ground [soaked] with the rain of the previous day, exposed to the heat of the sun and suffering keenly from the cords binding my wrists and straining my muscles. And, if I dared the presumption, I should say that I caught a glimpse of heavenly pity. I wept, not so much from my own suffering as from sorrow that such things should be in our own country. . . . And I was sad, that one endeavoring to follow our dear Master should be so generally regarded as a despicable and stubborn culprit.

Evidently, this represented a last attempt to cow Pringle into submission, for—unknown to him—an order had already been sent from

Washington, as a result of Quaker intervention there, to bring to the capital not only Pringle and his two companions but several other Quaker objectors who had ended up in the military camps of Virginia, as a preliminary to their eventual release from the service. On 7 November they received their paroles, and at last Pringle was able to return home—to quote the concluding words in his diary—"through the mercy and favor of Him, who in all this trial had been our guide and strength and comfort."

It was Friends of military age, of course, who had had to bear the main burden of war resistance. But the dilemma of conscience also presented itself in one form or another during these war years to many Quakers who were not challenged directly by the state's demand for military service. The Civil War took place before the coming of the age of total war, yet even then the threads of warmaking were subtly interwoven with the whole social fabric. To detach oneself from activities which helped, albeit indirectly, in the prosecution of the war was becoming increasingly difficult. The Society of Friends, more wary of rendering Caesar more than his due than were the American peace sects of German origin, had always striven to guard against a peace testimony which refused participation in war while at the same time acquiescing in activities which made the waging of war possible. We have seen this scrupulousness exemplified in their refusal to accept exemption from combatant duties through any form of alternative service, even where this was otherwise of an unobjectionable nature. But every activity, so their most concerned members constantly urged, must be carefully scrutinized to see if it did not contain hidden within itself the seeds of war.

This is the message of many of their wartime utterances, both those for public consumption and those intended primarily for the edification of members, documents that often appear platitudinous in their repeated exhortations to eschew evil and smugly moralistic in their style and whole approach. Yet in this very fastidiousness in the search for righteousness, despite the danger (by no means always avoided) that it would slide over into priggishness and a moral pharisaism, lay one of the sources of strength in the Society's peace testimony that has never entirely disappeared.

Consider, for instance, two documents drawn up in the first year of war by meetings from the two main branches of the Society. In an address of 23 April 1861 we find a special Representative Meeting of the New York (Orthodox) Yearly Meeting calling on members to "guard most watchfully against every temptation in any manner or degree to foster or encourage the spirit of war and strife" and "to be very careful in conversation upon passing events, both among themselves and with others—that nothing be allowed to escape their lips that may promote or countenance an appeal to arms or reliance upon them."[80] The same care to see that Friends should make their actions conform to the spirit as well as to the letter of their pacifism is shown in the minutes of the Western Quarterly Meeting of Philadelphia (Hicksite) Yearly Meeting. There the monthly meetings were urged to diligently exercise "a more watchful Christian care over the conduct of their members, especially in regard to the support of our testimony against War, and all warlike preparations; in order that they may be preserved within the pale of our Religious Society."[81] True, such pastoral care was often needed and not always exerted. Nevertheless, the Society's history during the period of the Civil War provides plenty of evidence that the thoughts and prayers of a considerable number of Quakers were directed toward the steady perfecting of their witness for peace.

The relationship between the exercise of civil government and the waging of war had occupied the minds of more thoughtful Friends ever since the days of the Quaker experiment in Pennsylvania. The coming of war had served to sharpen the issue, and it seemed to some that it was just here that the Quaker peace testimony of the day was weakest. Friends in large numbers had helped to vote the war administration into office. Was this (for all the admirable qualities of the President and his colleagues and Friends' sympathies with them in their task) a proper outcome of Quaker principles in politics? And then there was the knotty problem of the nature of the conflict: whether it was properly speaking a war between two states or a rebellion within the framework of civil government. In the latter case, and if its suppression were a legitimate function of the United States government, was not perhaps a complete and unequivocal withdrawal from political life, as a handful of Friends had been advocating for many decades, the only consistent policy for members of the Society to adopt?

These issues probably troubled only a minority of Friends. For most of those who remained according to their lights loyal to the peace testimony, upholding law and government—insofar as this did not entail a directly warlike function—and voting in elections did not appear to be un-Quakerly activities. The *Weltanschauung* of their fellow pacifists of the Mennonite and Dunker persuasions was fairly remote from the frame of mind of most American Quakers of that day.

[80] *Friend*, 22 June 1861. See also Wright, pp. 43, 44.
[81] *Friends' Intelligencer*, 16 Nov. 1861.

A keen pacifist like the clerk of Genesee (Hicksite) Yearly Meeting in upstate New York, John J. Cornell (whose peace pamphlet has been discussed earlier in this chapter), felt able to answer affirmatively the query whether a Quaker could properly claim "protection" from a government like their own, which relied ultimately on the sanction of the sword, provided such protection did not involve the use of armed force. The example of Quaker Pennsylvania, he believed, had shown that government need not necessarily involve injurious force and might be based on Christian principles of redeeming the wrong-doer, and not on retributive punishment. Meanwhile, until such government were established again, since some form of decent administration was essential for human well-being, the individual might give it his general support without being personally responsible for those of its actions of which he could not approve.[82]

Cornell's views were probably fairly typical of the main trend of opinion within the Society at this time. They were contested both from within the Society and from outside. Of outside criticism we may take as an example the views of the *Advocate of Peace*, the organ of the pro-war peace men who now controlled the rather conservative American Peace Society. The *Advocate*, as one might expect, was by no means unsympathetic to Quaker and other religious objectors. It stressed on several occasions that these men, for all their refusal to take part in the war, were staunchly antislavery and anti-secessionist. But, asked an article published in the spring of 1864, how far could their form of pacifism in fact be squared with civil government? "If a Quaker were mayor of Philadelphia, . . . how would he deal with a gang of burglars, incendiaries or murderers infesting the city?" It went on to cite the actual case of a mayor of a city in New England who belonged to the Society of Friends. "Would you censure him for the use of such force as he would find necessary in executing the laws?" And what if he had been, instead, mayor of New York during the previous summer's "copperhead" riots in that city. "Ought he on Christian principles to let the rioters have their way in their work of robbery, murder, and conflagration?" Finally, and inevitably, the article raised the question: what if a Quaker were President of the United States? Would he permit the rebels to flout the law of the Union with impunity and not take active measures to prevent it? "We regret to find Friends . . . treating such an enforcement of law as the same thing in principle with an ordinary war between nations."[83]

[82] Letter dated 8 Feb. 1862 in *Autobiography of John J. Cornell*, pp. 124-26.
[83] *Advocate of Peace*, XV, March-April 1864, 46, 47.

For the members of the American Peace Society and the millions of their more belligerent fellow citizens who also supported the war, the Quaker position appeared equivocal on account of its failure to endorse the full extent of governmental authority. In the eyes of its critics within the Society, on the other hand, its inadequacy lay in the degree of approval it was prepared to give government. It was in particular the question of voting at elections, when, as in wartime, most candidates were likely to be in favor of prosecuting the war (except those who had a secret partiality with the enemy cause), that aroused serious reservations among some Friends. The conservative Wilburite, Joshua Maule, for instance, had exercised the franchise before hostilities, but the coming of war led him to the conclusion that a consistent Friend must practice total abstinence in the realm of politics.[84] A contributor to the Hicksite *Intelligencer* on one occasion raised a problem that may have bothered many Friends of military age when he wrote:

> The President we have aided to elect, in the fulfillment of his official duty, calls upon us, through his subordinate, to do our share of military service. We unhesitatingly object, and proceed, forthwith, to state the grounds of the objection—that we are Christians, therefore cannot fight. . . . Our demanding officer is struck with surprise, and inquiries where our christianity and conscientious scruples were at the time we voted for the President, whose official duties, in part, we knew to be of a military character, and were now only in proper progress of fulfillment; and further urging that they who place a man in office, pledge themselves to the observance of all such requisitions upon them as the duties of that office in its execution may require.[85]

The approach of the presidential election of 1864 again faced the Quakers with a difficult choice. Many Friends were enthusiastic supporters of Lincoln; few wished to give their votes to his rival, McClellan. But some had serious doubts whether they could consistently vote for a war leader, however unquestionable his integrity. No ruling was ever issued by any of the branches of the Society: the discipline remained silent, and the matter was left for decision to the individual conscience of each Friend.[86]

If there was some difference among the Quakers concerning the degree to which they might properly become engaged in politics—especially in time of war—opinion in the Society was also divided to

[84] Joshua Maule, *Transactions and Changes in the Society of Friends*, p. 267.
[85] Quoted in Wright, p. 41. [86] Wright, pp. 87, 88.

QUAKERS

some extent as to how far certain civilian activities, otherwise unobjectionable, were permissible when their beneficiaries were soldiers.
Naturally, if personal profit was involved, as in selling horses or grain
for the use of the army, at least the stricter Friends registered strong
disapproval. And there was an even more general reprobation of any
business that had become associated directly with the waging of war.
Thus, we hear of Benjamin Tatham, Jr., a New York Friend who had
emigrated from England in 1841, turning over his firm from its prewar business of making shot to the manufacture of lead piping, which
even in wartime did not offend against his Society's peace testimony.[87]
As an epistle of Philadelphia (Orthodox) Yearly Meeting of 9 January
1864 put it:

> Keep clear of business of any kind, which depends for its emolu-
> ments on its connection with war. Sorrowful indeed will it be, if
> any of the professed advocates of peace are found engaged in busi-
> ness which, in the eyes of a quick-sighted world, may cause the
> sincerity of our testimony to the peaceable principles of the gospel
> to be doubted, and give occasion for the charge of inconsistency, if
> not of hypocrisy, to be made against our religious profession.[88]

But it was not so easy to make a hard and fast ruling (and still
more difficult to persuade Friends to keep to one) when it was a question of humanitarian aid to the army's soldiers. We have seen that
all branches of the Society officially, and many Friends individually,
refused such work if it was offered as an alternative to direct combatant service. But what if it were undertaken voluntarily, as an expression of the humanitarian impulse that led the best elements in
nineteenth-century Quakerism out into the highways and byways of
philanthropy? Was it to fall under a ban just because the recipients
of Quaker relief happened to wear a soldier's uniform? Quaker women,
in particular, felt the urge to join in the work of providing various
comforts for the men in the army and of thus helping, if only indirectly in their homes, the sick and wounded especially. The young
Mitchell sisters, for instance, children of a respected Nantucket Quaker, were engaged in such work, striving in this way to give expression
both to the Quaker message of goodwill to all men and to their emotional attachment to the Northern cause, when a member of their
meeting raised the question with them whether as good Quakers they
should participate in such "war" work. They referred the matter to

[87] John Cox, Jr., *Quakerism in the City of New York*, p. 129. Tatham was offered
the post of Commissioner for Indian Affairs by Lincoln, but he refused it on the
grounds that it was too much of a worldly honor.
[88] *Friend*, 9 Jan. 1864.

their father, whose strict adherence to the discipline was well known among New England Friends. "I think the Good Samaritan would not have asked [what was] the cause of suffering where suffering existed," he told them, and the sisters now felt able to continue their work with an easy conscience.[89] We find, indeed, no less a person than the English-born Mrs. Elizabeth L. Comstock, wife of a Midwest Friend and herself a minister influential in the counsels of the Orthodox Quakers of that region, extremely active in humanitarian work on behalf of sick and wounded soldiers in military hospitals and camps. Her labors gained high praise from Lincoln himself and other government officials.[90] It should be pointed out, however, that this work was part of her general concern for all sufferers—prisoners, the insane, as well as the freedmen and Southern prisoners of war—and in this way harmonized with the Quaker concept of service.

Nevertheless, strong sentiment existed, at least in regard to donations of clothing and other gifts for the troops, that this was a mistaken form of expressing the Quaker concern to relieve suffering. Although its mainspring was not any selfish motive, as it was for those whose businesses led them to deal in articles which promoted the war effort, still it contributed to the support of war, if in a more subtle way. In the eyes of such critics, it represented a compromising of the peace testimony and would easily be misinterpreted by outsiders as tacit support for the war. The Philadelphia *Friend*, in an editorial condemning such relief efforts as misplaced, reported the following remarks of a high-ranking officer in Washington spoken in the writer's hearing: "I understand your testimony against war, but the Friends at ―――― have sent several barrels of articles for the soldiers; they must certainly believe in war."[91]

This issue, the problem of deciding where to draw the line so that what was intended as labor on behalf of suffering humanity should not prove an unwitting abetment of the act of destruction, was to present itself again to the Society of Friends during the two world wars of our century.

From the eighteenth to the twentieth century American Friends have, as we have already seen, had to face another and perhaps more difficult question: the relationship of their peace testimony to the tax demands of a war-making government. The call for service, whether a compulsory requirement of state or federal law or a voluntary outgrowth of the inner conscience, affected the individual person who

[89] *Recollections of Lydia S. (Mitchell) Hinchman*, pp. 45, 46.
[90] See *Life and Letters of Elizabeth L. Comstock*, chaps. VIII-XIII.
[91] *Friend*, 29 Oct. 1864. See also *Friends' Review*, 9 Nov. 1861.

must bear responsibility for his own actions. But taxes affected property on which state and society had legitimate claims irrespective of use, which the majority of Quakers as well as the more quietist Mennonites and Dunkers acknowledged as ordained by God. During the Civil War the general sentiment among Friends, not only the Orthodox but Hicksites and Wilburites as well, remained that state and federal taxes "in the mixture," that is, those taxes that were not *in toto* allocated specifically for the purposes of war, should be paid without further questioning. "We feel," stated the Western Yearly Meeting of Friends in September 1861, "that we escape condemnation when the Magistrate and not the tax payer assumes the responsibility of its specific appropriations." And New England Yearly Meeting, a year later, was even more emphatic, urging members to continue to pay their taxes "cheerfully . . . without attempting to make any impracticable distinctions respecting such taxes as may be imposed upon them for the support of our Government."[92] This was, in fact, the traditional standpoint, although from time to time some sensitive spirit had arisen to challenge it; a period of war brought the whole issue more forcibly before Friends. While most, therefore, paid their ordinary taxes willingly, there was no attempt to bring into line the minority who refused by any kind of disciplinary action. Mutual toleration was to be observed in regard to honest differences of opinion between the moderates, who believed that a prompt and full rendering of tribute was essential in the present state of the world for good governance, and the more radical, who felt payment of such taxes meant a watering down of their peace testimony.[93]

Of these radicals an excellent example is to be found in the person of the Ohio Quaker, Joshua Maule, whose protest against voting has been mentioned above. Maule, who was already middle-aged when war broke out, had been an active member of the Conservative or Wilburite branch of the Society, which had begun to separate in the 1840's and 1850's. In 1861 he sided with a small splinter group within the Conservative Yearly Meeting of Ohio, which took the name of Ohio Primitive General Meeting. From these few details of his career we can see that Maule was a man who cleaved to the old ways and wished to see at least his branch of the Society maintain the letter as well as the spirit of the discipline in regard to Quaker peace principles. Wilburite Friends in Ohio, he tells us, when the test came, "flinched and failed" to bear a consistent testimony in this matter of paying taxes in wartime. He would have liked to see them

[92] Quoted in Wright, p. 48. See also, e.g., *Friend*, 1 Aug. 1863.
[93] See, e.g., *Friends' Intelligencer*, 26 Oct. 1861.

adopt the stand of eighteenth-century Friends like John Churchman or Job Scott or John Woolman (his belief that their view was the same as that of all early Friends was, of course, mistaken).

Throughout the period of the war Maule was considerably troubled by what he regarded as a general apostasy on the part of Friends, who for the most part consented to paying general taxes as in peacetime. They had failed, in his view, to think through consistently the full implications of their pacifism; he attributed this failure in large part to the influence of certain weighty Friends, who had advised compliance. A highly respected Wilburite elder told Maule: "I have not yet felt at liberty to withhold the just dues of government on account of a portion being woven in with it that I do not approve of." But it was just this view that Maule contested; he tried to disentangle in the case of his own tax returns the portion that was destined for war purposes. He did not, it is true, feel that he could hold back the money which he gave the government in the form of various trading licenses and purchase taxes levied in connection with his business, since it was impossible to determine what percentage of the whole was allocated to war. But at the end of 1861 we do find Maule going down to the county treasurer's office and, when handing in his total tax payment, deducting from it the 8½%, "which was the part expressly named in the tax list as for the war," and explaining at the same time the reasons for his somewhat unusual behavior. A few weeks later some pieces of his property were distrained in lieu of the unpaid amount. "And so what appeared at the first like a mountain of difficulty has passed comfortably away," Maule recorded.

In the following year he followed the same procedure; this time the county treasurer accepted Maule's explanations, telling him, "I have known you well; you are a consistent man: I will take your tax as you desire." True, in the remaining years of war Maule did not get off quite so easily, since he notes that distraint was made on his goods on these occasions. But his standpoint appears to have found more understanding among the tax-gatherers than in the circle of his own brethren, who may, indeed, have found his accusations of complicity in bloodshed a little trying. A few Quakers in Maule's area followed the same policy of not paying taxes "in the mixture," and there were others elsewhere; but the overwhelming majority saw no inconsistency between pacifism and payment.[94]

It was quite a different matter, however, with the special war taxes

[94] Maule, *Transactions and Changes in the Society of Friends*, pp. 220-24, 233-46, 251, 261-65, 271, 282-85, 299, 315. See Wright, pp. 46, 47.

of the period and the semi-voluntary contributions to the county fund for subsidizing recruits, where in each case the object was solely the more efficacious prosecution of hostilities, which was therefore objectionable to the spirit, if not also to the letter, of the Quaker discipline. As a Hicksite Friend from Duchess County (N.Y.) wrote of county taxes: "What a man does by the hand of another, he does himself."[95] Bounty money appeared in the eyes of Friends as being more tainted with blood than other special war taxes, since it was used to hire men for war rather than to provide only the indirect means for waging war. Although there were differences in practice (once again Baltimore [Hicksite] Yearly Meeting proved more accommodating to variation in opinion then did some other yearly meetings), the records show many Friends undergoing distraint of their property for nonpayment of such levies. "The object of refusing to pay a specific war tax," stated a special committee set up by the New York (Orthodox) Yearly Meeting to consider the whole question, "is to bear our testimony against war, and not to embarrass government, nor to avoid our share of the public burdens which can be paid without violating our religious principles."[96] Those Friends whose high regard for the rights of government ("the best civil government, as we believe, that has ever been established among men," in the words of Baltimore [Hicksite] Yearly Meeting)—or, perhaps, whose disinclination to face the economic disadvantages of defying the law—overrode their religious scruples against payment do not appear to have been called to account in any way by their meetings. This situation led to complaints in some quarters about the unfairness of penalizing, even to the point of disownment, young and inexperienced members who had risked their lives as soldiers in their country's service, while older and more mature Friends who had likewise transgressed, by complying with the state's demands in the way of bounties and special war taxation and sometimes also, as we know, by purchasing government bonds whose only object was the financing of the war, continued to sit unscathed on the elders' benches.

It is interesting to note that the question of paper currency, which had played so large a role at the time of the American Revolution in Friends' thinking on the wartime implications of their pacifism and had stirred up so much dissension within the Society, did not become an issue during the Civil War. Even a tax radical like the Conservative Joshua Maule did not see anything wrong in handling paper money, although apparently some of his Quaker opponents, in their efforts to show that Maule himself was not altogether consistent in his testi-

[95] *Friends' Intelligencer*, 17 June 1865.
[96] Wright, pp. 44, 183, 184, 186, 196, 197, 211.

mony for peace, did urge that notes were in part utilized by the government to finance the war.[97] Both Maule and his adversaries were obviously acquainted with the earlier controversy among Friends on the question, but paper money had by this date become firmly entrenched in public life. And, most important of all, the legitimacy of the issuing government was in no way in doubt now among Quakers, as it had been in the case of the Revolutionary authorities.

The Quaker civilian in the Northern states, if he aimed at giving consistent expression to his Society's stand against war, confronted some difficult problems of inner conscience. But his life on the whole continued in its accustomed way. His material prosperity was untouched, apart possibly from some losses from the distraint of goods taken for nonpayment of war taxes. He belonged to a religious denomination which, if it was still considered by some to be rather eccentric, yet enjoyed widespread respect among all sections of the population, from the administration in Washington downward. The loyalty of Quakers to the Union and their long and devoted antislavery record protected them on the whole from suspicion of sympathy with the enemy. They were not subject to the bitter hostility and even violence that some pacifist groups have experienced in time of war, before and since. And even those young men, like Cyrus Pringle, who had to witness to their pacifism in army camps and barracks often met with unexpected consideration and courtesy from officers and men alike. Some of them did, of course, become the victims of harsh and cruel treatment, but this was of short duration and was the result, not of official policy, but of the actions of some local military bully.

III

We must now turn our attention to the wartime experience of the considerably smaller group of Quakers whose homes were in the Confederate states. Friends were still to be found in Virginia, although the Virginia yearly meeting had been "laid down" in 1844 as a result of the large-scale migration of members to the West: only five monthly meetings now remained within the borders of the Old Commonwealth. Most Southern Quakers were to be found in North Carolina, which had its own yearly meeting of about 2,000 members,[98] where Friends were concentrated in the central and northwestern parts of the state and in a few small meetings in the east. The Quaker groups in Georgia

---

[97] Maule, *Transactions and Changes*, p. 250.

[98] *An Account of the Sufferings of Friends of North Carolina Yearly Meeting,* . . . *1861-1865*, p. 6. This Y. M. had also diminished greatly in numbers over the preceding decades as a result of emigration of its members to the West.

were extinct by this date, but three monthly meetings continued to exist in eastern Tennessee. Southern Quakers, like their Northern brethren, were opposed to slavery and strongly attached to the Union—yet in a land that was fighting to maintain its peculiar institution of slavery in independence of the Union. These circumstances, added to the fact that the Society here was numerically weak and comparatively little known in the community at large, account for the harsher treatment meted out to many Southern Quakers who refused to bear arms for the Confederacy and for the hardships suffered by a number of Friends who were not liable themselves for military service.

The contrast between the situation created by the antisecessionist, antislavery, and pacifist sentiments of Southern Friends and the mild hostility with which, at worst, Quakers in the North were sometimes confronted was brought out very well by North Carolina Yearly Meeting when Quakers there wrote in their records: "Unlike our Friends in the Northern States, it was not on the few that the trial came, but on the many, and in another more important respect our position differed widely from them. In our own case, the existing government and the officers were far from having sympathy with us."[99]

During the first year of war, however, Southern Friends received comparatively mild treatment despite their declared opposition to the war. On 1 July 1861 the Meeting for Sufferings of North Carolina Yearly Meeting approved a statement drawn up by a subcommittee specially appointed for that purpose, setting forth the Quaker position; "it was directed that each of the monthly meetings be furnished with a copy." Petitions were also prepared for dispatch to the two contending governments, earnestly begging them to make peace. The yearly meeting, when it assembled in the fall, followed the earlier example of Virginia Half-Year's Meeting in reiterating its old objection to paying commutation fines in lieu of military service, while at the same time expressing willingness to pay ordinary taxes and to do all possible to relieve war sufferers "(soldiers as well as others)." Several monthly meetings in Virginia likewise drew up declarations of their pacifist faith for the information of outsiders and the edification of their own members. The Goose Creek Monthly Meeting stated: "In as much as a state of war, now unhappily exists in this country, we deem it our religious duty to take no part in it; and to abstain from every act that would give aid in its prosecution." If members of the meeting were ordered to perform any duty that ran contrary to their conscience, "our principles and clear sense of religious duty would forbid our active compliance, even though there was connected therewith the

[99] Quoted in Fernando G. Cartland, *Southern Heroes*, pp. 125, 126.

heaviest penalty." They would, however, suffer the consequences of disobeying the law passively and would under no circumstances attempt any kind of active opposition to the government, for that would be entirely repugnant to their conscience.[100]

Half-Year's Meeting in Virginia, as a result of hostile comments in some local papers to the effect that the record of Quakers in the North proved all Friends to be radical abolitionists in their sympathies, also felt it incumbent upon themselves to publicly disclaim such insinuations. They pointed out, first, that Quakers wherever they were to be found were noncombatants on principle. If some young Friends had joined the Union army—just as a few had joined the Confederate forces —they had thereby separated themselves from the rest of the Society. In the second place, referring to the militant abolitionist group known as Antislavery Friends, they stated: "We here take occasion to say that several years ago some of our members in the West withdrew from their connection with us because the body of the Society *would not* unite with them in taking an active part in the Abolition movements of that day." They had no connection with this group, they said, and could not be held responsible for its actions.[101]

While making sure so far as they could by means of public statements that the religious basis of their opposition to war was rendered clear, Friends at the same time busied themselves with lobbying the state legislatures of North Carolina and Virginia, both of which were known to be preparing new military laws. North Carolina passed hers in September 1861, but Virginia not until March 1862, on the eve of the introduction of Confederate conscription. In each case, religious objectors were exempted on payment of a commutation fee, which was not, of course, acceptable to many Friends. North Carolina did not at first specify the sum required but eventually, in the early summer of 1862, set it at $100. Virginia demanded the much higher figure of $500 plus 2% of the value of the applicant's taxable property.[102]

[100] Wright, pp. 92-93, 97.

[101] *Encyclopedia of American Quaker Genealogy*, VI: *Virginia*, W. W. Hinshaw *et al.* (eds.), 48.

[102] Wright, pp. 93-99. An attempt made in December 1861 to push an act through the North Carolina legislature making it obligatory on every free male over the age of 16 to renounce his allegiance to the United States government and to assert his readiness to defend the Confederate States—on pain of banishment in case of refusal—was unsuccessful. Friends were active in lobbying against the bill. And the state governor, William Graham, himself opposed its passage, declaring in the course of his speech (cited in Wright, p. 146): "This ordinance wholly disregards their [the Quakers'] peculiar belief, and converts every man of them into a warrior or an exile. . . . This ordinance, therefore, is nothing less than a decree of banishment to them. . . . From the expulsion from among us of such a people, the civilized world would cry, shame!"

Some Friends were drafted during this early period of the war, but their release from service was obtained without too much difficulty. A number of Quakers of military age decided to escape across the lines to the Union side. A few were captured and brought back; others were successful in the attempt. Thus, we find an entry dated 7 March 1866, in the Minute Book of Hopewell Monthly Meeting near Winchester (Va.), recording: "The first summer of the war a few of our young men were forced out in the Militia, and placed to work on fortifications, but through the favor of a kind Providence were soon enabled to obtain their enlargement and escaped as refugees into the loyal states."[103]

The coming of Confederate conscription in 1862 made the situation considerably more serious for the Quakers. Now, in addition to their own state legislatures, to many of whose members their pacifist principles were fairly well known,[104] they had to deal with the Confederate Congress and administration, made up for the most part of men for whom the word "Quaker," if known at all, was a symbol of disloyalty to all that the South stood for. There were exceptions, of course: Friends were lucky to find a sympathetic ear and genuine understanding in no less a person, for instance, than the assistant secretary of war, Judge John A. Campbell. After the war was over, while Judge Campbell was in prison for his association with the defeated government, the Meeting for Sufferings of North Carolina Yearly Meeting petitioned the Federal government on his behalf, citing as part of the evidence in his favor the kindness and help the Quakers had received from him during the war.[105]

The first measure of Confederate conscription was passed on 16 April 1862. Although substitutes might be furnished in place of personal service in the army, conscientious objection was not provided for, and the position of Friends and the other peace sects seemed precarious. After some preparatory work, including the presentation of a memorial to the Confederate Congress asking for unconditional exemption for Friends, a delegation consisting of four leading members of North Carolina Yearly Meeting and John B. Crenshaw from Virginia was appointed in August to intervene personally in the Confederate capital of Rich-

[103] *Ibid.*, p. 173. Hopewell M. M. belonged directly to Baltimore Y. M. and did not form part of the Half-Year's Meeting of Virginia. See also *An Account of the Sufferings*, p. 7.

[104] E.g., Jonathan Worth, state senator, later treasurer, and then governor of North Carolina, was of Nantucket Quaker ancestry and genuinely anxious to avoid anything in the nature of a persecution of Friends on account of their pacifism. We frequently find him interceding on their behalf. See Wright, pp. 100, 146-48; Cartland, *Southern Heroes*, pp. 144-46.

[105] Wright, pp. 138-42.

mond. Jefferson Davis, whom they succeeded in seeing, was courteous but noncommittal. They also stated their case before the military committee of Congress, prefacing the presentation of their evidence by several minutes of silence after the manner of an informal Quaker meeting—much to the astonishment of the congressmen present. One of them later in the proceedings asked the Quaker minister, Isham Cox: "Doubtless your people are in the Northern army fighting us, and why should you not join us in fighting them?" To which Cox at once replied: "I am not afraid to agree to fight, single handed, every true Friend in the Northern army."[106] As a result of such efforts, as well as those of the Mennonite and Brethren congregations with whom Southern Quakers cooperated fairly closely in working for exemption, the draft law of 11 October 1862 contained a clause excusing all who were at that date members of these three peace sects (or of the "Nazarenes," a name which hides the identity of the Christadelphians) from the performance of military duties on payment of the sum of $500.

The exemption granted in the act proved satisfactory to the Mennonites and Dunkers, but it fell short of the unconditional status that the Quakers had requested. At their yearly meeting held at the beginning of November, North Carolina Friends expressed in the following minute a mixture both of disappointment and of gratitude for goodwill shown:

> We have had the subject under serious consideration, and while in accordance with our last yearly meeting we do pay all taxes imposed on us as citizens and property-holders in common with other citizens, remembering the injunction, "tribute to whom tribute is due, custom to whom custom," yet we cannot conscientiously pay the specified tax, it being imposed upon us on account of our principles, as the price exacted of us for religious liberty. Yet we do appreciate the good intentions of those members of Congress who had it in their hearts to do something for our relief; and we recommend that those parents who, moved by sympathy, or those young men, who dreading the evils of a military camp, have availed themselves of this law, shall be treated in a tender manner by their monthly meetings.

Nevertheless, despite the fact that Friends had once again come out publicly against paying commutation, many Quakers—as had been envisaged—did, in fact, avail themselves of their statutory right to exemption set down in the act of October 1862, a privilege which remained in force until the end of the war. (By that time, wartime inflation had so depreciated the real value of the Confederate currency

106 *Ibid.*, pp. 100-102; Cartland, *Southern Heroes*, pp. 125-28.

that the commutation fine of $500 had ceased to be much of a financial burden.) North Carolina Yearly Meeting instructed the clerks of its constituent monthly meetings, in conjunction with committees specially appointed for that purpose, to provide applicants for exemption with the certificates of membership that the authorities required. "By this action," says Wright, "the Yearly Meeting definitely allowed its members to avail themselves of the exemption privilege if they could conscientiously do so."[107] A similar position, if anything a little more compliant, was taken up by Half-Year's Meeting in Virginia. In a memorial, dated 5 October 1863 and addressed to the state legislature, they stated that, since in wartime no legal machinery existed for distraint on the property of those who refused commutation, Friends were paying the fines "under protest," regarding this as in line with Christ's injunction when he "directed the tribute money to be paid—That we offend them not.' "[108] The explanation is a little disingenuous: undoubtedly, the very considerable pressure to which Southern Friends were subjected made it much harder for them than for Quakers in the North to take up an uncompromisingly absolutist stand. The more yielding attitude of Virginia Friends perhaps explains why their sufferings were less than those of their brethren in North Carolina.

The position of the Quakers and the other peace sects in the South remained uncertain right up to the day when the surrender of Appomattox brought the conflict to a close. Not merely were there periodic threats to abolish the exemption granted conscientious objectors, but, with the widening of the age of those liable for the federal draft, the net of conscription encompassed an ever larger number of men. In mid-1862 the age limits were set at 18 to 35, but the upper limit was raised in 1863 to 45. In 1864 all men between 17 and 50 became liable, and in the last few weeks of the war a further extension of the age limits was about to come into force. Friends, therefore, lived in a continual state of crisis, and it often became necessary for their representative bodies to petition or memorialize either the Confederate Congress or the state legislatures of North Carolina and Virginia in defense of their pacifist position.

Leading Friends were active, too, in visiting prominent government and state officials. The name of John Bacon Crenshaw (1820-1889), a Quaker minister in Richmond (Va.), constantly occurs in this connection in the documents of the time. He was on friendly terms with Judge John A. Campbell, and his residence in the Confederate capital made

[107] Wright, pp. 104-10.
[108] *Memorial to Legislature of Virginia*, p. 2. The *Memorial* was reprinted in part in S. F. Sanger and D. Hays, *The Olive Branch*, pp. 229-31.

it easier for him to maintain contacts in government circles than it was for the more distant meetings in North Carolina. Crenshaw was immensely energetic—not only in lobbying government and legislature but in working for the release of drafted conscientious objectors, both Quaker and non-Quakers, from prisons and army camps and in raising money to pay the fines of those willing to accept commutation. He helped, too, in the relief of sick and wounded soldiers of both sides and in work for Northern prisoners of war. And, finally, he was able to promote a fair degree of cooperation between his own Friends and the Mennonites and Dunkers (not so simple an undertaking as it might sound).[109] Among the North Carolina Quakers the most outstanding personality at this time was the well-known educationalist, Nereus Mendenhall. Of Mendenhall's fearless advocacy of Quaker pacifism it has been said: "He did not hesitate to maintain the principles which it professed, on the street, in the railway trains, anywhere and everywhere he would show the incompatibility of all war with the spirit and teaching of Christ."[110]

We must now turn to the experiences of those Friends who were drafted after the introduction of Confederate conscription in 1862. A few young men from the meetings had volunteered for service, but a considerably smaller proportion than in the North since, quite apart from the question of pacifism, the Confederate cause had little appeal for those reared in the staunchly antislavery atmosphere of the Society. We read, too, of one Friend—Isaac Harvey of New Garden Monthly Meeting in North Carolina—who, upon being drafted and after resisting service for several weeks, yielded and agreed to bear arms. As soon as his meeting heard what he had done, it took steps to disown him.[111] All those who served voluntarily in a combatant capacity were naturally disowned by their meetings, also.[112] A number of young men of military age continued to escape to the North in order to avoid conscription. Others hid for a time in the forests; sometimes, local home guards hunting for the escapees would torture their parents in an effort to get them to reveal their sons' whereabouts. These draft dodgers for conscience' sake were, of course, but a small proportion of those potential conscripts who, either by hiding in the woods or by fleeing

[109] Margaret E. Crenshaw, "John Bacon Crenshaw" in *Quaker Biographies*, 2nd ser., III, 173-85. See also Wright, pp. 199-202.

[110] Quoted in Wright, p. 203.

[111] Cartland, *Southern Heroes*, p. 223.

[112] Wright, pp. 187, 188. Disciplinary action was also taken against any who furnished a substitute. We hear in 1865 of a Friend being "eldered" for hiring an armed guard to watch his property; after being dealt with, he acknowledged his conduct "to be inconsistent" with Quaker principles.

westward or northward, were attempting to escape fighting in a cause which, for one reason or another, they did not feel to be theirs.

Some who tried to escape were captured before they succeeded in crossing into Northern territory, like the Quaker brothers from North Carolina, Mahlon and Joshua Kemp. They were placed in the army and were present in December 1862 at the battle of Fredericksburg, where they consented to look after the wounded, helping to remove them from the battlefield at the risk of their lives. Perhaps as a result of the courage they displayed in action, the Kemps were released shortly afterward on paying the $500 commutation. We read of another young Quaker from the same state, William Woody, entering the army when called up, accepting a gun (although with the firm intention of never using it), and then taking the first opportunity to desert to the enemy. After arriving in Union territory, he made his way to Indiana without further mishap.[113]

Among those Quaker conscientious objectors who successfully made the journey across the lines was 18-year-old A. Marshall Elliott (1846-1910), who was later to become a professor of Romance languages at Johns Hopkins University and a prominent scholar in that field. Elliott's father was a Quaker farmer in North Carolina. In the summer of 1862, finding that the authorities would not recognize the conscientious objection to fighting which he had learned in his home and suffering from bad health, which made his position additionally precarious, the boy decided to escape to the North. Quaker neighbors helped conceal him and smuggle him across the boundary. "Once over it," he wrote later, "my next object was to make all possible speed for the headquarters of the Federal Army stationed then at Suffolk, Va. General Mansfield was at this time in command of the department of East Virginia, and through his kindness I was furnished with an escort of two soldiers to Baltimore and with a free passport to Philadelphia." The remainder of the war he spent as a student at Haverford College.[114]

Among the small group of Friends still remaining in the eastern part of Tennessee, those who were unwilling or unable to pay the commutation fine hid themselves in a large cave, the entrance to which was concealed from sight by thick undergrowth. Leading members of the local Quaker community, who were not liable themselves to military service, acted as contacts with the outer world and helped keep the men supplied with food and drink.[115] Most Friends, however, remained

---

113 Cartland, *Southern Heroes*, pp. 225-27.
114 George C. Keidel, *The Early Life of Professor Elliott.*
115 Cartland, *Southern Heroes*, chap. XV.

at home and awaited whatever might befall them at the hands of the authorities. In North Carolina some accepted employment in a reserved occupation, such as the state salt works; "not a few" of these, however, records the official account of North Carolina Friends' wartime experiences, "finding their work too closely connected with war, relinquished it."[116]

As mentioned above, many Friends were prepared to pay the commutation fine of $500, which was acceptable to the meetings. After the Confederate Congress had passed this exemption, there remained three groups of Friends (or near Friends) who found themselves in difficulties with the military authorities and in many cases suffered severe hardship, sometimes becoming the victims of considerable brutality.

There were, in the first place, some Quakers who were drafted into the army "under irregular proceedings" (to use the phrase in North Carolina Yearly Meeting's official account).[117] These were men who were legally entitled to exemption and willing to take advantage of it but who had been refused their rights by the local military authorities. Usually the matter was corrected in a fairly short time: both John B. Crenshaw and leading Friends in North Carolina were active in intervening on behalf of such men. Wright cites the case of three Quakers—Nere and Seth Cox and Eli Macon—who appealed to the sympathetic and influential non-Quaker Jonathan Worth for help, writing to him rather quaintly as follows: "There is three in Camp Holmes members of the society of Friends and we want thee to come over immediately on receiving these lines in order to pay our exemption tax and let us go home. If thee cannot furnish us with the money we want thee to come and see us any how."[118]

More serious was the position of the second group: those who had joined the Society only after 11 October 1862, thereby being excluded from the provisions of the act's exemption clause, and sympathizers with Quakerism who were not actual members of the Society. Many of those who eventually escaped from the Confederate states belonged to this category. About 600 persons (including the womenfolk and children) were admitted into membership during the course of the war. The pacifism of the Quakers was undoubtedly one of the tenets which attracted many of the new members (as it was in the wars of this century); for the suspicions of some government officials that the So-

---

[116] *An Account of the Sufferings*, p. 9. The state authorities were favorably inclined toward employment in the salt works as a recognized form of alternative service for Quaker objectors. But the yearly meeting rejected the idea when it was proposed. See Wright, p. 100.

[117] *An Account of the Sufferings*, p. 8.

[118] Wright, p. 146.

ciety was gaining recruits from political malcontents or physical cowards, however, there was no evidence. The hardships that some of these men had to bear as a result of their antiwar stand indicates rather the reverse. In addition, some in this group had been brought up in a Quaker environment; for one reason or another, however, usually because only one parent had been a Friend, they had not become birthright members of the Society and were therefore in the position of the much larger group of young Mennonites and Brethren, whose churches only accepted their young people into membership after reaching adult life. Most of these men were willing to pay the commutation fine if given the opportunity to do so.

Cartland in his *Southern Heroes* gives many instances of harsh and repeated punishment being meted out to these men while under military command.[119] Prolonged periods of "bucking down" were frequently imposed in the attempt to subdue their spirit (as it was with other recalcitrant soldiers) and to force them to accept combatant service. Cartland describes this punishment as follows:

> The man who is condemned to this trying ordeal is made to sit down on the ground; his wrists are firmly bound together by strong cord or withes; drawing up the knees his arms are pressed over them until a stout stick can be thrust over the elbows, under the knees, and thus the man's feet and hands are rendered useless for the time being.

Other cruelties inflicted included piercing repeatedly with a bayonet, hanging up by the thumbs, beatings and kickings, gagging with an open bayonet, deprivation of sleep, long periods on a bread and water diet, incarceration in filthy cells, and deprivation of means of washing. Frequently, the men were threatened with shooting or hanging. (Gideon Macon was about to be strung up on a tree when the regiment to which he had been assigned was forced to beat a hasty retreat by the advancing Northern army, and Seth Loflin would have been shot, following a court-martial sentence, had not the twelve men in the firing squad, overcome by his calm courage, refused to carry out the sentence and thus given time for it to be reconsidered.) In many cases, with their rifles forcibly strapped to their backs, they were compelled to accompany the army on active service, their position becoming increasingly precarious as they were brought into contact with the actual fighting.

Yet none were in fact executed (although several died from illness

119 See, e.g., pp. 181-94, 201-11, 222, 376-79. See also Wright, pp. 116-20; *An Account of the Sufferings*, pp. 10-18.

induced by their previous sufferings). Moreover, ill-treatment was usually the result of excessive zeal on the part of junior officers and not of orders from the higher command. There were sometimes abuse and rough usage at first from the ordinary soldiers; many, however, showed sympathy and appreciation of the men's courage and endurance and a growing awareness of the depths of conviction from which their resistance derived. "Taking all things into consideration," Wright remarks judiciously, "it is apparent that the cases of excessive severity in the South were the exception rather than the rule."[120]

Those who remained adamant in rejecting commutation were sometimes kept in army camp or army prison for several years, being released only as a result of the final collapse of the Confederate war effort. The refusal of these absolutists to compromise by undertaking any, even seemingly unobjectionable, duties done under military orders—cooking or orderly chores or carrying officers' baggage, for instance—brought added punishment. "We are in the entrenchments near Petersburg, in Company F. 27th regiment," Seth W. Loflin and J. A. Hill wrote home in September 1864 on behalf of nearly a dozen young men from Marlboro and Springfield Monthly Meetings in Randolph County (N.C.). "We have thus far refused to take any part in military duty, for which we are receiving severe punishment. . . . They say we must suffer until we drill. We still expect, by the Grace of God, and the help of your prayers, to be faithful to our profession." One of those who maintained a rigidly unconditionalist stand after being forced into the army was the 18-year-old potter's apprentice, Tilghman Ross Vestal, from near Columbia, Tennessee. A high-ranking Confederate officer, who knew him in camp, wrote later of this "remarkable boy": "He refused . . . to do the least thing that could be tortured or construed into military duty." When Vestal, who was not yet himself a member of the Society but whose mother, a Quaker, had brought him up in that persuasion, learned that the North Carolina Yearly Meeting, to which his mother belonged, did not disapprove of those in his situation taking advantage of the legal exemption, he agreed to allow Friends to petition President Davis on his behalf for permission to pay the commutation tax. As a result of their intervention, the boy was finally released from prison, after enduring many months of almost continuous ill-treatment.[121]

[120] Wright, p. 179.

[121] *Ibid.*, pp. 142-44; Cartland, *Southern Heroes*, chap. XVI. After attempting to prove Vestal wrong on the basis of the New Testament in his refusal to fight, former Governor Henry S. Foote of Mississippi was forced to admit: "I believe he knows more about that than I do."

In some instances, the military authorities even allowed unconditionalists to return home eventually. And if a "new" Quaker was willing to gain his release by paying his commutation fee, the Confederate government was usually willing (as in Vestal's case) to stretch a point and grant him in the end the exemption to which he was not entitled according to the exact letter of the law. The same accommodating spirit, as in the cases of men who were brought up in the Quaker environment but were not themselves members or who had recently joined the Society, was not infrequently shown by the Confederate authorities in dealing with those who held Quaker views but were not as closely connected with the Society. We read in John B. Crenshaw's diary, for instance, the following entry for 18 October 1862: "Put in a petition for Jesse Gordon, who professes to be a Friend in principle. The Secretary of War agreed to pass him as a Friend, much to our relief." Or again, for 7 February 1863: "Interceded for M. H. Bradshaw, not a Friend. Secretary of War agreed to pass him as a Friend. I paid the tax and brought him home with me."[122] Another case that may be cited at this point is that of "J. G.," a North Carolina man, who was a Methodist when fighting broke out, although he held Quaker views on war. Not eligible for exemption, he attempted to escape to the West when threatened with the draft in the autumn of 1862 but was arrested and put in an army camp. "Just put away your Quaker notions" if you wish to escape the firing squad, the officers told him when he refused to accept military orders or wear a uniform. Somehow his plight reached the ears of North Carolina Friends, who succeeded in obtaining exemption for him from the authorities in Richmond. Not long after his release, "J. G." was formally accepted into membership of the Society of Friends.[123]

Others in this class, however, had a harder road to travel. Take the story of Jesse Buckner of Chatham County (N.C.), a Baptist and colonel in the local militia at the time of the outbreak of the war. Puzzled to find that no members of the Society of Friends, which he held in respect although he had only a very passing acquaintance with its doctrines, had joined up, he was led on from discovering that they objected to war on principle to ponder the matter more deeply in his own mind. By the autumn of 1861 he had become convinced of the incompatibility of war with the Christian religion, and he resigned his commission in the militia. His troubles began when he was drafted in the following March and only ended with the Confederate surrender. Although he finally joined Friends in the spring of 1863, he still

[122] Cartland, *Southern Heroes*, pp. 353, 355.
[123] *Ibid.*, pp. 150-52.

had to face several lengthy spells in army camps, where he was subjected to almost continuous ridicule, threats, and harsh treatment in an attempt to break his spirit.[124]

Perhaps the strangest story of all is that of Rufus P. King (1843-1923), an illiterate North Carolina country boy, who was conscripted into the Confederate army early in 1862. His natural religious bent, strengthened by the experience of "conversion" which he underwent at a Methodist revivalist meeting during a furlough, had produced in him a strong repugnance to the idea of shedding blood. He had had no contact with Quakers, nor was he in touch, apparently, with any others holding pacifist views. Yet he determined, whatever the consequences, not to be instrumental in taking life. A seemingly chance assignment to work with the ambulance corps King saw as an answer to his prayers. Later he was present at the battle of Gettysburg, acting as a stretcher-bearer; during the subsequent retreat he was taken prisoner by the Union forces. After a year in Point Lookout prison, he was returned to the South as a result of an exchange of prisoners between the two sides. Called back into the army, King succeeded in deserting to the North and was able to make his way finally to Indiana. Here it was that he first became acquainted with Friends, who helped him get an education. He joined the Society in 1865 and returned thirteen years later to North Carolina, where his natural gifts brought him leadership in the Society's work and counsels.[125]

The third group of Quaker conscripts in the South who had to suffer severe hardship on account of their conscientious objector stand—probably the least numerous of the three, although no exact figures are available—were the men who, although members of the Society prior to the passing of the act of 11 October 1862 and, therefore, fully eligible for the exemption then granted, refused to avail themselves of this on the grounds of the traditional Quaker objection to accepting any alternative in exchange for permission to do what they believed was right. We have seen that at least the higher civil and military authorities were not anxious, if some way out could be devised, to add to their problems by having on their hands men who, it became increasingly obvious, would never make fighting material. We have seen, too, that Friends in both North Carolina and Virginia, while acknowledging it to be to some extent a compromise of their principles, were prepared *faute de mieux* to sanction the payment of commutation money by drafted members, if they were conscientiously able to pay.

[124] *Ibid.*, pp. 146-50; Wright, pp. 175, 176.
[125] Emma King, "Rufus P. King" in *Quaker Biographies*, 2nd ser., II, esp. 177-82; Cartland, *Southern Heroes*, pp. 290-98.

There were still, however, not a few who felt called to testify to the full Quaker witness for peace. For them, the position was hard indeed, for there was no legal machinery through which they could be released from liability for military service. In theory, therefore, they might find themselves under army command and driven from army camp to army camp, and even into the battle zone, until defeat brought about the dissolution of the Confederate armies. In practice, however, this situation rarely occurred: more often, means were found in the end to furlough an individual of this kind, if no other opportunity of ridding the army of him had occurred earlier.

The best known instance among the Southern Friends of this type of Quaker absolutist is that of the three Hockett brothers from Center Meeting near Greensboro in Guilford County (N.C.): William, Himelius, and Jesse. Himelius and Jesse were called up first, in April 1862. The provost marshal used the fact that a fellow Quaker, who had been drafted with them, had consented to pay the commutation tax, in order to persuade the two brothers to follow his example. They could, however, point to their yearly meeting's minutes of the previous year, a copy of which Himelius had luckily brought with him, to show that their own position was the official one of the Society. There ensued for the brothers over six months of continuous pressure to get them to obey military orders, including hanging by the thumbs, pricking with a bayonet, and nearly five days without food or drink, which they stubbornly resisted. Himelius was confined for a while in a military fortress with a heavy ball and chain attached to his legs. Of his prison he wrote in the journal he kept: "Notwithstanding its gloomy appearance, it seemed to me as a secret hiding-place, and my chains as jewels, for they were taken as an evidence of my suffering for Christ's sake." Their release, when it came, was the work of another Quaker, who paid the commutation on their behalf, but without their knowledge or consent.

Their brother William had had his call-up deferred by the military authorities from the fall of 1862 until June of the following year. Refusing to pay commutation, he was placed with the 21st North Carolina regiment and sent to join it near the battle front in northern Virginia. The nearness of the front line made his position extremely dangerous, since he refused both to wear army uniform and to drill or perform any tasks when ordered. As he wrote in the journal which he kept, comparing his present position with that of Shadrach, Meschach, and Abednego in the fiery furnace or Daniel's in the lions' den: "The army is a very trying place for a Christian to be in, because there are so many things that we cannot for conscience' sake do that must be

done if the war goes on. So we are constantly beset on every side."
During his sojourn in the army William experienced both kindness and
sympathy from the ordinary soldiers and considerable cruelty from
some of the officers, who were angered by his refusal to carry out orders
and to perform any kind of work. With his gun forcibly strapped on
to his back, he spent what leisure time was allowed him reading his
Bible. In July 1863 William was taken prisoner by the Union forces,
and, freed eventually from captivity by the ending of hostilities, he
made his way back to his home in North Carolina.[126]

The Quaker absolutists of the South and the new and near Quakers
were the ones who had had to bear the most heavy burden in witnessing to Quaker pacifism in time of war. All Friends in that sector who
were of military age had had to face difficult decisions, if not actual
suffering. As in the North the war had brought its special problems,
too, for those Southern Quakers who on account of age, sex, or sickness
were not liable for military service; in addition, many suffered considerable material losses, which their Northern brethren were spared. The
question of whether Friends should pay special war taxes bothered
Friends in the Confederate as well as in the Union states. In the summer of 1863, for instance, when a "tax in kind" was imposed to help
subsidize the war effort, the North Carolina Meeting for Sufferings reported that, in the past,

> Friends have not felt at liberty to pay such taxes. Such we think
> should be the case with the demand for the tenth part of the pro-
> duce of our lands. We believe that this is designed for the direct
> support of the army. It is strictly a *war measure.* Hence believing
> as we do that all wars are contrary to the Spirit of the Gospel of our
> Lord and Savior Jesus Christ, and that by the payment of this tithe,
> we are directly aiding to prolong these evils; it is the sense and judg-
> ment of this meeting that we cannot consistently pay said tithe.[127]

That all Friends were prepared to incur the heavy losses through distraint of their property which would probably have resulted from not
paying the tithe is unlikely. But some undoubtedly there were who
chose this way of bearing a clear witness to the Quaker peace
testimony.

The Quaker communities, along with the rest of the civilian population, suffered severe damage to their property from the depredations
of occupying Northern troops whenever they visited the area. Their
treatment by the Confederate military was often just as bad, and some-

---

[126] Cartland, *Southern Heroes*, chaps. XII, XIII; *An Account of the Sufferings,*
pp. 19-22; Wright, pp. 177-79.
[127] Wright, pp. 110, 111.

times even worse.[128] Some older Friends were arrested on suspicion (not unfounded, though hardly deserving such treatment) of being pro-Unionist in sympathies and were kept in confinement for periods from a few days to two years and over. A number of Friends were active in helping men of military age, whether pacifists or non-pacifist opponents of the Confederate war effort, to escape over the lines into Northern territory. If caught aiding such runaways, they were liable to be severely punished.

Thus the war years were in many ways even more of a testing time for Southern Friends than for those living in the Northern states. Nevertheless, if the physical hardships Quakers in the South had to endure were considerably more severe than in the North, the refusal to fight on behalf of a government that had implanted the maintenance of slavery and the destruction of the Union in the center of its war aims, on the other hand, caused less soul-searching and mental stress. The main dilemma faced by Friends in the North had been to reconcile their peace testimony with their equally strong desire to see the whole country rid of slavery. A few years after Appomattox, a Northern Quaker minister then traveling in the South, who was later to become the first historian of the Southern Quakers' wartime experiences, felt a sudden surge of emotion when he saw the Stars and Stripes flying in a small North Carolina town. His feelings would have been shared by most Friends on both sides of the former battle lines. The sight of the national flag, he wrote,

. . . filled his soul with feelings of patriotism such as a peace-loving Friend might safely indulge. There, in the heart of the land which had been so recently under the Confederate government and so long the land of slavery, the writer bowed before the God of all grace and thanked Him that the struggle was ended; that slavery . . . was a thing of the past; and that the dear old flag could once more be unfurled in . . . the Southland, and be recognized as the flag of "Our Country."[129]

[128] See An Account of the Sufferings, p. 25, for details on the material losses suffered during the war by Friends in North Carolina.
[129] Cartland, Southern Heroes, pp. 176, 177.

Chapter 7

●●

The Quaker Peace Testimony,
1865-1914

Almost half a century elapsed between Appomattox and the firing of
the guns of August 1914. Although the war in Europe appeared to have
its roots in events remote from the North American continent, it involved the United States as an active combatant within three years of
its outbreak. The First World War ultimately proved to be a landmark in American history, almost as much as it did in the history of the
rest of the world. Within the narrower limits of the peace movement,
too, we find that 1914 marked for both its pacifist and nonpacifist
wings a turning point; the war years saw the creation of a new movement which was to evolve new ideas and new techniques of action
in response to a vastly changed situation.

Yet the pacifism of the post-1914 period was, for all the differences
that clearly existed between the two periods, embedded in the past.
The half-century which preceded 1914 is particularly significant, because it was during these years that the changes that eventually produced these new ideas and new techniques were taking place within
the whole movement. But when we come to consider the story of
absolute pacifism (which is the particular theme of the full version
of this book) during this period, it is difficult to avoid a certain
sense of frustration. Pacifism appears to have been at a standstill: older
groups, like the Society of Friends or the German-speaking sects
(which were becoming increasingly English-speaking), seemed as a
whole relatively unconcerned with the issue of peace, while new organizations based on a pacifist platform, such as the Universal Peace
Union, were singularly ineffective. No outstanding leader—or even
any person of middling stature—arose to challenge the surrounding
apathy of an age of materialism.

The sources for many aspects of the story are meager—or submerged
in a vast sea of reports and periodical literature dealing primarily with
other topics. The most important elements, we begin to feel, are perhaps to be sought elsewhere: in the social transformation which was
bringing Mennonites and Dunkers and their like out of their rural isolation, in the theological revolution within the American Society of
Friends that was subtly undermining Quaker pacifism in large sections
of the Society, in new ideologies that had as yet little or no contact

with religious pacifism, like international socialism with its ideal of the brotherhood of man or anarchism with its goal of maximum freedom for all human beings. These forces—and others—were at work beneath the surface, but their effect was not to show itself properly until after the events of August 1914 engulfed the nations in war.

During the preceding half-century the Society of Friends remained the most active and concerned element within the pacifist movement. The Society was divided theologically and organizationally, but, despite the inroads that the Civil War had made in the ranks of its younger members in particular, the overwhelming weight of opinion within it still stood solidly behind the traditional Quaker peace testimony. No detailed study has been made of this period in the history of Quaker pacifism, and generalizations based on examination of only part of the evidence can only be provisional.

The Quaker press at this time was for a small denomination fairly large. The Hicksites had their *Friends' Intelligencer*, and from 1873 to 1882 they published, also in Philadelphia, a second periodical entitled the *Journal*. The Orthodox branch was represented as earlier by the Philadelphia *Friend* and the more evangelical *Friends' Review*. This paper merged in 1894 with the *Christian Worker*, founded in 1871 as an organ of the pastoral element which was growing increasingly strong among Friends, to become the *American Friend* under the editorship of the young Rufus M. Jones (1863-1948). In addition, there were other ephemeral and less important periodicals published in the Quaker spirit.

From a perusal of the Quaker press it would seem that, after the turmoil of the Civil War years had begun to subside, the Society's interest in questions of peace and war declined considerably. True, articles on Christian pacifism, as well as interpretations of world events from a Quaker angle and support for the efforts on behalf of international peace being made by the wider peace movement, did appear from time to time. There is rather more space devoted to peace in the Orthodox *Friend* than in the other papers.

A distinct change is noticeable toward the end of the last century and in the early years of the present one—largely owing to the efforts of some outstanding figures in the new generation of Friends then coming to maturity, men like Rufus Jones, Dr. Richard H. Thomas (1854-1904), Elbert Russell (1871-1951), and others. It cannot be said that at this time the Quaker press reflected any striking innovations in the theoretical groundwork of pacifism. But its columns were devoted to peace issues more often than in the previous decades. The discussion was more intelligent, better informed, and, above all, wider in scope; it included more frequent articles on arbitration and the various economic and political aspects of pacifism (in addition to pacifism's strictly religious aspects), as well as protests against the growing militarism and expansionism displayed by the United States.

A second method by which the Quakers continued to express their pacifism was the time-honored one of issuing public statements giving their views on the subject. These were frequently styled "addresses," sometimes "appeals" or "testimonies" or some similar title, and were usually issued in the name of a yearly meeting, which published them in pamphlet or leaflet form. Their contents followed a fairly uniform pattern. In the first place, they restated briefly the Christian case for pacifism, quoting a cloud of witnesses from the history of early Christianity, drawn almost invariably from the writings of Jonathan Dymond. Secondly, these documents usually went on to discuss, from the Quaker viewpoint, a number of topics connected with current affairs. They pleaded both the desirability and the practicability of disarmament, including unilateral disarmament, and preached the folly, even on the material plane, of piling up armaments indefinitely. They called for the adoption by their government of the principle of international arbitration to replace the final arbitrament of war. They protested against various manifestations of the militarist spirit in national life: the activities of the veterans associated with the Grand Army of the Republic, the pomp connected with Memorial Day, the militarization of youth through boys' brigades, and drilling in schools and colleges, etc. During the last two decades or so before 1914, these arguments tended to increase in proportion to the space devoted to discussion of the principles of religious pacifism. However, although the yearly meetings of the various branches of the Society were considerably more busy than the other peace sects in producing peace literature of this kind, it does not appear to have figured with them as a primary concern in comparison with such activities as education, foreign missions and Sunday schools, Indian work, temperance, prison reform, and even, in some quarters, revivalism.

In the postbellum period the main product of organized Quaker activity for peace was the founding in 1867 of the Peace Association of Friends in America. This association resulted from the initiative of a number of Orthodox yearly meetings—Baltimore, Indiana, Ohio, and Western—which were among those that came together eventually to form the strongly evangelical Five Years' Meeting. They were joined a little later as sponsors of the Peace Association by other Orthodox yearly meetings with an evangelical bent, including Iowa, Kansas, New York, and North Carolina. Their war experiences had brought about a revival of Friends' active concern for peace in the immediate postwar period. A rather inward-looking testimony was given a new outreach.[1] That it was the Orthodox branch that took the lead now was understandable, not only because the Hicksites had been more deeply divided on the war issue but because the evangelical sympathies of the Orthodox prompted them to use the new techniques of publicity that had been evolved by the evangelical movement for the furtherance of both their religious and philanthropic aims. That later some of the evangelical yearly meetings of Orthodox origin in the West came very largely to abandon pacifism in actual fact—insofar, that is, as individual members were concerned, and not the official doctrine in the book of discipline—is due to the peculiar developments in religious life in this area. This matter will be dealt with a little later in this chapter.

The Peace Association grew out of two peace conferences initiated by Ohio Yearly Meeting and held at Baltimore in November 1866 and at Richmond (Ind.) in March 1867.[2] Only Orthodox yearly meetings were represented (the delegates formed *ad hoc* peace committees of their respective meetings), although one non-Quaker sympathizer attended the second gathering. At the first conference two problems in particular were wrestled with. The number of Friends, especially in the West, who had abandoned pacifism during the war was evidently worrying concerned members (even if some of the figures for such delinquency were much exaggerated). And so the sponsors of the conference asked delegates to consider in the first place: "In what manner can we promote with the greatest efficiency amongst our own members, a more enlightened understanding of the Gospel of Christ as a gospel of Peace?" For the time being, no more startling recommendation was adopted than the printing and circulation in 20,000 copies among members of the Society of an address on peace, which was drafted by a committee of the conference. The second problem discussed by the gathering centered on methods by which Quaker peace principles could be spread among other denominations, and among the clergy in particular.

The dissemination of Quaker pacifism among non-Quakers was also one of the chief subjects of discussion at the Richmond conference early in the next year. And the methods suggested to achieve that end included writing memorials to Congress urging that body to promote the settlement of international disputes by peaceful means (a congress of nations and an international court were favored by some dele-

[1] See the *Advocate of Peace*, 1867, p. 283, for comments in the American Peace Society's annual report on this renewed peace activity among Quakers.
[2] *American Friend*, I (1867), no. 1, 5-10; no. 4, 88-97.

gates), allocation of money by yearly meetings to finance permanent committees for peace, and collaboration in peace work with "other Christian Professors" (not excluding Unitarians, some delegates thought, while others strongly dissented). Several delegates, it was reported, "spoke of the necessity of being willing to labor and patiently wait the Lord's time for the result, of the slowness of the progress that peace principles could reasonably be expected to make in the world." And, indeed, the time proved premature for the setting up of standing peace committees, which were to be a vital element in twentieth-century Quaker work on behalf of peace. But Charles F. Coffin's remark that "we must keep up a *continuance* of effort" found general agreement among the assembled Friends. And even if all the conference's proposals for further activities did not bear immediate fruit, it was out of this widespread desire not to allow the enthusiasm generated by the two conferences to dissipate without result that the Peace Association of Friends in America was born.

The prime mover in getting the Association started was Daniel Hill of New Vienna (Ohio), who acted as its secretary until his death in 1899.[3] A 4-page explanatory leaflet which Hill issued, probably in the 1880's, had this to say on its origins: "After the close of the late terrible rebellion in this country, the horrors of war were so freshly and vividly brought to light that many Friends were led to believe that the time had fully come for more energetic and persistent efforts to be put forth to try to prevent wars in the future." It defined the Association's objective as the advocacy in a Christian spirit of "the brotherhood of mankind" and of the idea "that we can not injure another without injuring ourselves." The Association believed "that war is unchristian, inhuman and unnecessary" and that it could be banished from human society if men so wished.[4]

At first, at any rate, Hill and his fellow workers were able to achieve a considerable amount in the way of publishing books, pamphlets, and leaflets. But the Association aspired to be more than a tract society, and we find it also organizing a limited number of public meetings and lecture tours by its agents and setting up prizes for essays on peace topics. Beginning in October 1870 there appeared in New Vienna under Hill's editorship the Association's own monthly journal, the *Messenger of Peace*, which continued publication in one form or another until 1943, although in much reduced format during the last three decades

---

[3] His successor was Allen D. Hole, who remained secretary until 1927. Although the Association finally ceased activities only in the 1930's, it had long been superseded in importance by other Quaker bodies concerned with work for peace.

[4] The leaflet is undated and is in the S.C.P.C. The statement quoted appears also in some of the Association's publications.

and more of its existence.[5] Ohio remained the center of the Association's activities as long as Daniel Hill was alive.

Most of the classics of the peace movement of the first half of the century, British and American, were reprinted by the Association, often in abridged form. So we find in their list of publications such staples of the older peace movement as Dr. David Bogue's lecture *On Universal Peace*, Thomas Chalmers's *Thoughts on Universal Peace*, Whelpley's *Letters* to Governor Strong, Sumner's oration on *The True Grandeur of Nations*, Thomas Thrush's *Letter addressed to the King*, the works of Elihu Burritt, as well, of course as the essays of Jonathan Dymond on war and Joseph John Guerney's little tract on the same subject.[6] There were peace pamphlets for children—including stories from the pen of that stalwart of New England nonresistance, Henry C. Wright—and anthologies of writings exemplifying the horrors of war and commending the virtues of peace. There were biographies of leading pacifists and of other outstanding peace workers. By no means all the Association's publications were reprints of older works, though it is not without significance that the most important items were not new. We find Hill himself issuing an exposition of the scriptural testimony against war and compiling a slim booklet giving the evidence why Christians might not fight with carnal weapons. Among the more interesting of the Association's original publications was a small volume by Josiah W. Leeds (1841-1908) entitled *The Primitive Christians' Estimate of War and Self-Defense*, which consisted mainly of short biographies of the early church fathers with copious extracts from their writings against war and military service.

The Association's main effort, however, was concentrated on producing the *Messenger of Peace*. Until it temporarily ceased separate publication in 1894, the paper had a circulation of between three and four

[5] Hill remained editor until the end of 1894, transferring the paper in August 1887 from New Vienna to Richmond (Ind.). In January 1890 it began to appear under the title *Christian Arbitrator and Messenger of Peace* as the organ of the Christian Arbitration and Peace Society with its headquarters in Philadelphia. From Hill's resignation until April 1900, the paper was not published separately, appearing only as a section of the *American Friend*. From 1900 the *Messenger* was edited in succession by Anna Thomas (1900-1905), H. Lavinia Bailey (1905-1913), and Allen D. Hole (1913-1923). In 1869 the evangelical wing of Orthodox Quakerism had a second and short-lived peace organ in the Chicago *Herald of Peace*, edited by W. E. Hathaway and Willet Dorland.

[6] A personal link with antebellum pacifism was provided by the New England Congregationalist John Hemmenway, William Ladd's friend and biographer and his associate in the earlier peace movement. Hemmenway frequently contributed to the *Messenger of Peace*. As he wrote in its issue of July 1872 (II, no. 10, 146): "Though I am not of Quaker profession and religion, but a Puritan, yet, on *War*, I am, and for thirty years have been, a *Quaker of the Quakers*."

thousand; after its revival in 1900 the number was probably less. Copies were distributed free to the clergy, as well as to colleges and libraries expressing an interest in receiving them. The paper certainly dealt with a wide range of topics connected with peace, although there was little discussion on the economic aspects of war and little or no original thinking on pacifist theory. During the nineteenth century, at least, the paper was conducted in a strongly evangelical spirit with emphasis on the Quaker pacifist case against war. Articles printed were usually didactic in tone and were not perhaps on a very high level, but a fairly consistent degree of competence was maintained. The public declarations against war of both Friends and of non-Quaker peace groups were given prominence in the columns of the *Messenger*, as were reports of peace meetings held in different parts of the country. The historical heritage of Christian pacifism was emphasized, and stories and extracts illustrating this theme were frequently published. International arbitration was constantly advocated as a solution for disputes between countries, and we find the annual Lake Mohonk Conferences on International Arbitration, organized by the Quaker Albert K. Smiley (1828-1912), well reported in the *Messenger*. More space came to be devoted to news of the European peace movement and to comment on world affairs from a Quaker point of view. From 1900 onward protests against the increasingly militaristic spirit being displayed in the domestic life and foreign policy of the United States and against the nation's growing expenditure on armaments grew stronger. This last factor gave rise, too, to a revived interest in the problem of paying taxes to a government preparing for war.

The *Messenger of Peace*, at least if we compare its circulation with the number of Quakers in the country, appears to have enjoyed rather meager support within the Society, especially considering that some of its readers and subscribers were non-Friends. The activities of the Peace Association were in part subsidized, as we have seen, by a number of Orthodox yearly meetings. But the initiative and drive to carry on the work was supplied by a small group of enthusiastic pacifists, who, despite endeavors stretching over half a century, evidently failed to inspire the bulk of members with their ardor for peace. In the twentieth century the Association and its journal played only a minor role in the Quaker quest for peace. For some three decades after its foundation, however, the Association—in spite of its somewhat narrow approach to the problems of peace, stemming from the doctrinaire evangelicalism of its sponsors and its simplified view of affairs that often bordered on the naive—fulfilled a useful function in keeping the issue of pacifism before a Society whose attention was focused for the most part on other, and what then seemed to many Quakers more urgent, problems.

In the period between the Civil War and the coming of world war, their environment, indeed, presented the Quakers with much fewer direct challenges to their pacifist beliefs than the preceding centuries had done. Although in the immediate postwar period we hear of small distraints being levied on Friends in Pennsylvania and some other states for nonpayment of the militia taxes which had replaced the old annual muster, this matter was of only very minor and passing concern to Friends. Federal conscription had come to an end, and the state militias were a dead letter. Toward the end of the century the imposition of compulsory military drill in some schools and colleges and the militarization of youth implied in the training given in the boys' brigade aroused Friends' attention. Quakers were also busy early in the new century in seeing that provision for religious objectors was included in legislation for mobilization of a national militia in the event of war. But all this activity was of only peripheral importance. During this period the decision whether the Quaker testimony against participation in war was in fact meaningful enough for them personally to face some sacrifice on its behalf confronted few members of the Society of Friends.

Nevertheless, a personal and direct witness for peace was sometimes called for even at this time. There was once again, for instance, the old problem of war pensions in the case of Friends who had served in the armed forces during the Civil War. Some of these Quaker veterans may have been converts to the Society in the years succeeding the war; others were members who had joined the army and who had subsequently, for this infraction of the discipline, been received back into the Society only after confession of error or after remission of this penalty by an indulgent meeting. In some cases, these men drew their pension apparently without feeling that they were compromising their Society's peace testimony. In many other cases, however, they refused to do so, even though there may have been no formal ruling against it in the discipline. We read—to give only one example—of an Iowa Friend, a small farmer who had been severely crippled in action and was therefore eligible to draw an annual amount of $30, consistently refusing to accept the money over a period of some forty years, even though he was himself in straitened circumstances.[7]

Occasionally we hear of a Quaker manufacturer or businessman curtailing his profits in order to avoid involvement with war preparations. The Lukens Iron and Steel Company of Coatesville (Pa.), a Quaker

[7] *Friend* (London), XLV, no. 52 (29 Dec. 1905), 860.

firm, received toward the end of the last century a lucrative order from the United States Navy for 10,000 tons of "protective armor plate." Its president, Dr. Charles Huston, turned down this and subsequent government orders connected with armaments on the grounds that they clashed with his Quaker pacifism. "War," he explained, "only decides which of the combatants has the superior strength, and it is more expensive than arbitration, as well as destructive to life and property."[8] Scrupulous conduct in business had long been a characteristic of the Quaker commercial ethos; the same scrupulousness was manifested by many Friends then, as at other times in their history, in seeing that their day-to-day activities conformed to the Society's testimonies on peace and other related issues.

The Quaker of military age no longer had to face the issue of conscription, at least for the time being. But all male adult Friends had to come to a decision whether to exercise their democratic right to the franchise or whether to refrain on principle because of a possible connection with the warmaking power. They might have to decide, too, whether political office of any kind was compatible with Quaker pacifism. And considerations of this sort might lead on to reflections on the general character of civil government and its relation to the peace testimony of Friends. A not uncommon feeling continued among some Friends in the postbellum period that voting and officeholding were incompatible with a consistent pacifism. On the whole, however, a majority of Quakers of the period would probably have agreed with the opinion expressed in the New York *Friend*, an organ of the liberal Hicksites, that "the higher executive offices are the only ones in which direct participation in military matters cannot readily be avoided" and that, therefore, taking part in elections and acceptance of local office and of seats in state legislatures represented, at least in peacetime, a commendable outlet for Friends' energies.[9]

Increased participation in public life marks the history of the Society from this time onward. True, the element of coercion in all existing government continued to trouble many Friends, as it had done earlier. On the other hand, for a small—but growing—number it presented little difficulty since, while retaining membership in, and usually a warm regard for, the Society, they had come to disagree with its pacifism, considering this as a non-essential component in its beliefs. Thus, for them, entry into political life was hedged around by few reservations or doubts such as afflicted many other Friends who were also drawn to politics. For the latter, however, the positive good that

[8] Fernando G. Cartland, *Southern Heroes*, pp. 16, 17.
[9] *Friend* (New York), I, no. 4 (April 1866), 48, 49.

might result from public service outbalanced in the final analysis the possible risk of involvement in the use of coercive force—and this might be dealt with, when the problem arose directly, by a strategic withdrawal from association with the agents of coercion. Government, they believed, was capable of being purged of the element of injurious force, as it had been in Quaker Pennsylvania, if enough citizens in a democracy so wished; meanwhile, such government, even if it rested on a foundation of force, was essential for civilized life.

A committee of Philadelphia (Hicksite) Yearly Meeting in 1871 went further than many of its fellow members could go when it stated in a minute (which in fact was withdrawn on account of the opposition it met in the meeting):

> Bad as war is, it is not the worst of evils. Anarchy, riot and mob violence, in which innocent women and children indiscriminately suffer, are even worse. Hence the necessity in our large cities of a police, sustained by military force, to check these in their early stages, to which arrangement the inhabitants are indebted for their quiet and security.[10]

But views not far removed from this in their conditional justification of violent coercion in the work of government are to be found not infrequently among responsible Friends of this period. This may be seen, for instance, in the following rather involved entry under the heading "War," which appears in the book of discipline issued by the Illinois (Hicksite) Yearly Meeting in 1878. It states:

> While we recognize the need of law and order, which in the present condition of mankind can perhaps only be maintained by governments resting on human authority, we believe that in the degree that we come individually under the government of that principle of justice and unselfish regard for the welfare of others, that lies at the foundation of the Christian faith, we shall render governments sustained by force, unnecessary, and build up through self-restraint, the government of Righteousness in the earth.[11]

The degree of coercive action that was permissible within the framework of civil government, the amount of approval that might be given to the application of injurious force by properly appointed officers of the law, had always been a debatable question for Quakers, as for other pacifists and supporters of the peace movement.

[10] *Autobiography of Benjamin Hallowell*, p. 334.
[11] *Rules of Discipline and Advices of Illinois Yearly Meeting of Friends* (1878), p. 11.

But with the Quakers, at any rate, the problem of war had been more clear-cut. The discipline forbade members to participate in any activities connected with war, and, although it was not always easy to know where the line should be drawn, especially in actual wartime, the intent was clear. True, insofar as many of the younger men who had entered military service were never disciplined in some sections of the Society and other Friends not liable to the draft who had given support in one way or another to the war effort were also untouched, the Civil War may be said to have marked a relaxation of the discipline in regard to war. But, despite individual deviations, the general consensus of feeling in the Society still regarded the peace testimony as an essential element in the Quaker faith.

It was in the post-Civil War period that a very significant trend began, especially in certain yearly meetings, away from the traditional Quaker attitude toward war. Its stages are not at all easy to trace, however, since during these years the peace issue had retreated into the background of Friends' concerns: there was no conscription to test the strength of pacifism within the various branches of Quakerism. The factors that brought about this change were often only indirectly linked with Quaker thinking on peace and war, though their influence was no less effective for being remote.

It was in the more newly established Western yearly meetings of the Orthodox branch that we find the first large-scale retreat from Quaker pacifism, a transformation that occurred slowly and almost imperceptibly and without the conscious knowledge of those involved. The full dimensions of the change were only observable in this century, when the small numbers of conscientious objectors supplied by these meetings in the two world wars revealed the extent of the loss of ground which pacifism had suffered there.

Various factors were at work. The most important of these was the strong influence exercised by the religious revivals of the 1870's and 1880's on Friends in the West, bringing in a host of new recruits to the Society from other denominations. "The converts who joined Quakerism accepted it for other reasons than its peace views. In fact many of them never really accepted" Quaker pacifism, even if this still remained the official doctrine of their yearly meetings. And no issue presented itself before 1914 to force them to clarify their own individual stand. For this trend in Quakerism the most important object appeared to be to bring Christ to the people as their Savior, to win souls for salvation. Mission work, not pacifism, was their major concern. Not merely in their theology but also in their whole mode of worship these Quakers drew closer to Protestant fundamentalism and away from the more traditional type of Quakerism, and even away from some groups that, like them, had adopted the pastoral system.

A second factor contributing to the decline of pacifism among large groups of Western Friends lay in the deepening suspicion with which some Friends in the West regarded Eastern Quakerism, a suspicion that had originated in the isolation, both physical and intellectual, of pioneer life (an isolation that had also been a prime factor leading to the adoption of the pastoral system). Now, for many Western Friends, Friends in the East appeared to have become increasingly tainted with theological liberalism, and the peace testimony, still maintained as a central concern in this area, suffered through guilt by association. In the twentieth century the fundamentalist majorities in the Orthodox yearly meetings of Ohio, Kansas, and Oregon withdrew from their association with other pastoral Friends in the Five Years' Meeting, and within these newly independent yearly meetings pacifism was to wither away almost entirely.[12]

A special study has been made by Cecil B. Currey of the development of the peace testimony among the Friends of Kansas Yearly Meeting, which was set up in 1872—in the period, that is, of strong revivalist influence. In the following year the meeting established a peace committee that under successive changes of name continued to lead a rather vegetating existence. In 1875 the committee reported: "The membership of this Yearly Meeting, as a mass—are not well informed in the Gospel matter of peace." But little seems to have been done at this time, beyond the printing and distribution of a small number of tracts and the preaching by pastors of an occasional peace sermon, to deepen members' understanding of Quaker peace principles. "Friends came to feel," Currey writes of the period from the late seventies on, "that the testimony of pacifism would develop in new converts without special instruction. . . . This doctrine did not seem to be considered an integral part of Quaker teaching. The exposition of pacifism was included in the Yearly Meeting *Discipline* and was available to all who wished to learn of it but the viewpoint was no longer stressed." There was some revival of interest in the subject of peace from the mid-1890's on. "Many of our ministers," it was remarked, "make the subject of Peace a prominent feature in their sermons." In 1911 we find Kansas Yearly Meeting petitioning President Taft in support of international arbitration. But, despite these signs of a growing concern with the practical implementation of Quaker pacifism on the

[12] See *Report of American Commissions of the Conference of All Friends* (1920): *Report of Commission V*, pp. 13-16; Cecil B. Currey, "Quaker Revivalism and the Peace Testimony," *Friends Journal*, vol. 8, no. 4 (15 Feb. 1962), pp. 75-77.

part of a small number of Kansas Friends, it is clear that on the membership as a whole the peace testimony had only a slight hold.[13]

Currey sums up well the position in which Quaker pacifism stood among the fundamentalist yearly meetings of the West during the early years of this century when he writes:

> Proclamation of the peace testimony was acceptable only if directed toward those already accepting it. For those whose conscience dictated otherwise, pacifism was irrelevant. Closed circles of believers were created who could discuss the tenet among themselves but who were frowned upon when they advocated it for others. Growing numbers of Evangelicals regarded the doctrine as superfluous.[14]

The younger generation, when a major war eventually involved the country in 1917, were in many cases insufficiently grounded or largely unacquainted from their home and meeting background with the Quaker pacifist position. The proportion of young men who entered the army from these yearly meetings, though considerable in the First World War, reached an even higher figure in the Second. In this section of the Quaker community the tide had turned against pacifism, seemingly irrevocably.

But the tide was also on the turn in other and less extreme sections of the Society. The process was advanced farther perhaps among pastoral Friends of the former frontier areas, where the same factors were at work as we have seen in the case of the meetings captured by the fundamentalism of the revivals, but the same process was also taking place among more traditional Orthodox groups as well as in Hicksite meetings. The prime cause of this defection from pacifism seems to be twofold. In the first place, there was, as we have seen above, a lessening interest in the peace testimony during the long years of peace and of freedom from conscription, an absence of challenge in this area, a concentration of effort on other "causes." Secondly, the abandonment (except among Wilburite Conservatives) of disownment as a means of enforcing the discipline,[15] combined with increasing

[13] Currey, "Quaker Pacifism in Kansas, 1833-1945," M.Sc. thesis, Fort Hays Kansas State College, pp. 41-49; "Quakers in 'Bleeding' Kansas," BFHA, vol. 50, no. 2 (Autumn 1961), pp. 100, 101.

[14] Currey, *Friends Journal*, 15 Feb. 1962, p. 76.

[15] Among the Protestant churches as a whole, a decline in membership standards can be observed in the second half of the nineteenth century. This, as in the case of the Quakers, was part result, part cause of the influx of large numbers of new members who were not properly initiated into the beliefs and practices of the denomination they had joined. After small groups of conservative and rigorist old believers had broken away on one pretext or another, the churches emerged with

integration of rural as well as urban Quakers into the surrounding society (which was not, of course, pacifist), made it possible for members to reject pacifism as a personal faith while adhering to a denomination which still maintained pacifism as a tenet of its collective witness.

The extent of this change in the attitude of Friends to war must not, however, be exaggerated. Up to 1914 and beyond that date, pacifism still held the allegiance of a large number of the most active and concerned Quakers in the West[16] as in the East, if we except the fundamentalist yearly meetings dealt with above. Even here the remnant remained faithful, and we find in this section of the Quaker community a man like Cyrus W. Harvey, a birthright Friend from Indiana and a Civil War veteran turned pacifist (see earlier), becoming a leading figure among Kansas Friends and a fervent upholder of the peace testimony. His pacifism, as we see it set forth in a small tract which he published in 1901 under the title of *The Prince of Peace or the Bible on Non-Resistance and War*, represented the narrowly scriptural approach, which by this date was already being leavened among some Quaker groups in the East by a concern for wider issues connected with peace. Harvey might have been old-fashioned, but his approach was forthright. "How can a Bible reader," he asks, "read all this, in faith, believing his own Bible, and find a place in his own conscience for war or self-defense?"[17]

Nevertheless, as a more significant figure for the future than Harvey, we may take a Quaker of the type of Joseph Gurney ("Uncle Joe") Cannon (1836-1926), also a birthright Friend from the Midwest, who was elected to Congress in 1872 and eventually reached the position of Speaker of the House of Representatives, which he held for many years. Although he remained a loyal member of the Society of Friends until his death at the age of 90, Cannon was avowedly not a pacifist and in politics belonged to the more reactionary wing of the Republican Party.[18] Cannon has his successor in our day in Richard M. Nixon; there have been few from this section of the Society, however, who have followed in Harvey's footsteps.

If the peace testimony was beginning to wither in some parts of the

---

their discipline relaxed and the traditional dogmas diluted. In large sections of the Quaker community pacifism, along with the plain dress and the plain speech, was among the items eventually discarded.

[16] Indeed, pastoral meetings in the West have produced quite a few of the most able and devoted exponents of Quaker pacifism in the present century.

[17] Cyrus W. Harvey, *The Prince of Peace*, p. 15.

[18] See L. White Busbey (ed.), *Uncle Joe Cannon.*

Society of Friends, renewal was slowly coming about elsewhere among Quakers from the 1890's onward. This process was operative mainly, though by no means exclusively, in the Orthodox and Hicksite meetings of the East.[19] Its chief characteristic lay in an increased awareness of the need to extend the boundaries of the traditional peace witness from a simple exposition of New Testament nonresistance to consideration of possible causes of war in the economic and social order, as well as in the political sphere, and of methods for their eradication. Analysis had still not gone very deep: international arbitration continued to be generally put forward as a kind of cure-all,[20] and there was little consciousness as yet of the need for any radical changes in the existing social structure. Although the Quakers' work for peace remained firmly anchored in their total rejection of the war method and any kind of social revolutionary approach to peace was quite alien to even the more politically liberal Friends, the emphasis nevertheless was gradually changing.

We can see this—to give only a few examples—in the work of such Friends as Benjamin F. Trueblood (1847-1916), Hannah J. (Mrs. Moses) Bailey, or William I. Hull. All three were active in the peace movement from around the end of the last century, and all three, though convinced pacifists themselves, collaborated closely with individuals and organizations which were not based on an absolute pacifist platform—a contrast to the narrowly sectarian position which we have seen the Society taking up earlier in relation to peace societies outside the Quaker enclosure.

Trueblood was secretary of the American Peace Society from 1892 to 1915 and editor of its journal, the *Advocate of Peace*. An ardent proponent of international arbitration, he represented the older and more conservative school of peace men. Nevertheless, in his international politics he was a unilateralist, urging on his country that to lead the way in disarmament, though clearly entailing risks, was the

[19] The Conservative or Wilburite Friends, who were considerably fewer in numbers than the other two main groups, maintained strict adherence to the peace testimony as part of their general traditionalism. The conservative nature of this witness is illustrated by the persistence into the twentieth century in the sections on war of their books of disciplines of items which had long lost all relevance to the existing situation. In the *Discipline* of their Iowa Y. M. published in 1914 (pp. 87-90), for instance, we still find advices inserted against paying taxes to buy drums and military colors, against buying or selling prize goods or being concerned in any way with men-of-war, and against paying militia fines. These advices were long out of date, but style and content in several cases differed little, if at all, from the eighteenth-century wording.

[20] In the books of discipline of some Hicksite yearly meetings early in this century were included items urging Friends to support arbitration as a method of settling international disputes.

only moral policy, the only one worthy of a Christian nation and one that had (he believed) every chance of success. "No nation," we find him saying in an essay written in 1895, "would think of attacking us if we had not one single war-ship, not one coast-defense gun."[21] For all the shortcomings of his type of peace action, his attitude, with its attempt to investigate in association with other men of goodwill how "the Christian law of love" could be made effective short of the millennium, represented a definite advance on the ingrown witness of the previous generations—a return, in fact, to the American Quaker tradition that had been cut short as a result of the fall of Quaker rule in Pennsylvania.

Hannah J. Bailey (1887-1923) was another Quaker pacifist who went out from the closed Quaker circle, and from her home at Winthrop Center in Maine she carried on the work of the Peace and Arbitration Department of the National Women's Christian Temperance Union. Pacifism for her was but a part of what she called, in the first number of the periodical, the *Pacific Banner*, which she edited between 1889 and 1895, "the grand work of moral reform": it was one issue alongside prison reform and temperance and Sabbath observance. This approach was in the style of the great antebellum reform movement, but now Quakers like Mrs. Bailey, instead of being looked at askance by large numbers in the Society as their predecessors had been, gained widespread support among their fellow members.

The active life of William I. Hull (1868-1939), the well-known Quaker historian and educationalist, lasted well into the period after 1914. He may be taken here as a representative of a school of thought that would gain increased support in our time among Friends on both sides of the Atlantic: he is typical of those personal pacifists who were prepared to grant a conditional sanction to the use of armed force in support of international law. "Peace *and* Justice," Hull wrote in 1909, were the aims of the contemporary peace movement, in which he hoped Quakers would take their part alongside other peace workers who did not share their unconditional pacifism. The immediate goals of the movement he defined as "International Courts of Law, the Limitation of Armaments and their sole use as a genuine International Police Force." Hull rejected any analogy between an international police force and national armies. Not merely was the source of their authority completely different, but the police force would be controlled by a power above the contestants, while a national army was the instrument of one side only in the quarrel. An international force, moreover, would act only to carry out the verdict of an impartial court.

[21] Benjamin F. Trueblood, *The Development of the Peace Idea and Other Essays*, p. 92.

Soldiers, of course, are sometimes used in aid of the police to enforce law and order within the jurisdiction of the soldiers' own country. At such times, they form in no true sense of the word an *army*; but are an auxiliary of the *police* force, subject to the same sovereignty and law to which those who threaten violence are subject; and even when acting in this police capacity, they are rightfully ... carefully circumscribed by the civil authority.

Further proof to Hull of the fundamental difference in character between police action and the employment of national armies lay in the fact that in war guilty and innocent suffer alike and indiscriminately, in contrast to the punishment of the guilty party in proportion to his offense, which, along with the prevention of crime before it happens, was the object of force used in support of law. Moreover, whereas the aim of army training was to kill as many of the enemy as possible, a police force was either unarmed or only lightly armed for self-defense, being "made to feel that homicide is absolutely the last resort."

How fallacious [Hull writes] is the analogy drawn between armaments and a true police system, may be readily seen when one compares the present system of national armaments with a system under which all the world's armies and navies, vastly reduced in size, would form part of an international force, and would act against any member of the family of nations only when it received a warrant for so doing from an international court, before which the delinquent member had been legally and impartially tried and sentenced. Such an armament would indeed be a genuine police force both for the punishment and prevention of genuine international crime and for the enforcement of genuine international justice.[22]

Hull was a pioneer in the kind of internationalism that has since gained widespread support as a result of the experiences of two world wars. Some of his thinking proved unrealistic, particularly his failure to recognize that the imposition by an international authority of military sanctions against a delinquent nation, especially if it were a major power, might easily result in a situation that was in fact little, if at all, removed from a state of war. (In the interwar years Hull entertained strong misgivings about the League of Nations in connection with its powers of enforcing military sanctions.) The nature of an international sovereign body and the extent of its powers were problems which were inadequately dealt with, too, in his writings of this period.

[22] William I. Hull, *The New Peace Movement* (published as *Swarthmore College Bulletin*, VII, no. 9 [Sept. 1909], 6, 7, 12-24).

What is particularly interesting for our purposes, however, is the rather uneasy combination which he contrived of nonpacifist internationalism on a lower, with Quaker pacifism on a higher, plane of morality, his attempt—not altogether successful—to attain "an intermediate resting-place in the world's journey upward towards Christ's goal of Love thine enemy." He called on men to refuse "uncompromisingly and inevasively" to "take the lives of their fellow men under any pretext whatsoever." To maintain that war was not just murder on a large scale was, in his opinion, mere sophistry.[23] Yet international arbitration and Hague Conferences seem today an insufficient response, a somewhat ineffectual compromise between the way of radical nonviolence such as was being propounded contemporaneously by Tolstoy and Gandhi and their disciples, on the one hand, and the increasingly influential school of internationalist thought that wished to see effective force placed at the disposal of a supranational authority, on the other.

The opening of the twentieth century, then, found the Society of Friends less united than in past centuries on their attitude toward war. Some sections, especially the Western yearly meetings that had been strongly influenced by the late nineteenth-century revival movements, and individuals in all branches of the Society had moved away from pacifism. Elsewhere, on the other hand, there had been a revival of interest in the peace testimony and a desire to give it new life, both by exploring its relationship to the facts of international politics and by bringing it into touch with the efforts of the non-Quaker and nonpacifist peace movement, which was growing in strength and influence. Both Hicksite and Orthodox yearly meetings in the East began to establish permanent peace committees from the 1890's on and to show renewed interest on an official level in the problems of peace and war. Although Quakers, like other pacifists, were not affected directly by war, the Spanish-American War of 1898 and American imperialist designs in regard to Cuba and the Philippines gave an added impulse to Friends to reconsider the implications of their peace testimony.

In December 1901 a three-day peace conference was held in Philadelphia, to which Quakers of all branches of the Society on the North American continent were invited. Among those who played a leading role in its initiation and proceedings we find the names of most prominent Friends who were helping at this time to refurbish Quaker pacifism: Benjamin F. Trueblood, Rufus M. Jones, Hannah J. Bailey, Alexander C. Wood, Howard M. Jenkins (the editor at that time of the *Friends' Intelligencer*), Alfred K. Smiley (the organizer of the

[23] *Ibid.*, pp. 26-28, 31, 33.

annual Lake Mohonk International Arbitration Conferences where in the previous year the idea of this gathering of all Friends was conceived), and many others. The conference itself, which its sponsors planned as both a public demonstration of Friends' continued concern as a body for the peace of the world and as a forthright protest against "the awful iniquities and crushing burdens of modern militarism," consisted mainly of a series of papers given by leading Friends on various aspects of the peace testimony. Many of them seem rather platitudinous today. The pacifist basis of Friends' concern for peace was stressed, but collaboration with nonpacifists was urged by many of the speakers. "The outcome of this Conference," said M. Carey Thomas (1857-1935), president of Bryn Mawr College, "should be an aggressive peace propaganda, not carried on separately by the Quaker Church, but in concerted effort with all believers in peace and arbitration." Friends, with their long pacifist tradition, she thought, "should become the backbone of such a propaganda." Rufus Jones suggested that it would help the cause if American Friends would imitate British Friends who, although much fewer in number, were well represented in the House of Commons, and send some ten to twenty of their members to Congress. "We must accomplish something with those who determine the destiny of nations," he added.[24]

The conference had little to say about the economic causation of war or about the clash of rival imperialisms and the search of finance capitalism for overseas markets, subjects to which the socialist and labor movements of the day were giving widespread publicity as being among the major causes of international conflict. But, at the same time, the gathering, in the way it put stress on the political aspects of pacifism and in its call for cooperation with the wider peace movement that had grown up outside the Society of Friends (although, of course, this call was made within the framework of the religious inspiration of the Quaker peace testimony), demonstrated that a new era was beginning in the history of Quaker pacifism. Men like Rufus Jones or Alexander C. Wood, who did much to shape the direction of Quaker peace efforts in the postwar period, were active, as we have seen, in the 1901 conference and during the next decade and a half. The full effects of the new spirit now beginning to reinvigorate Quaker pacifism were not to become completely apparent, however, until the United States' involvement in world war began a new epoch in American history.

[24] *The American Friends' Peace Conference . . . 1901*, pp. 3, 4, 83, 104, 105. See pp. 30, 54, for evidence of nonpacifist feeling within the Society. This report on the conference was published in the following year as a volume of 236 pages.

====================== *Bibliography* ======================

A. PRIMARY SOURCES

1. *Archival Materials*

Haverford College Quaker Collection:
Allinson, Samuel, "Reasons against War, and paying Taxes for its Support" (1780), MS.
New England Yearly Meeting MS Discipline [1781?], °BX 7617 N5C5 1781.

Philadelphia Yearly Meeting, Department of Records:
"Minutes of the Yearly Meeting of Friends at Philadelphia" for 1749-1779.

Swarthmore College, Friends Historical Library:
"A Collection of Christian and Brotherly Advices given forth from time to time by the Yearly Meeting of Friends for Pennsylvania and New Jersey . . . Alphabetically Digested under Proper Heads" (1762), MS.
"A General Testimony against all looseness and vanity or what else may tend to the hurt of the souls of youth or others" (1694), MS.
Thomas Jenkins Papers (R G 5).
Kennett Monthly Meeting Sufferings 1757-1791.
Mifflin, Warner, "Statement concerning his refusal to use and circulate Continental currency" (1779), misc. MSS.
New Garden Monthly Meeting Committee on Sufferings, Minutes 1777-1778.
Radnor Monthly Meeting, Minutes of Sufferings 1776-1779.
7 misc. items (incl. Ferris, Janney, and Whittier Collections).

2. *Newspapers and Journals*

Advocate of Peace (Boston—later Washington, D.C.).
American Friend (Richmond, Ind.).
Calumet (New York).
Friend (New York).
Friend (Philadelphia).
Friend; or, Advocate of Truth (Philadelphia).
Friends' Miscellany (Philadelphia).
Friends' Review (Philadelphia).
Friends' [Weekly] Intelligencer (Philadelphia).
Messenger of Peace (New Vienna, Ohio, and later Richmond, Ind. and still later Baltimore, Md.).
Moral Advocate, A Monthly Publication, on War, Duelling, Capital Punishments, and Prison Discipline (Mt. Pleasant, Ohio).
Non-Resistant (Boston).
Non-Resistant and Practical Christian, 1848 (Hopedale, Mass.).
Practical Christian (Hopedale, Mass.).

3. *Books and Pamphlets: Contemporary Printings*

An Account of the Sufferings of Friends of North Carolina Yearly Meeting, in Support of their Testimony against War, from 1861 to 1865, Baltimore (Md.), 1868.

An Address on Peace. Issued by the Yearly Meeting of Friends for New England, n.p.p., 1854.

Address of the Wilmington Monthly Meeting of Friends, to Its Members, on the Subject of the Militia Law, enacted at the last Session of the Legislature of Delaware, Wilmington, 1827.

Allinson, William J., *Right in the Abstract,* Philadelphia, 1862.

The American Friends' Peace Conference held at Philadelphia Twelfth Month 12th, 13th and 14th 1901, Philadelphia, 1902.

The Ancient Testimony of the People called Quakers, reviv'd. By the Order and Approbation of the Yearly Meeting, held for the Provinces of Pennsylvania and New Jersey, 1722, Philadelphia, 1773 edn.

Bates, Elisha, *The Doctrines of Friends; or, Principles of the Christian Religion, as held by the Society of Friends, commonly called Quakers* (1825), 5th edn., Providence, 1843.

Benezet, Anthony, *The Plainness and Innocent Simplicity of the Christian Religion with its Salutary Effects, compared to the Corrupting Nature and Dreadful Effects of War,* Philadelphia, 1782 edn.

———, *Serious Considerations on Several Important Subjects; . . . ,* Philadelphia, 1778.

Besse, Joseph, *A Collection of the Sufferings of the People called Quakers for the Testimony of a Good Conscience,* vol. II, London, 1753.

The Book of Discipline, Agreed on by the Yearly Meeting of Friends for New England . . . , Providence (R.I.), 1785.

Bownas, Samuel, *An Account of the Life, Travels, Christian Experiences in the Work of the Ministry of Samuel Bownas,* London, 1756.

A Brief Account of the Sufferings of the Servants of the Lord called Quakers: From their first Arrival in the Island of Antegoa, under the several Governours; from the Year 1660, to 1695, London, 1706.

Chalkley, Thomas, *A Journal or, Historical Account, of the Life, Travels, and Christian Experiences, of that Antient, Faithful Servant of Jesus Christ, Thomas Chalkley,* Philadelphia, 1754 edn.

Chew, Samuel, *The Speech of Samuel Chew, Esq., Chief Justice of the Government of Newcastle, Kent and Sussex upon Delaware; Delivered from the Bench to the Grand-Jury of the County of New-Castle, Nov. 21, 1741; and now published at their Request,* Philadelphia, 1741.

———, *The Speech of Samuel Chew, Esq., Chief Justice of the Government of Newcastle, Kent and Sussex upon Delaware; Delivered from the Bench to the Grand-Jury of the County of New-Castle, Aug. 20, 1742; and now published at their Request,* Philadelphia, 1742.

Christian Advices: published by the Yearly Meeting of Friends held in Philadelphia, Philadelphia, 1808.

Churchman, John, *An Account of the Gospel Labours and Christian Experiences of a Faithful Minister of Christ, John Churchman, Late of Nottingham in Pennsylvania, deceased,* Philadelphia, 1779.

Considerations respecting the Lawfulness of War under the Gospel Dispensation addressed to the Teachers and Professors of Christianity in the United States of America, New York, 1848.

Cornell, John J., *An Address to the Members of Genesee Yearly Meeting of Friends, in Relation to a Testimony against War,* Rochester (N.Y.), 1862.

——, *Autobiography of John J. Cornell*, Baltimore (Md.), 1906.

Cornell, W. T., *On the Incompatibility of War with the Spirit of Christianity*, Catskill (N.Y.), 1862.

Correspondence between Oliver Johnson and George F. White, a Minister of the Society of Friends, New York, 1841.

Cox, Samuel Hanson, *Quakerism not Christianity*, New York 1833.

Davis, Timothy, *A Letter from a Friend to some of his Intimate Friends, on the Subject of paying Taxes, &*, Watertown (Mass.), 1776.

Dickinson, James, *A Journal of the Life, Travels, and Labours in the Work of the Ministry, of that Worthy Elder, and Faithful Servant of Jesus Christ, James Dickinson*, London, 1745.

The Discipline of Iowa Yearly Meeting of the Society of Friends revised and printed by Direction of the Meeting held at West Branch, Iowa, in the Year 1914, n.p.p.

Discipline of the Yearly Meeting of Friends, held in New York, for the State of New York, and parts adjacent, . . ., New York, 1810.

Edmundson, William, *A Journal of the Life, Travels, Sufferings, and Labour of Love in the Work of the Ministry, of that Worthy Elder, and Faithful Servant of Jesus Christ, William Edmundson*, Dublin, 1715.

Evans, Joshua, *A Journal of the Life, Travels, Religious Exercises, and Labours in the Work of the Ministry of Joshua Evans, late of Newton Township, Gloucester County, New Jersey*, Byberry (Pa.), 1837.

Evans, William, *Journal of the Life and Religious Services of William Evans, a Ministry of the Gospel in the Society of Friends*, Philadelphia, 1870.

Extracts from Several Writers on Militia Fines and War, n.p.p., n.d.

Fisher, William Logan, *A Review of the Doctrines and Discipline of the Society of Friends*, 2nd edn., Philadelphia, 1854.

Foster, John W., *War and Christianity Irreconcilable. An Address to Christians*, Providence (R.I.), 1861.

Foster, Thomas, *An Appeal to the Society of Friends, on the Primitive Simplicity of their Christian Principles and Church Discipline; and on some Recent Proceedings in the Said Society*, London, 1801.

——, *A Narrative of the Proceedings in America of the Society called Quakers, in the case of Hannah Barnard. With a Brief Review of the Previous Transactions in Great Britain and Ireland . . .*, London, 1804.

Garrison, William Lloyd, *Selections from the Writings and Speeches of William Lloyd Garrison*, Boston, 1852.

Grey, Isaac, *A Serious Address to Such of the People called Quakers, on the Continent of North America, as profess Scruples relative to the Present Government: exhibiting the Ancient Real Testimony of that People, concerning Obedience to Civil Authority*, Philadelphia, 1778.

Hall, Rufus, *A Journal of the Life, Religious Exercises, and Travels in the Work of the Ministry of Rufus Hall*, Byberry (Pa.), 1840.

Hallowell, Benjamin, *Autobiography of Benjamin Hallowell*, Philadelphia, 1883.

Harvey, Cyrus W., *The Prince of Peace or the Bible on Non-Resistance and War*, Galena (Kan.), 1901.

Heaton, Adna, *War and Christianity Contrasted; with a Comparative View of their Nature and Effects. Recommended to the Serious and Impartial Consideration of the Professors of the Christian Religion*, New York, 1816.

Hicks, Edward, *Memoirs of the Life and Religious Labors of Edward Hicks, late of Newtown, Bucks County, Pennsylvania. Written by himself,* Philadelphia, 1851.

Hinchman, Lydia S., *Recollections of Lydia S. (Mitchell) Hinchman,* n.p.p., 1929.

Hoag, Joseph, *A Journal of the Life and Gospel Labors of that Devoted Servant and Minister of Christ, Joseph Hoag,* Sherwoods (N.Y.), 1860.

Hull, Henry, *Memoir of the Life and Religious Labours of Henry Hull,* Philadelphia, 1858.

Hull, William I., *The New Peace Movement,* Swarthmore (published as *Swarthmore College Bulletin,* vol. VII, no. 1, Sept. 1909).

Jackson, John, *Considerations on the Impropriety of Friends participating in the Administration of Political Governments,* Philadelphia, 1840.

——, *Reflections on Peace and War,* Philadelphia, 1846.

Janney, Samuel M., *Peace Principles exemplified in the Early History of Pennsylvania,* Philadelphia, 1876.

Jay, Allen, *Autobiography of Allen Jay,* Philadelphia, 1910.

Keith, George, et al., *An Appeal from the Twenty Eight Judges to the Spirit of Truth & true Judgement in all Faithful Friends . . . ,* Philadelphia, 1692.

Kersey, Jesse, *A Narrative of the Early Life, Travels and Gospel Labors of Jesse Kersey, late of Chester County, Pennsylvania,* Philadelphia, 1851.

——, *A Treatise on Fundamental Doctrines of the Christian Religion: in which are illustrated the Profession, Ministry, Worship, and Faith of the Society of Friends,* Philadelphia, 1815.

Leeds, Joseph W., *The Primitive Christians' Estimate of War and Self-Defense,* New Vienna (Ohio), 1876.

A Letter from One of the Society of Friends, Relative to the Conscientious Scrupulousness of Its Members to Bear Arms, n.p.p., 1795.

Lewis, Enoch, *Some Observations on the Militia System, Addressed to the Serious Consideration of the Citizens of Pennsylvania,* Philadelphia, 1831.

Love, Alfred H., *An Appeal in Vindication of Peace Principles, and against Resistance by Force of Arms,* 2nd edn., Philadelphia, 1862.

Martin, Isaac, *A Journal of the Life, Travels, Labours and Religious Exercises of Isaac Martin, Late of Rahway, in East Jersey, Deceased,* Philadelphia, 1834.

Maule, Joshua, *Transactions and Changes in the Society of Friends, and Incidents in the Life and Experience of Joshua Maule,* Philadelphia, 1886.

Memorial and Address of Friends on Military Exactions, [Philadelphia], 1837.

Memorial of Cyrus W. Harvey, Philadelphia, 1918.

Memorial to the Legislature of Virginia. Issued by the Religious Society of Friends, at their Half Yearly Meeting, held at Richmond 10th m. 5th, 1863, Richmond, 1863.

Memorial of Sarah Pugh. A Tribute of Respect from her Cousins, Philadelphia, 1888.

The Memorial of the Society of Friends, to the Legislature of the State of New York, on the Subject of Imprisonment, for Non-Compliance with Military Requisitions, New York, 1830.

Michener, Ezra, *A Brief Exposition of the Testimony to Peace, as exempli-*

fied by the Life and Precepts of Jesus Christ, and the Early Christians, and held by the Religious Society of Friends, Philadelphia, 1862.

Mifflin, Warner, *The Defence of Warner Mifflin Against Aspersions cast on him on Account of his Endeavours to promote Righteousness, Mercy and Peace Among Mankind*, Philadelphia, 1796.

Mott, James, Sr., *The Lawfulness of War for Christians, examined*, New York, 1814.

XV. *Papers relating to Quakers and Moravians*, n.p.p., n.d. [in Columbia University Library].

"Philalethes," *Tribute to Caesar, How paid by the Best Christians, And to What Purpose*, [Philadelphia], n.d.

Phillips, Catherine, *Memoirs of the Life of Catherine Phillips*, London, 1797.

Proceedings of the Pennsylvania Yearly Meeting of Progressive Friends, held at Longwood, Chester County, for 1862 and 1864, New York.

Proud, Robert, *The History of Pennsylvania . . .* , vol. I (1797) and vol. II (1798), Philadelphia.

Reckitt, William, *Some Account of the Life and Gospel Labours of William Reckitt*, London, 1776.

Remarks by a Member of the Society of Friends on the Subject of War, in reply to A.M., who addressed the Society on that Subject, n.p.p., n.d. [1847?].

Richardson, John, *An Account of the Life of that ancient Servant of Jesus Christ, John Richardson*, London, 1757.

Rules of Discipline and Advices of Illinois Yearly Meeting of Friends, Chicago, 1878.

Rules of Discipline and Christian Advices of the Yearly Meeting of Friends for Pennsylvania and New Jersey, . . . , Philadelphia, 1797.

Scott, Job, *Journal of the Life, Travels, and Gospel Labours of that Faithful Servant and Minister of Christ, Job Scott*, Wilmington (Del.), 1797.

A Serious Expostulation with the Society of Friends in Pennsylvania, and Parts Adjacent, being a Sincere Endeavour in the Spirit of Christian Duty and Affection, to point out the Propriety and Necessity of Preserving, in their Political Conduct, a Consistency with their Religious Opinions. By Pacificus, Philadelphia, 1808.

Smith, John, *The Doctrine of Christianity, as Held by the People called Quakers, Vindicated: In Answer to Gilbert Tennent's Sermon on the Lawfulness of War*, Philadelphia, 1748.

Smith, Samuel, *Necessary Truth: Or Seasonable Considerations for the Inhabitants of the City of Philadelphia and Province of Pennsylvania. In Relation to the Pamphlet call'd Plain Truth: And Two Other Writers in the News-Paper*, Philadelphia, 1748.

Smith, William, *A Brief State of the Province of Pennsylvania*, London, 1755.

―――, *A Brief View of the Conduct of Pennsylvania, for the Year 1756*, London, 1756.

Story, Thomas, *A Journal of the Life of Thomas Story*, Newcastle upon Tyne, 1747.

Taber, Joseph, *An Address to the People called Quakers*, Boston, 1784.

A Testimony and Caution to such as do make a Profession of Truth, who are in scorn called Quakers, and more especially such who profess to be Ministers of the Gospel of Peace, That they should not be concerned in Worldly Government, [Philadelphia], 1692.

The Testimony of the Society of Friends on the Continent of America, Philadelphia, 1830.

To Our Fellow Citizens of the United States. [Philadelphia Yearly Meeting], Philadelphia, 1814.

To Pacificus, in Reply to his Essay, entitled "A Serious Expostulation . . . ," showing wherein he has partially and unfairly represented Political Transactions, and answering the Aggravated Charges exhibited against the Society. By Philo Veritatis, Philadelphia, 1808.

A Treatise showing the Need we have to rely upon God as sole Protector of this Province . . . , Philadelphia, 1748.

Tryon, Thomas, *The Planter's Speech to his Neighbours & Country-Men of Pennsylvania, East & West-Jersey, and to all such as have transported themselves into New-Colonies for the Sake of a Quiet Retired Life,* London, 1684.

The Unlawfulness of All Wars and Fightings under the Gospel, Baltimore, 1846.

Washburn, John M., *Reason vs the Sword, A Treatise,* New York, 1873.

Watson, Thomas, *Some Account of the Life, Convincement, and Religious Experience of Thomas Watson, Late of Bolton, Massachusetts. Written by Himself . . . ,* New York, 1836.

Wells, J. I., *An Essay on War,* Hartford, 1808.

Wetherill, Samuel, *An Apology for the Religious Society, called Free Quakers, in the City of Philadelphia,* Philadelphia, n.d.

Wright, Henry C., *Six Months at Graeffenberg; with Conversations in the Saloon, on Nonresistance and other Subjects,* London, 1845.

4. Later Edited Works and Documentary Collections

Ashbridge, Elizabeth, "Some Account of the Life of Elizabeth Ashbridge. Written by Herself" in *The Friends' Library,* vol. IV, Philadelphia, 1840.

Brissot de Warville, J. P., *New Travels in the United States of America 1788,* tr. and ed. M. S. Vamos and D. Echeverria, Cambridge (Mass.), 1964.

"Bucks County Quakers and Revolution," *The Pennsylvania Genealogical Magazine* (Phila.), vol. XXIV, no. 4 (1966).

Byrd, William, *The Secret Diary of William Byrd of Westover 1709-1712,* ed. Louis B. Wright and Marion Tinling, Richmond (Va.), 1941.

Cadbury, Henry J. (ed.), *John Farmer's First American Journey 1711-1714,* Worcester, 1944.

————, "A Quaker Travelling in the Wake of War, 1781," *NEQ,* vol. XXIII, no. 3 (Sept. 1950).

————, "Some Anecdotes of John Woolman: Recorded by John Cox," *Journal of the Friends' Historical Society* (London), vol. XXXVIII (1946).

Charter to William Penn, and Laws of the Province of Pennsylvania passed between the Years 1682 and 1700, ed. George Staughton, Benjamin M. Nead, and Thomas McCamant, Harrisburg, 1879.

Coffin, William H., "Settlement of the Friends in Kansas," *Transactions of the Kansas State Historical Society, 1901-1902,* Topeka, 1902.

Comstock, Elizabeth L., *Life and Letters of Elizabeth L. Comstock*, ed. C. Hare, London, 1895.

Copy of a Memorial and Petition of the Society of Friends, to the Legislature of Virginia: with a Letter of Benjamin Bates, on the Subject of Militia Fines, Providence (R.I.), 1863.

Correspondence between William Penn and James Logan, Secretary of the Province of Pennsylvania, and Others, vol. I (1870) and vol. II (1872), ed. Edward Armstrong and included in *Memoirs of the Historical Society of Pennsylvania* as vols. IX and X, Philadelphia.

Fisher, S. R., "Journal of Samuel Rowland Fisher, of Philadelphia, 1779-1781," ed. Anna Wharton Morris, *PMHB*, vol. XLI, nos. 2-4 (1917).

Franklin, Benjamin, *The Autobiography of Benjamin Franklin*, ed. Leonard W. Labaree *et al.*, New Haven, 1964.

———, *The Papers of Benjamin Franklin*, ed. Leonard W. Labaree *et al.*, vol. 3, New Haven, 1961.

Gibbons, A. H., *The Life of Abby Hopper Gibbons told chiefly through her Correspondence*, ed. Sarah Hopper Emerson, vol. I, New York, 1897.

Gilpin, Thomas (ed.), *Exiles in Virginia: With Observations on the Conduct of the Society of Friends during the Revolutionary War*, Philadelphia, 1848.

Gurney, Eliza P., *Memoir and Correspondence of Eliza P. Gurney*, ed. Richard F. Mott, Philadelphia, 1884.

Hobbs, William, *Autobiography of William Hobbs*, Indianapolis (Ind.), 1962 edn.

Lincoln, Charles H. (ed.), *Narratives of the Indian Wars 1675-1699*, New York, 1952 edn.

Logan, James, "James Logan on Defensive War, or Pennsylvania Politics in 1741," *PMHB*, vol. VI, no. 4 (1882).

———, "Two Logan Letters," ed. Amelia Mott Gummere, *Journal of the Friends Historical Society*, vol. IX, no. 2 (April 1912).

Macy, Jesse, *An Autobiography*, ed. Katharine Macy Noyes, Springfield (Ill.) and Baltimore (Md.), 1933.

Mekeel, Arthur J. (ed.), "New York Quakers in the American Revolution," *BFHA*, vol. 29, no. 1 (1940).

Michener, Ezra (ed.), *A Retrospect of Early Quakerism; being Extracts from the Records of Philadelphia Yearly Meeting and the Meetings composing it*, Philadelphia, 1860.

Moore, James W. (ed.), *Records of the Kingswood Monthly Meeting of Friends, Hunterdon County, New Jersey*, Flemington (N.J.), 1900.

Myers, Alfred Cook (ed.), *Hannah Logan's Courtship*, Philadelphia, 1904.

Paine, Thomas, *The Writings of Thomas Paine*, ed. Moncure Daniel Conway, vol. I, New York, 1894.

Palmer, William J., *Letters 1853-1868: Gen'l Wm. J. Palmer*, ed. Isaac H. Clothier, Philadelphia, 1906.

The Paxton Papers, ed. John R. Dunbar, The Hague, 1957.

Pemberton, John, *The Life and Travels of John Pemberton, A Minister of the Gospel of Christ*, London, 1844.

Pennsylvania Archives:
1st ser., ed. Samuel Hazard: vols. II, III, VI, IX, Philadelphia, 1853-1854.
2nd ser., ed. John B. Linn and William H. Egle, vol. VII, Harrisburg, 1878.

4th ser., ed. George Edward Reed, vol. II, Harrisburg, 1900.
Pennsylvania Colonial Records:
  Minutes of the Provincial Council of Pennsylvania,
    vols. I-III, Philadelphia, 1852;
    vols. IV-VII, Harrisburg, 1851.
  Minutes of the Supreme Executive Council of Pennsylvania,
    vol. XV, Harrisburg, 1853.
Pringle, Cyrus, *The Civil War Diary of Cyrus Pringle*, Wallingford (Pa.), 1962.
Records of the Colony of Rhode Island and Providence Plantations in New England, ed. John Russell Bartlett, vol. I (1856) and vol. II (1857), Providence.
Rotch, William, *Memorandum written by William Rotch in the Eightieth Year of His Age*, Boston and New York, 1916.
Savery, William, *A Journal of the Life, Travels and Religious Labours, of William Savery*, ed. Jonathan Evans, London, 1844.
Schlissel, Lillian D. (ed.), *Conscience in America: A Documentary History of Conscientious Objection in America, 1757-1967*, New York, 1968.
Skeel, C.A.J. (ed.), "The Letter-book of a Quaker Merchant, 1756-8," *EHR*, vol. XXXI, no. CXXI (Jan. 1916).
Smith, John, *A Narrative of Some Sufferings for His Christian Peaceable Testimony, by John Smith, Late of Chester County, Deceased*, Philadelphia, 1800.
Smith, Samuel, *History of the Province of Pennsylvania*, ed. William M. Mervine, Philadelphia, 1913.
———, "The History of the Province of Pennsylvania" in *The Register of Pennsylvania* (Phila.), vol. VI, 1830.
Spotswood, Alexander, *The Official Letters of Alexander Spotswood*, ed. R. A. Brock, vol. I (1882), Richmond (Va.).
Taylor, Bayard, *Life and Letters of Bayard Taylor*, ed. Marie Hansen-Taylor and Horace E. Scudder, 5th edn., Boston, 1895.
Tolles, Frederick B. (ed.), "The Twilight of the Holy Experiment: A Contemporary View," *BFHA*, vol. 45, no. 1 (1956).
———, "Two Quaker Memorials for Abraham Lincoln," *BFHA*, vol. 46, no. 1 (1957).
Trueblood, Benjamin F., *The Development of the Peace Idea and Other Essays*, Boston, 1932.
Votes and Proceedings of the House of Representatives of the Province of Pennsylvania in *Pennsylvania Archives*, 8th ser., vols. I-V, ed. Gertrude MacKinney, Harrisburg (Pa.), 1931; vol. VIII, ed. Charles F. Hoban, Harrisburg (Pa.), 1935.
Woods, John A. (ed.), "The Correspondence of Benjamin Rush and Granville Sharp 1773-1809," *Journal of American Studies* (Cambridge, England), vol. I, no. 1 (April 1967).
Woolman, John, *The Journal and Essays of John Woolman*, ed. Amelia Mott Gummere, London, 1922.
———, "From a Letter from John Woolman to Abraham Farrington," *PMHB*, vol. XVII, no. 3 (1893).

BIBLIOGRAPHY

B. SECONDARY WORKS

Books, Articles, and Dissertations

Anscombe, Francis Charles, *I have Called You Friends: The Story of Quakerism in North Carolina*, Boston, 1959.
Archer, Adair P., "The Quaker's Attitude toward the Revolution," *William and Mary College Quarterly*, 2nd ser., vol. I, no. 3 (July 1921).
Barksdale, Brent E., *Pacifism and Democracy in Colonial Pennsylvania*, Stanford (Calif.), 1961.
Bartlett, John Russell, *History of the Wanton Family of Newport, Rhode Island*, Providence, 1878.
Beatty, Edward Corbyn Obert, *William Penn as Social Philosopher*, New York, 1939.
Bell, J. P. (ed.), *Our Quaker Friends of Ye Olden Time*, Lynchburg (Va.), 1905.
Bi-Centennial of Brick Meeting-House, Calvert, Cecil County, Maryland, 1701-1901, Lancaster (Pa.), 1902.
Biographical Sketches and Anecdotes of Members of the Religious Society of Friends, Philadelphia, 1870.
Bishop, Martha H., "Ann Branson" in *Quaker Biographies*, 2nd ser., vol. II, Philadelphia, n.d.
Boller, Paul B., Jr., "George Washington and the Quakers," *BFHA*, vol. 49, no. 2, 1960.
Bolles, John R., and Anna B. Williams, *The Rogerenes: Some Hitherto Unpublished Annals belonging to the Colonial History of Connecticut*, Boston, 1904.
Boorstin, Daniel J., *The Americans: The Colonial Experience*, New York, 1964 edn.
Brinton, Ellen Starr, "The Rogerenes," *NEQ*, vol. XVI, no. 1 (March 1943).
Brock, Peter, "Colonel Washington and the Quaker Conscientious Objectors," *Quaker History* (Swarthmore, Pa.), vol. 53, no. 1 (Spring 1964).
———, "The Peace Testimony in 'a Garden Enclosed'," *Quaker History*, vol. 54, no. 2 (Autumn 1965).
———, "The Spiritual Pilgrimage of Thomas Watson: From British Soldier to American Friend," *Quaker History*, vol. 53, no. 2 (Autumn 1964).
Brodin, Pierre, *Les Quakers en Amérique au dix-septième siècle et au début du dix-huitième*, Saint-Amand (Cher), 1935.
Bromley, Ernest R., "Did Early Friends pay War Taxes?" *Friends Intelligencer*, vol. 105, no. 42 (16 Oct. 1948).
Bronner, Edwin B., "The Quakers and Non-Violence in Pennsylvania," *Pennsylvania History*, XXXV, no. 1 (Jan. 1968).
———, *William Penn's "Holy Experiment": The Founding of Pennsylvania 1681-1701*, New York, 1962.
Brookes, George S., *Friend Anthony Benezet*, Philadelphia, 1937.
Busbey, L. White (ed.), *Uncle Joe Cannon*, New York, 1927.
Byrd, Robert O., *Quaker Ways in Foreign Policy*, Toronto, 1960.
Cadbury, Henry J., "History of Quakers in Jamaica" (*MS* in microfilm, F.H.L.S.C.).

———, "Nonpayment of Provincial War Tax," *Friends Journal* (Phila.), vol. 12, no. 17 (1 Sept. 1966).

———, "Penn as a Pacifist," *Friends Intelligencer*, vol. 101, no. 43 (21 Oct. 1944).

———, *Quaker Relief during the Siege of Boston*, [Wallingford (Pa.), 1943].

Cadbury, William W., "How Friends of Over a Century Ago addressed the Pennsylvania Legislature on Behalf of Conscientious Objectors," *Friend*, vol. 119, no. 10 (8 Nov. 1945).

Carroll, Kenneth Lane, *Joseph Nichols and the Nicholites*, Easton (Md.), 1962.

———, "Persecution of Quakers in Early Maryland (1658-1661)," *Quaker History*, vol. 53, no. 2 (Autumn 1964).

———, "Talbot County Quakerism in the Colonial Period," *Maryland Historical Magazine*, vol. 53, no. 4 (Dec. 1958).

Cartland, Fernando G., *Southern Heroes or the Friends in War Time*, Cambridge (Mass.), 1895.

Cope, Gilbert, "Chester County Quakers during the Revolution," *Bulletins of the Chester County Historical Society 1902-3*.

Cox, John, Jr., *Quakerism in the City of New York 1657-1930*, New York, 1930.

Crenshaw, Margaret E., "John Bacon Crenshaw" in *Quaker Biographies*, 2nd ser., vol. III, Philadelphia, n.d.

Cromwell, Otelia, *Lucretia Mott*, Cambridge (Mass.), 1958.

Crosfield, George, *Memoirs of the Life and Gospel Labours of Samuel Fothergill*, Liverpool (England), 1843.

Currey, Cecil B., "Quaker Pacifism in Kansas, 1833-1945," M.Sc. thesis, Fort Hays Kansas State College, n.d.

———, "Quaker Revivalism and the Peace Testimony," *Friends Journal*, vol. 8, no. 4 (15 Feb. 1962).

———, "Quakers in 'Bleeding Kansas'," *BFHA*, vol. 50, no. 2 (Autumn 1961).

Curti, Merle Eugene, *The American Peace Crusade, 1815-1860*, Durham (N.C.), 1929.

———, *Peace or War: The American Struggle, 1636-1936*, New York, 1936.

——— "Poets of Peace and the Civil War," *World Unity* (N.Y.), vol. X, no. 3 (June 1932).

Davidson, Robert L.D., *War Comes to Quaker Pennsylvania 1682-1756*, New York, 1957.

Davison, Robert A., *Isaac Hicks, New York Merchant and Quaker 1767-1820*, Cambridge (Mass.), 1964.

Dingwall, E., and E. A. Heard, *Pennsylvania 1681-1756: The State without an Army*, London, 1937.

Dorland, Arthur Garratt, *A History of the Society of Friends (Quakers) in Canada*, Toronto, 1927.

Drake, Thomas E., *Quakers and Slavery in America*, New Haven, 1950.

Dunn, Mary Maples, *William Penn: Politics and Conscience*, Princeton (N.J.), 1967.

Durnbaugh, Donald Floyd, "Relationships of the Brethren with the Mennonites and Quakers, 1708-1865," *Church History*, vol. XXXV, no. 1 (March 1966).

Ellsworth, Clayton Sumner, "The American Churches and the Mexican War," *AHR*, vol. XLV, no. 2 (Jan. 1940).

Encyclopedia of American Quaker Genealogy, vol. VI: *Virginia*, ed. William Wade Hinshaw, Thomas Worth Marshall, and Douglas Summers Brown, Ann Arbor (Mich.), 1950.

Falk, Robert P. "Thomas Paine and the Attitude of the Quakers to the American Revolution," *PMHB*, vol. LXIII, no. 3 (July 1939).

Ferguson, LeRoy C., "The Quakers in Midwestern Politics," *Papers of the Michigan Academy of Science, Arts and Letters*, vol. XXXII (1946), Ann Arbor, 1948.

Fitzroy, Herbert William Keith, "The Punishment of Crime in Provincial Pennsylvania," *PMHB*, vol. LX, no. 3 (July 1936).

Forbush, Bliss, *Elias Hicks: Quaker Liberal*, New York, 1956.

Forbush, LaVerne Hill, "The Suffering of Friends in Maryland," *The Maryland and Delaware Genealogist* (Washington, D.C.), vol. 3, no. 2 (Winter 1961-1962) and no. 3 (Spring 1962).

Foster, Ethan, *The Conscript Quakers, Being a Narrative of the Distress and Relief of Four Young Men from the Draft for the War in 1863*, Cambridge (Mass.), 1883.

Foulke, Joseph, *Memoirs of Jacob Ritter, a faithful Minister in the Society of Friends*, Philadelphia, 1844.

Fox, R. Hingston, *Dr. John Fothergill and His Friends*, London, 1919.

Friends in Wilmington 1738-1938, n.p.p., n.d.

Gary, A. T. [Pennell], "The Political and Economic Relations of English and American Quakers (1750-1785)," D.Phil. thesis, Oxford, 1935.

Gipson, Lawrence H., "Crime and Its Punishment in Provincial Pennsylvania," *Pennsylvania History*, vol. II, no. 1 (Jan. 1935).

Given, Lois V., "Burlington County Friends in the American Revolution," *Proceedings of the New Jersey Historical Society*, vol. 69, no. 3 (July 1951).

Gummere, Amelia Mott, *Friends in Burlington*, Philadelphia, 1884.

Hallowell, Anna Davis, *James and Lucretia Mott. Life and Letters*, Boston, 1884.

Hanna, William S., *Benjamin Franklin and Pennsylvania Politics*, Stanford (Calif.), 1964.

Hazard, Caroline, *The Narragansett Friends' Meeting in the XVIII Century*, Cambridge (Mass.), 1899.

Hershberger, Guy Franklin, "Pacifism and the State in Colonial Pennsylvania," *Church History* (Chicago), vol. VIII, no. 1 (March 1939).

———, "The Pennsylvania Quaker Experiment in Politics, 1682-1756," *MQR*, vol. X, no. 4 (Oct. 1936).

———, "Quaker Pacifism and the Provincial Government of Pennsylvania, 1682-1756," Ph.D., diss., U. of Iowa, 1935; summary in *University of Iowa Studies: Studies in the Social Sciences*, vol. X, no. 4 (1937): *Abstracts in History III* (Iowa City, Iowa); also typescript draft of book on this subject.

Hirst, Margaret E., *The Quakers in Peace and War*, London, 1923.

Hopewell Friends History 1734-1934, Frederick County, Virginia, Strasburg (Va.), 1936.

Hull, William I., *William Penn and the Dutch Quaker Migration to Pennsylvania*, Swarthmore (Pa.), 1935.

Illick, Joseph E., *William Penn the Politician*, Ithaca (N.Y.), 1965.

James, Sydney V., "The Impact of the American Revolution on Quakers' Ideas about Their Sect," *William and Mary Quarterly*, 3rd ser., vol. XIX, no. 3 (July 1962).

————, *A People Among Peoples: Quaker Benevolence in Eighteenth-Century America*, Cambridge (Mass.), 1963.

Jenkins, Charles F., "Joseph Hewes, the Quaker Signer" in *Children of Light*, ed. Howard H. Brinton, New York, 1938.

————, *Tortola: A Quaker Experiment of Long Ago in the Tropics*, London, 1923.

Jennings, Francis, "Thomas Penn's Loyalty Oath," *American Journal of Legal History* (Phila.), vol. 8, no. 4 (Oct. 1964).

Jericho Friends' Meeting and its Community, Ann Arbor (Mich.), 1958.

Jones, Louis Thomas, *The Quakers of Iowa*, Iowa City (Iowa), 1914.

Jones, Rufus M., *The Later Periods of Quakerism*, 2 vols., London, 1921.

————, *The Society of Friends in Kennebec County, Maine*, New York, 1892.

———— et al., *The Quakers in the American Colonies*, London, 1911.

Justice, Hilda, *Life and Ancestry of Warner Mifflin*, Philadelphia, 1905.

Keith, Charles P., *Chronicles of Pennsylvania from the English Revolution to the Peace of Aix-la-Chapelle 1688-1748*, 2 vols., Philadelphia, 1917.

Kelsey, Rayner Wickersham, *Friends and the Indians 1655-1917*, Philadelphia, 1917.

Ketcham, Ralph L., "Conscience, War, and Politics in Pennsylvania, 1755-1757," *William and Mary Quarterly*, 3rd ser., vol. XX, no. 3 (July 1963).

King, Emma, "Rufus P. King" in *Quaker Biographies*, 2nd ser., vol. II, Philadelphia, n.d.

Kirby, Ethlyn Williams, *George Keith (1638-1716)*, New York, 1942.

Knollenberg, Bernhard, *Pioneer Sketches of the Upper Whitewater Valley: Quaker Stronghold of the West*, Indianapolis (Ind.), 1945.

Knowles, James Purdie, *Samuel A. Purdie*, Plainfield (Ind.), [1908].

Konkle, Burton Alva, *Benjamin Chew 1722-1810*, Philadelphia, 1932.

Kreidel, George C., *The Early Life of Professor Elliott*, Washington (D.C.), 1917.

Leach, Douglas Edward, *Flintlock and Tomahawk: New England in King Philip's War*, New York, 1958.

Leach, Robert J., "Elisha Bates, 1817-1827: The Influence of an Early Ohio Publisher upon Quaker Reform," M.A. thesis, Ohio State U., 1939.

————, "Nantucket Quakerism 1661-1763" (typescript in F.H.L.S.C.).

Lerner, Gerda, *The Grimké Sisters from North Carolina: Rebels Against Slavery*, Boston, 1967.

Lewis, Joseph L., *A Memoir of Enoch Lewis*, West Chester (Pa.), 1882.

Littrell, Mary P., Mary E. Outland, and Janie O. Sams, *A History of Rich Monthly Meeting of Friends, 1760-1960*, Woodland (N.C.), [1960].

Lokken, Roy N., *David Lloyd, Colonial Lawmaker*, Seattle (Wash.), 1959.

Mekeel, Arthur J., "Free Quaker Movement in New England during the American Revolution," *BFHA*, vol. 27, no. 2 (1938).

———, "New England Quakers and Military Service in the American Revolution" in *Children of Light*, ed. Howard H. Brinton, New York, 1938.
———, "The Quakers in the American Revolution," Ph.D. diss., Harvard U., 1939 (copy in H.C.Q.C.).

Moore, Emily E., *Travelling with Thomas Story*, Letchworth (Herts.), 1947.

Morgan, Robert H., "John Wells and Adna Heaton: Early American Exponents of Quaker Pacifism," *Friend*, vol. 114, no. 6 (19 Sept. 1940).

Morlan, Charles P., *A Brief History of Ohio Yearly Meeting of the Religious Society of Friends (Conservative)*, Barnesville (Ohio), 1959.

Morse, Kenneth S.P., *Baltimore Yearly Meeting 1672-1830*, n.p.p., 1961.

Munroe, James A., *Federalist Delaware 1775-1815*, New Brunswick (N.J.), 1954.

Murray, Augustus Taber, "Whittier's Attitude Toward War," *Present Day Papers* (Haverford, Pa.), vol. II, no. 7 (July 1915).

Myers, Albert Cook, *Immigration of the Irish Quakers into Pennsylvania 1682-1750*, Swarthmore (Pa.), 1902.

Nash, Gary B., *Quakers and Politics: Pennsylvania, 1681-1726*, Princeton (N.J.), 1968.

Osgood, Herbert L., *The American Colonies in the Eighteenth Century*, vol. IV, New York, 1924.

Palimpsest (Iowa City, Iowa), vol. XLI, no. 1 (Jan. 1960): "John Brown among the Quakers."

Peare, Catherine Owens, *William Penn*, Philadelphia and New York, 1957.

Pickard, Samuel T., *Life and Letters of John Greenleaf Whittier*, vol. II, Cambridge (Mass.), 1894.

Pomfret, John E., "West New Jersey: A Quaker Society 1675-1775," *William and Mary Quarterly*, 3rd ser., vol. VIII, no. 4 (Oct. 1951).

Report of American Commissions of the Conference of All Friends. The Relation of the Life of the Society of Friends to the Peace Testimony. Being Report of Commission V, Philadelphia, 1920.

Root, Winfred Trexler, *The Relations of Pennsylvania with the British Government, 1696-1765*, New York, 1912.

Sanders, Thomas G., *Protestant Concepts of Church and State*, New York, 1964.

Sanger, S. F., and D. Hays, *The Olive Branch of Peace and Good Will to Men*, Elgin (Ill.), 1907.

Seibert, Russell Howard, "The Treatment of Conscientious Objectors in War Time, 1775-1920," Ph.D. diss., Ohio State U., 1936.

Semi-Centennial Anniversary Western Yearly Meeting of Friends Church, 1858-1908, Plainfield (Ind.), 1908.

Sharpless, Isaac, *Political Leaders of Provincial Pennsylvania*, New York, 1919.

———, *A Quaker Experiment in Government*, 2 vols. in 1 edn. (vol I: *History of Quaker Government in Pennsylvania 1682-1756*; vol. II: *The Quakers in the Revolution*), 1902.

———, *Quakerism and Politics*, Philadelphia, 1905.

Smith, C. Henry, *The Mennonite Immigration to Pennsylvania in the Eighteenth Century*, Norristown (Pa.), 1929.

Smith, H. E., *The Quakers, Their Migration to the Upper Ohio, Their Customs and Discipline*, n.p.p., 1928.

Smith, Joseph, *A Descriptive Catalogue of Friends' Books*, 2 vols., London, 1867.

Sowle, Patrick, "The Quaker Conscript in Confederate North Carolina," *Quaker History*, vol. 56, no. 2 (Autumn 1967).

Stewart, Frank H., "The Quakers of the Revolution," *Year Book. The New Jersey Society of Pennsylvania, 1907-1921*, n.p.p., n.d.

Stillé, Charles J., "The Attitude of the Quakers in the Provincial Wars," *PMHB*, vol. X, no. 3 (1886).

Sturge, Charles D., "Friends in Barbadoes," *Friends' Quarterly Examiner* (London), vol. XXVI, no. 104 (Oct. 1892).

Swansen, H. F., "The Norwegian Quakers of Marshall County, Iowa," *Norwegian-American Studies and Records* (Northfield, Minn.), vol. X (1938).

Thayer, Theodore, "The Friendly Association," *PMHB*, vol. LXVII, no. 4 (Oct. 1943).

————, *Israel Pemberton, King of the Quakers*, New York, 1943.

————, *Pennsylvania Politics and the Growth of Democracy 1740-1776*, Harrisburg (Pa.), 1953.

————, "The Quaker Party of Pennsylvania, 1755-1765," *PMHB*, vol. LXXI, no. 1 (Jan. 1947).

Thistlethwaite, Frank, *America and the Atlantic Community: Anglo-American Aspects, 1790-1850*, New York, 1963 edn.

Thompson, Mack, *Moses Brown: Reluctant Reformer*, Chapel Hill (N.C.), 1962.

Thorne, Dorothy Gilbert, "North Carolina Friends and the Revolution," *The North Carolina Historical Review*, vol. XXXVIII, no. 3 (July 1961).

Tolles, Frederick B., *George Logan of Philadelphia*, New York, 1953.

————, *James Logan and the Culture of Provincial America*, Boston, 1957.

————, "A Literary Quaker: John Smith of Burlington and Philadelphia," *PMHB*, vol. LXV, no. 3 (July 1941).

————, *Meeting House and Counting House: The Quaker Merchants of Colonial Philadelphia 1682-1763*, Chapel Hill (N.C.), 1948.

————, *Quakers and the Atlantic Culture*, New York, 1960.

Tooker, Elva, *Nathan Trotter, Philadelphia Merchant, 1787-1853*, Cambridge (Mass.), 1955.

Two Hundredth Anniversary of the Establishment of the Friends Meeting at New Garden, Chester County, Pennsylvania, 1715-1915, n.p.p., [1915].

Uhler, Sherman P., *Pennsylvania's Indian Relations to 1754*, Allentown (Pa.), 1951.

Wagenknecht, Edward, *John Greenleaf Whittier: A Portrait in Paradox*, New York, 1967.

Waterston, Elizabeth, *Churches in Delaware during the Revolution*, Wilmington, 1925.

Weeks, Stephen B., *Southern Quakers and Slavery*, Baltimore (Md.), 1896.

Wetherill, Charles, *History of the Religious Society of Friends called by some the Free Quakers, in the City of Philadelphia*, [Philadelphia], 1894.

Wherry, Noel M., *Conscientious Objection*, vol. I, Washington (D.C.), 1950.

White, Julia S., "The Peace Testimony of North Carolina Friends prior to 1860," *BFHA*, vol. 16, no. 2 (1927).

Whitney, Janet, *John Woolman, American Quaker*, Boston, 1942.

Windhausen, John D., "Quaker Pacifism and the Image of Isaac Norris II," *Pennsylvania History*, XXXIV, no. 4 (Oct. 1967).

Wisbey, Herbert A., Jr., *Pioneer Prophetess: Jemima Wilkinson, the Publick Universal Friend*, Ithaca (N.Y.), 1964.

Wright, Edward Needles, *Conscientious Objectors in the Civil War*, New York, 1961 edn.

Wyman, Lillie Buffum Chace, and Arthur Crawford Wyman, *Elizabeth Buffum Chace 1806-1899: Her Life and Its Environment*, vol. I, Boston, 1914.

Zimmerman, John J., "Benjamin Franklin and the Quaker Party, 1755-1756," *William and Mary Quarterly*, 3rd ser., vol. XVII, no. 3 (July 1960).

Author's Note: Carleton Mabee, *Black Freedom: The Nonviolent Abolitionists from 1830 through the Civil War* (New York, 1970) has appeared just as the present volume goes to press. Mabee's book constitutes an important contribution to the history of mid-nineteenth-century pacifism in the United States. Among subjects discussed are the relations between American Quakers and the "nonviolent abolitionists."

INDEX

Johnson, Oliver, Garrisonian
abolitionist and nonresistant,
268, 285
Jones, Griffith, 80
Jones, Rufus M., 341, 357
Jones, Sybil and Eli, 286
Jost Van Dyke, Quakers on island of,
62

Kansas, 242; Quakers in, 244-46, 290,
291, 342, 351-53
Keene, Richard, 37
Keith, George, 73-76
Kemp, Joshua and Mahlon, 331
Kersey, Jesse, 241, 264
"Kickapoo Rangers," 246
King Philip's War, 12, 17, 20, 22-24
King, Rufus P., 336
Kinsey, John, 97, 113, 115, 139
Kossuth, Lajos, Magyar patriot, 266

Ladd, William, peace advocate, 261
Lake Mohonk Conferences on
International Arbitration, 346, 358
Lamborn, Thomas, 204
Law, William, English theologian, 150
Lee, General Robert E., 227
Leeds, Josiah W., 345
Leib, Michael, Pennsylvania
politician, 221
Lewis, Enoch, 233, 234
Lincoln, President Abraham, 276,
277, 295, 297, 304, 308, 309,
318-20
Lloyd, David, 71, 82, 86, 90-93, 139
Lloyd, Thomas, 71
Loflin, Seth W., 333, 334
Logan, George, son of William Logan,
disownment of, 234
Logan, James, 4, 67, 88, 89, 95, 101-5,
110, 116
Logan, William, son of James,
102, 127, 134
London Peace Society, 261
Love, Alfred H., nonresistant and
reformer, 280, 284
Lowe, Emmanuel, 47
Lower, Thomas, 58
Lukens Iron and Steel Company,
347, 348
Lurting, Thomas, 15

McCarty, Ellen, 258
Maccomber, Thomas, 12, 13
Macon, Eli and Gideon, 332, 333

Macy, Elwood, 310, 311
Macy, Jesse, 308-11
Maine, Quakers in, 3, 203, 233, 258,
259, 286, 355
Markham, Captain, William Penn's
deputy in Pennsylvania, 82
Marshall, Christopher, 193
Martin, Isaac, 238
Maryland, Quakers in, 3, 7, 10, 37-
39, 157, 159, 179-81, 186, 192,
209, 223, 226, 227, 253, 274ff.,
292, 293, 300, 323, 342
Massachusetts, 22; Quakers in, 3,
10-19, 157, 159, 184, 199-203,
232; early persecution of Quakers
in, 10-12
Matthew, Governor-General William,
60, 61
Matlack, Timothy, 192, 193, 210
Maule, Joshua, 318, 321-24
May, Rev. Samuel Joseph, Unitarian
minister and reformer, 284
Mendenhall, Nereus, 330
Menno (Simons), Dutch founder of
Mennonitism, 141
Mennonites, xi-xiii, xv, xvi, 68, 74-76,
131, 213, 218, 270, 316, 321; in the
Confederate states, 328, 330, 333
Michener, Ezra, 265, 280, 281
Mifflin, John, 107
Mifflin, Jonathan, 131
Mifflin, Thomas, 161
Mifflin, Warner, 166, 186, 189,
212, 219, 238
Miller, Joseph G., 306-8
Mitchell sisters, 319, 320
Montserrat, Quakers on, 49, 54
Moore, Benjamin P., 308
Moravians, 137, 213
Morris, Joshua, 120
Morris, Governor Lewis, 31
Morris, Governor Robert Hunter, 121
Mott, James, Sr., 249, 250
Mott, James, Jr., 228
Mott, Lucretia, wife of James Mott,
Jr., 228, 249, 255, 266, 267-69, 292
Mühlenberg, Rev. Henry Melchior,
Pennsylvania Lutheran pastor, 138
Mullen, Rev. William J.,
ex-pacifist, 280

Nantucket, Quakers on, 26, 153,
187, 208, 213, 319
National Women's Christian
Temperance Union, 355